Themes in Religion
and American Culture

Edited by

Philip Goff and Paul Harvey

Themes in

The University of North Carolina Press

Chapel Hill and London

RELIGION and
American Culture

© 2004 The University of North Carolina Press
All rights reserved

Designed by April Leidig-Higgins
Set in Ehrhardt by Copperline Book Services, Inc.
Manufactured in the United States of America

Library of Congress Cataloging-in-Publication Data
Themes in religion and American culture / edited by
Philip Goff and Paul Harvey.
p. cm. Includes bibliographical references and index.
ISBN 0-8078-2890-4 (cloth: alk. paper)
ISBN 0-8078-5559-6 (pbk.: alk. paper)
1. Religion and culture—United States. 2. United
States—Religion. I. Goff, Philip, 1964–
II. Harvey, Paul, 1961–
BL2525.T48 2004
200'.973—dc22   2004007409

cloth   08 07 06 05 04   5 4 3 2 1
paper   08 07 06 05 04   5 4 3 2 1

To Conrad Cherry and to
Rowland A. Sherrill (1944–2003),
friends to young scholars
in American religion

Contents

Introduction 1

1 Theologies
David L. Weaver-Zercher 5

Precolonial Era 7
Colonial North America 10
Revolutionary and Early Republican America 14
Antebellum Nineteenth Century 17
Postbellum and Industrial Nineteenth Century 21
Early Twentieth Century 26
Modern America 31

2 Proselytization
Paul Harvey 39

Precolonial Era 41
Colonial North America 42
Revolutionary and Early Republican America 47
Antebellum Nineteenth Century 49
Postbellum and Industrial Nineteenth Century 53
Early Twentieth Century 57
Modern America 61

3 Supernaturalism

Yvonne Chireau 71

Precolonial Era 73
Colonial North America 74
Revolutionary and Early Republican America 79
Antebellum Nineteenth Century 82
Postbellum and Industrial Nineteenth Century 85
Early Twentieth Century 88
Modern America 91

4 Cosmology

Sue Marasco 99

Precolonial Era 102
Colonial North America 107
Revolutionary and Early Republican America 112
Antebellum Nineteenth Century 114
Postbellum and Industrial Nineteenth Century 117
Early Twentieth Century 122
Modern America 123

5 Race

Tracy Fessenden 129

Precolonial Era 132
Colonial North America 136
Revolutionary and Early Republican America 140
Antebellum Nineteenth Century 145
Postbellum and Industrial Nineteenth Century 147
Early Twentieth Century 151
Modern America 155

6 Ethnicity

Roberto Treviño 163

Precolonial Era 167
Colonial North America 169
Revolutionary and Early Republican America 174
Antebellum Nineteenth Century 176
Postbellum and Industrial Nineteenth Century 181
Early Twentieth Century 185
Modern America 189

7 Gender

Amy DeRogatis 197

Precolonial Era 200
Colonial North America 205
Revolutionary and Early Republican America 208
Antebellum Nineteenth Century 211
Postbellum and Industrial Nineteenth Century 215
Early Twentieth Century 217
Modern America 219

8 The State

Winnifred Fallers Sullivan 227

Precolonial Era 229
Colonial North America 232
Revolutionary and Early Republican America 238
Antebellum Nineteenth Century 241
Postbellum and Industrial Nineteenth Century 244
Early Twentieth Century 249
Modern America 252

9 Economy

James German 261

Precolonial Era 263
Colonial North America 268
Revolutionary and Early Republican America 273
Antebellum Nineteenth Century 275
Postbellum and Industrial Nineteenth Century 279
Early Twentieth Century 281
Modern America 286

10 Science

William A. Durbin 293

Precolonial Era 294
Colonial North America 295
Revolutionary and Early Republican America 301
Antebellum Nineteenth Century 305
Postbellum and Industrial Nineteenth Century 309
Early Twentieth Century 314
Modern America 318

11 Diversity and Region
Philip Goff 327

Precolonial Era 330
Colonial North America 334
Revolutionary and Early Republican America 338
Antebellum Nineteenth Century 342
Postbellum and Industrial Nineteenth Century 346
Early Twentieth Century 349
Modern America 352

Glossary 361

Notes on the Contributors 377

Index 379

Introduction

We offer this book as something unique in the field of American religious studies. We made it purposefully so.

The text reflects the changes in our field of study. During the 1980s, scholars challenged many aspects of the traditional narrative of American religious history. Like its secular counterpart, religious history had for decades highlighted the thoughts of men, mostly white, as the "real story," while everyone else who was religious provided either background or alternatives that were usually understood merely as foils to the metanarrative. The past decade saw those walls fall, as many scholars situated themselves outside the traditional places from which the story was told—highlighting instead the roles of women, or various regions, or ethnicities that were usually ignored. Together, they effectively demolished the long-standing narrative of the cultural hegemony of (particularly) Protestant ideas played out against the backdrop of America, a "decentralization" of the story in order to include more of its components.

The toughest criticism to be made against this new approach is that it leaves too little coherence to the story—if the metanarrative is broken, like Humpty-Dumpty's shell, it can never be patched together or replaced by another coherent structure. This criticism is less academic than it is practical, for how are we to teach about America's religious past if, in fact, it can only be understood in pieces, never as a whole? Can students really be asked to understand the intricacies and complexities of religion in America without some sort of a clothesline on which to hang the events, people, and interpretations? Isn't the old narrative necessary, if for no other reason than to offer structure to the many elements that constitute the whole story?

This volume was born out of the struggle to hew the line between the two poles in this debate. We have sought to do so with an intellectual integrity that recognizes both the demise of the old way of doing things and the need for some constructed narrative for people to understand the past. Therefore we have chosen to consider significant perspectives that offer different viewpoints—or, as Thomas Tweed would say, "sites"—on religion in America. We have elected to stand both inside and outside the doors of faith in offering this unique analysis of America's religious past. About one-third of the book situates itself inside those aspects of faith that are common to most groups; the remainder of the volume positions itself outside the church, synagogue, or temple in order to study relationships between religion and other aspects of American culture.

In each case, though, chapters are clearly chronological and narrative driven. This nod to traditional understandings of history, we feel, is important, particularly in the classroom. Although readers who eventually go beyond this introductory text might someday find its structure too linear and conventional, given academic debates over the past generation, they no doubt will have benefited from its arrangement. They will know that religion in America, indeed, has many components—which are often defined according to different perspectives—but they will understand those components as existing with beginnings and periods of development, change, and challenge and as full of interesting and important people throughout. In other words, even though we have abandoned the *traditional narrative*, we have not discarded the *tradition of narrative*.

It must be made clear from the outset that these essays are not meant to turn the field on its head. That has already been accomplished by the myriad monographs that have pushed aside traditional ways of understanding America's religious past. Rather, these chapters are syntheses of those pathbreaking works; they are attempts to bring together into a coherent whole the concepts put forth by those books that, quite literally, rewrote history. Whereas most of these books were confined to a specific region or era, our authors have presented their information and arguments under broad themes for the entirety of American history.

We arranged this volume to be read in various possible fashions. For those interested in a topical approach to American religion, we offer eleven perspectives that run through its history. Some of these themes are constituents of religion itself—such as theology and proselytization. Others—like race, gender, and regionalism—are elements of larger cultural forces that have interacted with religion in America over time. Indeed, one can easily understand religion existing in a symbiotic relationship with those aspects of life as they twist and turn around, against, and even through one another over time. For instance, race, ethnicity, gender, the state, economy, science, diversity, and region have all played important roles in shaping religion in America and, in turn, have been deeply influenced by religion.

One should not read too much into the order in which these thematic essays are presented. Each one is meant to stand alone and thus can be read in any order. The topics offered do not constitute all the possible themes but are the ones that we feel cover the key elements and encompass many of the other issues that one might wish to see developed under the broad heading of the section. For instance, "denominations" is a significant feature in America's religious history. But it might best be understood as a protoform of the religious diversity we see today. Therefore, denominations are discussed in the chapter entitled "Diversity and Region." Immigration is covered in the chapters on region and ethnicity. Such topics as capitalism, Americanization, nationalism, and democracy are addressed directly in chapters on economics, ethnicity, and the state. Likewise, the topic of scripture is central to the chapter on theology and plays a lesser but still significant role in virtually every other essay.

Another way to read this book is chronologically. We have divided each chapter into the same historical periods:

- precolonial era
- colonial North America
- revolutionary and early republican America
- antebellum nineteenth century
- postbellum and industrial nineteenth century
- early twentieth century
- modern America

By doing this, we hope that those who want a slice of American religious life in, say, the 1830s or the turbulent 1960s can read "across" the book, skipping from chapter to chapter to read only the pertinent chronological sections. For that purpose, we have broken out these periods in the table of contents to track the pages in which each era is discussed.

No doubt, some specialists in the field will read the volume closely and ask, "But what about [fill in your own blank]?" and question the gaps created by our approach. The point was never to cover everything. Rather, we have attempted to include as many large aspects of the relationship of religion to American culture as can be analyzed in one attempt. We sought to discover the common denominators of a number of similar topics and, in doing so, to simplify matters to thematic narratives that tell the story—or better, stories—of religion in America.

A glance through the table of contents would not necessarily suggest that this is a history book, but it is. Each author is, in fact, a historian of one sort or another specializing in an area of the American religious past. Yet, at the same time, although a quick look through any given chapter might tell the volume's historical bent, it might not reveal the book's overall thematic breadth. One can readily see how a chapter progresses from the precolonial period to modern America, but the slender slice of the American pie it offers topically would not disclose just how much territory the book explores.

We believe both that religion is a prism on culture and that culture can be a prism on religion. When "sited" correctly, given the questions one seeks to ask, each can refract the other, offering new perspectives and deeper understandings. Because of that firm conviction, we offer this volume as a "middle ground" in the debates that drive academics to perpetual rethinking but students to distraction.

Philip Goff   Paul Harvey
Indianapolis, Indiana   Colorado Springs, Colorado

Theologies

Literally speaking, the word *theology* means "words about God." Derived from the Greek terms for God (*theos*) and word (*logos*), *theology* is the process of thinking about God and putting those ideas into words. In much the same way that biology is the process of putting ideas about life (*bios*) into words and anthropology is the process of putting ideas about humanity (*anthropos*) into words, to engage in theology means to participate in the process of thinking and talking about God. Theology is often taught normatively, an approach in which students are instructed to embrace certain ideas about God, since these ideas are held to be uniquely true. Theology can also be taught descriptively. Instead of deeming a particular view of God the right view, an instructor or textbook may describe a variety of ways in which people in different times and places have thought about God.

This chapter assumes the second approach—the descriptive one—and therefore carries a plural word as its title, *theologies*. In this chapter we will explore a multitude of ideas about God held by a variety of Americans throughout American history. In the course of our exploration, we will see how adherents of different religions have embraced different theologies. More than that, we will see how adherents of the same religion have sometimes possessed divergent theologies and how these theologies have changed over time.

In some respects the term *theology* is not precise enough to describe this chapter's contents because, literally speaking, it implies thinking about *God*. Although this implication is appropriate in most cases, some American religions do not include the notion of a singular supreme being, embracing instead the idea of many gods or perhaps no god at all. It will therefore be useful to us to assume a broader definition of *theology* than the strictly literal one. Throughout this chapter, then, the term *theology* refers to a particular religion's notions about the sacred power(s) that control, sustain, and/or give meaning to the universe. Whether that sacred power is one particular God (monotheism), a pantheon of gods (polytheism), or an impersonal force, religious adherents typically believe something about the nature of this power. They also believe something about their position as human beings relative to this power. Indeed, one of the chief concerns of all religious people is to orient themselves appropriately with respect to the powers that maintain the universe. That being the case, our examination of various American theologies will go beyond exploring notions about the sacred powers to examining ideas about the status and obligations of human beings relative to these powers.

As we explore the conceptual differences between America's various theologies (e.g., one God versus many gods), we will find these theologies taking various forms, shaped for various purposes. For instance, some theologies are formulated by religious leaders with the goal of helping others think orthodox (correct) thoughts about the sacred powers. These *formal theologies*, devised by people with advanced theological training, are often written down, and they typically reveal a high regard for logical consistency. In other instances, however, theological beliefs are produced by ordinary men and women in the course of their everyday lives. Often called *popular theology*, this type of theological reflection is rarely written down, and its adherents exhibit relatively little concern for developing belief systems that address every theological problem. Still another form of American theology is *civil theology*. Most often formulated by political leaders in times of social upheaval, this theological type endeavors to relate current political events to sacred purposes, perhaps even a divine plan.

Whether systematically formulated or informally devised, America's theologies have shaped the ways in which Americans have thought about themselves as individuals and, in some cases, the way they've thought about themselves as a people. This chapter focuses on how Americans, both past and present, have conceived their sacred universes and found their places within them.

Precolonial Era

The diversity of North American religious life is nothing new. Thousands of years before European explorers "discovered" the New World, Native Americans inhabited the landscape. As tribal groups settled in different geographical regions with varying ecologies and climates, their styles of living diverged from one another, as did their religious thoughts and practices. Although pre-Columbian Native Americans did not think in terms of "practicing a religion" or of "having a theology" (notions that are largely European in origin), they exhibited an array of ideas about the sacred powers, as well as humanity's potential for relating to these powers.

Despite the theological diversity that existed among these precolonial Americans, some commonalities can be identified. For instance, most precolonial Native American religions did not envision a significant divide between the natural and supernatural worlds or between a powerful creator and a subservient created order. To the contrary, Native Americans saw all of the known universe—including the sky, trees, soil, water, and animal life—as endowed with sacred power and sacred significance. At the same time, Native Americans believed that all these powers related to one another *and* to them, creating a large and all-encompassing kinship network. Sometimes this kinship focus was expressed in explicit phrases, as in the Pueblo Indians' notion of superhuman Corn Mothers, who, in some primordial age, had given life to all plants and animals. In contrast to the Europeans who would later confiscate their lands, Native Americans understood nature to be more than simply the creation of a supernatural deity. For them, nature was itself sacred and spiritually alive.

In addition to rejecting a separation between the natural and supernatural worlds, most Native Americans possessed myths that explained the origin of the universe and their tribe's place in it. (In the field of religious studies, the term *myth* refers to a story about the sacred realm; it should not be interpreted to mean a *false* account.) Some Native American myths featured mysterious, nonhuman figures who helped bring order to the world or, conversely, sought to bring disorder. One of the most widespread creation myths among Native American tribes was the earth-diver story, in which birds and animals dove to the bottom of a primordial sea to retrieve bits of soil for making dry, inhabitable land. In this case, as in many Native American creation stories, there was no sense of a transcendent God standing over the world and creating the world from nothing. Creation, rather, was a cooperative effort among nature's inhabitants to fashion something new. Even though Native American creation myths varied from tribe to tribe, most celebrated the power of nature to provide all that was needed for human existence.

Not surprisingly, Native Americans sought above all else to cultivate a harmonious relationship with nature and the powers that animated it. Whether male or female, young or old, Native Americans participated in community rituals that kept the spirit-filled world in order and the spirits themselves satisfied. For instance, the Zuni Indians of Arizona and New Mexico sought blessings for their infants by offering sacrifices of cornmeal to the sun god. In Native American cultures more oriented to hunting, successful hunters offered apologies to animal spirits when these animals were killed. Similarly, they promised the spirits that the slain animal would be fully used, with no parts wasted. Still other Native American rituals revolved around healing and the maintenance of good health. Many Native American tribes had at least one shaman, a person who possessed extraordinary abilities to influence the world with spiritual power. By reciting certain words or dramatizing certain realities, shamans sought to bring diseased persons into harmony with the universe and thereby provide them with newfound strength.

Across the Atlantic Ocean from the North American continent, West Africans (who would soon become American slaves) likewise assembled themselves into discrete tribal groups. Historians have noted certain modes of thinking among West Africans that, according to our definition, constitute a common theology. For instance, most West African groups believed in a High God who had created all things, including the human race. Often associated with the sky, this High God was sometimes considered the parent of other, secondary gods. Whereas the High God demonstrated a removal from the world's ongoing affairs, the secondary gods were intimately involved with the world. For instance, the sky gods controlled rain, lightning, and thunder; the earth gods controlled fertility and vegetation; and the water gods superintended the rivers and the lakes. Given the impact these lesser gods could have on the world, for good or for ill, West Africans sought regular and repeated contact with them through worship and various forms of sacrifice.

In addition to placating the secondary gods, West Africans sought to maintain healthy relationships with their ancestors. Kinship ties were exceedingly important to West Africans, for these connections continued far beyond death. Indeed, West Africans believed that the spirits of their deceased ancestors lived all around them, granting health to descendants who properly revered them and punishing those who neglected them or violated tribal customs. Religious practices connected West Africans to a host of spiritual powers. For instance, various kinds of magic fostered healing, predicted the future, and, in some cases, brought harm to one's enemies.

Standing in sharp contrast to the religions of Africa and North America was Christianity, the official religion of Europe in the precolonial era. It shared many theological assumptions with Judaism, including the belief in one God, who created the universe and everything in it. Christianity also maintained Judaism's belief that humanity, having fallen into sin, was in need of God's mercy. In the first century C.E., a handful of Jews became convinced that a preacher named Jesus was both God's son and their long-awaited Messiah (or Christ), who would save them from sin and its terrible consequences. Although Jesus was eventually killed by his enemies, his followers claimed that he rose from the dead and returned to heaven. Early Christians believed that Jesus' death was propitiatory, appeasing God's anger toward sinful human beings. Moreover, they asserted that Jesus' resurrection proved his power over death, securing eternal life for his followers. Over time, Christians came to acknowledge Jesus Christ as a divine being equal with God the Father. Indeed, most Christians throughout history have affirmed the idea that a Trinity of divine beings (God the Father, God the Son, and God the Holy Spirit) rules the universe as a unified entity.

In the European nations that would colonize the New World, the long-predominant form of Christianity was Roman Catholicism. In addition to the theological beliefs identified in the previous paragraph, Roman Catholics stressed the importance of the institutional church—including the bishop of Rome (the pope) and the hierarchy of other clergymen beneath him—in mediating the salvation made available through Jesus' life, death, and resurrection. According to most Roman Catholic theologians of the time, salvation outside the church was not possible, meaning that ordinary human beings were entirely dependent on the church to provide them with the means to be saved from their sin. These means, also called sacraments, began with infant baptism, a ritual in which a priest sprinkled water on an infant's head to alleviate the penalty of original sin (inherited sin). For adults, the church provided two other sacraments to heal their sinful souls: the Eucharist, a shared meal of bread and wine that presented the body and blood of Jesus, and penance, the practice of confessing one's sins to a Catholic priest and performing certain activities assigned by that priest. Much as infant baptism alleviated the penalty of original sin, penance annulled the penalty of actual sin, thereby facilitating the sinner's entrance into heaven.

Beginning with Martin Luther in 1517, a succession of Christian theological reformers emerged in Europe who contested various aspects of Roman

Catholic thought, especially its ideas regarding the church's role in the salvation process. These theological reformers produced a movement now known as the Reformation, and their spirited protests against the Roman Catholic Church earned them the name "Protestants." So even as the rulers of Spain, France, and England set out to colonize the New World, they found the dominant religion of the Old World under theological attack from many different quarters.

Colonial North America

As European Christians from different nations and church traditions settled North America, the New World began to exhibit a theological overlay that in some ways mirrored the theological differences that existed in western Europe. With Spanish and French explorers leading the way, the Roman Catholic Church established theological outposts on the North American continent far earlier than Protestants. In fact, when Christopher Columbus arrived in the New World in 1492, the beginning of the Protestant Reformation was still twenty-five years in the future. But even as the Roman Catholic Church was establishing itself in the New World—organizing missions in Florida, New Mexico, and other parts of New Spain—Protestant theological reformers were undermining the Roman Catholic theological monopoly in the Old World.

The earliest and most prominent of these Protestant reformers was Martin Luther, a Roman Catholic priest who taught theology at Germany's Wittenberg University. According to Luther, the Catholic Church had lost sight of Christianity's most basic tenet: that God granted salvation freely to those who trusted in Jesus Christ to cover their sin with his righteousness. *Sola fide*, "by faith alone," became Luther's theological battle cry, a statement he used to challenge the Roman Catholic notion that doing penance contributed to one's salvation. When the Catholic Church condemned Luther's ideas, Luther responded that, in matters of theology, he must ultimately take his cues from the Bible, not the pope. *Sola scriptura*, "by Scripture alone," thus became the second pillar of Luther's theological reform. If Luther was right—if individual Christians could determine theological truth via their own reading of the Bible—the authority of the Roman Catholic Church would be undermined and perhaps erased altogether.

Roman Catholic leaders who feared the consequences of Luther's new ideas were justifiably concerned, for soon other western European Christians found reasons to assert their theological authority over that of the Catholic Church. Perhaps most unusual in this regard was England's King Henry VIII, who, for much of his life, was an ardent defender of the Roman Catholic Church and its theology. But in the early 1530s, in the wake of a personal dispute with the pope, Henry pronounced himself the head of the Church of England and placed all of England's church matters under his authority. From one perspective, the change that Henry engineered was very slight, since the theology of the churches involved did not really change, at least at first. But from another perspective, Henry's assertion of power was a radical one. With the pope no longer in authority over the Church of England, England's residents were no longer Roman Catholics but something else.

But what exactly were they? Over the course of the next century—a century during which England would begin to colonize the New World—the Church of England sought to define itself theologically. In contrast to its worship practices, which continued to manifest a very Roman Catholic feel, the Church of England (also called the Anglican Church) embraced certain theological ideas from the European continent that were distinctly Protestant.

Those ideas came from a second-generation Protestant reformer named John Calvin. Although he helped convey Luther's ideas to other parts of Europe, Calvin formulated a detailed theological system that was distinctly his own. The cornerstone of his theological system was God's sovereignty (control) over all creation. According to Calvin, absolutely nothing happened in the universe apart from God's sovereign control, including the salvation of human beings. Indeed, since all human beings were marked by total depravity (utter sinfulness), gaining salvation by their own merit, even their own choice, was entirely impossible. In the latter half of the sixteenth century, Calvin's theological ideas found favor among many Anglicans, most of whom found ways to combine his distinctive form of Protestant theology with the church's Catholic-like liturgy. But some Anglicans—the ones most impressed by Calvin's theology—complained that the Church of England was still too Catholic. These Anglicans soon gained the nickname "puritans," for more than anything else they wanted to purify the Church of England of its Catholic vestiges.

Like the French and Spanish before them, the English had various motives for colonizing America, many of them nonreligious. For the Puritans, however, theological commitments fueled their appetites for creating a "New England." The Puritans believed that God worked in the world by establishing covenants (solemn agreements) with groups of people, covenants that promised blessings to groups that lived faithfully to God and judgment to groups that did not. Since the Puritans understood that God had established one of these covenants with the nation of England, they naturally despaired when their fellow Englanders disobeyed God's commands. Fearing that God's wrath would soon fall on the Anglican Church and the English nation, some yearned for a place where they could build a Christian commonwealth more pleasing to God. Thus in the 1620s and 1630s ships carrying English Puritans arrived in New England, where, according to a surviving Puritan sermon, they sought to create "a model of Christian charity" for all the world to see. The sermon, delivered aboard an America-bound ship, reflected the Puritans' beliefs in both covenant blessing and covenant judgment. By keeping their covenant with God, the sermon reminded them, the Puritans could anticipate a long and happy experience in the New World; but if the Puritans failed to uphold their end of the agreement, "we shall surely perish out of this good land."

Given the theological basis of the Puritans' colonizing endeavors, it is hardly surprising that the Puritan colonies exceeded all the others in theological training and debate. One of the early debates involved Anne Hutchinson, a well-educated woman who led weekly theological discussions. Hutchinson, it appears, pushed Puritan theology to its logical extreme, arguing that works (pious actions) had absolutely nothing to do with one's salvation, and she correspondingly accused some Puritan ministers of overemphasizing righteous living. It was difficult for Puritan church leaders to dispute Hutchinson's claim that salvation came entirely by God's initiative, but her vigorous dismissal of righteous living threatened to undermine the Puritan goal of building a godly society. In that sense, Hutchinson's arguments against works exposed a troubling inconsistency in the Puritan theological system, an inconsistency best summarized with this question: How can God's salvation be an unmerited gift and yet God's covenant blessings be dependent on the righteous actions of men and women? In the end, Hutchinson was banished from New England. Her experience reveals that New England's Puritan leaders were far more devoted to strict, Puritan orthodoxy than they were to modern American notions of religious freedom.

Passionate disputes over the nature of true religion continued to plague New England throughout the seventeenth and eighteenth centuries. Even here, in this wellspring of Calvinist theology, many colonists possessed notions about magic that paralleled the folk theologies of Europe and West Africa. In a published sermon entitled "A Discourse on Witchcraft" (1689), minister Cotton Mather complained that some New Englanders found charms, enchantments, and even witchcraft more compelling than good Puritan preaching. But for many New Englanders, who modified their ministers' theologies as they saw fit, the use of magic was a logical way to secure supernatural protection in a frightening world. In that sense, the magical worldviews of ordinary New Englanders constituted a significant strand of popular theology, a strand most clergy found detestable. Salem's witch trials, which took place in 1692, betray the magnitude of this sort of belief in Puritan New England. Twenty people lost their lives in Salem, victims of a theologically based legal system that authorized the suppression of witchcraft.

Even as Salem's witch trials constituted the most intense theological dispute in America's seventeenth century, the most vigorous theological debates of the eighteenth century pertained to the Great Awakening. The Awakening, a period of heightened religious enthusiasm among America's Protestant Christians, helped launch the career of Jonathan Edwards, a minister whose church traced its theological roots to the Puritans. Edwards soon rose to prominence as the Awakening's most able defender, answering critics who denounced its emotional preaching and ecstatic conversions as counterfeit Christianity. In his *Faithful Narrative of the Surprising Work of God* (1736), Edwards described a period of heightened religious fervor in his own parish, attributing the revival (in good Calvinist fashion) to God alone. A few years later Edwards asserted that it was possible to determine which conversions were truly God's work, since they exhibited certain marks of Christian virtue. In *A Treatise Concerning Religious Affections* (1746), his most influential work, Edwards sought to define the essence of Christianity. Although refusing to set aside the core of Puritan theology (God's sovereignty, human depravity, and humanity's dependence on God's grace), Edwards creatively employed ideas he borrowed from new understandings of human psychology. According to Edwards, true Christianity existed when one's "affections" (emotions) were inclined toward God, a view that once again affirmed the Awakening's validity. Still, Edwards always took care to emphasize that the intensity of one's emotions said nothing about one's spiritual state. The key, said Edwards, was not the magnitude of people's emotions but whether their affections were directed toward God, an orientation of the heart that compelled true Christians to seek God's pleasure.

As articulate as he was, Edwards was unable to convince some New England ministers of the Awakening's integrity. Charles Chauncy emerged as the Awakening's most vigorous critic, charging that the revivals' participants were succumbing not to the Holy Spirit but to "enthusiasm." According to Chauncy, these enthusiasts falsely believed that God had visited them when in fact they had fallen victim to their own "overheated imaginations." He argued that the Christian scriptures placed a higher priority on godly conduct than on emotional experience. Not surprisingly, Chauncy was one of a number of New England ministers who, in the mid-eighteenth century, gave increasing weight to reason as means for knowing God. For Jonathan Mayhew, who joined Chauncy in condemning the Awakening, this devotion to reason meant rejecting the irrational arithmetic of the Trinity. Supplementing his unitarian theology (which defined God as a singular, unified being) with an emphasis on humanity's potential for good, Mayhew soon drew charges of heresy from those more committed to Calvinist conceptions of God, sin, and salvation.

Ironically, both parties in the Awakening controversy fed the colonists' growing hunger for liberty, a hunger that would eventually culminate in the American Revolution. As men devoted to reason, Chauncy and Mayhew both argued that rational people ought to pursue the truth freely and, when reason demanded it, oppose tyrannical powers that opposed that ability. Edwards's theology likewise had political implications. Indeed, his most enduring legacy may have been his ability to translate the conversion stories of ordinary Christians into a theology that affirmed their religious experiences and nourished their ability to interpret those experiences for themselves. Although America's Christian laypeople had never been completely controlled by their ministers' ideas, Edwards provided a powerful argument for resisting the clergy's theological domination. In that sense, his theology fanned the glowing embers of democracy that, in a few short decades, would burst into flame.

Revolutionary and Early Republican America

As talk of revolution gained strength, many European Americans began to envision a nation free from British control. Most of the Americans who championed freedom spoke the English language, and many of them had English roots and relatives. Nonetheless, even after the British colonies achieved their independence and became the United States of America, America's inhabitants continued to speak many different languages and worship many different gods.

Slaves, who arrived in great numbers between 1680 and 1760, brought with them their West African conceptions of the universe, conceptions that their European owners found strange, frightening, and deserving of contempt. More than the Europeans' disdain, however, slavery's social and demographic factors—the buying, selling, and dispersal of African people throughout the American colonies—fractured African tribal groups and destroyed their religious systems. Key religious myths thus faded from memory, and as these myths died, so too did certain African conceptions of the gods. Although discrete religious practices remained (for instance, burial customs, healing rites, and ritual dancing), these practices generally became divorced from the theological frameworks that existed in West Africa.

Over time, many African American slaves adopted Christian conceptions of the universe. Especially after 1760, as European American Christians increased their efforts to convert southern slaves, African Americans began to think in ways that reflected the theology of their owners, most of whom were Christians. Nevertheless, even as African American slaves embraced their masters' religion, they fashioned theological views that were uniquely their own. Whereas slave owners spoke of a Christian God who demanded order (an orderliness that placed whites over blacks), slaves spoke of a God who cherished freedom—not only freedom from personal sin but freedom from slavery's oppression. The Exodus, the biblical story of the Israelites' escape from Egypt, thrilled and inspired African Americans, who found the story to be indicative of God's desires for all enslaved people. Many slaves believed that, just as God helped the Israelites escape from bondage, so too would God lead them to a land of freedom. In the meantime, Jesus stood with them in the midst of their troubles, having himself experienced savage treatment at the hands of evil people. "Nobody knows the trouble I've seen," declared one African American spiritual. "Nobody knows but Jesus."

Other Christians in revolutionary America held views of God that, because of their political implications, scandalized their Christian neighbors. Quakers, whose name derived from their tendency to tremble when gripped by God's power, contended that humans could be filled with the Light of Christ, Jesus' immediate spiritual presence. With Christ's Inner Light to guide them, Quakers believed they could live intensely virtuous lives; consequently, they often offended their neighbors by taking extreme stands on certain moral issues. For instance, Quakers became America's first Christian denomination to condemn slavery, arguing that the Light of Christ forbid Christians to own other human beings. Perhaps more radical, Quakers rejected warfare as a Christian moral option, asserting that Jesus' teaching had prohibited it. Quakers thus mirrored the theological convictions of the Mennonites, a Pennsylvania German group whose theological roots lay in Anabaptism, the sixteenth century's most radical Protestant reform movement. According to Anabaptist theology, God demonstrated his love for his enemies by sending Jesus to earth to die for them. If Jesus' followers wished to live godly lives, they too should be willing to love their enemies. For Mennonites as well as for Quakers, demonstrating God's love meant renouncing the weapons of war.

In most cases, however, revolutionary Americans conceived of a God who supported warfare, at least in some circumstances. Especially in New England, where the strains of Puritan covenant theology still ran strong, but also in other regions of America, many Christians interpreted the emerging conflict with Britain as a struggle between good and evil. For them, faithfulness to God meant resisting tyranny in all its forms—not just the tyranny of sin, or even the tyranny of bad theology, but political tyranny as well. Some of these Christians recalled and rejuvenated the Puritan notion of chosenness, the idea that God had chosen America for a special mission and would thus support its cause. Over time, many Americans became convinced that resisting the British Crown was nothing less than a God-given duty. To be sure, not every Christian group in America sanctified rebellion. In addition to Quakers and Mennonites, who argued for Christian pacifism, Anglican loyalists contended that God required full obedience to earthly governments. Still, the theological consensus for opposing Britain's rule was so strong that it included many of the Roman Catholic communities in the English-speaking colonies.

Although Protestants and Catholics found common cause in the struggle for American independence, most of America's revolutionary leaders embraced a theological perspective that rejected Christian theology as traditionally conceived. As disciples of the Enlightenment, a European intellectual tradition esteeming reason over revelation in the search for truth, Thomas Jefferson, Benjamin Franklin, and many other upper-class Americans became Deists. In contrast to Christians and Jews, Deists asserted that God was uninvolved in the world's ongoing affairs (some have called this God the "watchmaker God," that is, the God who created the universe, wound it up like a watch, and then let it run its course). For Deists, this notion of a powerful but uninvolved God best explained a world in which people prayed for miracles but never saw them happen. Thomas Jefferson was himself so skeptical of miracles that he produced his own miracleless account of Jesus' life. From Jefferson's standpoint, this edited version of Jesus' life was far superior to standard New Testament accounts because it rescued Jesus' moral teachings from the fanciful stories that had grown up around him.

Despite such skepticism, many of Jefferson's contemporaries found ways to embrace both the claims of Enlightenment rationality and the doctrines of traditional Christian theology. Most prominent in this regard was the Presbyterian John Witherspoon, who drew on a stream of Enlightenment philosophy known as Scottish commonsense realism. Conceived largely by two Scots, Francis Hutcheson and Thomas Reid, commonsense philosophy appealed to universal human sensibilities (common sense) in the search for truth. For instance, most human beings knew that causes produced effects, that a First

Cause initiated the effects that brought the universe into being, and that this First Cause (God) possessed a moral perfection against which humanity would be judged. These ideas were simply "common sense." Clergymen like Witherspoon championed this notion to support traditional Christian ideas about a God who created the universe, participated in human history, and inspired sacred texts. Embracing commonsense philosophy may not have *necessitated* the acceptance of orthodox Christian theology, but many educated Christians found this Enlightenment contribution quite useful as they engineered arguments for the truth of Christianity's claims.

If Witherspoon's appropriation of Scottish common sense represents one kind of theological creativity in the early American Republic, the theological synthesis of two African American slaves, Gabriel Prosser and his brother Martin, represents quite another. Both Gabriel and Martin had been converted to Christianity by Protestant revivalists who, by the end of the eighteenth century, were making significant inroads among lower-class whites and African American slaves in the South. After his conversion to Christianity, Martin became a preacher to his fellow slaves. Soon, however, Martin's message exhibited something more than an other-worldly concern for heaven. Finding similarities between his people's situation and that of the ancient Israelites, Martin preached that God would assist them in a rebellion against their white oppressors. In addition to this Judeo-Christian impetus for launching "Gabriel's Rebellion," many would-be rebels drew inspiration from African theological notions. For example, some rebels believed that African-born slaves would be able to foretell the future and thereby help the slave warriors avoid disastrous battlefield decisions. Gabriel's Rebellion, planned for August 1800, was found out and quickly suppressed by authorities, and its leaders were put to death. For our purposes, however, the ability of these African American slaves to synthesize divergent theological beliefs reveals that America's theologies were far from static. It also reveals that America's theologians —even those with no formal education—often succeeded in inspiring their audiences to action. Other powerful and uniquely American theologies would appear in the decades ahead.

Antebellum Nineteenth Century

When the Frenchman Alexis de Tocqueville traveled throughout the United States in 1831, he observed that America's religious leaders demonstrated a great respect for "the intellectual supremacy exercised by the majority." As a consequence of their respect, America's ministers refused to challenge the status quo, adopting instead "the general opinions of their country and their age." Considering all the religious movements that filled America's antebellum landscape, Tocqueville was no doubt overstating the case. Still, it is hard to deny his contention that America's antebellum religious leaders were often "borne along" by the political winds and social currents of their day.

In the world of finely articulated, formal theology, Nathaniel Taylor's New Haven Theology exhibited this Americanizing tendency as clearly as any. A professor at Yale Divinity School from 1822 to 1858, Taylor championed a modified brand of Calvinist Christianity that scandalized many of his colleagues. He never rejected Calvinism outright, but he found certain aspects of Calvinist thought outmoded, even dangerous. Most notably, he rejected the notion that human depravity was a genetic defect passed down from Adam (the first human being) that caused all people to sin. For Taylor, sin was in the *act* of sinning, not in a person's hereditary nature. So while he continued to assert that sinning was inevitable, he nonetheless affirmed that all human beings had the "power to the contrary" and therefore did not *need* to sin. Taylor's theological contribution solved two problems that had long plagued Calvinist theology. First, it sidestepped the notion that every person's future had been determined by the sinful actions of one historical figure. Second, it avoided the conclusion that God held sinners responsible for something they did not choose themselves. More than anything, Taylor's New Haven Theology made human choice really matter. And in a nation enthusiastic about democracy, many Americans believed that even sinning should be a matter of personal choice.

Although Taylor argued that New Haven Theology was a modified form of Calvinism, his theological adjustments reveal that Christianity in antebellum America was growing more Arminian. Arminianism, which traces its name to the Dutch theologian Jacob Arminius (1560–1609), rejected the Calvinist doctrine of divine predestination in favor of human choice. Perhaps no ecclesiastical body reflected this Arminian emphasis as clearly as the Methodist Church. Founded by John Wesley in eighteenth-century England, Methodism became the largest religious movement in America by the time of the Civil War. Part of the Methodists' success can be attributed to their bold evangelization strategies, but in addition to using successful methods, Methodist ministers assured their listeners that they had the power to choose their own salvation. Poking fun at Calvinism's emphasis on predestination, one Methodist preacher ridiculed his theological competition like this: "You can and you can't / You will and you won't / You'll be damned if you do / And damned if you don't." Some Methodists extended this emphasis on human choice to promote *entire sanctification*, a postconversion blessing from God by which the sinner was made entirely holy. Few championed Holiness theology as effectively as Phoebe Palmer, who, in good Methodist fashion, assured her listeners of their ability to receive this blessing. Although never denying that holiness was a gift from God, Palmer contended that all who dedicated themselves fully to God could receive this second blessing. For Palmer, sanctification was no more complicated—and no less a choice—than conversion itself.

Methodists weren't the only antebellum Americans renouncing the intricacies of formal, academic theology. In the 1830s, a small but influential group of New Englanders emerged to challenge the reigning orthodoxies of educated, upper-class Americans. This group, the transcendentalists, argued that not only was Calvinism outdated but so was its more liberal successor, Unitarianism. Earlier in the century, Unitarians such as William Ellery Channing had drawn on Enlightenment thought to construct a more rational Christianity, disavowing traditional Christian doctrines (e.g., the doctrine of the Trinity) that seemed to them inadequately based in reason. Soon, however, the Unitarians suffered their own internal theological rebellion. The transcendentalists, led by Ralph Waldo Emerson, accused the Unitarians of promoting a "corpse-cold" religion consisting of sterile, cerebral doctrine. Building on the insights of European romantics, Emerson and his colleagues rejected the idea that religious truth derived from an objective analysis of the universe. For Emerson and others like him, true religion consisted of discovering "the God within," as well as experiencing God as revealed in the wonder of nature. Emerson once told his listeners that divine truth was far more accessible in a snowfall than in a sermon filled with doctrine.

Surprisingly enough, two of Emerson's contemporaries followed the transcendentalist road all the way to Rome, shocking their unorthodox colleagues by converting to Roman Catholicism. Orestes Brownson and Isaac Hecker both converted in 1844, initiating decades-long careers as advocates for Roman Catholicism on the North American landscape. Brownson, whose previous religious explorations had taken him from Calvinism to Arminianism, then to Unitarianism and transcendentalism, found something in Roman Catholicism that, from his vantage point, all these other theological perspectives lacked: a way to infuse the supernatural into the natural human life. Drawing on classic Catholic views about the church's mediating role in salvation, Brownson argued that true life was to be found only in communion with the church. He thus rooted his theology in the external authority of the church, whereas his associate Hecker chose interiority (the "aspirations of nature") as his theological starting point. For Hecker, these internal aspirations constituted evidence of the Holy Spirit's activity in the hearts of men and women, an activity that would compel them to advance God's work in the world. Hecker's emphasis on the interior life led some critics to accuse him of trivializing the externals of Roman Catholicism (e.g., the sacraments and the church hierarchy). For Hecker, however, such an emphasis was crucial for creating a renewed, vigorous Catholicism that could compete for souls on the theologically diverse American landscape.

Perhaps no group exemplified the theological ingenuity of antebellum Americans as fully as the Church of Jesus Christ of Latter-day Saints. In some respects, the Latter-day Saints (or Mormons) embraced the fundamental tenets of traditional Christianity: a loving God, a sinful human race, and God's saving grace offered through the death and resurrection of Jesus Christ. But the Latter-day Saints traveled beyond these traditional theological tenets to formulate a unique form of Christianity. Transplanting the story of redemption in American soil, Mormons contended that the lost tribes of Israel had settled in pre-Columbian America, where they lived out a history of faithfulness and unfaithfulness to God in a manner similar to that of the Old Testament Israelites. According to the Book of Mormon, the righteous Nephite tribe was eventually wiped out by the unrighteous Lamanites, the ancestors of the many Native American groups that inhabited antebellum America. In this way, the Book of Mormon answered one of many questions that vexed antebellum Americans, namely, From whom did the Native Americans derive? At the same time, the Book of Mormon sanctified the American landscape by indicating that God's plan of redemption was now centered in America, not Palestine.

More than simply relocating God's plan for redemption in America, however, Mormon theology located this plan in the Mormon Church. Chastising other Christian groups that spent their energies debating the Bible's meaning, Mormons asserted that God had supernaturally revealed the blueprint for salvation to Joseph Smith, their youthful and charismatic founder. Smith, the son of New York farmers, translated the Book of Mormon and claimed various other visions and revelations. More than that, he helped his followers envision themselves as the "latter-day saints," chosen by God to fulfill a special role in history's final epoch. By following God's commands, the Latter-day Saints would be a light to non-Mormons, pointing the way to God. Rejecting the strict dichotomy between humanity and divinity, the Latter-day Saints contended that faithful human beings would progress until they one day became "as gods," creating in Mormonism a polytheistic, evolutionary understanding of the sacred realm. In light of their theological understandings, it is hardly surprising that the Latter-day Saints interpreted their migration to Utah Territory in 1847 as an exodus, applying the same term to their own migration that the Israelites applied to their escape from Egypt three thousand years earlier.

In this way, the predominantly European American Mormons shared a particular theological notion with America's slaves, whose understanding of Christianity was increasingly oriented around the hope that God would once again deliver the oppressed from their oppressors. Nowhere was this hope expressed more clearly than in the lyrics of African American spirituals, many of which possessed politically liberating double meanings. For instance, in addition to referring to spiritual rest, "Steal Away to Jesus" evoked the idea of stealing oneself away from one's master to freedom. Spirituals also provided slaves with a way to articulate their particular understanding of the sacred universe. Unpersuaded by the Calvinist ideas of many southern whites (since whites often justified slavery as God's predestined plan for blacks), slaves created spirituals that focused less on individual sin and human depravity and more on endurance and communal triumph. To be sure, some spirituals revealed a sense of abandonment by God ("sometimes I feel like a motherless child"), while others exhibited a rejection of the material world ("this world is not my home"). By and large, however, spirituals exhibited a remarkable sense of hope and self-worth, providing evidence that those who sang them believed in a benevolent God who would eventually come to their rescue.

Postbellum and Industrial Nineteenth Century

If theology was meant to be the exclusive domain of trained theologians—or at least reserved for churches, synagogues, and secret slave gatherings—no one told Abraham Lincoln. In his second inaugural address, delivered just one month before the Civil War's end, President Lincoln tried to make sense of the bloodshed. He understood well the war's political causes, but he was less certain how to fit the conflict into his sacred universe. Aware that both warring factions prayed to the same God, Lincoln realized that the notion of God fighting for one side was overly simplistic. Indeed, the very notion that one side was evil and the other was good was, to Lincoln, indefensible. Lincoln finally had to admit that God had "His own purposes" for the war, some of which were beyond human comprehension. Still, he was willing to draw some theological conclusions. Lincoln suggested that God had given this war to both the North and the South as a way to purge the nation of slavery, an "offense" that had come to America by God's providence "but which having continued through His appointed time, He now wills to remove." According to Lincoln, the misery of the war was intimately connected to the suffering that had been inflicted on America's slaves. Moreover, this second round of suffering was actually purging America of its 250 years of sin.

Lincoln's notion of a purified people would take deep root in post–Civil War America, though it developed in a way that he would not have blessed. Like Lincoln, white southerners also needed to make theological sense of America's Civil War, a difficult task in light of their deeply held notion that God had approved their cause. How could it be, white southerners asked, that their rebellion had failed when a just and powerful God ruled the universe? From such nagging questions emerged a peculiarly southern understanding of history called "the Lost Cause," an interpretation of God's purposes that sustained white southerners' twin beliefs that God was just *and* the South was righteous in its cause. According to Lost Cause theology, God had punished the South for various sins, including worldliness and greed (but not slavery itself). This chastisement was painful, to be sure, but Lost Cause theologians asserted that divine chastisement was ultimately a good thing, for it indicated that God still had great plans for the South.

If postbellum southern Protestants needed any more evidence to prove their moral superiority, they found it in the social and theological innovations that were taking place in the North. One innovator was Methodist social activist Frances Willard, who drew on orthodox Christian themes to advance the role of the church in American society and the role of women generally. As the longtime president of the Woman's Christian Temperance Union, Willard promoted not only temperance but women's education, medical care for the poor, and prison reform. Her goal of Christianizing American society anticipated the work of many late-nineteenth-century social gospelers (see the section "Early Twentieth Century," later in this chapter), and her contention that women needed to take the lead in this work anticipated more thorough-going renditions of feminist theology. Woman is "first of all a daughter of God," wrote Willard, and her "relation to the state should be equal to that of her brother, man." Although later observers might deem this a rather moderate viewpoint, Willard's theologically based egalitarianism received a cool welcome from many postbellum Christians, including those in her own Methodist denomination.

Even more troubling to conservative Christians—and to all theists, for that matter—was the growing number of American atheists. Atheism, the belief that a supernatural being or divine force does not exist, has a long history in America—that is, it did not arise in the postbellum era. Still, this theological perspective attracted a number of prominent adherents in the 1870s and 1880s, most of whom were educated, upper-class northerners. The advance of atheism in the United States is often attributed to Charles Darwin, a British scientist whose *On the Origin of Species* (1859) challenged the notion that a Divine Designer had created a purposeful universe. Although many who embraced Darwin's scientific theories continued to espouse theism (the belief in God), the growing influence of science as an alternate and naturalistic way to explain reality convinced more than a handful of postbellum Americans that theism was now untenable.

Ironically, even as atheism was winning adherents on American soil, one of the world's oldest theistic traditions was gathering strength. Judaism was not new to North America in the late nineteenth century, but it became much more prominent with the arrival of eastern European immigrants in the 1880s and 1890s. Like its theological descendant Christianity, Judaism first developed in the Middle East as a monotheistic (single god) religion, identifying the universe's all-powerful God as Yahweh. According to Jewish thought, Yahweh had long ago established a covenant with a man named Abraham, the children of whom became Yahweh's chosen people, the Israelites. Yahweh's greatest gift to the Israelites was the Torah (the Law), which informed the people of Israel what Yahweh expected from them—expectations that were coupled with Yahweh's promise to bless obedience and punish disobedience. Because Yahweh's judgment was believed to extend beyond individuals to the Jewish people as a whole, Jews developed an elaborate system of sacrifices and ceremonies for demonstrating devotion to God and repentance from sin. Many nineteenth-century Jews continued to perform rituals that reenacted Yahweh's powerful acts and repaired breeches that developed from human disobedience.

The migration of European Jews to late-nineteenth-century America brought two forms of Judaism into stark contrast. Reform Judaism, which consisted mostly of ethnic German Jews who had lived in America for decades, sought to reduce the tensions between Judaism and the larger American culture by abandoning traditional Jewish practices (e.g., strict dietary laws). More than rejecting certain practices, however, the Reform movement encouraged Jews to think differently about their place in the world and God's relationship to them as Jews. For instance, Reform theologians rejected the notion that a Messiah would one day gather the Jewish people and return them to Palestine, their homeland. Reformers similarly rejected the authority of the Talmud, a commentary on the Torah that helped Jews understand God's expectations. Moreover, given the Jews' relatively happy existence in

America, the notion that God would send a Messiah to deliver them to Palestine made very little sense. What *did* make sense to them was the idea that modern people would understand God quite differently from premodern people and would therefore view God's expectations differently. According to the Reformers' Pittsburgh Platform (1885), present-day Jews should "accept as binding only the moral laws, and maintain only such ceremonies as elevate and sanctify our lives."

Reform Judaism appealed to the most Americanized segment of America's Jewish community, but the majority of late-nineteenth-century Jewish immigrants joined Orthodox synagogues. Unlike the Reformers, who sought to maintain the moral emphases of Judaism but otherwise adapt their religion to modern America, Orthodox Jews endeavored to preserve traditional ideas and practices. Deeply committed to both the Torah and the Talmud, Orthodox Jews accused their Reform counterparts of abandoning the essence of the Jewish faith and becoming little more than Gentiles (non-Jews) in the process. Soon a third party emerged within American Judaism, seeking a middle way. In many ways, Conservative Judaism expressed sympathy for Orthodox theological assumptions, maintaining, for instance, that fidelity to the law could not be compromised. Solomon Schechter, the most influential of all Conservative leaders, argued that America's religious freedoms meant that "we Jews need not sacrifice a single iota of our Torah." Nevertheless, even as the Conservative Jews argued for fidelity to tradition, they admitted that certain nonessential practices could be set aside. Although Orthodox Judaism continued to flourish on American soil, many of the immigrants' children eventually found homes in Conservative synagogues.

Late-nineteenth-century Catholics likewise reflected a variety of theological perspectives, some of them traditional, others rather innovative. For their part, immigrant Catholics often gave priority to devotional practices such as praying to saints, saying the rosary, visiting shrines, and handling relics. These deeply rooted practices manifested a theological framework in which God was always near at hand and was able (if not always willing) to grant supernatural favors to those who asked. Even nearer at hand were various Christian saints who could be called on to persuade God to act in benevolent ways. Needless to say, the saints who succeeded in that regard became very popular among those whose family members experienced healing or protection. These saints were less popular, however, among Roman Catholics who were invested in Americanizing the immigrant Catholics; the Americanist Catholics criticized the immigrant Catholics for their excessive commitment to "religious sentimentality," which, in the Americanists' view, led to intellectual and social passivity. In the view of one Americanist, Archbishop John Ireland, Catholics would be better served by recognizing "the new age" and "extend[ing] to it the conciliatory hand of friendship." Ireland's Americanizing views were never universally embraced, but they were certainly more welcome in the United States than they were in Rome. In 1899, Pope Leo XIII issued an encyclical condemning Americanism as muting crucial aspects of traditional Catholic theology.

Jews and Catholics were not the only postbellum Americans whose traditional theology was challenged by modern intellectual currents. Indeed, the growing prestige of science compelled many Americans to reformulate their theologies, mostly in the attempt to maintain theistic conceptions of the universe. In the realm of American Protestantism, the most celebrated reformulation was the New Theology, best articulated by Theodore Munger. Munger knew that many of his fellow Protestants had been disconcerted by Darwin's theories as well as by higher criticism, a way of studying texts that raised questions about the Bible's trustworthiness. In response to these intellectual crises, Munger published *The Freedom of Faith* (1883), in which he advocated not a retreat from science but a "broader use of reason in religion." According to Munger, the sacred and secular worlds had too long been held apart, resulting in Christian theologies that were overly "magical." By overcoming this divide, Munger continued, Christians could finally understand the historical and scientific processes by which God's reign was being established on earth. Of course, harmonizing the laws of nature with the Christian faith meant radically reinterpreting the nature of God, who in Munger's New Theology was much less transcendent (acting over and above human history) and far more immanent (acting in and through historical events). In Munger's scheme, even doctrines such as the resurrection of Jesus needed to be redefined, since the idea of a decomposing body being reconstituted could not be harmonized with the laws of nature. Needless to say, many Christians complained that Munger's naturalistic theology was nothing less than a rejection of true, supernatural Christianity.

In contrast to Theodore Munger, who tended to equate God's activity in the world with naturally explainable phenomena, Mary Baker Eddy preserved supernatural religion by adopting and adapting the language of science. Eddy's reformulated theology, Christian Science, was intimately connected to her past. Having experienced intense physical suffering during her early adult years, she found immediate relief one day while reading a New Testament story about Jesus healing a palsied man. Eddy attributed her sudden healing to a revelation of spiritual truth, which she eagerly shared with others. According to Eddy, every human possessed the potential to live an authentic and suffering-free existence, an existence that found its ultimate expression in Jesus Christ. The problem for most people was that they held very limited views of themselves, thinking about themselves primarily as material beings controlled by the laws of nature. Eddy sought to destroy this "illusion" by informing people that God, the Infinite Mind, had created all things (including humanity) as a reflection of that Mind. The secret to well-being, then, was for people to gain a correct understanding about the true nature of reality, which would in turn set them free from the illusory laws of nature.

In addition to retaining Jesus as her key religious figure, Eddy argued that the universe operated according to metaphysical laws (literally, above-physical laws) that humans could apprehend and follow. At their best, said Eddy, Christian Science practitioners—those who practiced these laws on behalf of others —could produce observable results again and again, just like scientists carrying out laboratory experiments. Thus, Eddy's new religion was not only *Christian*, it was *science*.

Other theologians proposed models harmonizing Christianity and science, giving Americans a growing number of theological options. Many Americans, however, were less than enamored with these mediating options. For these Americans, committed as they were to traditional theologies, it was not the time to search for middle ground. Rather, it was the time to choose sides.

Early Twentieth Century

In 1893, the World's Parliament of Religions met in Chicago. Held in conjunction with the Columbian Exposition, which celebrated the four hundredth anniversary of Columbus's arrival in North America, the parliament gathered representatives of the major world religions, including Hinduism and Buddhism. Some Americans had already encountered these Eastern religious traditions, but the World's Parliament of Religions gave these faiths a level of publicity they had never before enjoyed in North America. Even though these ancient Eastern religions gained only a handful of adherents in the parliament's aftermath, the excitement they generated reminded many Americans that theological diversity meant far more than just debating interpretations of the Christian Bible.

One American who found this theological diversity both fascinating and troubling was the philosopher and psychologist William James. Like so many others in his time, James stood at the intersection of science and religion, but instead of trying to harmonize them in some way (like Theodore Munger), he attempted to use science to explain religion. In his most famous study, *The Varieties of Religious Experience* (1902), James recorded and categorized the experience-based testimonies of all kinds of religious people. For James, the truth of these diverse testimonies did not reside in a particular theological conception of the universe; rather, the truth resided in the way these experiences (and the verbal testimonies that resulted from them) were morally and psychologically helpful to the persons who experienced them. James, who wanted desperately to believe in God, was unable to say anything definitive about a supreme being and, in that sense, did not have his own theology. At the same time, he was willing to consider another person's theology to be true as long as it helped that person make sense of his or her religious experiences and the universe in which these experiences occurred. For James, this pragmatic approach to truth made it possible for the scientifically minded person to take other people's religious experiences, and the theologies that explained them, seriously.

Even as James was conducting his scientific research, students at a small Kansas Bible college were interpreting their own religious experiences as mighty visitations from God. Earlier, the college's founder, Charles Parham, had taught his students about the "latter rain," a special outpouring of God's Spirit on humanity. Believing that the Holy Spirit's blessings had long been absent from earth, Parham and other latter-rain proponents forecast that the Spirit would once again shower the earth. When Agnes Ozman, one of Parham's students, began speaking in "unknown tongues" (a language unknown to the speaker) at a January 1, 1901, prayer service, Parham interpreted this activity as the baptism of the Holy Spirit. News quickly spread about Ozman's experience, and the Pentecostal movement was born, taking its name from a biblical account in which the Holy Spirit fell on early Christians at a festival called Pentecost. According to Pentecostal theology, God promised a threefold blessing to people who properly prepared themselves. Not only would God save them from their sins (the first blessing), but God's Spirit would cleanse them of their sinful nature (the second blessing). Christians in America's Holiness tradition had previously outlined this two-step process of conversion and sanctification, but Pentecostal theologians added to it by arguing that a third blessing was now in store for faithful Christians, namely, Holy Spirit baptism. How would one know whether he or she had experienced this Spirit baptism? For early Pentecostals the answer was clear: speaking in unknown tongues was the unmistakable sign.

The thrill of the latter rain, then, distinguished Pentecostalism in the early twentieth century. By this time, however, many other American Christians had arrived at the conclusion that they were living in history's last days. This sense that history would soon expire derived largely from a British theological import called dispensational premillennialism. Dispensational premillennialists interpreted the Bible to say that the world would become increasingly evil before Jesus returned to establish the last dispensation, a thousand-year period of peace and righteousness called the millennium. Some Christians criticized dispensational premillennialism as dangerously pessimistic, contending that it undermined the incentive to work for society's improvement in the here and now. The premillennialists' most relentless critics were advocates of the social gospel, a reform movement that sought to apply Jesus' teachings to contemporary social problems. Combining an emphasis on God's immanence (God working in and through history) with a *post*millennial view of history (in which Jesus would return *after* God's kingdom had been established on earth through Christian efforts), social gospel advocates rejected the notion that Christians should focus their attention on Jesus' return. For their part, premillennialists accused social gospel proponents of overestimating humanity's potential for improving a sin-ridden world. They believed that no one but Jesus himself could reverse the downward slide of history—and the sooner Jesus returned to do it, the better.

Premillennialism was simply one of many theological touchstones for fundamentalism, a Protestant theological perspective that rose to prominence during the century's first quarter. Emerging in response to evolutionary theory, scientific naturalism, and modernist theology, fundamentalists argued that there were certain fundamentals that one needed to believe to be a true Christian—not only premillennialism but the absolute inerrancy of the Bible, the virgin birth of Jesus, and Jesus' bodily resurrection. As we have seen, modernists found beliefs such as these intellectually problematic and argued that the essence of Christianity lay in its ability to elevate the human spirit and foster ethical activity. Why spend time arguing doctrinal trivialities, asked the modernist Harry Emerson Fosdick, when the world needs Christians working for justice? Fosdick may have perceived the fundamentalists' ideas to be peripheral to Christianity's core, but fundamentalists, who saw themselves as defenders of the true Christian faith, believed that Fosdick and his modernist friends had gutted Christianity of its supernatural basis. And the fundamentalists were right: the modernists *had* depreciated the value of the supernatural. At the same time, the fundamentalists had themselves been theologically innovative, making some formerly minor doctrines major and thereby redefining Christianity's essence.

The tensions generated by modern intellectual currents sparked theological disagreements among Roman Catholics as well. Of course, Roman Catholic theologians had something their Protestant counterparts lacked: an earthly authority who, by virtue of his office, had the final say in these theological disputes. In 1907, after a lengthy period of debate, Pope Pius X issued *Pascendi Dominici Gregis*, a statement in which he condemned modernism as "the heresy of all heresies." In this intellectual context, most American Catholic theologians sought to ground their thinking in the medieval philosophy of Thomas Aquinas. Neo-Thomism, as this school of thought was called, reaffirmed the idea that theological authority lay in the church's hierarchy, and it also affirmed the notion that the sacraments of baptism and the Eucharist ensured the spiritual unity of the Catholic Church. Much like the Protestant fundamentalists, neo-Thomists fashioned themselves as the defenders of traditional Christianity, although for them traditional meant straight from the thirteenth century. "A Catholic thinker should be . . . so wholly permeated with medieval thought," said one neo-Thomist, "that anything he says or does, even though it looks new, should be but a natural, immediate, and spontaneous expression of that everlasting tradition."

Although the effects of *Pascendi Dominici Gregis* continued to shape American Catholicism through the 1950s, it would be wrong to assume that there was no Catholic theological ferment in the intervening years. The most provocative contribution came from the Catholic Worker Movement, founded in 1933 by Dorothy Day and Peter Maurin. Distressed by the ruthlessness of industrial capitalism, Day and Maurin found theological resources within Catholicism to address the needs of working-class Americans. Their solution, sometimes called personalism, asserted that God's Spirit was most present in the world in personal acts of love. In other words, God's redemptive love, once embodied by Jesus Christ, was now revealed through Christians who devoted themselves to the same people Jesus did: the poor and the oppressed. In certain instances, Day was extremely critical of the American Catholic Church, expressing dismay with its "business-like priests" and its "lack of a sense of responsibility for the poor." At the same time, Day believed that the church's sacraments made God present to humanity in a loving way, thereby affirming a key tenet of traditional Catholicism. From that theological perspective, it only made sense to Day that to be truly Christian meant to engage in regular and unreciprocated acts of mercy.

As much as Catholics and Protestants adjusted and readjusted their theologies in the early twentieth century, a significant number of African Americans found them inadequate. Troubled by the inability of white Christians to renounce the racism in their midst, some African Americans concluded that this evil stemmed from the deep-seated European assumption that God was white. How else could one explain the pictures of a white Jesus, as well as white people's tendency to believe they were superior to blacks? In response to these realities, some African Americans began to formulate Christian theologies in which blackness assumed a central role. In the case of the African Orthodox Church, George Alexander McGuire encouraged African Americans to think of God "as black." Although he admitted that God was spirit and was therefore devoid of color, he nonetheless argued that humans could think of God only in anthropomorphic (humanlike) terms. That being the case, African Americans were entirely justified to think of God as black, "since we are created in His image and likeness."

Despite McGuire's attempts to reconceptualize the God of Christianity, some African Americans found it preferable to reject Christianity altogether. Wallace Fard and Elijah Poole (later Muhammad) were particularly creative in this regard, organizing in the 1930s the Nation of Islam. In some respects, the Nation of Islam mirrored the theology of Islam, a centuries-old monotheistic religion of Africa and the Middle East. For example, both Islam and the Nation of Islam proclaimed the existence of one God, Allah, whose ways were revealed by the seventh-century prophet Muhammad. But even as these two religions shared some beliefs, Black Muslims (adherents of the Nation of Islam) advocated certain ideas that other Muslims considered unorthodox. For instance, after Fard's disappearance in 1934, Black Muslims increasingly identified Fard with Allah himself. Poole, who then assumed the title "Messenger of Allah," outlined a series of beliefs that stressed the significance of blackness. In addition to arguing that the first human being was black, Elijah Muhammad taught his followers that a deranged black scientist had long ago created a "white beast" that multiplied out of control, creating the oppressive white race. According to Black Muslim teaching, the twentieth century would culminate in a colossal battle between good and evil, resulting in the return of black dominance under Allah's rule. In the meantime, blacks should endeavor to separate themselves from all aspects of white society, including "the white man's religion," Christianity.

In their attempt to formulate a meaningful theology, Black Muslims paralleled the activity of America's other theologians, both past and present. On the one hand, Black Muslims embraced traditional ideas that had been handed down through many generations. On the other hand, they sought to adapt these traditional ideas to their lived experience, which in their case was the experience of severe oppression. White Americans, most of whom showed little concern for the plight of blacks, paid little attention to this new theology in their midst. Indeed, only when Malcolm X gained the media's spotlight in the early 1960s did the Nation of Islam become a nationally recognized religious movement. As the twentieth century passed, other theologians would draw inspiration from him as they sought to connect their theological understandings to their political goals.

Modern America

No twentieth-century event shook America to the extent that World War II did, and theological systems were not immune to the tumult. Casualties mounted into the tens of millions, and the race to win the war produced a weapon that, for the first time, gave humans the godlike power to destroy the world. Moreover, Hitler's plan to exterminate every Jew in Europe came perilously close to succeeding, a reality that raised every sort of theological question. What did it say about God's love and power—and even God's existence—that an event as horrible as the Holocaust could occur?

One American theologian who was asking such questions before World War II was Reinhold Niebuhr. A professor at New York's Union Theological Seminary, Niebuhr criticized the optimism he saw in other Christian theologians, particularly those who considered themselves modernists, or liberals. Throughout his career, Niebuhr questioned the liberal assumption that education and religious inspiration would eventually eliminate self-centeredness and produce a peaceful world. To Niebuhr, this optimism not only ignored history but also disregarded the fundamental Christian truth that humans possessed significant potential for evil. Niebuhr's pessimistic appraisal of humanity, best expressed in *Moral Man and Immoral Society* (1932), won numerous adherents in the 1930s, especially as Americans gained knowledge of events transpiring in Germany. Later, Niebuhr remarked that he should have entitled his book "Immoral Man and Even More Immoral Society," a comment indicating his desire to revitalize Christianity's emphasis on human sinfulness. Even though Niebuhr's theology conflicted on many issues with that of Christian fundamentalists, the fundamentalists could give their heartiest assent to Niebuhr's scathing summary of liberal theology. According to Niebuhr, Christian liberals believed that "a God without wrath brought men without sin into a kingdom without judgment through the ministrations of a Christ without a cross." In other words, liberals (according to Niebuhr, at least) misunderstood the nature of God, history, and humanity on every point.

If the horror of the Holocaust compelled Christians to reevaluate their ideas about moral progress, it forced Jews to ask more agonizing questions about God's very existence. Some Jews found themselves drawn to the judgment of Richard Rubenstein, whose *After Auschwitz* (1966) argued that the Holocaust destroyed once and for all traditional Jewish notions about God. "How can Jews believe in an omnipotent, beneficent God after Auschwitz?" asked Rubenstein, who concluded that Jews had now entered "an age of no God." Rubenstein's answer to "the God problem" in the wake of Nazi death camps was more radical than most, but all Jewish theologians needed to offer some response. In *Faith after the Holocaust* (1973), Eliezer Berkovits suggested that God, despite being alive, chose to remain "hidden" from day-to-day human affairs. This hiddenness was necessary, said Berkovits, because if God constantly interfered in the world's affairs, humans would be deprived of both freedom and responsibility and would therefore cease to be human. Berkovits was careful to note, however, that God had not *completely* withdrawn from the world, for even though God remained hidden for long periods of time, God providentially guided history in the right direction. Hans Jonas offered yet a third Jewish answer to the God problem, explicitly rejecting Berkovits's notion of divine hiddenness. It wasn't that God *chose* to remain hidden, wrote Jonas; it was that God "has divested himself of any power to interfere with the physical course of things." In other words, God was not omnipotent. To some theists, Jonas's contention that God was not all-powerful flew in the face of reason, for to them omnipotence was the very definition of God. Jonas's response to this critique was penetratingly simple: How could a loving, all-powerful God stand by and watch Hitler kill millions of people? Jonas's theological solution to this haunting question was to sacrifice the notion of divine omnipotence for the sake of divine goodness.

Jews weren't the only Americans trying to make sense of God in the wake of World War II. Despite increasing attendance at worship services throughout the 1950s, some Americans were arguing that a transcendent, God-centered worldview was outdated and potentially destructive. In *The Secular City* (1965), theologian Harvey Cox suggested that modern people were increasingly finding meaning in the here and now, not in traditional religious dogma that promised a glorious afterlife. This rising secularity was not to be deplored, Cox said; it was to be celebrated, for it meant that the church could finally be relevant to society's needs. Redefining *theology* to fit his argument, Cox wrote that "theology . . . is concerned *first* with finding out where the action is." Cox's book may have been the most provocative theological treatise of the 1960s, but other theologians were even more blunt about the demise of traditional theology. Calling themselves "Death of God" theologians, these writers contended that God language no longer made sense to modern ears and should therefore be abandoned once and for all. The modern theologian, wrote one Death of God thinker in 1966, was "a man without faith, without hope, with only the present, with only love to guide him."

Despite extensive media coverage of the Death of God movement, the vast majority of twentieth-century Americans found God language very meaningful indeed. Few Americans expressed their God-centered convictions as eloquently as Martin Luther King Jr., whose charisma and intellect thrust him into the forefront of the civil rights movement. The son of a Baptist minister, King earned a divinity degree from Crozer Theological Seminary in 1951 and a Ph.D. in theology from Boston University in 1955, discovering along the way the writings of Reinhold Niebuhr and Mahatma Gandhi, the Hindu pacifist. But equally significant to King's theology was the black church tradition in which he was raised, a tradition that conceived of God as One who heard the cry of the oppressed. This theological perspective, often called liberation theology, would soon be articulated by Roman Catholics working among the poor in Latin America. In the United States, however, liberation theology emerged most prominently among those who campaigned for civil rights. These activists did not believe that God was dead, nor did they perceive God to be hidden. Rather, they saw God as empowering those who stood on the righteous side of the civil rights struggle. Later, African American theologians such as James Cone would extend these liberationist critiques of white oppression. According to Cone, who published *A Black Theology of Liberation* in 1970, the black experience provided the normative context for understanding Christianity, since the gospel of Jesus Christ was first and foremost a call for the liberation of the poor and oppressed.

The desire to overcome oppression inspired other twentieth-century liberation movements, many of which linked political action to theological reflection. Most notable in this regard was the feminist movement and its theological complement, feminist theology. Various feminist theologies had circulated in nineteenth-century America, but the nation's growing gender-consciousness in the 1960s and 1970s opened spaces for a new round of theologians to critique the patriarchy of Christianity and other male-dominated religions. Few feminist theologians spoke as powerfully as Mary Daly, whose book *The Church and the Second Sex* (1968) contended that traditional Christian theology had made God into "an old man with a beard" and thereby made women less than fully human. Other feminists advanced Daly's work, refining her notion that God exceeded the capacity of human language and that God therefore transcended the maleness assumed and assigned by biblical writers. Women of color, both black and Latina, pressed the discussion even further by combining critiques of racism and sexism. From the viewpoint of womanist theologians like Delores Williams, the black church was profoundly patriarchal, and the feminist movement was economically elitist, if not racist. Though acknowledging some commonalities between white feminist theologians and African American womanist theologians, Williams and others contended that the experiences of black and Latina women gave them unique vantage points for understanding God's activity in the world.

When Daly first published *The Church and the Second Sex* in 1968, she considered herself a Catholic and, like many feminist theologians, sought to transform Christian theology from the inside. Eventually, however, Daly concluded that the Christian religion was hopelessly sexist, and she joined a growing number of women who embraced alternate theologies that, in their view, more fully affirmed the female experience. Goddess religion, as these alternatives were sometimes called, revived ancient, matriarchal religious traditions that, instead of espousing a God with masculine characteristics, envisioned a feminine Goddess. According to adherents of Goddess religion, the Goddess possessed the power to infuse the world with feminine qualities that patriarchal religion and male-dominated bureaucracies had smothered. In addition to helping women challenge the world's patriarchies, the Goddess sanctified female strength and sexuality, two realities that were often demonized in patriarchal religious traditions. According to Goddess religion, even nature itself exhibited feminine power, demonstrating the Goddess's potency in rounds of birth and rebirth.

Feminism's reappropriation of Goddess religion signifies the usefulness of ancient religious ideas to late-twentieth-century Americans, a usefulness that others discovered through their association with New Age religion. Since its emergence as a self-conscious religious tradition in the 1970s, New Age religion (so called because it projects a wholesale human transformation that will introduce a harmonious new age) has never been a unified theological entity, but the books, practices, and training institutes that share the New Age name do manifest some common theological traits. Perhaps most significant, New Age religion exhibits an optimistic view of humanity, asserting that individuals can achieve salvation through immediate transformations of consciousness. These transformations, which overcome a false consciousness that limits human potential, can be nurtured by various means (e.g., meditation and channeling), all of which function to awaken practitioners to the divine that exists within them. In the strictest sense of the term, then, New Age thought is not really a theology, for it rejects the idea of a God who exists separately from humanity and offers salvation to the human race. Rather, New Age religion locates divine power in humans themselves and in the energy of the universe. Correspondingly, the goal of many New Age practices is to help practitioners become properly aligned with the life force of the universe, that is, with the energy that brings healing and releases unrealized human potential.

New Age religion embraces many of the theological assumptions of some of the world's oldest religious traditions. For instance, the New Age emphasis on self-realization through meditation reflects an Eastern understanding of sacred power that is evident in various strands of Buddhism. In addition to Eastern spiritual resources, New Age practitioners have found Native American traditions especially useful in their quest for self-realization and societal transformation. For instance, the Bear Tribe Medicine Society, an intentional community founded by the Ojibwa Indian Sun Bear, has endeavored to connect Native Americans and other Americans who share similar religious philosophies. Drawing on Native American ideas and practices, Medicine Society members seek to understand their place in the sacred universe, which, in Native American fashion, means realizing that the earth is a living being in need of care and healing. Indeed, an emphasis on ecological responsibility has been prevalent among various strands of New Age religion.

Conclusion

Not only today but throughout American history, many Americans have resisted being told by religious authorities what they should believe and have instead formulated belief systems that help them make sense of their worlds. Given the theological choices most Americans have had at their disposal, it should not surprise us that some seventeenth-century Puritans embraced Calvinist theology *and* a magical worldview. Nor should it surprise us that some twenty-first-century Americans discuss Christian theology on Sunday morning and manipulate New Age crystals on Friday night.

The tendency of Americans to combine seemingly contradictory theologies has led some observers to conclude that theology does not really matter or at least to claim that theological distinctions are lost on all but the highly educated. But lest we deem theology to be irrelevant to the lives of ordinary Americans, we should recall the astounding resilience of theistic belief in American life: despite the advance of modern, scientific thinking—an advance that led many observers to forecast the demise of traditional theology—a late-twentieth-century survey of religious beliefs revealed that the vast majority of Americans believed in God (95 percent), heaven (85 percent), and life after death (70 percent). Not only did these Americans maintain theistic conceptions of the universe, but many devoted their time, energy, and resources to converting others to their way of thinking.

Of course, the seriousness with which Americans approach theology should come as no surprise to students of American religious history. Since the Europeans arrived in the New World more than five centuries ago, theological discussions and disagreements have been a constant element of American life, spawning everything from bloodshed in the streets to friendly debates in college dormitories. For good and for ill, Americans have been—and will be—a theological people.

SUGGESTED READINGS

Albanese, Catherine L. *Nature Religion in America: From the Algonkian Indians to the New Age*. Chicago: University of Chicago Press, 1990.

Boyer, Paul. *When Time Shall Be No More: Prophecy Belief in Modern American Culture*. Cambridge: Harvard University Press, 1992.

Campbell, Robert A., and James E. Curtis. "Religious Involvement across Societies: Analyses for Alternative Measures in National Settings." *Journal for the Scientific Study of Religion* 33, no. 3 (1994): 215–29.

Carey, Patrick W. *American Catholic Religious Thought: The Shaping of a Theological and Social Tradition*. New York: Paulist Press, 1987.

Dayton, Donald W. *Theological Roots of Pentecostalism*. Peabody, Mass.: Hendrickson Publishers, 1987.

Hall, David D. *Worlds of Wonder, Days of Judgment: Popular Religious Belief in Early New England*. Cambridge: Harvard University Press, 1990.

Hatch, Nathan O. *The Democratization of American Christianity*. New Haven: Yale University Press, 1989.

Hutchison, William R. *The Modernist Impulse in American Protestantism*. Durham, N.C.: Duke University Press, 1992.

Karp, Deborah B., and Abraham J. Karp. "Jewish Literature and Religious Thought." In *Encyclopedia of the American Religious Experience*, edited by Charles H. Lippy and Peter W. Williams, 1015–38. New York: Scribner's, 1988.

Kuklick, Bruce. *Churchmen and Philosophers: From Jonathan Edwards to John Dewey*. New Haven: Yale University Press, 1985.

Marsden, George M. *Fundamentalism and American Culture: The Shaping of Twentieth-Century Evangelicalism: 1870–1925*. New York: Oxford University Press, 1980.

Noll, Mark A. *A History of Christianity in the United States and Canada*. Grand Rapids, Mich.: Eerdmans, 1992.

Raboteau, Albert J. *Slave Religion: The "Invisible Institution" in the Antebellum South.* New York: Oxford University Press, 1978.

Shipps, Jan. *Mormonism: The Story of a New Religious Tradition.* Urbana: University of Illinois Press, 1985.

Turner, James. *Without God, Without Creed: The Origins of Unbelief in America.* Baltimore: Johns Hopkins University Press, 1985.

Wilson, Charles Reagan. *Baptized in Blood: The Religion of the Lost Cause, 1865–1920.* Athens: University of Georgia Press, 1980.

Wright, Conrad. *The Beginnings of Unitarianism in America.* Boston: Starr King Press, 1955.

Proselytization

The Man Nobody Knows was a bestseller in 1925 and 1926. It was a biography of Jesus, depicting Christ as the world's greatest businessman. "He picked up twelve men from the bottom ranks of business and forged them into an organization that conquered the world," wrote author Bruce Barton, a minister's son and corporate public relations specialist. The parables of Jesus were not only pearls of wisdom but also the "most powerful advertisements of all time." Barton crudely expressed common views about the selling of religion, converting people to the faith—proselytization. Certainly the minister in the 1920s who advertised his weekly sermon with a sign for "Three-in-One Oil" as the image for the Holy Trinity understood that marketing ploys might entice converts—or at least inquiries.

Such religious advertising and recruiting—whether they come from the Protestant, Catholic, Mormon, Jewish, Islamic, Buddhist, Theosophist, Zoroastrian, or any other faith found (or founded) in the United States—were hardly new to the 1920s. Believers from diverse traditions have perfected techniques of aggressive salesmanship, active recruitment, niche marketing, and promoting brand loyalty. To be sure, recruitment into religious groups does not amount simply to market competition. Religious conversion involves complicated human desires, not simply targeted pitches. Yet the market analogy provides one useful way to understand how faiths solicit, recruit, and hold members.

This chapter considers varieties of religious proselytization. Innovators have adapted religious traditions to the American free market of conversion. Obviously this is true of evangelical groups, who are proselytizers by definition. To a remarkable extent it is true also of Jews, Catholics, Asian religious groupings, and others. But what is proselytization? Simply put, it is the action or practice of converting a person or people to a different opinion, political party, or faith, especially from one religious faith to another. Ironically, the term *proselyte* biblically and etymologically means a Gentile who has fully converted to Judaism, but in more recent times the term usually refers to evangelical conversion. Beyond these dictionary definitions, we will explore the cultural meanings of proselytization in American religious history. In taking up this task, a number of questions immediately arise. What are the motivations of the proselytizers and the proselytes—that is, the converts? Where does persuasion end and coercion begin? Does proselytization come down (in the cynical interpretation) to the creation and marketing of a brand name? Is the concept of proselytization itself based on a model of conversion that simply ill fits groups other than the self-consciously evangelical ones? To what extent, for example, can ethnically based religious groups (the German Lutherans, the Pennsylvania Dutch, East Indian Sikhs, the Acoma Puebloans, or the African American Nation of Islam) be said to proselytize? What about Judaism and other religions into which adherents are normally born (rather than actively being "born again")?

The free market of religion in America, protected by the Constitution ("Congress shall make no law respecting the establishment of religion, or prohibiting the free exercise thereof") and practiced in the daily spiritual quests of Americans, means that groups use persuasion to attract and hold converts. And the reality of the free market means that the winners (who for much of American history have been Protestants, especially of the evangelical variety) have written their own histories in triumphalist terms—as if the person who has the most souls wins the game. But proselytizers come in all shapes and sizes. They come with all sorts of motivations, too. Proselytizers generally see themselves as genuine and altruistic persuaders, as carriers of a message that may transform individual lives and perhaps even rectify injustices in the social order. Critics often see them as naive cultural imperialists, brainwashers, or accomplices in one or another project of political or psychological coercion. Discerning the "true" motivation is difficult, perhaps impossible; altruistic persuasion and cultural imperialism, for example, may often be two sides of the same coin. The methods and effects of proselytization are easier to assess. The evangelical model has been adapted by various traditions to suit their own purposes, whether New York City Presbyterians, the League of the Iroquois, slave preachers, Reform Jews, or American Zen Buddhists.

Precolonial America

Without a separate concept of "religion" as distinct from other rituals of life, Native Americans could not engage in, or even conceive of, proselytization. Recruiting people into a separate and identifiable faith was far removed from their cosmos. The Iroquois in New York and Canada did not send religious emissaries to the Catawba of the Carolinas or the Creeks of the Southeast. Rather, recruitment into a particular way of practicing faith came through other means. One of those was adoption, that is, literally incorporating members into the tribe (and into the tribe's religious practices) through adopting them as family members. The adoptees might be prisoners of war taken in skirmishes with other groups. They could also be marriage partners selected from outside the immediate tribal domains, or wandering individuals picked up while on hunting expeditions, or Europeans who through coercion or choice simply changed their identity and became "Indian." Mohawk Indians who besieged Deerfield, Massachusetts, in 1703 dragged off several white settlers, including a very young Eunice Williams and her father, a well-regarded minister. The white prisoners of war later were redeemed, save for Eunice. She refused ransom, choosing instead to stay with her Indian captors, now her adopted family, and practice their ways. No amount of negotiations and pleas from home could dissuade her. She had converted.

Native religions usually were tied to particular tribal groupings and geographies. With spirit invested in local ecologies—animals, flora, fauna, rocks, and other natural objects—native religions hardly were transferable to other tribes or places. When tribes federated into larger political entities, such as the Five Nations of the Iroquois, ceremonial rituals might be invoked, or invented, to sacralize the new entities, but this qualified less as proselytization than as assimilation. Seeking to recruit members to a faith outside the place and group was inconceivable—at least until Europeans, with their aggressively proselytizing ways, entered the Americas and conjured up a new world for everyone.

If American Indian religion had no concept of conversion, the peoples that the Indians were soon to encounter—the Europeans and Africans—espoused or already had been exposed to proselytizing religions that were based on universal claims. In England, a group of rowdy early Protestant Christians challenged the state-sanctioned Anglican Church, some trying to reform it and others decrying it as hopelessly corrupt. For these English Christians, derisively called Puritans, religion was an internal experience, one that required a complete transformation of the soul, rather than something based on good works and external forms. Despite persecution, the Puritans had already learned to proselytize for their radical religious ideas among a small but increasingly influential set of English men and women, most of them from the middle class or the ranks of the minor gentry. For Puritans, preaching the Word was foremost.

Meanwhile, in Catholic Europe, especially Spain and France, Catholic leaders fought the Protestant Reformation, themselves proselytizing for Catholicism in what historians call the Counter-Reformation. Catholic leaders formed new brotherhoods, notably the Society of Jesus (the Jesuits), which were soon key to the global spread of the Catholic version of Christianity. In Spain, leaders of the Inquisition punished those who deviated from orthodoxy, developing modes of religious coercion that would soon be applied to American Indians in Florida, Mexico, and the North American Southwest. In Africa, during these same years, Islamic proselytizers marched from their northern strongholds southward to sub-Saharan Africa, the center of the new westward slave trade, and brought many Africans into Muslim beliefs and practices. Meanwhile, European (especially Portuguese) missionaries experienced considerable success among the Kongolese and other groups. Thus, even though most Africans continued to practice tribal religions that (like those of American Indians) were localized and nonproselytizing, the missionary religions of Christianity and Islam made a considerable impact among the African peoples who were already in the process of being forcibly transported to the Americas.

Colonial North America

The narrative of Christian proselytization in the Americas begins with European Catholics—specifically, the Spanish and the French. They carried the struggle for Christ and against the Protestant Reformation to different parts of the New World—the Spanish to the Southwest, California, and Florida and the French to upper New York, Canada, and the Mississippi Valley. The Jesuits in New France (around the Great Lakes and the Mississippi Valley), faithful chroniclers of their missionary expeditions, never wielded the same proselytizing authority as did the Franciscans in the Southwest, mostly because they were not generally associated with a military force intent on settlement. In reports to their superior in France, the Jesuits wrote soberly of their experience, apoplectic that the savages were content with their own cultural customs. Complaints of the language barrier and the hard work and expense of missionary life dominate the French missionaries' reports. "Instead of being a master and great Theologian as in France, you must reckon on being here a humble Scholar, and then, good God! With what masters—women, little children, and all the Savages—and exposed to their laughter," a discouraged missionary wrote home in 1636. Yet the proselytizing zeal remained. He urged others to join in the perilous work: "It is to souls like yours that God has appointed the conquest of so many other souls whom the Devil holds yet in his power."

In the sixteenth-century Southwest, the incoming Spanish invoked magical enticement and practiced brutal coercion in their proselytizing efforts. Don Juan de Onate and several hundred Franciscan friars and their military escorts on horses traveled northward to New Mexico, establishing the town of San Juan in 1598. The Puebloans, themselves migrants to the region a few hundred years before the Spanish, attempted to bring these European newcomers into their world, using gifts of corn and other goods and offering their women to cool the fires of the European men. The friars responded strangely, in the eyes of the Puebloans. The friars came with crosses held high, and soon the southwestern natives (such as residents of the Acoma Pueblo) took the crosses as the functional equivalent of their own prayer sticks.

Unlike Protestants, who emphasized preaching the Word, the Franciscans in the Southwest saw practicing the Word as the foremost means of proselytization. First, the Indian soul had to be purged, a task the friars attempted by confiscating kachinas (doll-like icons of Pueblo cosmology), prayer sticks, and other items of material culture. The padres invaded the kivas (cone-shaped interior sacred spaces in which gods could be summoned) and planted crosses in the middle, symbolizing the triumph of Christ over pagan forces. Purification also meant rooting out Indian sexual mores. Here, the (theoretically) celibate world of the Franciscans encountered the highly sexualized cosmos of the Puebloans, with its imagery of rain fructifying the earth like a man's semen fertilized a woman and with an institutionalized social role for homosexuals and transvestites. Franciscans meted out special punishments to those engaged in what the Europeans disgustedly viewed as sexual perversion. Friars whipped, shaved, and on occasion sodomized or painfully twisted the testicles of the male neophytes. The "warriors of Christ" displayed their might in front of Pueblo children, who were supposed to see the power of the padres and the relative impotence of the native gods. If such coercive practices were the stick, the European abundance offered to children at the missions was the carrot. For example, by dispensing livestock to young men, the friars broke the dominance of revered older natives and enticed younger Puebloans into the Christian fold. This was proselytization by material acculturation. The friars also staged theatrical productions, teaching the events of the Christian narrative and thus displacing the temporal seasonal yearly rhythms ingrained in southwestern native cultures—proselytization through drama.

The great Pueblo revolt of 1680 vividly displayed the anger at such coercive proselytization. The Puebloans burned churches, demolished crosses and chapels, and tortured and killed friars. The first century of Christian proselytization in the Southwest thus ended in violent revenge by the very natives who supposedly had been made children of the Christian God. But the Spanish in the Southwest by no means were cowed by uprisings. By the eighteenth century, after two centuries of Franciscan proselytization and the Puebloans' complicated response, traditions melded. The best example of this may be the appearance, in parades and festivals, of the Virgin Mary, draped in flowers, her ears sprouting corn stalks. In southwestern festivals and parades, the Catholic Virgin adopted the trappings of the Pueblo Corn Mother, whose fertility brought forth crops and children.

Coercive proselytization also characterized the California missions in the eighteenth century, notably in the person of the Franciscan Junípero Serra. The idea of the missions—Spanish-style compounds built from San Diego to San Francisco—was to take California Indians, the neophytes, and gradually civilize them, which necessarily meant Christianizing them. As with the Franciscans in New Mexico, the proselytizing padres used material enticement to attract American Indians (especially younger men) into the fold and then worked them and disciplined them harshly for their "barbarism." Father Serra readily admitted that the California padres whipped their native children, assuming that this rendered them spiritual aid. By the end of the missions period, the 1830s and 1840s, the padres had overseen the near total extinction of the California natives through the breakdown of tribal ways coupled with the spread of disease, alcohol, and warfare. In this case, proselytization was the means to a final solution of the Indian question.

In New England, the Puritans, who begin arriving in large numbers in the 1630s, also proselytized among native populations, in fits and starts. John Eliot, a New England divine, translated the Bible into Algonquian, intending to teach American Indians the Word and train some of them to be ministers. "Some of them began to be seriously affected, and to understand the things of God," wrote Puritan leader John Winthrop in his journal, describing the effect of Eliot's preaching, "and they were generally ready to reform whatsoever they were told be against the word of God, as their sorcery (which they call powwowing,) their whoredomes, etc., idleness, etc." But Eliot's well-intentioned endeavor could not prevent King Philip's War of the 1670s, an East Coast debacle of destruction that paralleled the contemporaneous Pueblo revolt in northern New Mexico. During the war, Eliot's praying Indians huddled on Martha's Vineyard without food, clothing, and fuel. But by that time, few New Englanders cared to distinguish any longer between praying Indians and preying barbarians. The preeminent Puritan divine of the late seventeenth century, Cotton Mather, rejoiced at the victories of white New Englanders, convinced that God's plan called for less proselytization and more subjugation.

The Puritans envisioned creating a "city set upon a hill," a beacon of holiness that would shine on the corrupt Old World. They excised all manner of churchly ornamentation, in architectural style, priestly garb, and worship practice. Puritan divines outlined a covenant theology, a belief system positing a kind of cosmic contract between the elect and God, who offered salvation by grace in exchange for human submission to God's omnipotent power. Inheritors of Calvinism, which stressed the total depravity of humans and the infinitely mysterious power of God, the Puritans knew that grace alone —not infant baptism, good works, indulgences for the church, or personal yearning for piety—sufficed for salvation. Yet they faced the problem inherent in Calvinism: Who knew who was of the elect, those chosen to receive God's grace? And who might be fooling whom? God's unfathomable grace, after all, works in mysterious ways. In theory, it could be possible for the most pious Puritan to be denied God's grace, for reasons beyond human determination, while another apparently less worthy soul might luck into salvation. Moreover, the fierce litigiousness of New Englanders—their constant legal battles over whose property line ended where, whose cow might traipse on whose property, and whose servant had bewitched or hexed another's household— suggested the human frailties even of the saints, let alone the sinners.

Grappling with this dilemma, Puritan theologians reasoned that, even if God's grace was mysterious and indefinable, in practice men more or less knew who was of the elect. Personal behavior told. Puritans referred to as "visible saints" those whose piety, godly ways, and public professions of faith indicated outwardly that they were almost surely God's children inwardly. This hardly settled the philosophical quandary, but it provided a theological mechanism for a workable social order. Over several generations, as New England society prospered, Puritans evolved into Yankees. Not all were happy with what they saw as the spiritual decline that accompanied material comforts. They yearned for revival and got it in the mid-eighteenth century.

American evangelicalism took off with a series of revivals in the American colonies in the eighteenth century, collectively known as the Great Awakening. Appearing sporadically from New England and the Middle Colonies in the 1740s to the Chesapeake and coastal lowland South in the 1760s, the Great Awakening featured new styles of popular public evangelicalism. Challenging the authority of older, established ministers, the so-called New Lights convicted the seemingly pious of sin and brought a new message of born-again Christianity. The greatest theologian in American history, Jonathan Edwards, provided a substantial intellectual framework for new modes of evangelization. He outlined a philosophy for and psychology of the conversion experience, in terms made familiar by John Locke and other leading philosophers of the time.

The Great Awakeners attacked "dead" (unconverted) ministers and established churches. Gilbert Tennent's famous sermon "The Danger of an Unconverted Ministry" ignited a bitter exchange of words between the established Old Lights and the upstart New Lights. In some places, female and black revivalists carried the Word to the sinners and fiercely defended the right of social inferiors to declaim the word of God. August divines such as the Bostonian Charles Chauncy insisted that preaching the Word could not be entrusted to roving packs of untested and theologically naive proselytizers. "What is the Tendency of the Practice, but Confusion and Disorder," he asked. "If one Pastor may neglect his own People to take Care of others, who are already taken care of; . . . why not another, and another still, and so on, 'till there is no such Thing as Social Order in the Land." Despite such withering criticism, there would be no turning back from the democratization of proselytization.

The eighteenth-century revivals were a transatlantic phenomenon, a fact exemplified in the life of George Whitefield. Born to a devout Anglican family, Whitefield attended Oxford as a servitor, a gopher boy for sons of the gentry. While there, he fell under the sway of John Wesley, who had begun an informal fellowship of pietists later pejoratively dubbed the "Methodists," referring to their emphasis on cultivating a method for spiritual practice. In 1740 and 1741, Whitefield preached in the northern colonies. Americans responded enthusiastically to his thunderous appeals. His journals were widely read in England and the colonies, turning him into a celebrity speaker. Whitefield yearned for reconciliation between the warring Old Lights and New Lights, aiming to make America safe for evangelical democracy. As the years progressed, Whitefield's public presence, adroit use of theatrical tactics, and unctuous earnestness turned him into a kind of colonial Billy Graham, a unifying presence wholly unthreatening to authorities. He developed a friendship with Benjamin Franklin, whose *Poor Richard's Almanack* placed alongside Whitefield's sermons as classics of eighteenth-century American expression. In their own very different ways, the two famous Americans proposed that the wisdom of common men should form the basis of authority. These evangelists for commonsense enlightened rationalism (Franklin) and evangelical fire (Whitefield) both pointed to the coming revolutions in politics and religion.

Revolutionary and Early Republican America

During the American revolutionary era, the new techniques of popular communication developed in part by Whitefield and other evangelists (as well as by newspapers and pamphleteers such as Thomas Paine) inspired colonists to defeat the greatest Western imperial power of that era, centered in London. Ministers first rallied parishioners to holy war against the French in the Great War for the Empire, also known as the French and Indian War, from 1754 to 1763. Colonial religious elites depicted this complicated transatlantic conflict as a sort of Protestant crusade against "papists" in the western wilderness (notwithstanding the fact that substantial numbers of colonial American Catholics, including a large percentage of the population of Maryland, had also caught the contagion for liberty). Such revolutionary rhetoric, communicated through the same popular means employed by evangelists in the Great Awakening, soon ignited popular understanding of the struggle against British rule. Ministers again invoked the sacred cause of liberty. The British pharaoh could not stand against the American Moses. Religious and political liberty were intertwined, allowing evangelical ministers and antievangelical elites (such as Thomas Jefferson and other enlightened Deists) to make common cause.

For American Indians, the rapid westward expansion of Anglo-Americans throughout the eighteenth century spelled not liberty but disaster. Westward settlers encountering Indians deployed a range of cultural intermediaries — traders, government officials, missionaries, and others. Even in a relatively promising situation of a middle ground between Indians and whites, however, conflict ruled the day. In Pennsylvania, the founding vision of peaceful coexistence of peoples gave way to constant and murderous skirmishes. Christian proselytizers, go-betweens in an increasingly hostile environment, met failure. As one native informed a missionary on the Pennsylvania frontier in 1745, "We are Indians and don't wish to be transformed into white men. The English are our Brethren, but we never promised to become what they are."

American Indian leaders used religious awakenings to revitalize their beleaguered communities. One religious seer, an Iroquois from New York named Handsome Lake, went through a series of visionary journeys in the late eighteenth century, a time when the historical dominance of the Iroquois nations in the region fell prey to a rapidly advancing American civilization. Handsome Lake's original message melded Iroquois lore and Christian beliefs learned from Quaker missionaries. "Our lands are decaying because we do not think on the Great Spirit," Handsome Lake had written to President Thomas Jefferson, "but we are now going to renew our Minds and think on the great Being who made us all, that when we put our seeds in the Earth they may grow and increase like the leaves on our Trees." Originally consumed with apocalyptic visions of Iroquois destiny, in later years Handsome Lake turned to a gospel of sobriety and industry among American Indians, peace with whites, and preservation of Iroquois lands. In the religion of Handsome Lake, salvation came through following the code of Gaiwiio (the Good Message), with a mixture of Iroquois practices (including a traditional ceremonial calendar and a mythology consonant with older beliefs) and Christian influences (temperance, confession, and a notion of conversion to a new religion). Handsome Lake presented himself originally as a messenger of the new code, a preacher, but later claimed special supernatural revelations and divine powers.

The religious ferment of the new Republic came to a head in the early nineteenth century. One scholar has labeled this era the "democratization of American Christianity." Other historians have referred to this time as the "Methodist century." During the period from 1800 to 1850, church membership increased tenfold. In 1800 one out of every fifteen Americans was a Protestant church member; by 1850 that number was one in seven. The Methodists, a small sect in the late eighteenth century, numbered more than one million by midcentury. With circuit-riding preachers combing the countryside on their horses, preaching to congregations throughout the newly settled areas, Methodists proved flexible enough to meet the need for religious organization on the frontier. Using their centralized church governance, Methodist leaders harnessed and controlled their expanding empire. Methodist theology, moreover, highlighted free will in accepting or rejecting God's grace, ideal for a society in which men seemed to control their own destinies. In short, Methodists were perfect for this new religious environment of westward expansion and permanent religious competition.

The revivals in the newly settled region around Cane Ridge, Kentucky, kicked off decades of camp meetings. Americans found in the camp meeting setting a peculiarly satisfying combination of religious edification, social communion, and theatrical entertainments. At these countryside fests, several ministers simultaneously preached in large communal services, while families (including slaves) camped out along the grounds. The day alternated between devotions and prayers, meals, and ecstatic religious experiences. Peter Cartwright, a tireless Methodist camp meeting exhorter in the early nineteenth century, recalled that, even though the preachers of the time "murdered the king's English almost every lick," nevertheless "Divine unction attended the word preached, and thousands fell under the power of God." Up to ten thousand people gathered from miles around and heard a dozen or more ministers of various denominations exhort. "I have seen more than a hundred sinners fall like dead men under one powerful sermon, and I have seen and heard more than five hundred Christians all shouting aloud the high praises of God at once," Cartwright later wrote. Converts at the early, most enthusiastic meetings, from 1801 to 1805, recounted "trances and visions" and engaged in what one observer called "the running, jumping, barking exercise." In later decades, religious leaders enforced stricter codes of decorum, hoping to tame such backwoods frenzies, but the camp meeting remained a popular and effective tool of democratic Protestant proselytizers.

Antebellum Nineteenth Century

Proselytizers enjoyed stunning successes in the religious democracy of antebellum America. Congregationalists and Presbyterians united their plans to send home missionaries westward to establish churches for the expanding population and evangelize among the Indians. Methodist circuit riders and Baptist farmer-preachers by the thousands exhorted in brush arbors and log cabin churches, drawing tens of thousands to their fold. Tens of thousands more flocked to camp meetings. Denominational proselytization through debate became mass entertainment. In multiday oral sparring matches, Baptists disputed with Methodists over the proper mode of baptism, and Presbyterians feuded with Methodists over the finer points of Calvinist determinism versus free will. Some Protestants advocated a return to the original New Testament church (hence their historical designation as "primitivists"). Groups such as the Disciples of Christ, led by former Baptist ministers Alexander Campbell and Barton Stone, proselytized for "no creed but the Bible," believing themselves to be the contemporary manifestation of the ancient church. But the Disciples soon divided into various factions, not fully agreed on just what the Bible taught. Presbyterians, Methodists, several varieties of Baptists, Disciples of Christ, Shakers, Quakers, transcendentalists, Mormons, "Millerites" (Adventist Christians who believed that Jesus would return exactly in 1843)—the list of proselytizers goes on. Antebellum religious expression increasingly appeared to be infinitely divisible. Evangelical workers may have gathered a bountiful harvest, but they also sowed the seeds of religious chaos.

In upstate New York, a religious seeker named Joseph Smith, distraught over this Christian disunity, claimed to have discovered some tablets, placed there by the angel Moroni. The newfound text, which became the Book of Mormon, revealed the place of America in the ancient Christian narrative. In America, according to his revelation, the saints would gather in Zion and create the Kingdom of God on earth. Smith converted others, first in the area in upstate New York from which he hailed. Later, Mormon proselytizers found much success in the newly developing regions of what would become the Midwest, such as the present-day states of Indiana, Illinois, and Missouri. All male members of Mormon churches were priests, expected to preach at every opportunity—and they did. A hierarchy of male priesthood orders honored those with seniority in the mission field. Only Joseph Smith held the complete revelation, but elders were to sermonize as the Spirit moved them. Centralized doctrinal control combined with decentralized means of proselytization served Mormons as well as it did Methodists.

Charles G. Finney, the great Protestant preacher of that era, eased northern (especially New England) suspicions about the social turmoil that might be unleashed by potent plain-folk revivalism. Not exactly of the plain folk himself—he was a lawyer and college president as well as an evangelist—Finney articulated theological reasoning common to antebellum Christians. A revival, he explained, was simply "the *right* use of the appropriate means." Revival preachers sowed the seed. Ultimately, only God's blessing allowed the seed to blossom and the harvest to come. What was the result, Finney asked, of the older doctrine of divine sovereignty, that men had no agency in their own salvation? Finney's answer: while the church fiddled, America burned. Millions had "gone down to hell, while the church has been dreaming, and waiting for God to save them without the use of means. It has been the devil's most successful means of destroying souls." Just as political campaigning brought out the vote, revivalism produced sure results. Churches were "awakened and reformed," sinners saved, profligates reclaimed, "harlots, and drunkards, and infidels, and all sorts of abandoned characters, are awakened and converted. The worst part of human society are softened, and reclaimed, and made to appear as lovely specimens of the beauty of holiness." Finney also imparted his own strongly perfectionist streak to the Second Great Awakening, a movement that fed directly into abolitionism, women's rights, Spiritualism, and communal living experiments.

Many antebellum Christians argued that, with freedom of religion (and freedom not to attend church, the case for most Americans), moral order could come about only through an intense voluntarism. And voluntarism required committed activists, virtuosos of religion and social reform. William Lloyd Garrison, leader of the abolitionist movement, was one such perfectionist. With financing from well-off and socially conscious philanthropists, Garrison and others pounded the pulpit for the cause of cleansing the nation of its original sin, slavery. Antislavery societies engaged lecturers as itinerant proselytizers, a method drawn from the Methodists. They produced an avalanche of printed material, paralleling similar publishing feats from the American Tract Society and other religious print agencies. The abolitionists, however, converted relatively few to their cause of immediate, unconditional, uncompensated emancipation.

Antislavery advocates found a powerful voice in Frederick Douglass. After escaping from his Maryland plantation in the 1830s, Douglass embarked on a remarkable career as an internationally known evangelist for human freedom. A brilliant writer and polemicist, Douglass was probably the single most effective proselytizer for the antislavery cause. In the 1840s and 1850s, while residing in Rochester, New York, and publishing the black abolitionist organ the *North Star*, he rhetorically devastated the slave system and the so-called revivalism that accompanied the spread of the iniquitous institution. As Douglass told one gathering, "Revivals in religion, and revivals in the slave trade, go hand in hand together. The church and the slave prison stand next to each other, the groans and cries of the heartbroken slave are often drowned in the pious devotions of his religious master . . . while the blood-stained gold goes to support the pulpit, the pulpit covers the infernal business with the garb of Christianity." Equally effective in the antislavery ministry was Sojourner Truth, the black abolitionist who once purportedly bared her breast in front of detractors who doubted that she was a woman (at the same time offering to suckle those skeptics with the same breast that had nursed many white babies). "This unlearned African woman, with her deeply religious and trustful nature burning in her soul like fire, has a magnetic power over an audience perfectly astounding," wrote one admirer.

The abolitionists blanketed the North with powerful visuals, including the famous image of the chained slave kneeling before a standing white man, the slave asking, "Am I not a man and a brother?" Most important for this strategy of sentimentalism, however, was Harriet Beecher Stowe's melodramatic masterpiece *Uncle Tom's Cabin*, the best-selling book in America (save for the Bible) in the nineteenth century. Stowe's work exposed slavery's inevitable degradation of both slave and master. Stowe's angelic heroine, Little Eva, daughter of a dissolute but sympathetically portrayed slaveholder in New Orleans, communicates the moral: slavery is wrong because it is cruel and heartless. Stowe clinched the tale with the evil Yankee slave driver Simon Legree presiding over the horrific beating of Uncle Tom, the pious slave. In the story's epilogue, the major black characters who have managed to escape to the North (including Eliza, after her famous tiptoeing across the ice floes of the Ohio River to the shores of freedom, carrying her child in her arms) set sail for Africa, where they proselytize for the Christian faith among their benighted African brothers.

In the South, antislavery sentiments stood no chance against the grim reality that slavery was profitable and gave even poor whites a chance at wealth. Here, the major proselytizers were not the famous preachers such as Whitefield but instead relatively anonymous plain-folk evangelicals who transformed this region of backwoods indifference into the Bible Belt, the land of conservative Christianity. Early colonial efforts at proselytization, led by the Anglican Society for the Propagation of the Gospel in Foreign Parts, experienced limited success with whites and virtually none among slaves. Virginia Anglicans struggled throughout the eighteenth century, attracting colonial elites but few others. Later in the century, the Baptists in Jefferson's Virginia shocked their world. They refused to pay taxes to the Anglican Church, condemned horse racing and its attendant gambling as sinful, and met in biracial groupings to celebrate their salvation from eternal damnation, sometimes hearing black or female exhorters in such meetings. Those under conviction—often women, sometimes black, generally younger, and often of modest wealth—narrated their quests for glory. Though these seekers couched their stories in the expected self-abasing idiom—"a wretch like me," as the phrase from the first lines of "Amazing Grace" goes—salvation for them meant that their private turmoil assumed cosmic significance. Initially, the southern elites scorned the evangelicals. Yet by the 1830s, and even more so by the Civil War, wealthy men and women filled the pews in the churches of the same incipient denominations whose forebears they had disdained as zealous ranters. As spired steeples replaced log churches and unlettered exhorters gave way (at least in cities) to gentleman theologians, southern clergymen propounded their own social vision of God, country, family, and slavery. In other words, they sold out.

Into such a milieu came the mission to the slaves, led most prominently by Charles Colcock Jones, a Presbyterian minister and slave-owning planter from Savannah. He urged on a reluctant planter class the need to spread the gospel to enslaved people. It was a difficult sell in a region that constantly surveilled black gatherings. A South Carolina rice baron noted the prevalent white fears that slaves who listened to the evangelical preachers might "imbibe . . . the notions of equality and liberty, maintained in the gospel." Jones crafted his message carefully. He told planters that religious instruction would create "a greater subordination" and would teach "respect and obedience [to] all those whom God in his providence has placed in authority over them." He assured slaves that submitting to their earthly rulers and heavenly master ensured their reward in another life.

Slaves also preached the Word. Mostly denied the written Word, slave preachers mastered the art of oral religious expression. Sometimes they preached in public, in separately organized black churches that remained under close white monitoring. In public their message was carefully contained. In private, however, when slaves spread the gospel among themselves, the preaching took flight. One black Texas minister, told by the master to preach obedience, subverted that message when he could: "I knew there was something better for them but I darsn't tell them so lest I done it on the sly. That I did lots." He told the slaves, "but not so Master could hear it, if they kept praying that the Lord would hear their prayers and set them free." Antebellum slave preachers thus became agents of covert proselytization, precisely what Charles Colcock Jones's critics feared would happen.

Postbellum and Industrial Nineteenth Century

After the Civil War, proselytization entered a new age of mass-marketed evangelism, even while other groups carved out their own space in a Protestant-dominated America.

Black churches experienced a remarkably rapid growth after the Civil War: black missionaries fanned out across the country; prominent churches in major cities erected impressive edifices; and black religious entrepreneurs established presses and publishing houses to provide edifying material for their own people. Baptist and Methodist churches claimed more than 90 percent of black churchgoers, no accident because these two denominations took the lead in converting slaves and free blacks and because these populist evangelicals required no education or formal training of preachers or converts. Few matched the tireless organizing for African American rights in church and state of Henry McNeal Turner. Turner is known mostly for his advocacy (later in his life) of black American emigration to Africa, but his major achievement was the establishment of the African Methodist Episcopal (AME) Church in the South after the Civil War. Born free in South Carolina, in the 1850s Turner established residence and began to make his name and career in Georgia. Stunned by the erudition Turner displayed in the Methodist pulpit, some claimed that he was a "*white man galvanized.*" After service as a Union army chaplain, Turner set about organizing the AME Church in Georgia, a black denomination banned from the South in the 1820s when black Methodists in Charleston were implicated in an aborted slave rebellion. When southern-style racism swept the country in the 1890s, Turner made his name as a progenitor of black theology, advocate of black American emigration to Africa, and organizer of AME missions work in South Africa.

White southerners after the war created their own civil religion, featuring its own theology, myths, rituals, and saints. Evangelists for the Lost Cause, notably the elite Virginia minister and historian John William Jones, propounded a mythical interpretation of the past that exalted the deeds of the fallen Confederate heroes. According to the tenets of Lost Cause theology, God's chosen people (white southerners) had been baptized in the blood of suffering and thus had been chastened and purified. In justifying the reimposition of white supremacist regimes in the southern states, religious proselytization compelled political activism.

Mainstream Protestantism in the post–Civil War North—victorious in war and complacent in peace—settled down to a comfortable existence, symbolized most prominently by Henry Ward Beecher's prosperous congregation in Brooklyn (as well as his astronomical yearly salary of thirty thousand dollars). Russell Conwell's famous oration "Acres of Diamonds," a sermon suggesting that God would financially reward the pious, set the tone for much popular preaching. Pulpiteers trumpeted the "Gospel of Success," and Americans purchased Horatio Alger's didactic children's novels, which taught the godly lessons of luck and pluck.

Evangelicals figured that the future of mass evangelism depended on conducting respectable, sober crusades that would undergird rather than undermine authority. Dwight Moody, the transatlantic evangelical phenomenon of the era, fit the bill perfectly. As a young entrepreneur, Moody set up shop in Chicago in the 1860s, recognizing that the city with broad shoulders needed boots and shoes. While Moody accumulated wealth, he poured energies into his own newly created Sunday school situated in a red-light district on Chicago's Near North Side. Here Moody conducted relentlessly friendly evan-

gelistic campaigns, pursuing children on the street, herding them into his informal church, and giving pithy exhortations. By the 1870s, Moody's evangelical meetings in England and throughout America attracted large crowds. Increasingly, he depended on financial support from the business community, a
fact entirely consonant with his own theology and social vision. The Philadelphia department store tycoon John Wanamaker, one of his primary patrons, turned an abandoned railroad depot into a tabernacle hall for a Moody
crusade there in 1876. Following the event, Wanamaker installed a new department store in the depot, reasoning that the meetings had familiarized Philadelphians with the location. Learning from his business cronies, Moody employed skillful techniques of preparation and persuasion. Volunteers planned
the actual meetings carefully and advertised them vigorously, setting precedents for later evangelical campaigners such as Billy Graham. Moody's de-
meanor was also a model. He seemed to speak spontaneously, from the heart,
even as he delivered well-practiced and perfectly timed pleas. Political radi-
cals derided mass evangelism as sugar coating on the raw will to power of
Gilded Age industrialists. Yet Moody remained a popular symbol, difficult
to dislike personally even though many liberal Protestants objected to him
ideologically.

Not all evangelical crusades were as quietist. The Woman's Christian Temperance Union (WCTU), the largest organization of women in American history up to that point, accomplished the era's greatest persuasive feat. Temperance advocacy had a long history throughout the nineteenth century, closely
paralleling the movement for woman suffrage. Protestant women, with some
male allies, led the movements. Both were originally associated with antebellum perfectionism but lapsed into a post–Civil War lull, as the conservatism
of the Gilded Age stifled reform. Finally, in the latter part of the nineteenth
century, both movements revived under the leadership of progressive women
such as Elizabeth Cady Stanton and her daughter Harriet Stanton Blanch
(suffragism) and Frances Willard (temperance). For the WCTU, eliminating
the scourge of alcohol assumed the same moral significance that exorcising
slavery held for an earlier generation. The WCTU, as well, debated the same
quandary—moral suasion versus political action—common to American
reform movements. The temperance movement followed both strategies at
various times and discovered that political victory did not bring about the
Kingdom of God on earth. Still, the WCTU's achievement was astonishing.
Antebellum America was an alcoholic republic. Citizens consumed mass quantities of alcoholic beverages, and political candidates regularly "treated" supporters to liquor on election days. By 1920, the same year women secured

their constitutional right to vote, America was the only Prohibitionist republic. Drinking itself, of course, hardly stopped, but Prohibition represented a progressive Protestant triumph, and women's activism was in good measure responsible for it.

While Protestants devised new ways of responding to corporate capitalist America, Catholics, Jews, and others formulated similar programs of proselytization. Fervent revivalism, for example, a practice normally associated with evangelical Protestants, had a close corollary in the missions and special services conducted by several generations of Catholic priests. From 1850 to 1920, Catholic congregants as a percentage of total church adherents in the United States doubled, from 14 to 28 percent; the percentage of Catholics in the total population rose from 5 to 16 percent. This was no accident, nor was it a function only of Catholic immigration to the country from Ireland, Italy, eastern Europe, and Mexico. Certainly this immigration was part of the story, yet many of the immigrants were only nominally Catholics. Church leaders in America, recognizing the dangers to the "one true faith" from the myriad Protestant sects in the United States (as well as from indifference and traditional anticlerical attitudes), sponsored intense programs of parish missions, the Catholic counterparts to revivals. During one such revival in New York City in 1867, for example, a diarist reported that "one woman began to cry aloud; twenty others joined in as a chorus; and the whole congregation showed similar symptoms when the preacher said: 'Don't cry now but cry at your confession: then bewail your sins.'" Itinerant priests such as Francis Xavier Weninger served as the equivalent to the frontier exhorters of the Methodists, gathering in a harvest of souls to the faith. Weninger wrote, "I continually am giving Missions in the woods as well as in the metropolis going to every chapel, no matter how many families there are. In the course of the year I am preaching over 1,000 times every year." Parochial schools planted throughout the country in the nineteenth century and staffed by nuns institutionalized devotional Catholicism as the faith of the sons and daughters of immigrants, especially in urban America. For many Catholic children, parochial school education was a rite of passage, and the nuns who taught in these schools became famous for their strict discipline in the classroom. The schools reinforced the growing tie between ethnic neighborhood enclaves and local parishes.

Jews likewise took part in adapting to the free market of American proselytization. Reform Jews were not seeking converts from outside Judaism, but they were attempting to attract disaffected Jews to a faith that responded to the realities of living in American society. Reform Judaism itself, as pioneered by Rabbi Isaac Mayer Wise in Cincinnati before the Civil War, was a recognition that Jews lived in an evangelical culture and would have to adapt accordingly. Reform Judaism thus jettisoned certain traditions viewed as archaic, modernized services, opened up seating to families (at about the same time that many conservative Protestants also did away with gender-segregated seating), and provided more open and inviting services. While Reform Jews in America (especially in areas of lesser Jewish concentration such as the South and Midwest) did their best to become American, many Conservative Jews pressed the cause of Zionism, the religio-political platform holding that only a separate and independent Jewish homeland would be the salvation of the race. In 1896 Theodor Herzl, a Hungarian Jewish intellectual, published *The Jewish State*, giving Zionism its manifesto for the next century. Conservative Judaism—whose members were not fully Orthodox but objected to the complete set of innovations introduced by Reform Jews—were especially effective advocates for the Zionist program.

Early Twentieth Century

The religious ferment on the West Coast in the early twentieth century illustrates the major themes of proselytization in twentieth-century America. The West Coast was less an orderly "free market" in spiritual choices than a huge, permanent, and disorderly street bazaar. Proselytizers of all types flourished. In Los Angeles, established white Protestant conservatives encountered Jewish and Catholic European immigrants, West Coast migrants seeking the good life, movie moguls, Latinos, Chinese, Japanese, and Sikhs. The area was a new world for everyone. In this milieu of heterogeneity and popular culture extravaganzas, some looked for religious familiarity, whereas others sought out new varieties of religious experience. Pentecostalism provided both.

In 1906, just before the San Francisco earthquake, William L. Seymour, a black minister originally from Louisiana, attracted a following to services held in a former horse stable in South Central Los Angeles. Seymour's preaching style was hardly the main draw. He turned his back to the audience, lowered his head into a shoebox, and delivered expositions of the strange new doctrines of Pentecostalism. Despite his deliberate lack of charisma, Seymour convinced many that speaking in tongues was God's evidence of the "third baptism" of the Spirit (following salvation, the first baptism, and complete sanctification, the second baptism). The early Pentecostals preached that the world was entering its last days—the devastating earthquake in San Francisco being a telltale sign. Before Jesus' Second Coming, his disciples would receive the power of the Holy Spirit and preach the gospel in all languages, just as early Christians experienced in the Book of Acts. Congregants, curiosity seekers, evangelists, rowdies, and reporters converged at the humble mission. "The night is made hideous," a *Los Angeles Times* correspondent reported, "by the howlings of the worshipers. The devotees of the weird doctrine practice the most fanatical rites, preach the wildest theories, and work themselves into a state of mad excitement." Over the next few years converts across the country heard the Word.

Pentecostalism initially remained a relatively small and obscure movement concentrated among the "disinherited." But then its message was taken up by new religious entrepreneurs such as Aimee Semple McPherson, who combined mass marketing and theatrical entertainments with a comforting message. McPherson's story shows that, for evangelical proselytizers as well as movie stars, there was no such thing as bad publicity.

Sister, as McPherson liked to be called, was born in Canada and grew up in a family active in the Salvation Army. After receiving the Pentecostal spirit baptism and speaking in tongues, she set sail for China as a missionary. Quickly giving up on this fledgling (and floundering) career, she was soon barnstorming on the revival circuits. In the South, she preached to whites and blacks alike and declared that God knew no color barrier (although in the 1920s she welcomed the verbal support of the Ku Klux Klan). In 1918, McPherson settled in Los Angeles, and by 1923 she had built her own temple, written her first autobiography, and used radio to transform herself into a nationally known personality. McPherson portrayed herself as "Everybody's Sister" even though she failed in maintaining close personal relationships with anyone, including her second and third husbands and her own mother and daughter. She proclaimed a simple "Foursquare Gospel" but utilized lush pageantry to preach it. She spurned controversy yet became a national spectacle when, after disappearing and suddenly reappearing in 1926, she claimed to have been kidnapped by a Mexican gang, when in fact she was hiding out with a new lover. Weaving together the strands of Methodist optimism, Salvation Army popular piety, and the Pentecostals' emphasis on the dramatic works of the Spirit and faith healing, Sister Aimee created a religious tapestry richly embroidered with her own personal self-mythologizing.

Whereas conservative evangelicals preached individual salvation and spirit baptism, believers from many other traditions were convinced that salvation of individual souls was lacking without a larger involvement in the social order. Advocates of the Christian social gospel were innovative and tireless proselytizers for a liberalized faith. "Let it never be forgotten," wrote Richard Ely, a social gospeler and economist at major American universities, that "salvation means infinitely more than the proclamation of glittering generalities and the utterance of sweet sentimentalities. Salvation means righteousness, positive righteousness, in all the earth, and its establishment means hard warfare. Preaching the gospel . . . means a never-ceasing attack on every wrong institution, until the earth becomes a new earth, and all its cities, cities of God." Walter Rauschenbusch, Baptist seminary professor and author of *A Theology for the Social Gospel*, called for the "spiritual force of Christianity" to be turned against "the materialism and mammonism of our industrial and social order." He condemned religious men as being too "cowed by the prevailing materialism and arrogant selfishness of our business world." Many Catholics also pushed for their own version of the social gospel. Parish priests were the rank and file of this movement, as Catholic immigrants (Poles, Italians, and others) manned heavy industry in the early twentieth century. American rabbis organized into the Commission on Social Justice gave another religious sanction for workers to organize for collective bargaining, urging that "the dignity of the individual soul before God cannot be lost sight of before men."

The gigantic foreign missionary enterprise conducted by American religious organizations during this era arose from a similar mixture of evangelical and socially progressive impulses. Today, American foreign mission efforts are dominated by conservative evangelical groups (the Southern Baptist Convention and the Assemblies of God, the largest Pentecostal denomination, are the two largest senders of career missionaries) and Mormons (by far the largest sender of noncareer missionaries). In the Gilded Age and Progressive Era, however, it was mainstream Protestant denominations that led the way, sending thousands of men and women to places such as China, Africa, Japan, India, Burma, and South America. Some of these were explicitly "heathen" (meaning non-Christian) places; others were Christian but considered so full of idolatrous Catholicism as to be equally pressing candidates for Christianization. Foreign missions had begun in the early nineteenth century with the formation of the American Board of Commissioners for Foreign Missions. In the late nineteenth century, as the non–Christian world seemed to be opening (owing largely to the Western powers' exercises in imperialism in Africa and Asia, where European powers especially exercised political authority), Christians took up the mantle laid down by Robert Speer, a recruiter and publicist for the foreign missions effort, who spoke of the opportunity for the "evangelization of the world in this generation." Although Speer and his colleagues were part of the "muscular Christianity" of their era, in reality it was women's missionary societies that raised the bulk of the funds for the huge effort at overseas proselytization. For example, the Woman's Missionary Union of the Southern Baptist Convention was largely responsible for turning the once rather provincial Southern Baptists into the largest career missionary-sending agency in the country in the post–World War II era, with a missionary force of more than seventy-five hundred by the 1970s. The convention's annual "Lottie Moon" offering, named after a longtime missionary heroine in China, raked in tens of millions of dollars annually. In this way, as in so many other eras of American religious history, women's behind-the-scenes work was instrumental to the proselytizing impulse in American religion. This "errand to the world" represented by the missionary enterprise showed Americans' great faith in proselytization itself. Americans actually took the imperious slogan "the evangelization of the world in this generation" as a serious goal. By the 1930s, many missionaries, less naive for their experiences, began to argue that American-style proselytization was not easily translatable to other cultures. They argued for more money and workers in educational enterprises. Conservative evangelicals, however, insisted on spreading the gospel in print and by word of mouth, just as they had always done, trusting that God would work results in people's hearts.

While socially conscious believers from many faiths exerted considerable influence on progressive political movements, nativist groups promoted a conservative agenda summarized in the slogan "100% Americanism." Ethnoreligious bigotry, some of them realized, could be mass-marketed. The second coming of the Ku Klux Klan in the early twentieth century serves as one chilling example. The motion picture blockbuster *Birth of a Nation*, which purportedly recounted the heroic defense of the "Aryan birthright" led by the first Klan during Reconstruction, directly inspired the Klan's rebirth in 1915. In 1919 William Simmons, a Georgia Baptist minister and founder of the second Klan, hired two advertising experts to stimulate recruitment. Over the next few years Klaverns (local Klan units) sprang up all over the country, and women's auxiliaries took their place alongside them. By the mid-1920s, the Klan claimed more than five million members. In the Midwest, where it attracted the largest membership, the Klan directed its animus mostly toward Catholics, Jews, and immigrant populations. The Klan staged huge community fests—parades, barbecues, carnivals, and the like—while retaining the aura of a secret fraternal organization, complete with robes, arcane ritual, and elaborate hierarchies. A separately organized Women's Ku Klux Klan, itself a huge national organization, dispatched "poison squads of whispering women" to organize boycotts against local Jewish and Catholic merchants. As Klan leader Hiram Wesley Evans explained in a high-toned publication,

"We know that we are right in the same sense that a good Christian knows that he has been saved and that Christ lives—a thing which the intellectual can never understand." He sought to explain Klan convictions "for the enlightenment and conversion of others."

The second Klan disintegrated in the late 1920s, a victim of its egregiously money-grubbing leaders and perhaps also its political successes. But American nativism never lacked for effective proselytizers. During the depression years, Father Charles Coughlin, the "radio priest," preached his mixture of Catholic conservative theology, populist criticism of national financial institutions, and hateful anti-Semitism to an audience of up to fifteen million radio listeners. This simple parish priest from Detroit exploited the same mass media revolution deployed by religious conservatives from Aimee McPherson in radio to Oral Roberts and other televangelists later in the century. Coughlin's earnest voice (reminiscent of Dwight Moody's), simple homilies, and radio presence (akin to that of another master of the medium, Franklin D. Roosevelt) captured a national audience. Coughlin initially supported Roosevelt's New Deal and later advocated a vaguely outlined financial revolution. His social gospel critique of wealth maldistribution melded into a nativist screed on an imagined Jewish banking conspiracy. Eventually, Coughlin's anti-Semitism caused the newly created Federal Communications Commission to yank him off the air. But his popular radio addresses set a precedent for future proselytization through mass media.

Modern America

After World War II, religious discourse pervaded American culture, undergirding the Cold War struggle. Americans flocked to church in record numbers. More than 60 percent of Americans attended some religious service every week. Mainstream religious leaders eased Americans' transitions to corporate capitalism and a therapeutic culture of self-realization and autonomy. Liberal Protestants, post–Vatican II Catholics, and Reform Jews carried their religion into corporate board rooms and neighborhood barbecues. Proselytization itself, among respectable Protestants at least, fell into disrepute. Believers from Christian evangelicals to Conservative Jews and traditional Catholics held no such compunction; recruitment was their stock-in-trade. Their efforts paid off.

The Southern Baptist Convention provides a case in point. Emerging from the ashes of the Civil War, this denomination of small farmers and plain townsfolk became the largest denomination in the South by 1900. As southerners migrated northward and westward in the twentieth century, the Southern Baptist Convention soon became the nation's largest Protestant denomination, numbering more than eighteen million adherents nationwide by the 1990s, with members spread throughout the country. The First Baptist Church of Dallas, Texas, pastored by the irascible fundamentalist W. A. Criswell, was the nation's single largest congregation. Southern Baptists perfected professionalized proselytization. A large denominational apparatus sent out thousands of home and foreign missionaries. The denomination's Sunday School Board churned out millions of pages of edifying age-graded instructional material, hymnals, and worship aid. The convention's church-building program loaned start-up money for congregations establishing outposts in new communities. Southern Baptists, in short, advertised and expanded in ways akin to those used by successful retail chains.

The success of the Southern Baptists might be compared to that of another group that grew to national prominence, the Church of Jesus Christ of Latter-day Saints—the Mormons. Like the Southern Baptists, the Mormons developed an entire subculture in which all members of a family might find fulfillment. The Latter-day Saints required of their faithful a two-year term of missionary work in whatever place the church might select, be it Samoa (where they experienced spectacular success), or France (where they did not), or Harlem. The Mormons also established a far-flung religious empire, based in Salt Lake City, that rivaled the Southern Baptist empire centered in Nashville. Both groups taught their members the religious duty to proselytize. For Southern Baptists, it was the "Great Commission," from the biblical verse commanding believers to spread the Word to every nation. For Mormons, this duty was based on the intense belief in family and community and the ultimate hope of reuniting family members in the afterlife (leading Mormons to baptize the dead symbolically in a kind of posthumous salvation).

American Judaism has also demonstrated remarkable flexibility, an ability to adapt to American life. Following World War II, although American Judaism's strength remained concentrated in the traditional Jewish enclaves in the Northeast (the Lower East Side of New York City and the New York and New Jersey suburbs), many other Jews followed jobs and opportunities to the Sunbelt and West Coast. There they discovered the same land of abundance and self-invention that other Americans found. Innovative and entrepreneurial rabbis, recognizing that some older customs of American Jewish life were ill suited to this new environment, developed new ways to organize this new Jewish generation. Leon Kronish, a Reform Rabbi in Miami, organized "congregational commandos" to bring unaffiliated Jews into his temple. His colleague in this rapidly growing city, a Conservative rabbi named Irving Lehrman, encouraged education for Jewish women, including instituting the new practice of bat mitzvah for Jewish girls (a parallel to the more established bar mitzvah custom for adolescent Jewish boys). Seeing the success of the Youth for Christ prayer movement, Lehrman suggested that Jewish young people, too, had been "given all sorts of lectures and forums and discussion groups —everything except old-fashioned prayer." His response was to cultivate a personal spirituality at his synagogue, to encourage Jews to find a personal meaning in their faith just as Protestant evangelicals urged their faithful to do. In such ways, American Judaism adapted to the culture of free-market proselytization. Rabbis were not evangelical preachers, yet Judaism incorporated certain aspects of the evangelical model of recruitment, for rabbis knew it worked.

As religious denominations and traditions replenish themselves through such means, individual religious evangelists and entrepreneurs have updated the techniques of mass proselytization. The obvious example of this is Billy Graham. Hailing from North Carolina, this evangelist extraordinaire burst on the scene following World War II, pulling off some of the largest religious crusades in American history. Graham's emotionally calibrated sermons moved Americans frightened by the Cold War and fearful for the moral fiber of the country. "We have seen a strange paradox that often confused and bewildered me," Graham wrote in the 1960s. "We have seen a revival of religious interest throughout the United States but an acceleration of crime, divorce and immorality. Within the church there is a new depth of commitment, a new sense of destiny and a spirit of revival, yet in the world there is an intensification of the forces of evil." Despite his pessimistic theology, Graham's lanky good looks, overwhelming sincerity, and comforting message—that "history is not wandering aimlessly, . . . [that] there is a plan and purpose in what often seems to us hopeless confusion"—attracted millions to his services and tens of millions to his nightly preaching on television. In the heyday of the Graham crusades, the choice for individual conversion was subsumed into a cataclysmic struggle between the Free World and the international Communist conspiracy.

While evangelists dispensed a highly personal gospel to ordinary Americans, a new version of the social gospel, one imbued with the vision of racial justice, spread from black churches to the national consciousness. Groups such as the Southern Christian Leadership Conference (SCLC) and the Student Nonviolent Coordinating Committee (SNCC) operated with the language of sin and redemption familiar to white and black alike, especially southerners, who instinctively understood such evangelical idioms. As one student activist put it, "The work abounded in the biblical ethos of the Southland, black and white." Or as a black female Mississippi sharecropper expressed her conversion to the movement: "Something hit me like a new religion." The SNCC was about building the "beloved community," an America cleansed of racial sin; the SCLC sought to "redeem the soul of America." Both used language descended from the tradition of American perfectionism. Americans from both the North and the South spoke of undergoing a racial conversion, of being redeemed from racism. Civil rights leaders harnessed this sentiment to proselytize for social justice.

No one functioned as a more effective evangelist for racial justice than Martin Luther King Jr., who hoped his epitaph would read that he was a drum major for righteousness. Scion of a prominent black Baptist family in Atlanta, King grew up privileged in some respects but also black in the Jim Crow South. He attended Morehouse College, a Baptist school for black men in Atlanta, and earned a Ph.D. in theology from Boston University. King studied the social gospel and other contemporary theological trends and studded his sermons with references to Reinhold Niebuhr and other contemporary theological authorities. King also drew inspiration from the black pulpit. Sketching out a "dream deeply rooted in the American dream," he hoped for a faith "able to work together, to pray together, to struggle together, to go to jail together, to stand up for freedom together." In Birmingham, Alabama, in 1963, King joined longtime civil rights stalwart and Baptist minister Fred Shuttlesworth, head of the Alabama Christian Movement for Human Rights. King and his colleagues led a series of demonstrations designed to dramatize the brutality of segregation in this racist southern city. After his arrest for violating a court order to cease the protests, King composed his masterpiece "Letter from a Birmingham Jail," modeled after the apostle Paul's letters from jail in the New Testament. In the letter, he explained that he was carrying "the gospel of freedom beyond my own home town. Like Paul, I must constantly respond to the Macedonian call for aid." He could not rest in his comfortable preaching post while Birmingham police attacked residents (including black children) with fire hoses and police dogs. "Injustice anywhere is a threat to justice everywhere," King reminded his listeners. He condemned white moderates who settled for order over justice and thus insidiously supported evil, just as the good Germans had done with Hitler. King's letter cogently explained the strategies, tactics, and philosophies of the civil rights movement.

The mainstream civil rights leadership held no monopoly on issuing persuasive calls for racial justice. Malcolm X, the former Malcolm Little, became in the 1960s the nation's foremost advocate for the Nation of Islam and black nationalism. Malcolm's own background could hardly be more different from that of King. Raised primarily by his mother and extended family, Malcolm moved from Omaha to Boston as a young man and fell in with street hustlers. In the 1950s Malcolm spent several years in jail, where he grew interested in the teachings of Elijah Muhammad, including Muhammad's stories of the demonic origins of white people. On his release from jail, Malcolm took the fledgling Nation of Islam into national prominence, furthered by the conversion of prominent figures such as Muhammad Ali. Malcolm's impact, however, stemmed less from his religious teachings than from his clarion call for black self-respect and nationalism. As a group, Black Muslims proselytized with great success among disaffected young black men in the prison system, men much like Malcolm X himself during his prison years. Largely outside the reach of the traditional black Protestant denominations, these men found a new meaning and self-respect in the world of African American Islam. They provided a ready audience for its message of breaking from the old "slave churches."

Beyond its success with African Americans, Islam more generally in contemporary America has discovered the prospects and perils of proselytization. Much like Catholics in earlier eras, American Islamic leaders face the suspicion that their religion is not quite "American." After the tragedy of September 11, 2001, American Muslims faced harassment and periodic searches and seizures by the FBI and other governmental agencies. They had to endure attacks on the Islamic religion by conservative Protestants who likened the prophet Muhammad to a "terrorist," in a manner similar to how Protestants of an earlier era referred to the Catholic pope as an Antichrist. Yet substantial immigration to America from the Islamic world, including not only the Arabic world but also Pakistanis, Indonesians, and African Muslims, feeds the growing presence of the religion in contemporary America, and the free market of proselytization will influence Islam's move beyond ethnic immigrant communities and into "mainstream" American life. A recent two-hour biography of the prophet Muhammad funded by American Islamic organizations and shown on public television demonstrates that the media will play a key role in educating Americans about the Islamic faith and reaching out to potential proselytes.

In contemporary America religious groups continue to expand their proselytizing efforts, now including billboards, Web sites, automated phone messaging systems, Christian rap music, guitar masses, yoga classes, audio books, theme parks, kitsch, and cable television channels. Evangelists still hawk all manner of religious wares, from straitlaced Protestant evangelicalism to New Age spirituality. The gospel of health through positive thinking, formerly personified by Norman Vincent Peale and his perennially popular *Power of Positive Thinking*, was broadcast on public television by Indian television guru Deepak Chopra. Stage and screen star Shirley MacLaine's various autobiographies and self-help books, including works such as *Out on a Limb* and *Dancing in the Light*, taught the concepts of New Age religion to millions of Americans. Millions more watched her famous 1987 television appearance in which a message from a spirit was "channeled" through the voice of MacLaine's guru. Throughout the twentieth century and into the twenty-first, intellectuals and artists have bemoaned, attacked, and lampooned this culture of persuasion and salesmanship—or, to use a harsher term, hucksterism. They point out that Americans inevitably dilute even the most ethereal or apparently dangerous of spiritualities, such as Zen Buddhism or witchcraft, into persuasive pitches.

The recent growth of megachurches also suggests that entertainment and theater remain central to religious persuasion, as they have been since the days of George Whitefield. Surveys have demonstrated that contemporary Americans distrust an excess of moral earnestness in preaching and desire anonymity as passionately as they ostensibly seek community. In response, interdenominational chapels and fellowships bring together congregants in mall-like structures, generally in suburbs, and present a generically Christian pitch in the format of an hour-long live television show. Indeed, many of these services are specifically made for television, with the live audience serving as a backdrop. These religious theaters provide a familiar setting for a predominantly white middle-class consumer shopping experience.

Although watered-down evangelicalism and theatrical megachurches mostly attract white suburbanites, the nation's increasingly multicultural character ensures that religious quests will be more diverse than ever. Periodic surges of interest in Asian religions, which peaked again in the 1990s, demonstrate that proselytizing skill is not limited to the traditional Protestant-Catholic-Jewish mainstream triad. American dabbling in Asian religions dates from the nineteenth century, when Henry Steel Olcott became America's "first [white] Buddhist" and when the World's Parliament of Religions, meeting at Chicago's mammoth World's Columbian Exposition in 1893, introduced many Americans to Asian religious ideas (despite the liberal Protestant cast of the parliament itself). But it was only after World War II that Asian religions attracted followers other than intellectuals and eccentrics. In a reverse missionary motion, figures such as the British Episcopalian intellectual Alan Watts and the

Japanese priest Shunryu Suzuki instructed a growing American audience in Japanese Buddhism and Taoism. "What I saw in Zen," Watts told his listeners in the 1950s, "was an intuitive way of understanding the sense of life by getting rid of silly quests and questions." Watts delivered more than a thousand lectures and published twenty-six books in the 1950s and 1960s, teaching countercultural luminaries such as the poets Allen Ginsberg (who was interested primarily in Tibetan Buddhism) and Gary Snyder. Watts himself remained at some distance from Asian religious practitioners in San Francisco, where he taught, having heard too many assimilated Japanese Buddhists chanting lines such as "Buddha loves me this I know / For the sutra tells me so." Under the guidance of Shunryu Suzuki, however, serious Japanese Buddhism established a strong presence on the West Coast. Suzuki touted the total meditative practice of zazen. "The state of mind that exists when you sit in the right posture is itself enlightenment," he explained to his mostly white audience. "In this posture there is no need to talk about the right state of mind. You already have it. This is the conclusion of Buddhism." The most recent Asian immigrants—Thais, Cambodians, and others—have brought their own Buddhist traditions (especially Theravada Buddhism) to the country. In 1999 the Dalai Lama, the exiled religious leader of Tibetan Buddhism, explained his philosophy to forty thousand interested listeners in New York's Central Park. He specifically rejected the role of proselytizer, but his celebrity presence served to spread his hopes for ecumenical peace and harmony.

Spreading from intellectuals on the coasts, Asian Buddhism as expressed through its acolytes has slowly found its way into the heartland. Growing up in Montana, future basketball guru Phil Jackson, son of a Pentecostal minister, sought religious enlightenment beyond his narrow upbringing. He eventually found it in the practice of zazen, and it did not hurt his basketball game, either. "The more skilled I became at watching my thoughts in zazen practice, the more focused I became as a player," he explained. Sitting zazen taught him to "*trust the moment*—to immerse myself in action as mindfully as possible, so that I could react spontaneously to whatever was taking place." Baseball player Yogi Berra's dictum—"You can't think and hit at the same time" —illustrates in a folk koan the same principles Jackson brought to Chicago Bulls players as diverse as megastar Michael Jordan, his sometimes pouting sidekick Scottie Pippen, and troubled cross-dressing rebounder Dennis Rodman. They might have been more interested in television endorsements than Eastern ways, but their disciplined yet creative playing symbolized the very virtues Jackson sought to teach.

Conclusion

The selling of Gautama Buddha's ancient teachings to American basketball players recapitulates the theme traced here. Religious traditions in America coexist in an environment of toleration and competition, of entrepreneurial drive and theological innovation. Evangelical proselytizers, by the very missionary nature of their faith, have had a natural advantage, but other groups have adapted and borrowed evangelical models successfully. All are peddlers in divinity.

SUGGESTED READINGS

Ahlstrom, Sydney E. *A Religious History of the American People*. New Haven: Yale University Press, 1972.

Angell, Stephen. *Bishop Henry McNeal Turner and African-American Religion in the South*. Knoxville: University of Tennessee Press, 1992.

Ariel, Yaakov. *Evangelizing the Chosen People: Missions to the Jews in America, 1880–2000*. Chapel Hill: University of North Carolina Press, 2000.

Blumhofer, Edith. *Aimee Semple McPherson: Everybody's Sister*. Grand Rapids, Mich.: Eerdmans, 1993.

Bonomi, Patricia. *Under the Cope of Heaven: Religion, Society, and Politics in Colonial America*. New York: Oxford University Press, 1986.

Demos, John. *The Unredeemed Captive: A Family Story from Early America*. New York: Knopf, 1994.

Findlay, James. *Dwight L. Moody: American Evangelist, 1837–1899*. Chicago: University of Chicago Press, 1969.

Gaustad, Edwin. *A Documentary History of Religion in America since 1865*. 2nd ed. Grand Rapids, Mich.: Eerdmans, 1993.

———. *A Documentary History of Religion in America to the Civil War*. 2nd ed. Grand Rapids, Mich.: Eerdmans, 1993.

———. *A Religious History of America*. Rev. ed. San Francisco: HarperCollins, 1990.

Gutiérrez, Ramón. *When Jesus Came the Corn Mothers Went Away: Marriage, Sexuality, and Power in Northern New Mexico, 1500–1846*. Stanford, Calif.: Stanford University Press, 1991.

Hackett, David. *Religion and American Culture: A Reader*. New York: Routledge, 1995.

Hatch, Nathan. *The Democratization of American Christianity*. New Haven: Yale University Press, 1989.

Heyrman, Christine Leigh. *Southern Cross: The Beginnings of the Bible Belt*. Chapel Hill: University of North Carolina Press, 1997.

King, Mary. *Freedom Song: A Personal Story of the 1960s Civil Rights Movement.*
New York: William Morrow and Co., 1987.

McLoughlin, William G. *Revivals, Awakenings, and Reform: An Essay on Religion
and Social Change in America, 1607–1977.* Chicago: University of Chicago Press,
1978.

Payne, Charles. *"I've Got the Light of Freedom": The Organizing Tradition and the
Mississippi Freedom Struggle.* Berkeley and Los Angeles: University of California
Press, 1994.

Tweed, Thomas A. *Retelling U.S. Religious History.* Berkeley: University of California Press, 1997.

Tweed, Thomas A., and Stephen Prothero. *Asian Religions in America: A Documentary History.* New York: Oxford University Press, 1999.

Wallace, Anthony F. C. *The Death and Rebirth of the Seneca.* New York: Vintage,
1969.

Supernaturalism

New England Puritans watched the skies for comets and astrological wonders —just as the Maya did—even as they were in the process of creating modern Protestantism. Nineteenth-century Americans loved machines and Yankee ingenuity, but they still combed for water and gold with divining rods, talked to their dead relatives in séances, and healed their own bodies through "mind-cures." White people in the American South, otherwise contemptuous of black slaves, often secretly consulted black conjurers and healers for advice on health, love affairs, and other personal matters. Tourists flock to New Orleans in part to purchase goods that are the commodified remnants of centuries-old traditions of voodoo. Contemporary Americans rely on science and technology and yet consult astrologers and psychics for important personal decisions, avoid stepping on cracks in the sidewalk, attend church, and profess strong belief in the afterlife. Why? How do we explain the American propensity for mixing religion, science, magic, folklore, and the occult?

Historians of American religion contest the meaning of *occultism*, *religion*, and *magic*. *Occultism* describes beliefs that have roots in older intellectual traditions and ancient philosophies. *Religion* suggests veneration of or devotion to divine beings, and *magic* is traditionally understood as an instrumental practice that is primarily concerned with efficacy, with "what works." In many contexts, however, the distinction between magic, occultism, and religion is blurred, especially when they are seen from opposing points of view. For example, acts that are deemed "religious," such as prayer or prophecy, might be virtually identical to some demonstrations of magic, which might be called "spells" and "divination" in the idiom of the latter.

The debate over the use and meaning of the term *magic* has a lengthy history. Scholars first defined *magic* as a mode of thought, in that it assumed that a particular relationship existed between causes and their effects. Theories of magic described this relationship as sympathetic (the idea that like produces like and that effects are similar to their causes) or contagious (objects that have been in contact with one another will continue to affect one another at a distance). In the late nineteenth century, the Scottish classicist Sir James George Frazer insisted that magic was an expression of the earliest stages of human belief and that magical practices revealed the spurious reasoning that characterized primitive modes of thought. Again, it is not entirely certain, according to this theory, whether magical approaches are completely different from religious (faith-oriented) or scientific (rational) ones. In fact, magical, religious, and scientific ways of thinking may overlap in any given historical moment.

For the purposes of this chapter, the term *supernaturalism* describes the myriad approaches human beings have used to interact with the unseen powers of the invisible world. The supernatural comprises a realm of forces and entities that might serve as the agents of such interactions, whether through ritual, intellectual theorizing, or practical experiments. Religion can speak of the supernatural, as it is included by the prior definition, among these agents. The chapters about cosmologies and science in this volume consider historical American ideas about humans' relation to the cosmos and the interaction between the invisible (spiritual) and visible (material) worlds. This chapter has a more specific and delimited aim: to focus topically on the magical and occult traditions, ranging from divination, fortune-telling, and Conjuring to harmonialism in twentieth-century New Age religions. The term *magic* is used to refer to specific techniques that involve the manipulation of supernatural agents for particular ends. Occultism is focused on the recovery of divine wisdom and other sources of esoteric knowledge. The terms *occult* and *occultism* describe systematic attempts to predict and interpret the workings of the world using higher forms of knowledge. Finally, the term *harmonialism*, as defined by the religious history scholar Sydney Ahlstrom, is "based on the premise that this-worldly phenomena are in correspondence with higher truths in other realms of being, which are ultimate objects of our ongoing quest. . . . What is sought after, fundamentally, is a state of harmony with the ultimate principles that underlie the universe." Obviously, the thought, behaviors, and beliefs epitomized by these terms are not exclusive of one another. They have often converged, as we will see, in the American context.

Precolonial Era

Magic and occult traditions have maintained an uneasy relationship with orthodox religion. Nevertheless, in societies both past and present, a fusion of ideas has occurred. Roman Catholicism in Europe provides one example. From the fifteenth through the seventeenth centuries Catholicism was infused with beliefs and behaviors that drew from vernacular sources. This was the spiritual practice of the masses, what is usually known as popular religion. Throughout Europe, faithful Catholics created shrines at holy sites, consecrated relics of the dead, and·brought their sick and afflicted before the priests, who petitioned the saints on their behalf. Above all, both laypersons and clergy possessed an awareness of the powers that were present in the invisible worlds of heaven and hell, including malevolent forces and satanic spirits, and took appropriate measures to ensure their well-being with talismans, amulets, and other protective devices. Some Catholics understood certain religious practices to be efficacious, such as the sacramental ritual of the Eucharist or the veneration of certain sacred objects, images, and other tokens of holiness. These beliefs were compatible with the official teachings of the church, but other activities, such as the unsanctioned use of ecclesiastical materials for personal gain, were not.

Roman Catholic Christians were heirs to a cosmology that presupposed the reality of an invisible, densely populated universe ruled from on high by an all-powerful creator. The creator, however, reigned at much more of a distance than the angels, saints, and other spiritual beings that were believed to inhabit the world in which people lived. From the Middle Ages onward, Roman Catholics speculated about the power of both God and his heavenly agents. Fear and fascination with unseen spirits, both divine and diabolic, formed the basis of a supernatural folklore that revolved around the angels, cherubim, and demons who regularly communicated with human beings. Other stories of miracles, such as the powerful acts of intercession by the saints, were passed on by believers from generation to generation. Over time, Catholics developed a pantheon of saints ranging from Saint Patrick, for whom the Irish day of celebration is named, to Saint Jude, the patron saint of hopeless causes.

In the wake of the Protestant Reformation, institutional Christianity fragmented, even as it remained the dominant faith of most Europeans in the sixteenth century. New spiritual alternatives, however, emerged that both complemented and competed with the formal doctrines of the Christian churches. In making the institutional church the central repository of divine power, Christian dogma granted to humans the ability to intercede in the invisible realm, a role reserved for select mediators, the clergy. But spiritual assistance was also provided by practitioners who remained outside the pale of the churches. In England, these were known as cunning folk, "white witches," or "wise men and women." Christians and non-Christians alike sought out cunning folk for their skills in healing sicknesses, providing charms to guard people from evil, and divining hidden knowledge. Some of the cunning persons utilized techniques that were adopted from ancient pagan traditions, but others made use of resources with explicit ecclesiastical origins, such as prayers, biblical verses, and devotional artifacts, including crosses and saints' images. Priests denounced such practices, but the institutional church found itself unable to weed out all the magical professionals. Laypersons continued to turn to them for their services and the promises of fertility, good fortune, and health that they offered.

Colonial North America

Even with the English migration to the American colonies in the seventeenth century, Old World supernatural beliefs continued. Some colonists adopted traditions that augmented their religious practices, such as divination and fortune-telling, spell casting, magical healing, and various styles of occultism. The mental world of colonial settlers bubbled over with a ferment of ideas that supplemented Christianity. Some beliefs and practices, such as witchcraft or *maleficium*, were imported by the settlers directly from their homelands. Others, such as serpent gazing and treasure hunting, were original American creations.

When compared with the peoples whom Europeans encountered in the New World, it appears that Anglo-Americans were not so unusual, considering the great range of spiritual beliefs they possessed. Native Americans, whose religious life was starkly supernatural, conceived of a universe in which the sacred was closely entwined with human existence. Native American religions presupposed a world that was alive with divine power, sacred entities, and other spiritual forces. Shamans, the religious leaders in American Indian communities, held a variety of roles, functioning as healers, spiritual protectors, and interpreters of divine mysteries. Perhaps the spiritual perspectives of American Indian peoples were not so completely different from the supernatural beliefs of many of the European settlers with whom they made contact. Indeed, there would later be some interaction between the two worldviews, as Native American beliefs would influence the development of certain Euro-American folk healing practices and herbal medicines.

A third group of people who came to America during this time period had distinctively supernatural worldviews and religious ideas. These were the enslaved Africans who were brought to the Western colonies during the seventeenth and eighteenth centuries, nearly eight million by the end of the 1700s. Although Africans subscribed to a variety of religions, most maintained a core belief in the existence of a supernatural world. African peoples viewed the supernatural world as a realm that was full of life-giving spiritual power. They tapped into and sometimes manipulated this power through ritual prayer, hypnotic song, and communal religious dance. Traditional African religions, like Native American religions, were based on worship of invisible entities, many of which were believed to have originated in nature. Like Anglo-Americans, Africans viewed the universe as an accessible territory of powerful forces. Africans in the New World passed down these beliefs to their children, creating the context in which future African American religions—from slave Christianity to Brazilian candomblé and Haitian Vodou—would evolve.

The newly arrived English Protestants forged an eclectic spiritual course in America. Many shunned what they viewed as the "priestly superstitions" of Catholic devotionalism, preferring a simpler style of ritual and worship. Leaders of the Protestant churches—including the Puritans of New England and the Anglicans in the colonial South—soundly condemned magic and occultism. Ironically, however, many Christians espoused beliefs that engaged the supernatural. Many Protestants, for instance, favored a lore of "wonders" that circulated in both oral and written form. This supernatural rhetoric held that the sovereignty of God was manifested in remarkable events that encompassed both the visible and invisible worlds, revealing the divine presence in natural elements, storms, meteors, comets, eclipses, rainbows, and other signs in the heavens. Other providential portents and miracles, from prophetic dreams to monstrous births, demonstrated God's divine purpose and judgment. These "worlds of wonder," as experienced by Anglo-American colonists, affirmed the faith of the collective community.

Other forms of supernaturalism surfaced among the colonists. Some traditions gave shape to the acute fears of the settlers as they negotiated the unknown physical terrain of the world in which they now lived. Lacking precise theological explanations for all the difficulties they faced, some Anglo-Americans enacted their anxieties by turning inward and identifying spiritual *maleficium*, or witchcraft, that they found to exist in their own communities.

For at least three generations, witchcraft accusations rent the fabric of early American culture, reverberating throughout the communities of Puritan New England (where the persecutions lasted up to the end of the seventeenth century) and the southern colonies as well (where the very first accused witches were identified). Accused witches were usually female, widowed or never married, and economically independent or well-off—a social profile suggestive of gender conflict in early America.

Supernaturalism in the colonies thrived independent of the churches. Despite state Christianity's monopoly on public religious expression, the spiritual inclinations of the population veered wildly, from the private magical experiments of curious individuals to the advanced occult investigations of learned elites. The variety of styles of supernaturalism in the seventeenth century reflected a diverse range of interests. Poor settlers and those on the frontiers bought and traded charms, amulets, and talismans for the health and protection of their families and communities. Some people turned to magical harming, using spells and incantations, in order to articulate their animosities and resentments. A minor conflict erupting between neighbors, for example, could have parties interpreting the sudden death of a farm animal as evidence of witchcraft.

Intellectuals in early America also adopted other, more sophisticated forms of supernatural practice. One of these was astrology, a system of prediction based on interpretations of the position of celestial bodies. Once the domain of medieval scientists and philosophers, astrology enjoyed a renaissance in the late seventeenth century among common folk as the result of the publication of almanacs, the colonial household guides of folk wisdom and farming lore. Widely available by the early 1700s, almanacs incorporated arcane astrological symbolism and prognostications on medicine and human anatomy, with calculations of the alignment of the planets and predictions of auspicious and inauspicious events, such as comets or eclipses. Aside from making use of almanacs, it was not uncommon for individuals to consult professional astrologers for insights on future trends or for guidance on conducting business. Merchants and shipping traders, for instance, sometimes utilized horoscopes in order to determine the most opportune times for securing new enterprises or preparing their departing vessels. In later years, a version of astrological insights would find its way into the *Farmer's Almanac*, which advised colonists on all manner of topics, including forthcoming weather patterns.

Colonial intellectuals also pursued alchemy, a pseudoscientific art of metallurgical and supernatural transformation. An acceptable subject of scholarly inquiry among elites in Europe, alchemy made its way into Anglo-American intellectual culture sometime during the first half of the eighteenth century. Its traditional object was to transform less-valued substances into those that were precious—as with the conversion of ordinary metal into gold. Like chemistry, alchemy was considered a form of scientific investigation with religious overtones. Alchemy posited that the metamorphosis of common metals corresponded with the transformation of the self during the process of inner spiritual purification. The knowledge that the alchemist obtained by ascetic means paralleled the achievement of mystical human perfection, or immortality. The most prized and sacred material goal of the alchemists was acquisition of the Philosopher's Stone, a fabled substance that, with the proper techniques, would allow the transmutation of any metal.

By the late seventeenth century, interest in many of these practices had subsided. Magic and occult traditions became "folklorized," meaning that they persisted, but in a less public, more attenuated fashion. Some supernatural beliefs became limited to narrower segments of the population. Many older traditions were incorporated into the subterranean culture of American folklore; others, as we will see, maintained a syncretic relationship with popular forms of Christianity.

Occult traditions in the eighteenth century emerged as an eclectic force, fusing the explanatory assumptions of reason with metaphysics. One influential occult movement in this period was Hermeticism, an esoteric system that followers purported to be rooted in a body of texts from second- and third-century Greco-Roman Egypt, written by one Hermes Trismegistros, the "Thrice-Greatest Hermes." Hermeticism was based on a complex theory of correspondences between matter and spirit, undergirded by a concept of the divine intellect of humanity.

At the end of the seventeenth century, Johann Kelpius (1673–1708) brought the Hermetic tradition from Germany to America, where it meshed with sectarian forms of Christianity and flourished within organized religious communities in eastern Pennsylvania. Offshoots of Hermetic thought filtered down for several generations and influenced the development of traditions such as Theosophy, Freemasonry, and Rosicrucianism, a secret order of occult mysteries (see the next section of this chapter). Some Christians blended mystical piety and occult beliefs—as, for example, the Pennsylvania Germans, whose particular brand of spirituality had found its initial expression in Kelpius's Hermetic tradition, and the Swedenborgians, discussed in the next paragraph. The German mystics were well known for their skills in finding lost and stolen items, curing witchcraft afflictions, and utilizing ceremonial magic, such as protective circles, for the common good.

Emanuel Swedenborg (1688–1772) was a figure of great importance in the literate culture of occult spirituality that had formed in America in the early 1700s. Swedenborg melded the diverse streams of liberal religious knowledge that were circulating at this time into a comprehensive spiritual tradition. An aristocratic Swedish scientist and engineer, Swedenborg wrote extensively on issues as broad and varied as philosophy, anatomy, geology, alchemy, and astronomy. He turned to religion sometime in the mid-eighteenth century after he claimed to have received a series of revelations from angelic beings. Inspired by these revelations, he expounded on biblical events and taught a Neoplatonic system of correspondences that proposed that the world was constituted by several orders of being, or spheres. These spheres—the natural, the spiritual, and the celestial—existed in association with the heavenly system of God. This doctrine of correspondences also posited the existence of a reality that was described as the continuity of human experience, which evolved throughout eternity. Swedenborg's writings were filled with detailed descriptions of a new world, including heavenly landscapes, personalities, and radical sexual relationships that Swedenborg believed showed humanity's true moral and spiritual potential. Swedenborg's followers eventually coalesced into a Christian denomination, the Church of the New Jerusalem. One of the most famous Swedenborgians was John Chapman (also known as Johnny Appleseed), the legendary figure of American folklore who traveled the frontier, planting apple trees and preaching what he called "good news fresh from heaven."

Some supernatural beliefs of the eighteenth century derived from the New World landscape. In the mid-1700s a strange new fascination gained the attention of people from various walks of life. Serpent gazing, a phenomenon described in a number of early folklore sources, reproduced many settlers' attitudes toward the strangeness of the natural environment, the animals, and the topography of America. Serpent gazing was based on the belief that human beings could be spellbound and captivated by some hidden power based in a snake's eye. Occult investigators insisted that there was an analogy between these fanciful descriptions of serpent fascination and the power attributed to some persons to harm others through the "evil eye." Although serpent-gazing stories became a trend within a number of literary works by English and Anglo-American naturalists, the actual origins of these ideas are obscure, although some scholars have suggested a Native American provenance for the beliefs.

Revolutionary and Early Republican America

The advent of the new nation saw a spectrum of developments in the arena of supernatural belief that reached across broad segments of the population. The early eighteenth century was a fertile period of alternative spiritual ideas. At that time older Renaissance traditions merged with new trends in both popular culture and intellectual thought. In the latter part of the century, with Enlightenment notions fostering religious doubt and skepticism, only some traditions retained the public acceptance that they had in earlier periods. Nevertheless, some significant spiritual novelties surfaced in this period.

In the postrevolutionary era, concerns for economic security were exemplified by pervasive materialism and self-interest, an outlook that was mirrored by a comparable phenomenon in supernatural practice—that of treasure seeking and money digging—frequently practiced in New England, western New York, Pennsylvania, and the southern states of North Carolina and Virginia. Treasure hunting, a mania that lured hopeful seekers of quick wealth to elaborate "money-digging" schemes, persisted in some areas for more than twenty years. The traditions surrounding these practices showed popular belief in a "supernatural economy," for the treasures themselves possessed obscure origins. Some were believed to be buried by pirates and protected by invisible forces and could be located only by those with special divining abilities. Ambitious seekers used dowsing boughs and rods, seer stones, and magical rituals to ward off evil spirits and ghosts in their quest for precious boxes of money, gold, and mines of concealed wealth. These beliefs paralleled alchemy and other occult traditions that emphasized the acquisition of hidden wisdom by means of both physical rigor and spiritual faith.

With the rise of the Republic also came a rebirth of organized traditions with occult overtones. Some of these had been imported from Europe, such as Rosicrucianism and Freemasonry. The Rosicrucians were a latter-day manifestation of a fifteenth-century order (the Fraternity of the Rose Cross) that claimed to be founded by a legendary figure, Christian Rosenkreuz. In the early 1600s, accounts of Rosenkreuz's initiation into Eastern mystery religions and his recruiting of monks into a fraternity called the Brotherhood of the Rose Cross were publicized by a Lutheran pastor, Johann Valentin Andreae (1586–1684), in a pamphlet, *Fama Fraternitatis*, in 1614. It was after the migration of German Protestants in the eighteenth century that the ideas of the secret society were introduced in the United States. The fraternity's teachings and activities were relatively obscure until the nineteenth century, when American Rosicrucians Pashal Beverly Randolph (1825–75) and Ethan

Allen Hitchcock (1798–1870) revived interest in the society through their sponsorship of lectures, publications, and organizational efforts on behalf of the mystical brotherhood.

Rosicrucianism synthesized a number of ideas, including those concerned with spiritual "illumination" and theurgy, or devotional magic. One of the central principles of Rosicrucian thought was the idea that the individual must engage in a personal, heroic quest for wisdom and hidden knowledge in order to attain the highest level of spiritual development. Through discipline, one would be gradually awakened to metaphysical truths not available to the uninitiated person. Rosenkreuz's teachings reflected the direct influences of Gnosticism, the esoteric teachings of an early Christian sect that espoused mystical insight over intellectual empowerment and promoted the idea of dualism, the body-spirit dichotomy.

Although details of Rosicrucian ritual and practice in America were shrouded in mystery, the organization of practitioners into orders reflected a pattern seen with other fraternal associations of the time, including the Freemasons. Deriving from a network of trade guilds founded in England and Scotland in the early eighteenth century, Freemasonry spread in America sometime in the late 1700s, mainly among male Protestants. The spiritual experience of the Freemason consisted of the attainment of "degrees" through a series of rituals and ceremonies designed to advance the initiate progressively through higher levels of knowledge. Some Masonic beliefs exhibited the rational orientation of eighteenth-century Enlightenment thought, with God represented as "Great Architect of the Universe" and an emphasis on human reason. There were, nevertheless, unelaborated references to "ancient mystery religions" from Greece and Egypt and a liberal use of symbols derived from older European occult traditions.

The spiritual practices of descendants of Africans in America evolved significantly in the latter part of the eighteenth century. The onset of the Haitian revolution in 1797 sent thousands of slaves and slaveholders fleeing to the French-held territory of Louisiana, transforming this swampy low country into the site of a second African diaspora. In New Orleans, large numbers of enslaved blacks created a unique synthesis of African, European, and American religious elements in the religion of voodoo. New Orleans at that time was home to the largest Haitian population in the United States. But because of the convergence of races and religions in this cosmopolitan port city, voodoo developed along a different trajectory than it did in Haiti. Haitian Vodou originated as a rural-kin-based religion with strong collective worship elements. Voodoo in early-nineteenth-century New Orleans, in contrast, involved more of an emphasis on private, client-based supernatural rituals, including divination, healing, and spiritual harming. Although maintaining ties to its African sources in its practice of ritual activities such as spiritual possession, animal sacrifice, and serpent handling, New Orleans–style voodoo became widely known for its integration of Catholic iconography and the use of negative magic (that is, magic employed for the purposes of harm).

The reputation of New Orleans as a capital of "black magic" was secured by Marie Laveau, the famous "Queen of Voodoo." Partly a real figure and partly a creation of myth and rumor, Laveau symbolized the mélange of cultural forces that eventuated in a unique form of voodoo practice. Laveau was a "free woman of color" (mixed race) who worked as a seamstress and hairdresser for the city's white and Creole elites. She was also associated with the public drum dances held in Congo Square by New Orleans's black community, whose members revitalized many of the African-based spiritual practices. Laveau became a legendary spiritual adviser to numerous clients, as well as an influential patron of the clandestine network of voodoo practitioners in the city. In keeping with her mysterious career, the date of her death is not certain. Nor is it clear whether there was even a single Marie Laveau or whether her name was adopted by other family members who were associated with New Orleans's unique voodoo tradition.

As the Revolutionary War fostered belief in the unrivaled potential of ordinary persons, so did conventional religious life begin to reflect a growing receptivity toward experimentation and spiritual innovation. No longer constrained by the limitations of state sponsorship, Protestant Christianity exploded with creative impulses. Evangelical religion, boosted by the potent, sweeping impact of the Second Great Awakening, manifested supernaturalism in its institutional dimensions as well as in its outward, experiential aspects. Evangelical Christians were encouraged to seek the divine presence in dreams and visionary episodes and to accept supernatural manifestations of God's grace. At the height of the revivalist furor in the late 1700s and early 1800s, Baptist and Methodist preachers promoted exuberant experiences and enthusiastic styles of worship for seekers and converts. Evangelical Methodists also institutionalized practices of supernatural healing, drawing from an older Wesleyan tradition of miraculous cures.

The postrevolutionary era witnessed a pervasive rise in claims of spiritual revelation by individuals. In some cases their inspired leadership resulted in the formation of new religious movements and sects. From the Mormons, the adherents of America's first homegrown religion, to utopian societies like the Shakers, institutional religious life in the United States articulated the yearning of believers for true spiritual experience. The Mormons were a prime example of a church that synthesized beliefs in magical healing, occult ritual, and divination. Such traditions had characterized the world inhabited by the church's founder, Joseph Smith. Described by contemporaries as a prophet, Smith received divine dreams and angelic visitations in his youth. He was well known as a powerful seer to the network of treasure diggers and Masonic initiates in western New York in the early 1800s. Supernaturalism clearly permeated the cultural milieu in which Smith and the early Latter-day Saints found themselves. An understanding of this supernaturalism is essential to a full comprehension of this period of American religious history.

Antebellum Nineteenth Century

In terms of supernatural beliefs, the United States during the mid- to late 1800s was particularly rich, as a number of new voices presenting claims to divine truth and unmediated access to spiritual experience came to the fore. Some movements in this period linked conventional religious beliefs with older occult traditions that had circulated for generations.

Many of these new movements were influenced by the ideas of Franz Anton Mesmer (1734–1815), an Austrian physician who developed an influential theory of affinity called "animal magnetism." Mesmer (from whose name the term *mesmerize* derives) believed that most diseases of the body were caused by imbalances in a vital invisible fluid, called animal magnetism, that surrounded all living organisms and physical matter. The imbalance of animal magnetism resulted in a deprivation of the energy of this invisible force, and with the proper techniques, a skillful practitioner could "magnetically" transfer the fluid and correct the imbalances. Mesmer's teachings became popular in the United States in the 1840s as they were joined with psychic practices such as clairvoyance and hypnotism. Although Mesmer's ideas were adopted by members of the sectarian healing culture in nineteenth-century America, the concept of animal magnetism was consistently denounced by religious, medical, and scientific authorities as false.

One of the most significant traditions to be given impetus by Mesmer was Spiritualism. This movement reflected the period's excitement with science, combined with atavistic longings for religious truth. The Spiritualist movement ostensibly began with events in 1847 at Hydesville, New York, where two sisters, Margaret and Katie Fox, were believed to have established contact with the dead through a series of mysterious "rappings," or knocking sounds, in their home. These rappings were taken to be messages from beyond the grave, delivered with the assistance of the sisters as mediums of contact. As more and more people became convinced that the rappings were legitimate communications, the publicity from these events grew, and a new religion was born.

For nearly thirty years, Spiritualism bridged the line between religious experience and commercial spectacle. In the stolid Victorian era, Americans experimented with Ouija boards, table turning, parlor séances, and, in some instances, spectral materializations, all efforts to communicate with the dead. To many, Spiritualism provided irrefutable confirmation of the immortality of the soul, the existence of heaven and an afterlife, and the presence of an immanent and benign deity. Because of Spiritualism's frank affirmation of the essential goodness of human beings and its denial of the existence of hell or the need for salvation, its followers believed it to be a more benevolent expression of Christianity than that which was taught in many of the churches. Many Americans of note were either avid Spiritualists or at least dabbled with the practice, including many antislavery activists and advocates of women's rights.

Although it was widely practiced in the United States, Spiritualism never achieved the status of a national church or a denomination. It was promoted through public lecture tours and séance demonstrations by mediums and trance speakers, many of whom who were activists in the progressive reform movements that surfaced in the latter part of the nineteenth century, such as temperance and suffrage. The movement's leading spokesperson was Andrew Jackson Davis (1826–1920). He was a prominent mesmerist who gave Spiritualist beliefs a consistent philosophical and theological foundation. A skillful medium, Davis was able to self-induce trance states, in which he would receive communications from departed spirits, such as Emanuel Swedenborg and other figures.

The attempt to reconcile science and religion found articulation in a number of new occult traditions that sought to address age-old religious problems such as the existence of life after death and the nature of the human soul. The so-called harmonial religions (so named by scholars who have studied this constellation of religious beliefs and institutions) were an example of the merging of occult ideas with late-nineteenth-century popular scientific thought. Harmonial groups shared belief in an underlying oneness, or harmony, that existed between all forces within the universe, in accordance with a correspondence between the visible and the invisible realm, or the material and the metaphysical world. Harmonial faiths also emphasized that well-being, health, and psychic enlightenment were contingent on one's ability to realize perfection, or one's fullest spiritual potential, by recognizing the fundamental hierarchy of spiritual development that existed in this world and the next and establishing a rapport between them. Lacking a firm dogma, harmonial religions embodied a rich variety of traditions and included some beliefs that resonated with mainstream religion, as well as a number of influences that eschewed historical commonalities with the Judeo-Christian tradition.

Supernaturalism also influenced the healing practices of blacks in the nineteenth century. African Americans, who had maintained traditions of magical therapy since the earliest days of their enslavement in America, engaged in a system of belief and practice known as Conjure, a form of healing and counterharming that adopted both Christian and African-based religious elements. Practitioners of Conjure posited the belief that body and spirit were connected and that certain untreatable illnesses stemmed from the animosity of other persons who possessed the ability to harm others using supernatural methods. Conjurers, who were also known as hoodoo doctors and rootworkers, treated physical ailments with magical medicines. Some conjurers used herbs; others cured stubborn afflictions with mysterious, handmade charms. During slavery, conjurers were often responsible for the physical well-being of members of black communities. In his famous autobiography, Frederick Douglass relates his experiences with a conjurer whose root charm, he suggests, had saved him from the violent advances of a ruthless overseer. Although operating without sanction from the churches, most conjurers drew from a familiar repertoire of religious symbols and beliefs, utilizing Christian talismans, Bibles, and prayers for their treatment of affliction.

In African American slave traditions, the roles of preacher and conjurer were sometimes shared by a single person. William Webb was one such individual, a bondsman who embodied the dual capacities of magician and minister. While enslaved in Kentucky in the early 1800s, Webb recalled that once he had prepared special bags of roots for other slaves to carry in order to keep peace between masters and bondspersons on local plantations. The roots, he explained, were to be used in conjunction with prayer. When asked by other slaves about the bags, he explained, "I told them those roots were able to make them faithful when they were calling on the Supreme Being, and to keep [their] mind at work all the time." A believer in the mystical significance of dreams, prophecy, and sleight of hand, Webb combined the characters of supernatural specialist and religious functionary. Webb was not unique. In the 1840s an observer described a black preacher she had met on a farm in Virginia. This "man of many gifts," she wrote, was simultaneously popular as "a conjurer who could raise evil spirits, and a god-man who wore a charm, and could become invisible at any moment." "Prophet" John Henry Kemp was another. This Mississippi-born man was a loyal representative of the "True Primitive Baptist Church" but was also gifted with the ability to determine the future, read palms, and cure sickness with the aid of "charms, roots, herbs, and magical incantations and formulae" for "those who believe[d] in him." Thus, as spiritual pragmatists, black Americans utilized both traditions of Christianity and conjuring as they responded to any number of concerns (illness, death, the brutality of a master, the fate of a love affair) they might face. Both conjuring and Christianity were anchored in their perceptions of a supernatural, responsive universe. Each met specific needs that the other did not.

The lack of a sharp dichotomy between the sacred and the secular led many blacks to view the supernatural world as directly impinging on human experience. From slavery, African Americans put a premium on spiritual empowerment, an empowerment that was potentially available to all believers. The exuberant practices of community worship, the Afro-Christian traditions of "shouting," spiritual possession, mystical revelation, and the drama of conversion—all of these might serve to bring the individual into a transcendent experience in which the boundaries between the self and the spirit were made permeable. Magic, as a practice intended for contacting and manipulating the spiritual, had similar goals. Black Americans placed a great emphasis on the acquisition of supernatural power and the practices by which persons could tap into that power to make it "work" for them. For some, conjuring and hoodoo were a legitimate appropriation of spiritual energies. For others, these traditions possessed a theurgic function and provided personal spiritual empowerment. The complementary nature of supernaturalism and religion produced much of the variety—and much of the tension—that existed in the cultural arena for slaves and their descendants. In the eyes of many blacks, supernatural practitioners bridged the heritage of their ancestors (hence the frequent description of conjurers as "full-blooded Africans") and the adopted cultures of North America.

Postbellum and Industrial Nineteenth Century

Nowhere were supernaturalism and occultism more pronounced than in the various strains of alternative healing that proliferated in America during the mid- to late 1800s. Healing physical affliction continued to be a central preoccupation for a number of spiritual traditions that arose during this time.

Christian Science and Seventh-Day Adventism were two denominations that institutionalized their approaches to healing and the body in a religious context. To a similar extent, each of these sects emphasized the supernatural origins of affliction and sickness, the distinction between spirit and body, and the efficacy of divine treatment of diseases.

Ellen Gould White (1827–1915) founded the Seventh-Day Adventist Church in 1863, following a divine vision she received in which she was instructed in the development of a new gospel of health. White was originally a convert to the Millerites, a loose collective of believers who were organized around their faith in the imminent return of Jesus Christ. White became an active promoter of the benefits of hydropathy, a water cure treatment that was popular among middle-class Americans who took part in alternative therapies at this time. After receiving her initial vision, White assumed the role of a prophetess. She preached and wrote on the practicality of healthful living. Under her prophetic authority, the Adventists taught the benefits of dietary correction through a vegetarian regimen and the avoidance of alcohol, coffee, and tobacco. Although White's spiritual understanding was obtained from her own supernatural experiences, she explicitly condemned the occult healing practices that were in vogue at the time, such as hypnotism, mesmerism, psychology, and "mind-cure."

The Seventh-Day Adventists' distinctive ideas coincided with those of another nineteenth-century healing movement, the Christian Scientists. Mary Baker Eddy (1821–1910) founded the Church of Christ, Scientist, in 1879. Eddy had been subject to nervous disorders since her youth, and in her adult life she had sought a variety of remedies, including the homeopathic treatments of Phineas Parkhurst Quimby, a healer who was well known in occult circles in the mid-nineteenth century (see below). In 1866, after spontaneously healing from a severe spinal injury, Eddy became convinced that reality itself was ultimately spiritual, that God is all that exists, and that all matter, evil, and even sin itself were illusory. This radical denial of the existence of matter, Eddy believed, formed the foundational principle through which physical healing could take place.

The Theosophists provided one of the most interesting alternatives to mainstream Christianity. Strongly influenced by Eastern religions such as Buddhism and Hinduism, the Theosophical movement brought a decidedly international flavor to American occultism. Theosophy was organized in the United States in 1875 with the founding of the American Theosophical Society by Helena Petrovna Blavatsky (1831–91) and Henry Steel Olcott (1832–1907). Both Blavatsky and Olcott had been deeply affected by the idea of mediumship, or communication with the spirit world, and created an organization that would function as an open platform for those who were interested in psychic and occult matters. In their travels throughout the world, particularly in the East, Blavatsky and Olcott studied the metaphysical concepts of Asian religions. Eventually they developed Theosophy into a system of belief that incorporated theological and philosophical ideas from many traditions.

Theosophy was centered around acquisition of "ancient wisdom" in the form of secret teachings from invisible masters, or adepts, who conveyed their messages through select spiritually evolved individuals. The invisible masters were also called mahatmas (after the adepts from the Hindu tradition). They were said to be part of the Great White Lodge, a mystical brotherhood of leaders whose role was to guide the world through its various stages of spiritual evolution. Theosophists believed in a single Infinite Reality, from which everything flowed and from which the key to all scientific and religious knowledge derived. All individuals, they believed, possessed the knowledge that enabled them to reach perfection, and hence harmony, with the Infinite Reality. In order to achieve this ascendancy in consciousness, however, one needed to acquire mystical insight through a series of spiritual initiations and ascend through the seven planes and cosmic cycles that constituted and defined the universe.

Although Theosophy was popular among members of the educated upper and middle social classes, other, less intellectualized traditions such as New Thought and I AM drew from its ideas, displaying the attraction of harmonialism across broad segments of the population. New Thought was initially established as an alternative to mainstream medicine. It would garner acclaim because of its influence on Mary Baker Eddy and Christian Science. New Thought practitioners conceived of their tradition as a form of mental healing, believing that the mind was the greatest source of power and that, with self-motivation and through true unity with the divine, all individuals could attain both health and material prosperity. These ideas were introduced by Phineas P. Quimby (1802–66), a former clockmaker from Maine who successfully cured patients using a vicarious treatment. Quimby would acquire the symptoms of the sick person while encouraging them to adopt a positive mental attitude by fixing on healing energy and the presence of God. Quimby believed that a person's mental conviction—his or her inward ideas and beliefs—was the key to sickness and health and that all healing derived from realization of the true divine within. Harmony with the divine occurred when one was awakened to an awareness of one's true spiritual nature. Therefore, as manifestations of bad thoughts or faulty ideas, all afflictions were seen to be rooted in the mind. By instilling balance of thought through positive affirmations, disease and sickness could be banished. The goal was to eliminate "wrong beliefs" so that harmony could be realized between divine and human being. New Thought had many followers in the late nineteenth and early twentieth centuries (most notably Mary Baker Eddy), yet even prior to Quimby's death, the movement was unable to sustain itself institutionally and remained a diffuse collective of believers.

One successful offshoot that emerged from New Thought was the Christian-based Unity school, a movement founded in 1889 that taught that good health and personal fulfillment could be achieved through prayer and unification with the "Christ mind." New Thought writers, moreover, were split between those who saw the goal of "harmony" as the ability to see beyond the material and others who touted New Thought as the key to achieving prosperity. The movement eventually produced popular writers such as Norman Vincent Peale, whose *Power of Positive Thinking* was a kind of popularization of what had been esoteric ideas in the nineteenth century, simplified now to a formula for success and prosperity.

In the years prior to the turn of the twentieth century, more and more Americans took an interest in the spiritual life of the "Orient," that is, the religions of the East, including Buddhism, Hinduism, and Islam. For many Americans, this exposure to the religious life of India, China, and Japan came about through the World's Parliament of Religions, an international exposition billed as an exhibition of the world's cultures and peoples at the Chicago World's Fair in 1893. After the parliament, some American occultists sought to develop a dialogue with non-Western spiritual practitioners by exploring some of the more obscure mystical practices and beliefs, such as yoga and reincarnation. Asian culture, with its venerable sacred traditions and its ancient texts, represented to many Westerners the unelaborated wisdom of the ages. For occultists, the appropriation of Asian culture represented a natural convergence of Eastern and Western mysticism and the apogee of harmonial enlightenment.

Early Twentieth Century

Occult and supernatural practice in the United States at the turn of the twentieth century was tenuously connected to institutional religious life. New ideas were continuously propagated by ambitious spokespeople who gave intellectual credence to their mystical visions. They sometimes attracted numerous disciples and created a vast synthesis of occult knowledge. Occult tradition in this period can be viewed as a form of piety that functioned as an alternative to conventional religious thought. In these belief systems, the supernatural world was verifiable, and God was not viewed as something outside being and consciousness. The divine was conceived as something within, a linking of finite and infinite personality, a cosmic extension of the human self.

A prominent early-twentieth-century group that integrated elements of Christianity while using the rhetoric of the Theosophists was the I AM Religious Activity, introduced in 1932 by Guy Ballard (1878–1939), a former miner from Arizona. Ballard claimed to have made contact with a great spiritual adept by the name of Saint Germain, who revealed to him instructions to the "Great Law of Life," the fundamental truths of the Ascended Masters. Ballard, who was chosen as their messenger, announced the advent of the "I Am" Age of Earthly Perfection, a golden age in which divine harmony would awaken humanity. Recording the messages of the Ascended Masters, Ballard held classes, gave lectures, and published several books with their verbatim dictations. Ballard's workshops and seminars, which were attended by thousands, also offered lessons and affirmations by which believers could tap into their own divine insight and communicate with the Ascended Masters themselves.

I AM grew into a national movement as Ballard and members of his immediate family promoted the teachings of the Ascended Masters. They emphasized human unity with the divine (I AM, the biblical name of God) and the existence of an invisible, spiritual hierarchy that was attainable by humans through personal elevation. I AM members considered their beliefs to be compatible with Christianity, as Jesus was himself represented as one of the highest Ascended Masters. Furthermore, in the name of "Jesus the Christ" all decrees, or affirmations, were repeated by I AM members for their own peace and self-empowerment. Similar groups, such as Alice Bailey's Arcane School and, most recently, Elizabeth Claire Prophet's Church Universal and Triumphant, have adopted many of the ideas and language of the original I AM organization.

Like their predecessors of the nineteenth century, harmonial religions emphasized healing as a practical consequence of spiritual development and placed a great importance on the power of mind over body. Even as it was believed to be centered in the realm of science, occultism gradually shifted to the realm of psychic phenomena. One reason for this shift had to do with the understandings of the causes of disease and sickness that harmonial religions promoted, which went against the grain of conventional medical thought. In the harmonial worldview, healing was not viewed as purely physiological in cause; rather, both affliction and health were nonmaterial in nature, with origins that were found in the spiritual and metaphysical arenas. In other words, the healing and rehabilitation of the body began with the mind and the spirit.

Protestant Christianity in the early twentieth century had also seen a greater openness to interpositions of the supernatural in everyday life, particularly in the area of miraculous healing. An emphasis on observable evidence and experiential spirituality was prominent in Pentecostalism, a Christian movement that sprang forth from a series of revivals dating from 1906 in Los Angeles. Pentecostals believed that the presence of God was manifested in the power of the Holy Spirit, as foretold in the New Testament Book of Acts. Pentecostal Christians witnessed the presence of God in supernatural events, which included the practice of speaking in tongues, visions, "signs and wonders" such as prophecy, and spontaneous healings. From an occult standpoint many of these experiences could be interpreted as paranormal phenomena, with the acting supernatural forces none other than God, Jesus, and the Holy Spirit. In any event, Pentecostal ideas of the supernatural met with great acceptance, for within two decades the movement had ignited a worldwide phenomenon.

Like their enslaved forebears of previous generations, blacks in the years of freedom relied on material objects for supernatural mediation. An array of amulets and talismans, called "hands," "MoJos," "gris-gris," "jacks," "tobies," "goopher bags," and "wangas," were utilized by practitioners for purposes of protection. The contents of the specialist's "trick bag" varied. One conjurer's favorite item included balls of tar, sulfur, and assorted lumps of color that blazed when set afire. The fabrication of "voodoo dolls," "luck balls," and other supernatural artifacts became the mainstay of successful practitioners. Other popular items in black American supernatural traditions included red flannel bags filled with dried leaves, potent crumbling powders, or metallic dust. Bottles of various liquids, pins, and needles were interred by practitioners or strung on trees as a snare for invisible forces.

In the twentieth century, African American conjuring traditions emerged as cultural icons, as they were appropriated by blues musicians and artists whose lyrics referred to supernatural practices (e.g., "I got my mojo working," "That ole black magic," "You put a spell on me," and many others). Conjuring also made its way (in remnant form) to the nation's cities, where practitioners or the merely curious could buy love potions, High John the Conqueror root, and numerous other items that were the commodified form of conjuring practice. One of the most important ingredients in the apothecary of African American supernaturalism consisted of organic roots taken from designated plants. In particular, the root of the High John the Conqueror vine, with its twisted or tuber-shaped body, was most valuable. Of all the charms carried by African American practitioners, these roots were especially prized for their potency and effectiveness. It may be that the prominence of the root in African American magic traditions harkens back to Kongo African beliefs in *minkisi*, the supernatural medicines that incarnated powerful spirit beings and divinities as composite and created artifacts. An early African American Pentecostal preacher named Charles Harrison Mason, founder of the Church of God in Christ (the nation's largest black Pentecostal denomination), often preached with strangely shaped roots, tubers, and other like objects in his hand, using them to impart spiritual lessons and power. Mason's practice shows how, among African Americans, the visual influence of conjuring traditions outlasted slavery and continued in various forms throughout the United States after the turn of the twentieth century.

Modern America

Like American religion generally, supernaturalism in the post–World War II years burgeoned and blossomed, took on characteristics from the faith in science and technology that followed the war, and deeply influenced (and was deeply influenced by) the counterculture and movements of alternative spiritualities that sprang up in the 1960s and 1970s. Americans' faith in the scientific and the material seemed as much complementary as contradictory to their fascination with the unseen, the esoteric, the strange, and the supernatural.

One kind of mixture of the scientific and the supernatural lay in America's simultaneous fascination with and horror of drugs—especially in the case of those drugs that affected the American middle classes in the 1960s and after. For decades prior to that, natural hallucinogens quietly had become part of Native American religious expression, namely, in the form of the peyote buttons taken by members of the Native American Church as part of all-night religious rituals. And for generations before that, mushrooms and other botanicals were part of the religions of many groups in the Americas. White Americans, however, remained largely ignorant of those traditions.

In the postwar era, drugs—marijuana, speed, and lysergic acid (LSD)—entered American life through the counterculture. They came from a variety of sources—from the black jazzmen emulated by the Beat poets to the controlled hallucinogenic experiments conducted by psychology professors such as Timothy Leary and Richard Alpert. One drug in particular, LSD, developed a small following in the early 1960s, when Leary conducted "trials" with it: groups of academics and (especially) divinity students came to Leary's home to ingest the drugs and reported on what happened to them. Eventually he formed the aptly named League for Spiritual Development to encourage mind-expanding drug-taking sessions in carefully controlled environments. Coming from a background of behavioralist psychology, Leary originally had little use for the religious terminology that would come to be associated with LSD. He quickly grew intrigued by the fact that it was divinity students, ministers, and others from religious backgrounds who were attracted to consciousness expansion through LSD. Leary placed himself in the tradition of William James and others earlier in the century who had been fascinated by the varieties of religious experience, including psychic phenomena such as hypnotism and mesmerism. One of Leary's coenthusiasts, another Harvard psychologist named Richard Alpert, also tried LSD, several hundred times. As he later said, "God came to the United States in the form of LSD." Later, he decided that LSD was a temporary expedient needed to introduce followers to the new realms of consciousness but that other religious traditions could produce the same effect without the need for drugs at all. Richard Alpert set off to India and Nepal to discover these traditions, just as the poet Gary Snyder had done in the 1950s during his twelve-year period of Zen Buddhist study in Japan. Alpert's stay was much shorter but profoundly influential. After taking the new name Ram Dass, he returned to the United States to spread the new gospel of natural enlightenment. His 1971 book *Remember, Be Here Now*, subtitled "cookbook for a sacred life," told of his spiritual quest. In easy 1-2-3 steps it introduced to Americans formerly exotic paths to the supernatural, including meditation and yoga.

If Timothy Leary was the sacred clown and enthusiast of drug-induced changes in consciousness, Alan Watts, an English-born scholar and popularizer of Eastern religious traditions in the United States, was its theoretician. In the 1960s Watts also experimented with psychedelics—a continuation, in his way of thinking, of the psychic experiments of the late nineteenth century and the religious explorations of William James in the early twentieth. Much like Leary, only with more self-consciously serious prose and manner, Watts saw psychedelics as one means to mystical experience. If this use of psychedelics was not "practical" in the Western sense, if the new consciousness broke down hierarchies and encouraged unorthodox visions, so much the better, Watts believed. Religious resistance to drug use, Watts argued, came in part because "our own Jewish and Christian theologies will not accept the idea that man's inmost self can be identical with the Godhead." Watts later turned away from psychedelics, seeing them as one baby step in Westerners' attempt to shed the skin of techno-rational culture along the path to spiritual enlightenment.

After World War II, occult and supernatural beliefs also took on other scientific, and pseudoscientific, forms. Beginning in the late 1940s, occult beliefs began to reflect the burgeoning fascination with the nascent fields of air and space technology, as well as the common concern for national security that gripped the country after World War II. In June 1947, a businessman named Kenneth Arnold reported to authorities that he had seen an inexplicable phenomenon while flying in a plane over Washington State. His report, in which he described several shiny saucerlike objects that moved in formation at more than twelve hundred miles per hour, gained national attention and immediately was followed by a number of accounts of additional sightings in other parts of the country. Thus began a new wave of excitement—and controversy —surrounding the existence of unidentified flying objects, or UFOs.

From that time, thousands of other sightings, encounters, and physical abductions of individuals by extraterrestrial beings were reported by witnesses in the United States. The rising Cold War fears of Americans may have contributed to an unusual surge of paranoia that was given graphic expression in stories of mysterious and potentially dangerous invaders. Accounts varied, from the credible to the incredible, with witnesses describing objects in the skies, anomalous lights, and strange visual phenomena. Some people claimed to have seen actual landings of spacecraft and their inhabitants, and others reported contact with the aliens, often described as short, hairless creatures with distended heads and orblike eyes. Other witnesses told of subsequent visits by persons dressed completely in black (the original "MIB") who, they claimed, discouraged them from telling others of their experiences.

Within a generation, a thriving subculture of believers in UFOs had formed, and occult interpretations filled the gap when the official explanations left many in doubt. For some occultists, the extraterrestrials were none other than the invisible Ascended Masters, who now sent their messages using different channels of communication. Some occultists claimed that the alien adepts actually lived on other "worlds" or planes of existence. The intent of these evolved entities was benign; their mission was to act as guides for human beings, who were stalled at a lower stage of spiritual evolution. Although scientific and government research into the existence of UFOs yielded little actual evidence, proponents of these beliefs, with their elaborate hypotheses of extraterrestrial invasions and alien transmissions, continued to gain adherents well into the 1970s. As was the case with mesmerism, Theosophy, and many other movements, the literature on UFOs mixes the supernatural and the superrational, occult belief and scientific explanations.

Interest in magic, occult, and supernatural phenomena in the United States underwent another resurgence in the 1960s and 1970s, one that replayed many of the themes of harmonial religions, healing therapies, and Spiritualist practices from the antebellum era. In films, books, and other media, popular culture promoted many of the ideas of previous decades. Some "new" occult and supernatural concepts were actually restatements or reinterpretations of former traditions. Spiritualism, or communication with the dead, for example, was now called "channeling." Such traditions as shamanism and witchcraft likewise incorporated beliefs from pagan religions that were purportedly thousands of years old.

The rise of alternative religions, the increasing viability of metaphysical healing techniques, and the growth of scientific investigation into paranormal phenomena renewed public interest in these ideas. This revival of the occult also coincided with major transformations in the social, political, and cultural environment of the United States between 1960 and 1980. Astrologers marked this period as the start of the Aquarian Age, referring to a two-thousand-year epoch of spiritual evolution that was concurrent with the entry of the spring equinox into the constellation Aquarius, believed officially to begin in the year 2740. For many, the Age of Aquarius represented the dawn of spiritual enlightenment on the earth and was evidenced by an abandonment of traditional cultural constraints, a new receptivity to holistic approaches to health, and positive developments in human consciousness.

The popular occult belief that the Ascended Masters were transmitting knowledge to specially chosen members of the human race gained wider acceptance in the 1970s and 1980s when a number of people claimed to be able to summon these forces from the invisible world. These persons, known as psychic channelers, were actually predated by others with such abilities, including Edgar Cayce (1877–1945), known as the "Sleeping Prophet," and Jane Roberts (1929–84), who relayed the communications of an entity named "Seth" in the 1970s. In the latter part of the twentieth century, the rise of numerous new channelers was accompanied by exceptional media attention and, with that, a greater potential for monetary profit and fame. In 1977, J. Z. Knight, a Washington housewife, made contact with a thirty-five-thousand-year-old entity named "Ramtha" while in a trance. Knight became one of the more successful of a number of psychics who widely promoted their abilities to communicate with a realm of unseen beings. Using Ramtha's channeled wisdom, Knight became a popular teacher, offering the ancient teachings of her spirit guide to audiences who paid as much as a thousand dollars per session.

Channeling in this period was viewed by many middle- and upper-class Americans a form of psychic therapy, particularly after its endorsement by the actress Shirley MacLaine. MacLaine wrote three books recounting her own experiences with spirit guides and reincarnation, two of which were produced as made-for-television movies in the late 1980s. In her successive autobiographies and self-help treatises, MacLaine narrated her religious pilgrimage toward "inner transformation." Her works crested along with the surge in popularity of the New Age movement, itself a descendant of the countercultural prophets of the 1950s and 1960s. MacLaine came to the conclusion that personal transformation would have to precede "transforming the world I live in," an argument ironically parallel to the long-standing evangelical call for personal salvation as the necessary prerequisite to any change in the social order. Practices of meditation, chanting, and reading crystals were all in pursuit of discovering the true "Higher Self" that lay trapped within the mortal self. MacLaine's popularity peaked in the mid-1980s, with a television special touting her guru's powers of levitation and reincarnation. Following the exposure of some prominent New Age teachers as fraudulent and the acknowledgment of some practitioners that their faith in crystals was just that—faith—and not verifiable in any sense, the movement went into decline. As was often the case with supernaturalism, the spiritual needed the complement of the scientific, as least as the "scientific" was defined in a particular age. The writings of MacLaine and other New Age adherents were a popularized form of a long American tradition of the quest for the true "higher" self, a common theme in the exploration of supernaturalism.

Gradually, the Aquarian Age gave way to the New Age of the 1980s. In the New Age, occult and supernatural traditions were promoted as spiritual resources that could engender transformations in every area, from prosperity and spiritual awakening to environmental reform and world peace. The tools of the New Age practitioner included healing crystals, tarot cards, and astrological charts, as well as a plethora of how-to publications. New Age products displayed a growing emphasis on commercialism. Like the older traditions of mesmerism, New Thought, and alternative medical therapies through spiritual practice, New Age became big business.

Some occult and supernatural traditions have drawn on the practices of marginalized or submerged religions in the United States. For example, shamanism, which called forth the primal sensibilities of New Agers, underwent a rebirth in the 1970s. Shamans are the magicians or medicine men of tribal societies who are believed to possess supernatural knowledge and special magical abilities. One current of shamanism's popularity was traced to the influence of a series of books by a Peruvian-born writer named Carlos Casteneda (1925–), who published accounts of his personal experiences with Don Juan

Matus, a Yaqui Indian mystic and sorcerer. Matus, or Don Juan, as he became known, acted as Casteneda's guide while he was doing anthropological research in California. Don Juan accompanied Casteneda during his apprenticeship in several mystical adventures and spiritual journeys that involved the use of mescaline, a mind-altering drug. Although certain characters and events in Casteneda's books were apparently fictionalized, the ideas concerning a higher reality and the emphasis on shamanic power stimulated the imagination of an entire generation of spiritual seekers.

Shamanism also figured in the New Age milieu as a form of religious practice. Whereas some Americans appropriated the spiritual traditions of Native American peoples by taking part in sweat lodges and vision quests, others sought a connection to shamanism in traditions that related to their own racial, ethnic, or cultural backgrounds. Many Anglo-Americans, for instance, turned to the ancient religions of pre-Christian Europe. This movement, known as neo-paganism (as opposed to paganism, which sometimes involved animal and human sacrifice), comprised a broad cluster of traditions, including the Wiccan, Celtic, Norse, and Druidic religions. Like other shamanistic religions, neo-paganism was a nature-based, polytheistic faith in which believers used ritual and magic to communicate with spiritual beings (practices that disturbed and frightened many conservative Christians).

Shamanism also flourished among minority group members. Two African-based religions from the islands of Haiti and Cuba, Vodou and Santeria, were brought to the United States by immigrants throughout the late twentieth century. Both Vodou and Santeria revolve around human interactions with the spirit world through ritual, animal sacrifice, drumming, and dance. In Vodou, bodily possession by invisible forces called *loas* is accomplished by invocation. Similarly, in the religion of Santeria, divine beings known as orisha enter the bodies of believers when called, much like the spirits of the dead in the nineteenth-century Spiritualist movement. While in the trance state, possessed persons walk, talk, and act as if they have become the spiritual beings who inhabit their bodies. Both Santeria and Vodou integrate practices from Christianity: hymns, chanted preaching, prayer, and testimony, for example. Although both religions celebrate the powers of the supernatural realm, their practitioners generally shun any association of their beliefs with sorcery, negative magic, and witchcraft.

Conclusion

At the turn of the twenty-first century, beliefs in magic, supernaturalism, and occultism show few signs of abating. Interest in these phenomena can be seen in their popularity in contemporary American culture. Films such as *Ghost* and, more recently, *The Sixth Sense* revisit the idea of human communication with the dead. Other media tap the public fascination with unsolved mysteries, such as the *National Enquirer*, a best-selling newspaper that presents weekly accounts of UFOs, angels visiting the earth, and local ghostly disturbances. Cable television's "Psychic Hotline" has exploded into a multi-million-dollar industry. The preoccupation with supernatural prediction has even reached the highest levels of government. In the 1980s, while Reagan administration officials relied on the system of technology known as "Star Wars" to defeat the Soviet threat, first lady Nancy Reagan admitted that she had consulted an astrologer in order to arrange her husband's schedule. The rational and the supernatural again commingled, this time in the political realm.

How do we understand the enduring grasp that magic, supernaturalism, and the occult have on American consciousness? To many scholars it is unclear why such ideas prevail in modern, technological, and scientifically minded societies. To be sure, for some people they are entertaining and function as little more than intellectual curiosities. To others, they are more meaningful. One explanation for the persistence of such beliefs may be that occult and supernatural traditions provide philosophical and theological perspectives that rival conventional views. For believers they offer a glimpse of a transcendent, self-sustaining reality. And because they emphasize spiritual development and therapy, they may supplement and support mainstream religious beliefs rather than challenge them.

Magic, supernaturalism, and the occult promote a vision of a universe that is powerful, mysterious, and infinite but at the same time accessible. These beliefs are essentially religious in that they appeal in compelling ways to the existence of an alternative realm. Far from being ephemeral, beliefs in magic, supernaturalism, and the occult display enduring qualities such as faith, the desire for spiritual advancement, and the relentless grasp for certainty in an uncertain world. In American history, they have persisted despite opposition, their premises accepted on faith when other explanations fall short.

SUGGESTED READINGS

Ahlstrom, Sydney E. *A Religious History of the American People*. New Haven: Yale University Press, 1972.

Albanese, Catherine. *America: Religion and Religions*. 3rd ed. Belmont, Calif.: Wadsworth Publishing, 1999.

Brooke, John. *The Refiner's Fire: The Making of Mormon Cosmology, 1644–1844*. Cambridge: Cambridge University Press, 1994.

Brown, Karen McCarthy. *Mama Lola: A Vodou Priestess in Brooklyn*. Berkeley and Los Angeles: University of California Press, 1991.

Carroll, Brett. *Spiritualism in Antebellum America*. Bloomington: Indiana University Press, 1997.

Chireau, Yvonne. *Black Magic: Dimensions of the Supernatural in African-American Religion*. Berkeley and Los Angeles: University of California Press, 2003.

Fauset, Arthur. *Black Gods of the Metropolis: Negro Religious Cults in the Urban North*. 1944. Reprint, New York: Octagon Books, 1970.

Ferguson, Marilyn. *The Aquarian Conspiracy: Personal and Social Transformation in the 1980s*. Los Angeles: J. P. Tarcher, 1980.

Frederickson, George. *The Black Image in the White Mind: The Debate on Afro-American Character and Destiny, 1817–1914*. New York: Harper and Row, 1971.

Hall, David. *Worlds of Wonder, Days of Judgment: Popular Religious Belief in Early New England*. New York: Knopf, 1989.

Jenkins, Philip. *Mystics and Messiahs: Cults and New Religions in American History*. New York: Oxford University Press, 2000.

Leary, Timothy. *Changing My Mind, among Others: Lifetime Writings*. Englewood Cliffs, N.J.: Prentice-Hall, 1982.

Levine, Lawrence. *Black Culture and Black Consciousness: Afro-American Folk Thought from Slavery to Freedom*. New York: Oxford University Press, 1977.

Lewis, James V. *Theosophy*. New York: Garland, 1990.

Raboteau, Albert. *Slave Religion: The "Invisible Institution" in the Antebellum South*. New York: Oxford University Press, 1978.

Rawick, George, ed. *The American Slave: A Composite Autobiography*. 41 vols. Westport, Conn.: Greenwood Press, 1972–79.

Smith, Theophus. *Conjuring Culture: Biblical Foundations of Black America*. New York: Oxford University Press, 1995.

Spencer, Jon. *Blues and Evil*. Knoxville: University of Tennessee Press, 1993.

Stuckey, Sterling. *Slave Culture: Nationalist Theory and the Foundations of Black America*. New York: Oxford University Press, 1988.

Tallant, Robert. *Voodoo in New Orleans*. New York: Macmillan, 1946.

Thomas, Keith. *Religion and the Decline of Magic*. New York: Scribner's, 1971.

Tweed, Thomas A., ed. *Retelling U.S. Religious History*. Berkeley: University of California Press, 1997.

Waters, Donald, ed. *Strange Ways and Sweet Dreams: Afro-American Folklore from the Hampton Institute*. Boston: G. K. Hall, 1983.

Williams, Peter. *America's Religions: From Their Origins to the Twenty-first Century*. Urbana: University of Illinois Press, 2001.

———. *America's Religions: Traditions and Cultures*. New York: Macmillan, 1990.

Cosmology

During the 1990s, the popular television show *The X-Files* entertained view-
ers with weekly discussions of the tension between science and faith, logic
and truth, and the individual's right to choose between competing ideas. Science often took the fall in *The X-Files*, as Native American shamans, Appa-
lachian witch doctors, and even children demonstrated a clearer perception
of the truth than the professionals sworn to tenets of logic and reason. The
main characters, Dana Scully and Fox Mulder, acted out for Americans their
own religious tension between what they believed to be true and what they
could prove exists. Can science explain the mysteries of the universe, or do
we accept our limited ability to understand the world beyond our immediate
environment? Do we remain tied to our terrestrial existence or entertain the
idea that we are part of a much larger cosmos?

Americans have been asking these questions for many generations, as perceptions of the continent expanded and then contracted with exploration
and settlement. Religion has played a key role in defining the relationship between Americans and the environment by setting precedents for how humans should approach their knowledge of the natural world and how that information regulates their daily existence.

Religion and the environment have an intimate relationship. Humans divide the earth into sacred and secular space, the calendar into sacred and sec-

ular time, and daily rituals into religious and profane practices. Most religions also prescribe human interaction with the natural world. Orthodox doctrine divides the earth into edible and inedible, the herbs that heal and the herbs that debauch, and divinely mandated and forbidden food. Sacred rules guide the preparation of the earth's bounty for consumption. Religions also designate natural and unnatural human behavior: when and whom to marry, how to react to or interact with outsiders, and how to regulate personal behavior. The right to punish lawbreakers is also defined by a religion's view of capital crimes and the right of fellow humans to exact corporeal punishments for crimes against nature and crimes against humankind. In essence, religious doctrine is a rule book defining human interaction with the environment. When a break with a mainstream religion occurs, such as the Protestant Reformation, revelations to Joseph Smith about Mormonism, or neo-pagan religions, these revolutionaries claim they are stripping away the falseness of former practices and rediscovering the true essence of humankind's relationship with the cosmos.

This chapter explores how Americans have conceptualized humanity's place on the earth and hence humans' relationship to God. Two distinct cultural patterns with supporting behaviors, social controls, and cosmological views have defined the relationship between religion and the environment throughout American history. These are best described as organicism and mechanism. *Organicism* comprehends the universe as an intimate place crowded with sacred forces made manifest in plants, animals, and humans as well as water, air, fire, and earth. Humans can neither control nor completely understand these forces. Thus, in an organic universe, the influence of these many powerful forces are feared, cajoled through sacrifice, summoned in ritual, and obeyed. In contrast, *mechanism* limits the number of sacred forces, usually concentrating them into one powerful deity without a fixed, terrestrial location. In a mechanistic universe, humans develop their relationship to the deity through laws the individual can understand, master, and manipulate.

The first of these two ideas, organicism, predominated before the Protestant colonization of the Americas in general and the Industrial Revolution in particular. Essentially, an organic universe is a closed system, like a human body, with all parts inextricably linked to the health of the whole. Likewise, the cosmos contained both deleterious and beneficial forces following one another in repeated cycles: health and growth followed by decay and death, fertile spring rains giving way to harvest and then frost. Religious forces permeated this world and included beneficial spirits as well as demons and tricksters.

Religious practices sought to minimize the impact of these deleterious forces, encourage the beneficial, and maintain the health and stability of society within its environment.

The second idea, mechanism, was not manifest fully in American society until the Industrial Revolution of the nineteenth century. However, ideas of mechanism emerged during the Enlightenment, through the emergence of Protestantism, and in the age of exploration. Scientific experimentation, navigation technology, enlightened humanism, and the protests against the Catholic hierarchy all encouraged individual knowledge of and responsibility toward the future of society and challenged the traditional ideas of cosmological maintenance. Increasingly, technology became a more effective means of understanding previously inscrutable processes. For example, the development of printed maps as well as Bibles in the vernacular rendered previously incomprehensible relationships to the cosmos within the mastery of the individual. Thus, rather than expecting the cycles of and spiritual elements within the earth to provide direction and expectations for human society, mechanism introduced ideas and tools that changed humans' relationship to both. As new tools of mechanism developed, the forces controlling the spiritual world and the geographical world became increasingly comprehensible.

The development of mechanism did not systematically eradicate organicism. To the contrary, organicism was and is a useful means of understanding the cosmos, and many belief systems contain elements of both mechanism and organicism; such belief systems exist across ethnic, racial, geographical, and religious boundaries. In its history, Christianity has been very willing to accept an organic cosmos consisting of beneficial and deleterious forces on the earth. Many New Age religions, ostensibly organicist, promote the mechanistic idea that the power on the planet can be manipulated with the human mind. Regardless of the overlap between organic and mechanistic beliefs, a definition relevant to both systems is important for clarity. A *cosmos* can be defined as the bounded space an individual or group conceptualizes as its known world and the spiritual forces that control it: the environment of seen and unseen forces and the rules, laws, and memory of historical experiences that govern the human interaction within this discrete space. A study of religion and the environment is a study of the geography of sacred forces: where the supernatural exists and how humans understand and interact with its power.

Precolonial Era

Societies in Africa, Europe, and America needed tight social organization and cooperation to ward off invading neighbors, natural disasters, and the ever present threat of hunger and disease. Hunting, gathering, and subsistence farming required the labor and discipline of every member of the group. Living in the deserts of the Middle East, Africa, and the American Southwest brought special concerns over water, hygiene, and food storage. From Exodus through Deuteronomy, the Bible's Old Testament contains excellent examples of religious doctrine's environmental prescriptions as well as specific food laws separating the clean from the unclean. In one passage, for example, God provided Moses with a means to purify water: "He appealed to the Lord, who pointed out a certain piece of wood. When he threw this into the water, the water became fresh" (Exod. 15:25); another passage concerned the equitable distribution of food: "When they measured it out by the omer, he who had gathered a large amount did not have too much, and he who had gathered a small amount did not have too little" (Exod. 16:18). The relationships between organic societies, their religions, and their physical environments were demanding, comprehensive, and very local. The cosmos before colonization was a very intimate place.

Many Native American groups shared narrated stories describing how humans emerged from nature (on the back of a turtle, or from under the soil, or in myriad other ways) and never fully separate from its force. For the Pueblo people of the Southwest, humans were born within the earth. The tribes of the Northeast believed they developed from animal ancestors or emerged as plants from the soil. Many animals and plants were held as sacred by different tribes: the corn of the Pueblos, the buffalo of the Plains tribes. Because humans were never completely separate from nature, there was no sense of taking the energy of the buffalo as it dies or hoarding the power of the sacred corn through its consumption. In an organic universe, the energy moves constantly through different manifestations of nature, whether they are plant, animal, human, a bolt of lightning, or a mountain stream. Rites, ceremonies, and daily activities promote beneficial agency from these sources while keeping malevolent forces at bay. Human behavior is regulated to remain sensitive to the needs of the system and maintain its balance.

Through their yearly migrations, nomadic tribes worked to fulfill bodily and community needs with little sense of material accumulation. Because these groups often returned to an area year after year, overuse one season could result in decreased productivity the next. Likewise, sedentary groups practiced crop rotation along with careful manipulation of forest, riparian, and uncultivated areas to encourage the prosperity of a diversity of beneficial plants and animals for their use and consumption. The health and prosperity of the population and environmental stability were intimately connected. Therefore, regulation, conservation, and constant vigilance of both the community and its food source remained at the center of daily life for Native American groups.

Native American spirituality cultivated the relationship with its environment, seeking to retain intimacy with the animals, plants, and nonhuman elements. The vision quest, common among tribes of the Plains, was a coming-of-age ceremony based on fasting, deprivation, and the discernment of the warrior's animal origin. Several Native American groups carried fetish bags, or medicine bundles; these were small bags containing representations of cherished elements, which created a composite representation of its wearer's identity and connection to particular elements in the environment. Shamans were understood to have retained their intimate knowledge of nature and could communicate with nonhuman forces, particularly animals.

Shamans discerned which practices were beneficial or malevolent and helped aid the tribe in propitiatory sacrifices and celebrations of gratitude. In times of drought, famine, disasters, and periods of prolonged and unsuccessful warfare, shamans distinguished what kind of sacrifice or penitential behavior would regain the beneficial agents in the cosmos. Fasting, dancing, sacrifice, and bodily mutilation were a few of a shaman's options, and the tribe would continue or even heighten the practices until the situation improved. At other times, propitiatory sacrifices were used as an insurance policy against disaster. In a circular cosmos in which the bad and the good rule equally, sacrifices were designed to fulfill the needs of the negative so that the positive forces could swing back around.

The circle is key to Native American religious symbolism. Shoshone tribes of the Great Basin (now Nevada and Utah) believed that the universe was created through four hoops. Likewise, the Lakota of the upper Midwest created their round dwellings to imitate the circular cosmos, and the Pueblo people maintained circular sacred kivas. The circle mimics the celestial and terrestrial boundaries of the earth as well as the cyclical fluctuations of the seasons. Native Americans remained sensitive to the natural changes in their cyclical environment and structured their lives accordingly.

In a cosmos based in maintenance and community security, those who threatened to disrupt stability were rarely allowed. A shaman could have special insight, and a chief or headman might gain exceptional status within the group, but the lone, misunderstood warrior or recalcitrant young woman was simply not tolerated. This was a closed system based on conserving resources. The elderly, the terminally ill, and the mentally handicapped were discarded when their existence threatened the security of the whole. This was particularly evident in the Plains tribes. The very elderly accepted their threat to the tribe and were left to die with few provisions in a makeshift shelter as their group went on without them.

Death in a closed, organic system was not a radical loss and a departure from the earth. Because energy was not lost but transferred, death was a transition from one kind of existence to another. George Catlin observed how, in the Mandan tribes of the upper Missouri River, death was made into a ceremony of reincorporation. At death, the corpse was dressed with the accoutrements of life, bound in wet buffalo hide, and placed on scaffolding in a separate "village" for the dead. Later, women retrieved the bleached skulls, brought them back into the community of the living, and placed them in a circle with their vacant sockets looking toward the center. Placing herbs under the skulls, the women would then sit and talk to their dead loved ones as they sewed beadwork. From birth, throughout life, and even into death, the cosmos of Native Americans remained a contained, intimate place.

The dead were also essential in African religions. Africans acknowledged the ever present influence of beneficial and malevolent spirits mixing on the earth. However, West African tribes, from which the majority of American slaves were taken, generally practiced religions focusing on the particular power of humans over their surroundings. Not only did these practices focus on ancestor worship, but there is evidence of chief cults venerating particularly powerful leaders. West Africans also recognized various gods with particular spheres of influence. Territorial gods protected distinct tribes, and household gods associated themselves with particular families or lineages. Family deities were almost always the spirits of dead ancestors, remaining to protect and influence their living progeny. Like the Mandan, West Africans reincorporated their dead into their daily lives with carved reliquary objects and symbols. Unlike the Mandan, Africans believed that the ancestors remained powerful immediate forces on the earth and possessed an unlimited ability to affect the lives of the living.

Because the natural environment was home simultaneously to the living and the dead, the oldest patriarch was the most powerful religious figure in West Africans' lives. He had the greatest knowledge of both the living and the dead and could act as an intermediary between them. Because the dead could affect weather, hunts, warfare, and community health, religious cere-

monies were designed to placate the ancestors and ask for their beneficial intercession for the group. Such a closed, conservative cosmos allowed the dead
to remain a powerful, even central factor in the corporeal world. So, whereas
Native American shamans regulated the animal and plant spirits as they mixed
with living humans, African American patriarchs negotiated relationships
between the living and the dead.

The belief that the physical environment held powerful and mysterious
forces was equally real for Europeans before colonization. For generations,
Europeans believed that God ordained kings and queens to rule through his
divine inspiration. At sanctified altars, priests turned bread and wine into the
body and blood of the risen Christ in transubstantiation. Priests also interpreted divine law, and through confessions they allowed individuals and the
community means to achieve God's forgiveness through ritual sacrifice and
repentance. Catholic saints, once living men and women, were venerated as
divine agents present on the earth after their death. Devils and angels were
equally present in the medieval world, and both could affect mortal lives. Yearly
cycles brought sacred celebrations when Europeans believed that mortals and
divine spirits walked in close proximity, bringing heaven and earth within the
same realm and reminding the living of the tangible power of the immortal.

In many religious practices, the divine inhabited the physical environment
in which people lived. In the tight quarters of a circumscribed, closed cosmos, Native Americans, West Africans, and medieval Europeans led lives in
reaction to these forces, changing their behavior in response to the whim of
the forces and managing their rituals to promote safety and cajole beneficial
agency from the environment. Living so close to the environment meant ad-
hering to the constraints of each season, strengthening the behavior of the
community, acknowledging powerful spiritual leaders, and remaining sensitive to the natural world. This tight, obedient social and religious structure
was also important because the environment was always in tension between
good and evil, beneficial and malevolent forces. Thus, humans were responsible for promoting the good and discouraging bad while simultaneously accepting that they could only exert influence, not control over their lives.

In some ways, the birth of mechanism is indicated in the failings of many
organic practices. When the sacrifices no longer worked, when the spiritual
leaders failed, when the God-ordained rulers rejected their divine dictates,
crises came. Furthermore, European individualism threatened the importance of community cohesiveness. The idea that a single person could achieve
success and safety without the help of others was a true revolution in the
fifteenth and sixteenth centuries. Markets and banks depended on the indi-

vidual's ability to achieve economic success and social mobility. Furthermore, plagues, famines, and other catastrophes hit cities in particular, demonstrating that close human contact could have deleterious effects. Behaviors emphasizing individual action became more beneficial than group interaction.

Just as people reassessed how they lived and worked together, new ideas about science, philosophy, and religion were also challenging the accepted ideas about the earth. Scientists such as Copernicus and Isaac Newton began to think the earth was just one part of a much larger cosmos. Their ideas that forces acted on the earth from outside the environment threatened the belief that people and their gods were crowded together on earth. By extending the cosmos out to planets, the sun, and the stars, science provided new places for the divine to exist away from the kitchen hearth, the forest glen, and the rivers and streams. Philosophers extolling logic and reason, like René Descartes, challenged tradition and an intimacy with the physical environment as the definition of knowledge. Instead, they saw individual knowledge as the starting place for understanding the rest of the world.

Science and reason became an alternative to mystery as the force controlling humans' place in the cosmos. Instead of propitiatory sacrifices that might or might not placate the spirits in the universe, science offered certain and replicable solutions to solve nature's mysteries. For many, the earth was rendered less mysterious and more benign under the rule of science. Scientists and philosophers encouraged Europeans to let go of their superstitions and encumbering attachments to a universe infested with spirits and uncontrollable forces. Descartes, for example, encouraged humans to declare their independence from these forces and become "masters and possessors of nature." He also suggested that individuals concentrate on eliminating the deleterious half of the human existence. Science, he reasoned, could rid society of an "infinity of maladies, both of body and mind, and enfeeblement brought on by old age." European thinking had presumed an environment filled equally with beneficial and deleterious forces. Enlightenment thought offered a way to promote the good and eliminate the bad while elevating the individual's ability to control these forces.

The Protestant Reformation also helped individuals remove themselves from a religious environment rife with uncontrollable forces. Luther protested the earthly and fallible priesthood serving as the convoluted mediator between Catholic believers and God. He sought to make the relationship between God and humans less corrupted by the complex web of church hierarchy, ritual, and mystery inherent in medieval beliefs. Like Descartes's "I think, therefore I am," Protestantism offered, "I think, therefore I am capable of comprehending and nurturing a relationship with my creator." Developments such as the Protestant Reformation and new ideas about science and reason, then, resulted in two competing ways of understanding the cosmos: as an environment filled with mysterious forces or as a nature controlled and understood by science. Even as Enlightenment ideas emboldened explorers, scientists, and philosophers to extend the boundaries of the known world, many groups continued to choose religious practices that made their environments predictable and their lives stable. On the eve of colonization, Native Americans, Africans, and most Catholics understood the earth to be a magical place, steeped in the spirits of good and evil. They each developed complex ritual communication with the seen and unseen worlds around them. Meanwhile, in western Europe, Protestantism freed humans from the unknown world and gave them essential control over life, faith, and the acquisition of knowledge.

Colonial North America

When southern Europeans landed in America in 1492, they were still steeped in an organic, medieval-Catholic religious tradition quite different from the religious thinking of post-Reformation European settlers. The differing views of the cosmos held by the Spanish Catholics and the Protestant northern Europeans each had profound consequences for the Native Americans. We now scoff at the European colonists' assumption that they had landed in a wilderness, but the physical environment of the Western Hemisphere was foreign, chaotic, unpredictable, and frightening to them. On the other hand, Native Americans saw their environment as carefully organized, and the European newcomers represented a scary new variable in an established plan. Religions in colonial America were forged at this crossroads of perception.

When exploration of the New World began in 1492, the organic Catholic practices of the Spanish met the organic practices of Native Americans. The Spanish clergy were on a special mission of conversion. They believed the millennial prophecy that the earth had already experienced the Age of the Father and the Age of the Son and was currently experiencing the Age of the Holy Spirit preceding the Second Coming of Christ. Conversion of non-Christians would hasten this event. Catholic baptism followed on the heels of military conquest on the American continent.

Catholics and Native Americans found common ground on several theological points. The Catholic belief in a father God, a mother Mary, the presence of the Holy Spirit, saints with particular spheres of influence, and the practices of sacrifice, deliverance, repentance, and celebration bore a resemblance to some native practices. Both cultures were tied to the cycles of the earth in subsistence farming and animal husbandry, which allowed an exchange of ideas rooted in a similar cosmological understanding.

Regardless of the similarities, converting Native Americans to Christianity was rarely characterized by acquiescence or peace. Natives resisted the invaders, and the Spanish used brutal tactics in pursuing converts. Once an area had been militarily conquered, friars frequently razed native temples, erecting Catholic churches, chapels, and cathedrals in their place. During the ritual of baptism, American Indians received new Christian names. All these changes were necessary to replace the gods of the Native Americans' cosmos with the Christian God.

The Native Americans continued an uneasy and complex relationship with Spanish colonizers, but later generations demonstrated how the worlds of the two cultures commingled. In Santa Fe, New Mexico, a statue of the Virgin, named La Conquistadora for the Iberian invaders, has been paraded through town for four hundred years. The statue is adorned with ears of corn fixed to its sides, betraying La Conquistadora's dual identity of half Corn Mother goddess and half mother of Jesus. The Virgin of Guadalupe is another representation of the Virgin Mary who first appeared in the central plateau of Mexico in December 1531. This Virgin appeared to a converted Native American, baptized Juan Diego, on a hill where an ancient Aztec temple to the Mother Goddess had once stood. She appeared on the first Sunday in the octave of the Immaculate Conception but spoke to Juan Diego in his native Nahuatl language. Both Virgins symbolize the relationships forged from two organic cultures and celebrate the cultures' shared belief in the sacred on American soil.

Because African Americans also shared this religious relationship with the environment, when they landed in the Western Hemisphere and began their new lives in slavery, they sought to establish a sacred relationship with their new homes. While humans enslaved them, they remained conscientious of their obligations to the spirits on the earth. African Americans living in close proximity with Spanish Catholics also blended aspects of Christianity into their religious practices. Like La Conquistadora with its ears of corn, Virgin statues appeared in Spanish territories in the Caribbean with African features and African-style amulets. In Haiti, one church had Spanish Catholic images in one room and an "African pegis, altars of the Orisha in their African manifestations as stones," in another. African American Christian leaders continued the art of African spirit coercion. Patriarchs who retained their memory of Africa served as historians and intercessors between the environment of the New World and the gods of the old. The American hemisphere may have been new to Africans, but they quickly developed an understanding of their new land that provided a means to negotiate their lives using the practices of and acknowledging the spirits from their old world.

In the early 1600s, the Puritans brought new religious ideas to structure their settlement of Massachusetts Bay. Because of the success they found in the growing trade in the expanding Atlantic world and the increased social mobility brought by the profits of a burgeoning capitalist marketplace, the Puritans may be one of the groups that benefited the most from mechanistic innovations. In their flight from Europe, they also sought to escape laws and practices that kept them from realizing their religious and community potential. Consequently, it is little wonder that the Puritans used their new religious beliefs to carefully plan and organize nearly every aspect of their American lives to limit old influences and promote new concepts of community cohesion and social responsibility. To assert this new structure, community leaders mandated village plans whereby houses and activities radiated from the meetinghouse and a central village green. Fields were likewise assigned to promote cooperative farming practices and discourage isolation. Communities sought to structure their lives by bringing unprecedented control to the environment and social activities. In Boston, Protestant leaders conscientiously attempted to eliminate the superstitious and environmentally entangling practices of more organic European traditions. Months were assigned numbers to replace names associated with pagan gods and any lingering power they retained on earth. The Puritan leaders mandated an end to other organic practices as well: there would be "no saints days or Christmas, no weddings, or church ales, no pilgrimages, nor sacred places, nor relics or ex-vetos: no 'churching' after childbirth, no godparents, or maypoles, no fairy tales, no dancing on the Sabbath, and no carnival." Like the specific plans for the design of their villages and fields, these changes were the Puritans' attempt to control both the seen and unseen worlds of New England to serve their religious ideals. The older popular habits diffused sacred power, and the Puritans sought to eliminate them in order to focus religious practice and belief on Bible reading, sermons preached by learned men, individual prayer, and the arduous path of personal salvation.

The Puritans brought unprecedented planning and forethought to their lives in North America in an attempt to start a new religiously based life free from Old World entanglements. However, their approach to New World problems remained permeated with organic Old World traditions. The logical origin of earthquakes, droughts, Native American attacks, sickness, and death confounded the Puritan community. Soon, prolonged environmental prob-lems caused church leaders to call for time-honored practices of fasting, sup-plication, and deprivation to regain God's favor and end the perceived pun-ishment. Cotton Mather analyzed deleterious phenomena as evidence of the devil's work among God's people: "We have seen likewise the *Plague* reach-ing afterwards into other Townes far and near, where the houses of *Good Men* have the Devil, filling them with terrible vexations." Even though many New Englanders were aware of the scientific explanation of earthquakes and comets, most could not shake the divine implications of such transfixing events. There-fore, when the environment proved unpredictable, religious leaders imposed greater control on human behavior.

Successive generations, however, became more comfortable with and ex-erted greater control over their physical environment. Burgeoning popula-tions moved farther from town centers, subdued the New England environ-ment, and pushed away Native Americans and the unknown wilds of forest and nature. Strict community rules had girded these Puritans' parents and grandparents in an effort to protect them from the unknown in the American "wilderness," but by the 1670s, younger couples maintained successful lives outside community oversight. Church elders, accustomed to exerting control over the community, sought to reign in this scattered generation and denied them church membership. Yet the real point of contention was control of the environment. As America became more predictable, tight communal prac-tices were unnecessary.

The First Great Awakening (1740s–1760s) was the event that broke these younger generations from the traditions of tight, local, tradition-bound church community structure. Many colonists anxiously sought a religious experi-ence devoid of contractual obligations to far-off parishes, church hierarchies, and distant religious traditions. For these believers, the American continent was no longer a scary place. Tight community structure and sacrificial behav-iors in response to environmental events were no longer necessary. Yet this Protestant worldview was not devoid of a spiritual landscape or emotional ex-perience. The Holy Spirit's presence on the earth, along with belief in the devil or demonic forces, was still an essential part of religious reality. How-ever, good and evil did not necessarily battle for possession of the earthly realm but for control over individual souls. The letters of Sarah Osborne, a spiri-tual seeker in New England, demonstrated this Protestant religious environ-ment. Osborne explained in great detail how the devil vied for control of her soul: "Uttering the language of hell, 'there is no hope! There is no help! The door of mercy's shut against me forever!'" Then God rescued her with comforting thoughts: "Your external day of grace is not over . . . it is the devil who has suggested this all to you and he is a liar from the beginning." This conversation took place in her mind. Instead of describing an external world full of good and evil forces, working for control over the earth, Osborne demonstrated how the First Great Awakening appealed to people who worried less about the external world and more about understanding their interior spiritual journey.

American Protestants brought Christianity to Native Americans using this concept of self-seeking conversion. English Protestants had a millennial tradition that also encouraged conversion to hasten the Second Coming. But the Anglo-European conversion practices were focused on individual, knowledge-derived conversion experiences, with little tolerance for the earth-encompassing sacred space as conceived by Catholic conquerors. Unlike the Spanish converters, the Protestants did not supplant Native American sacred space with Protestant alternatives. Rather, Protestants educated American Indians in reading, writing, and logical explanations of the scriptures. Meanwhile, Native Americans watched as their carefully organized environment disappeared under plows and fences. Anglo-American settlement broke their yearly migration patterns, and the areas they depended on for food and shelter vanished permanently. American Indians were not offered a spiritual alternative through Protestant conversion but rather a mandate that the earth was not sacred and their practices were no longer efficacious.

Colonizing America was a traumatic experience for all concerned. Each group had to negotiate a new relationship with its spiritual landscape along with facing the physical changes wrought by colonization. As the organic practices of Africans and Native Americans met those of the Catholics, all three groups adapted their communication about the inherent spiritual power of the environment. African worship rituals manifested themselves in Catholic symbols in the Caribbean, and American representations of the Virgin Mary, as we have seen, were suffused with Native American and Spanish symbolism. Protestant groups sought to leave organic traditions in Europe as they sailed to a pristine world in New England. Instead of the well-organized, rational universe their newfound faith promised, however, the American continent presented environmental challenges that sent these Protestants back to the safety and security of their organic traditions. For more than one hundred years, Anglo-Americans fought a battle between the logical cosmos of their religion and the inexplicable forces of their environment. By the end of the colonial period, an uneasy and sometimes violent relationship existed between Americans, their gods, and a cosmos in transition.

In the early Republic, land acquisition expanded the boundaries of the United States, and American citizens found freedom to move, increase their land holdings, and choose from different economic opportunities. Controlling land was equated with wielding power, and scientific advances made manipulating land easier. Farmers in the South could choose to move west when their land became overused and less productive. As people moved, not only did they uproot themselves from land that held homes, fields, and communities where they had lived for generations, but they also left family graves and memories of and relationships with the land. In addition, religious practices changed as people moved. For some, breaking ties and moving was liberating, and their religious relationships turned toward negotiating their new homes and changing work habits. For others, the ties to the land were essential to religious security. They fought to maintain and nurture connections to a spirit-filled earth. As people moved around the new nation, their cultures and religions collided. More important, each group had to face challenges to its cosmological integrity as it relocated or as its land was invaded by people with other conceptions of sacred place and religious practices.

Deism is a religious philosophy celebrating the power of science and machinery. A product of European liberalism reflecting the scientific ideas of the Enlightenment, Deism asserts that God designed the universe as a perfect machine, so complex and elegantly crafted that the Creator simply set the universe in motion and stepped back to watch his creation work flawlessly through time. There was no Holy Spirit in Deism because God's machine was so perfect that he never intervened in its workings. Deism was the ultimate fruition of intellectual mechanism because it removed the need for sacrifice and divine intervention and emphasized the use of scientific logic and reason to provide order in a perfectly crafted world. The popularity of Deism among patricians in the early Republic demonstrates their comfort with and sense of mastery over the American landscape. Thomas Jefferson, an advocate of Deism, edited his own version of the New Testament, removing the miracles and contradictions to create a logical and reasonable reflection of God's words. Jefferson's Bible conceptualized no sacred space on earth or idea of the supernatural on earth. Deism is symbolic of an era when humans celebrated mastery over nature.

Transcendentalism follows many aspects of Deism and includes many mechanistic ideas. Writers such as Henry David Thoreau and Ralph Waldo Emerson appreciated nature; they often wrote of society and nature as opposite and antagonistic entities. This is a break from an organic universe in which humans and nature are intimately connected. Both men delighted in learning about and explaining the processes of nature through the rational rules of science. Thoreau explained the chemicals of phosphorescence in the moss at Walden Pond. Emerson proclaimed that humans and nature are both innately good: "In the tranquil landscape, and especially in the distant line of the horizon, man beholds something as beautiful as his own nature." Nature, for both these men, was a welcoming place, where people could renew and reinvigorate themselves. Walden Pond was a destination for Thoreau when he felt overcivilized by living in a city crowded with people. Inherent in this attitude is the idea that nature is separate from civilization and that scientific, not spiritual, elements are at the heart of nature's awesome landscapes.

While Protestant Anglo-Americans took control over their personal salvation, Native Americans experienced crises as the land that held their gods and sacred space was taken through conquest. Their relationships with European colonists developed along a broad spectrum. Missionaries, trappers, and traders sought to develop friendly relationships with Native Americans. As Native Americans reached a religious crisis, their once knowable environment became a confusing struggle. Forced to abandon the land where their culture, religion, and history were rooted, many native groups lost their cultural anchors to the earth.

Many tribes split, as factions argued over the best approach to maintaining their tribal integrity in the face of Anglo aggression. There is perhaps no better example of this than the Cherokee tribe. The growing Métis class of Cherokee-Anglos developed a written language, a national constitution, and a political relationship with the American government and followed Protestant practices. However, the majority of the Cherokee were not interested in adapting to Anglo-American ways; nor did this approach offer any social stability or sense of control. Their traditional religious practices moved underground, out of sight of the Métis and outsiders.

Slaves had an intimacy with their environment that their masters could not share. They used their knowledge of the environment to bring a sense of security and stability into their daily lives. Several generations of African Americans used waterways and forests to cloak movement between plantations and practice religion away from their masters' control. Within communities, individuals emerged as conjurers who could manipulate the seen and unseen forces in the environment to bring spiritual answers to real world problems (see chapter 3 in this volume for more on conjurers). Using their knowledge of and sympathy with the processes of nature, African Americans supplemented their diets with wild plants and animals and made medicines and poisons from natural sources. Even as they lived under the arbitrary realities of slavery, African Americans used their intimacy with nature as an essential agency in their lives.

Regardless of how well African Americans may have negotiated a relationship with the American landscape, physical environments were not interchangeable. The spirits of Africa remained in Africa even when their descendants were taken away. Because their ancestors were not in America, it was an improper place for Africans to spend eternity. Charles Ball, a slave in western Maryland, described in his 1837 autobiography how African American slaves repatriated their departed loved ones to assure continuity in their afterlife. In the grave of a dead infant, the father placed "a small bow and several arrows; a little bag of parched meal; a miniature canoe, about a foot long, and a little paddle" for the child to row back across the ocean to Africa. The father also placed a piece of muslin with "curious and strange figures painted on it in blue and red, by which, he said, his relations would know the infant to be his son, and would receive it accordingly, on its arrival amongst them."

Emptying the earth of its sacred power was essential to Americans who wanted science and mobility to provide greater access to productive farmland. As plows and farms moved west, canals, roads, and railroads pushed deeper into America's interior. The nation was on the move. Conservative philosophies faced a daunting battle against strong cultural and religious forces more interested in moving forward than looking back.

Antebellum Nineteenth Century

As Americans became more confident about their environment, cataloging its elements and identifying its processes, they also grew more proficient at extracting its resources to feed a growing national economy. Interstate commerce resulted in an American landscape transformed by an interlaced network of canals, roads, and railroads. Americans made the earth conform to their needs. At Walden Pond, Thoreau contemplated the meaning of the railroad and its disruption of nature. While he venerated the beauty and complexity of his surroundings, he eventually decided the railroad was necessary for society's progress. Most Americans agreed with Thoreau's assessment and increasingly marked the landscape as an inert commodity rather than as a sphere of vital and dynamic elements.

The emerging market economy in the 1830s demanded accuracy, consistency, and days structured by clocks and weeks by timetables. Workers had to adjust to a workday and workplace dictated largely by others. The Second Great Awakening (1800–1840) marked a significant shift from religions that navigated the natural world to doctrines and practices that negotiated rapid change in a commercial and industrializing society. The Second Awakening also encouraged the development of social, educational, and moral reform movements to address this new, mechanistic world of work. In pointing out the need for such movements, Charles Finney (1792–1875), a minister and president of Oberlin College, used agricultural metaphors likening the workers to the raw materials they transformed: the workers were "fields ripe for harvest," and the revival's job was to "harvest" and process the crop into strong churches, temperance societies, schools, and mutual aid societies.

Many women joined in the restructuring efforts of the Second Great Awakening, but others took the revival spirit in another direction. Wives, mothers, and daughters did not live in an orderly and predictable cosmos in the antebellum era. Fathers and then husbands subsumed their identities, leaving their public lives in the hands of male relations. Women received a basic education but rarely had access to the study of philosophy, science, mathematics, and engineering, the subjects undergirding rational society. Childbirth remained difficult and infant mortality high. Consequently, women remained tied to a worldview whereby they had to negotiate their existence within an essentially closed system of intimate relationships. Drawn to the emotional conversion experience and enlivened by a dynamic religious environment and the sense of control the movement offered, women turned to the newly emerging practice of Spiritualism. Based on the manipulation of the human spirit, Spiritualism included séances and other rituals used to predict the future and contact dead loved ones. Annie Denton Cridge believed in Spiritualism and extolled its virtues in her newspaper the *Vanguard*. When her first child died within a month of his birth, she wrote about her pain but described how, in the final moments of her child's life, the spirits of her own dead parents appeared above the infant, "waiting to bear his sweet spirit away." She then watched the baby's spirit rise up to join them. After the baby's death, his spirit visited her often, showing signs that he "had recovered from the illness that took his life." Like the Mandan practice of reincorporating skulls into the tribe, Spiritualism offered a way for grieving women to reincorporate dead loved ones into their daily lives and circumscribe the world of the living and the dead to create an intimate space where they commingled. The Spiritualism described by Annie Denton Cridge can be considered an organic religious practice because it brought the worlds of the living and the dead together through practices meant to coerce and manipulate the energy in the universe.

While revivals took salvation to cities and towns, the Second Great Awakening also led certain groups to remove themselves to areas where they could practice new religious ideas in isolated, structured communities. One such movement, the Church of Jesus Christ of Latter-day Saints, developed in the early nineteenth century. Mormon cosmology included both organic and mechanistic impulses that can be traced to the seventeenth century. Mormonism acknowledged the superiority of humans over nature while maintaining that the earth still holds generative forces. Many Americans believed that these forces were made manifest in gold and treasure within the earth and that finding this treasure demonstrated unique individual powers as well as the inherent mysteries in the physical world. The gold tablets found and read by Joseph Smith in upstate New York in 1829 were just one aspect of Mormon cosmology that fit into a tradition of natural manipulation and human exceptionalism.

Mormon community structure, the importance of family, and the fusing of secular and religious authority were resurrected from an earlier time in American history. Smith reasserted the power and importance of sacred space on earth and the role of learned priests who could manipulate the forces between the visible and invisible worlds. God in Heaven was characterized as female as well as male (Father and Mother in Heaven). Mormon theology acknowledged the importance of growth of the community and the use of science and technology as tools to assure the success of the Mormon enterprise. Mormon communities embraced their weak and strong members within the body of the church but sought to eliminate deleterious agents like caffeine, alcohol, and tobacco.

In Utah, Latter-day Saints erected their sacred space, the Mormon Temple, at the center of a planned community. The Mormons spread through the sun-bleached desert, manipulating and managing scarce water resources to feed a burgeoning population. They used the bee and beehive as symbols of their place as productive workers in the natural order. Work and industry along with spiritual mystery created a mechanistic-organic synthesis in the Mormon religion.

The conquest of California provides another important example of the clash between more organic religions and the newer, more mobile practices. When a desire for markets, raw materials, and shipping ports brought Anglo-Americans to California, these entrepreneurs encountered wealthy Spanish families ruling the Far West in a feudal relationship with their Native American workforce. The church supported this association by Christianizing the

Native Americans and encouraging their subservience while their landlords clothed, fed, and housed them in return. This organic social structure was predicated on reciprocity and obligation as Native Americans, Spanish landlords, and the church all worked to keep their relationships stable. The Anglo-Americans, in contrast, had individualistic, laissez-faire ideas and sought to usurp the power of the Spanish landlords and hire the native workers in order to build a market economy using their inexpensive labor. When the Anglo-Americans fought and won claim over California in the late 1840s, they also broke the organic community structure of their Spanish predecessors. The transition to a market economy was traumatic for the native workers, leaving most in perpetual poverty and alienated from social progress.

The antebellum era gave birth to a national economy and a dominant culture embracing the idea that the earth was designed to benefit and serve humans. Deism celebrated the ultimate capabilities of machines by postulating that the universe was itself a perfect mechanism unfolding a promising and progressive world through time. The Second Great Awakening removed religion farther from nature by reacting to artificial environments transformed by factories, time clocks, markets, and banking systems. Religions embracing the earth increasingly defended themselves against invasion and continued to seek power and safety within established traditions. Preserving these behaviors included hiding them from outsiders and removing the customs from public view. The antebellum era created a gulf between religions that understood the earth to be filled with powerful sacred forces and those whose work increasingly depended on subduing and transforming the environment to yield to factories and schedules imposed by humans.

Postbellum and Industrial Nineteenth Century

With urbanization and the rise of cities, Americans could live and work in a world far from daily contact with natural surroundings. Humans and machines, not plants and animals, were the forces working in their daily lives. Conversely, Native and Latino American groups in the West, Southwest, and Northwest, rural Appalachians in the East, and many African Americans in the South maintained their intimate relationship with nature's fluctuations and continued to believe that the earth was alive with spiritual forces. Significantly, these two ways of living were increasingly alien to each other: Native Americans in Arizona could not fathom the daily work of the factory, and commodity traders in Chicago could not grasp the meaning of venerating corn as sacred.

To say that city dwellers all lost touch with an environment filled with spiritual forces or that all rural Americans believed in a sanctified earth is incorrect, however. The most tantalizing aspects of the relationship between the physical environment and religion during the industrial era were the complex locations of earth-bound religions. Good and evil spirits, sacred objects, beneficial herbs, and other religious symbols could be found in inner-city neighborhoods and high-rise tenements. Likewise, the problems between native groups and intervening Anglo settlers in the West often arose around religious views of the earth. Was the environment sacred space or valuable commercial commodity?

In cities and towns, religious practices often turned toward the new factory model as the way to organize religious ethos. They venerated the factory assembly line more than the natural landscape. Many Protestant groups found the industrial ideal empowering. Progressive social reform became progressive Protestant religion: cleaner, whiter, brighter religious practices. The ministries of Dwight Moody and Josiah Strong are excellent examples of institutionalizing and mechanizing the conversion process. The teachings at the Moody Bible Institute in Chicago held that the process of "patience, prayer, Bible reading, and churchgoing" opened people's hearts and converted their souls. Dwight Moody preached that being born again was a thorough cleaning from the inside out. Congregationalist Josiah Strong protested the economic woes of capitalism but echoed its machinery by preaching that process, standardization, and uniformity were the hallmarks of a "true Christian people." Both men discouraged the made-at-home variety of religious practice. To be Christians, Americans were encouraged to submit to growing church institutions. Like a big healthy factory, mainstream Protestant churches took pride in their size and efficiency.

Separating religion so profoundly from the environment allowed many groups to move forward into modern society by severing traditional relationships with earth-bound spirits, sacred space, and tradition-bound theology. Many African Americans found the promises of a forward-looking, standardized, and logical Christian belief system liberating. Such practices released them from a painful past of enslavement and moved them toward a future of individual freedom and political equality. Men and women in the African Methodist Episcopal Church, among others, embraced the tenets of Progressive reform and moral uplift. Progressive black women in the South reached out with sanitary commissions, educational opportunities, and training facilities to eliminate the suspicious organic attitudes of the rural and urban poor. They practiced what has been termed "the politics of respectability," assuming that progress in black America would bring cleaner, brighter lives while showing white Americans that African Americans were worthy of respect.

Many immigrant groups, including reform-minded Jews, enjoyed the opportunity to adapt practices to fit the needs of modern, industrial society free from the strict and community-encompassing traditions of conservative self-regulating practices. Orthodox Judaism has all the elements of an organic, earth-bound religious system: food laws, ritual bathing, strict community structure, and tradition-based law. These ideas had protected Jews from larger, sometimes hostile communities in Germany and eastern Europe, but immigration to America was often seen as an opportunity to drop practices that separated them from mainstream society. Reform-minded Jews moved into New York tenements, worked alongside other ethnic groups, and allowed their religious calendars to accept working on the Sabbath. Women worked and attended school, and kosher food preparation declined. Such behaviors allowed greater economic opportunity and the chance to explore individualism and self-identity formerly restricted under Orthodox practices.

Yet, for many immigrants, American shores and city living did not sever religious ties. They understood that America meant freedom to reconstruct, not give up, traditional practices. Southern Italian and Greek immigrants came to America shored up by earth-bound Catholic practices. Although both groups gladly entered construction, mining, and manufacturing industries, their personal lives remained tied to communal, familial, and spiritual influences. Developed in reaction to a distant and hostile Roman hierarchy, southern Italian religion remained closely tied to medieval social and religious practices that mirrored, in many ways, the Spanish conquistadors four hundred years earlier. With pouches much like the medicine bags of Native Americans around their necks, Italian children were rendered safe from the "evil eye." Garlic, peppers, and various saints' medals were often added for special protection. Rejecting Irish domination of the Catholic hierarchy, Greeks and Italians replaced faithful church attendance with adherence to home altars and family worship services where they could nurture their ties to a world in which good and evil mixed freely in their urban neighborhoods.

Whereas many Jewish groups came to America to shed aspects of their ethnic and religious identities, others came to rebuild the Orthodox Judaism threatened in Europe and reestablish a religious connection to the soil. After the flood of Russian immigration in 1881, close to a hundred Orthodox Jewish communities developed across rural areas in the United States; these communities were devoted to rebuilding Jewish agricultural practices. From

1882 to 1959, the various communities supported their endeavors with the development of the Baron de Hirsch Agricultural School in Woodbine, New Jersey, organized the Federation of Jewish farmers, and published the *Jewish Farmer*. Although the various communities often included manufacturing enterprises, the Jewish communities demonstrated that land and religion remained inextricably linked.

In the West, ranchers, farmers, and other groups arrived to lay claim to land held by Native Americans. Bloody battles and publicized massacres prompted the U.S. government to turn from military to legislative action to pacify the West. The Dawes Severalty Act of 1887 was designed to bring Native Americans into line with mainstream American behavior. Because native religions were predicated on daily rituals, adherence to tradition, and an intimate relationship with the physical environment, the Dawes Act served to create a real religious crisis by forcing Native Americans to settle into agricultural lives, build square dwellings, and send their children to Indian schools to inculcate Anglo-American ideals. Young Native Americans were forced to cut their hair, and both sexes were given Anglo-American names. As reflected by the phrase "kill the Indian, save the man," Native Americans were regarded as another raw material to be fed through the machinery of American industrialization.

The impact on native culture was dramatic. Once a generation had been removed from the traditional cultural practices, those children lost the daily and seasonal relationships with their environment full of spiritual entities. Coming out of Indian schools, few Native Americans felt grounded in their new American identity or understood their traditional values. In his book *The Man Who Killed the Deer*, Frank Waters used the character of Martiniano, a young Apache returning to his tribe after six years in an Indian school, to demonstrate the confusion his schooling caused: "You grab us boys out of our houses and send us away to school and teach us all this nonsense, all those lies about becoming good citizens and being like white men." Martiniano laments his alienation from an ancient and innate relationship with his tribe's land, ancestors, and the cosmos from which his people drew their power. Consequently, he is left with a "profundity of immeasurable depths, the hidden, haunting mystery of his deeper self." Although his initiation into the mechanistic world was a matter of education and study, returning to organic practices was nearly impossible once the traditional relationships with the earth had been broken.

Official Catholic oversight in the Southwest had ended by the early nineteenth century, creating a religious culture where Catholic ideas and practices took on a life of their own. Willa Cather's *Death Comes for the Archbishop* is a fictional tale of the American Catholic Church attempting to control the newly incorporated Southwest. When the French-born bishop finds his way to a remote village, he finds that the lives of the saints have taken on American identities. He observes two statues, one of the Virgin Mary and another identified as Santiago, a "fierce little equestrian figure, a saint wearing the costume of a Mexican *ranchero*." In a conversation with a young boy, the bishop connects Santiago with his French counterpart: "'Oh yes, Santiago. He was a missionary, like me. In our country we call him St. Jacques, and he carries a staff and a wallet—but here he would need a horse, surely.' The boy looked at him with surprise. 'But he is the saint of horses. Isn't he that in your country? He blesses the mares and makes them fruitful. Even the Indians believe that. They know that if they neglect to pray to Santiago for a few years, the foals do not come right.'" Cather's book records how religious practices tied to the earth were organic and could adapt to the local religious environment. Such practices did not require the official church to keep the religious ideas alive.

Not only did these communities treat Catholic missionaries cautiously, but they repelled waves of Protestant missionaries who came to the West in the 1870s. From their *santos* carved from cottonwood trees along the Pecos and Rio Grande rivers, to *retablos* painted by local artists, to adobe chapels and Penitente *moradas* dotting the countryside, to their ancestors walking the earth with them, tripping them up and pointing out their follies, Latinos lived comfortably with their sacred universe. They were religously secure and culturally homogeneous, and outsider religions thus held little attraction.

Meanwhile, naturalist and future conservationist John Muir left his work at an Indianapolis carriage parts shop in 1867 and walked a thousand miles to the Gulf of Mexico. He suffered from cold, hot, wet, and dry weather as he walked but realized, despite his travails, how much more fulfilling and comfortable his life felt when he remained close to nature and attentive to the fluctuations of the earth. He articulated a need to preserve wilderness for its spiritual as well as aesthetic beauty. He saw urban Americans as "tired, nerve-shaken, over-civilized people" who needed to escape to the wilderness and realize "that going to the mountains is going home; that wilderness is a necessity." Just as he enticed Americans to get "in touch with the nerves of Mother Earth," he also fought to keep civilization away from beautiful areas. In 1914, Muir lost a fight to preserve Hetch Hetchy Valley from a dam project that would provide water for the expanding populations in California. When he died shortly after the fight, friends and family claimed that he had become so intertwined with the valley's destiny that he could not live past its demise. By returning to an organic understanding of the earth, Muir surrendered his individuality to the earth and suffered the consequences of becoming intimate with a resource desired by a growing and expanding America.

In his famous speech of 1893, historian Frederick Jackson Turner used U.S. census data to declare America settled and the frontier closed. Isolation and environmental security were precious commodities in the late nineteenth century. Cities became new, artificial environments where machines of industry demanded obedience from humans. Yet religious practices defied definition through an urban-rural dichotomy. In New York City, as in Santa Fe, New Mexico, statues of the Virgin Mary were paraded through Catholic crowds delighted with the representation of their sacred mother on their earthly streets during religious festivals. In rural areas missionaries and churches brought news that Christian salvation was not dependent on tradition or alliances to earth-bound rituals.

Early Twentieth Century

By the early twentieth century, most Americans had become quite alienated from any sense of sacred or beneficial forces in nature. In the late nineteenth and early twentieth centuries, mass-produced goods finally made their way into the lives of average Americans. Scientific study resulted in widely available and affordable medical and industrial advantages such as pasteurized milk and bottled beer. Electricity, telephones, and indoor plumbing became attainable for middle-class Americans by World War I. In general, the benefits of science, technology, and machines were more prevalent in homes, and Americans were more comfortable with their promises, just as they became more accustomed to modern workplaces. Industrial engineer Frederick Winslow Taylor's motto, "the gospel of efficiency," reveals how seriously Progressives took on mechanistic ideas for organizing society from the inside out. Americans were told to reject the old and embrace the new: paint over their wooden door frames, replace oil lamps with electricity, and create brighter, whiter living space. Society embraced machines and brought them into its inner sanctums.

Nature was equated with something raw, dirty, and dangerous. Folk medicines were banned in favor of professionally prescribed pills. Breast milk and nursing were discouraged in favor of formulas and bottles, which were touted as more sanitary, healthful, and "better than nature." Progressive reformers were less willing to allow Italian children to wear garlic around their neck or tolerate candles burning before home altars in urban tenements. Consequently, religious practitioners honoring sacred elements of the natural world had to choose to give up their practices or hide them far away from an invasive public eye.

Science, technology, and religion merged at several points. The practice of numerology, or the belief that the miracles and prophecies of the Bible can be explained mathematically, demonstrated that God's mysteries could be explained logically through science. Mary Baker Eddy's Christian Science presented a significant approach to mechanistic self-control. She saw each human as a deistic body, which held all the power of self-regulation, and believed that the mind and the spirit could control the ailments of the body. The church community, like the factory, came together to work for a product, and the efficiency and efficacy of the church were demonstrated by the health and well-being of its members.

For more than a hundred years, many Americans progressively embraced mechanism, its doctrines of knowledge, reason, and science and eschewed the religious value of the natural world. Machines, progress, and urbanization were seen as the key to a better life for all humans. The individual was made paramount through religious practices that elevated the unique soul and the relationship of the believer to a rational, reasonable God. Religious individualism was wrapped up with social prosperity.

Within a few short years on the battlefields of Europe, science and technology no longer seemed the ultimate gifts from God but perhaps the best-disguised evil. Turning away from science and a rational religious experience, many Americans sought to return to a belief that a divine, not a mechanical, force was truly in control of their lives. Many Americans did not want to give up the beneficial products the machines provided, but they also wanted the solace of organic religion's belief that God is present and acting for good on behalf of believers. In other words, Americans wanted the best of the organic and the mechanistic worlds: spirituality and science, community without commitment, and the sacred without the sacrifice.

Modern America

At the end of the twentieth century, Americans were preoccupied with who, or what, was at the helm of existence—in other words, how much they controlled the world around them. Their relationship with the natural environment was tense as they became farther from, not closer to, a relationship with the earth around them. Popular media in the modern world perennially ask who or what controls the universe and what is the relationship of humankind to the natural world. George Orwell had a particular sense of society's anxiety over its relationship to nature and science. Both *1984* and *Animal Farm* took a serious look at how humans use logic and reason to create a false relationship with one another and mask their inherent animal behavior. Such movies as *It's a Wonderful Life* demonstrate the presence of an omnipresent God capable of intervening in the worst human-caused catastrophes. *2001: A Space Odyssey* places machines in the ultimate position of control over human beings.

Beginning in the 1950s and 1960s, mainstream churches thrived as attendance rose and celebrated national solidarity and patriotism in the midst of a Cold War with an officially atheist nation. After Glen Canyon and Hoover Dam became monuments to technology and engineering, congregations built modern sanctuaries as feats of cutting-edge architectural design. Like the interstate highway system, modern evangelists such as Billy Graham spread across the nation. Symbolized by Graham's charisma and his message of immediate conversion through the work of the Holy Spirit, the revivals were by no means a one-person or one-spirit production. A complex support staff orchestrated each event with intensive planning. Magnificent dams, fabulous buildings, and larger-than-life preachers needed an increasingly complex infrastructure.

Modern Americans did not universally accept large-scale projects and celebrations of humans' control over nature. Throughout the latter half of the twentieth century and into the twenty-first, individuals and groups have publicly protested technological relationships with the earth. Significantly, many of them have been scientists. Rachel Carson's 1962 book *Silent Spring* articulated that human use of DDT to kill insects was infecting the food chain. She demonstrated that the health of humanity was intimately connected at all levels to the health of the earth as a whole.

At the end of the 1960s, modern media provided further evidence that humankind was confined together in a finite world. *Apollo 11* landed on the moon in 1969 and sent back images of a tiny, isolated blue ball, spinning in a sea of darkness. Although this image is commonplace now, it was an awesome and somewhat terrifying one for Americans at the time. *Apollo 11*'s images spurred the imagination and conscience of many and may have played a role in launching the modern environmental movement, as the first national Earth Day was held in 1970. A generation of Americans suddenly circumscribed their views of individual exceptionalism on a tiny planet.

Space exploration did not necessarily promote the preeminence of technology in shaping humans' relationship to the cosmos. Scientist James Lovelock's Gaia hypothesis, first articulated in 1977, essentially stated that science has served to reveal that humans have little control over the earth. Instead, according to Lovelock, the earth's breathing entity, called Gaia, coevolved with the plants and animals on her surface: "The name of the living planet, Gaia, is not a synonym for the biosphere—that part of the Earth where living things are seen normally to exist. . . . Just as the shell is part of the snail, so the rocks, the air, and the oceans are part of Gaia. Gaia, as we shall see, has continuity with the past back to the origins of life, and in the future as long as life persists. Gaia, as a total planetary being, has properties that are not necessarily discernable by just knowing individual species or populations of organisms living together." Every human action was met with Gaia's reaction, leaving little room for a mechanistic sense of control over her forces.

Lovelock, Carson, and *Apollo 11* all represent an America suddenly unsure of its control over earth but aware of humankind's culpability for its own health and well-being. In response to these scientifically derived ideas, some Americans eschewed many modern conveniences and went "back to nature" in the early 1970s. Rejecting TV dinners, donning prairie fashions, planting gardens, and eating whole grains, many young Americans sought to reintroduce themselves to the earth to learn more about the planet they had been trying to escape for so long.

For some, returning to the earth meant rediscovering organic religions left far behind in human history. Neo-paganism and witchcraft from pre-Christian Europe were both practices embracing male and female forces within the earth ready to be cajoled for human benefit. They encourage cyclical living and acknowledgment that the health of each practitioner is linked inextricably to the health of the community and the planet. Organizations like Wicca promote religion as a way of living, not just a weekly ritual. For most witches in modern America, however, their religious experience is an attempt to recover a lost past through research, reading, and reenacting their notion of ancient rituals in an attempt to rebuild that fabric of knowledge and tradition so key to an organic cosmos.

Many Native Americans face a similar quest as they seek to recapture the religious practices taken from them in the era of Indian school assimilation. Still under siege in many ways, Native Americans continue to fight court battles to maintain tribal integrity by preserving land and water rights, hunting practices, and religious ceremonies. Because their practices are tied to the natural world, they face constant threats. As John Muir and Frank Waters indicate, organic practices and practitioners often live or die depending on the health of their cosmos. Native Americans continue to negotiate between cultural memory and material prosperity in a modern economy. Latino Americans also face struggles to maintain traditional practices based on close community cohesiveness and environmental continuity. Losing water rights for subsistence farming breaks up many small communities, as children can no longer support themselves from their family's land. With their departure to the cities, communities dry up, and the continuity to the past is threatened. However, Penitente *moradas* exist in inner cities, and Latino neighborhoods retain their cultural cohesiveness across America, demonstrating a durability of belief that allows for geographical transplanting.

Nature continues to wrap itself around the lives of many rural Americans, especially in the harshest environs. On the vast, windswept plains of South Dakota, Kathleen Norris recorded the relationship between nature and humans through a quote from a Benedictine monk: "We built these buildings ourselves. We've cultivated these fields since the turn of the century. We watch from our dining room window the mirage of the Kildeer Mountains rise and fall on the horizon. . . . Fifty of our brothers lie down the hill in the cemetery. We have become as indigenous as the cottonwood trees . . . if you take us somewhere else, we lose our character, our history, maybe our soul." Even in a modern world, intimate relationships develop between humans and the earth that surrounds them.

Aldo Leopold recorded in the *Sand Creek Almanac* his belief that humans cannot discover their true self until they have wrestled with their inextricability from nature. Rediscovering what other groups have always recognized, many Americans have returned to a relationship with the earth to reassure themselves that they can find security in the natural processes of the earth. But intimacy also means vulnerability, and Leopold's life was shortened fighting a wildfire along the Wisconsin River in 1948. Contrary to romanticist visions of nature, an organic cosmos is not peaceful. Death remains a vital part of living close to the life processes of the earth.

The spinning blue marble presented by *Apollo 11* confirmed that humans were, for the time being, bound together in a complex, circumscribed biosphere. Consequently, at the end of the twentieth century, even broadcast media ministries were echoing the tenets of living closer to the earth. An evangelical Christian, Larry Burkett, and his popular radio show, "Money Matters," are excellent examples of organic principles applied to modern problems. Tithing, financial support for pastors, preparing for an unsure future, modest consumption, and community welfare are just a few of the ideas that place Burkett's ministry in an older tradition. In 1998 and 1999, articles in *Christianity Today* discuss the merits of Celtic Christianity and the movement to rethink completely urban lifestyles. These trends indicate the underlying existence of more circumscribed religious ideas even when science, technology, and urban living appear dominant.

Conclusion

In *The Production of Space*, Henri Lefebvre discusses how our seemingly solid homes are actually interconnected with one another and the environment in complex ways: "Our house would emerge as permeated from every direction by streams of energy which run in and out of every imaginable route: water, gas electricity, telephone lines, radio and television signals, and so on." Modern environmental historians often debate the definition of *natural* in a world where science and technology have become intertwined with the soil, water, and plants around us. With so many forces running through our lives, it is little wonder that American culture is constantly asking who or what is in control of the universe and how that power is conferred on humans.

Over the course of American history, two ways of answering that question have emerged. The first, organicism, demonstrates that the earth is a complete entity, full of dynamic, vital, generative forces, where energy is neither made nor destroyed. The Gaia hypothesis of 1977 reflects much of the meaning in John of Salisbury's fifteenth-century medieval body politic. Both are excellent symbols for organic religious ideas. They portray a world evolving as a single, interconnected community, echoing the precepts of Native Americans, medieval Europeans, and African American conjurers, as well as modern environmental science. The organic cosmos is finite, yet humans are inherently incapable of understanding its complexity. Religious practices therefore must involve worship of and surrender to the forces beyond humankind's control. This conservative ethos ensures maintenance of the known instead of expending energy moving into the unknown.

Mechanism, the second way of answering the question, developed when the organic ethos could no longer ensure the health of the community. The "scientific revolution," the Protestant Reformation, the First Great Awakening, Deism, and televangelism all liberate the believer from a constricting community. Some African Americans after the Civil War embraced mechanism to distance themselves from slavery for reasons similar to those of workers in New England mills flocking to evangelical revivals in the 1830s. Mechanism offered believers a way to cut ties with the past and elevate the conversion experience to an intimate and immediate contract between God and human. For them, religion became an internal matter, an intellectual exercise. Consequently, Sarah Osborne's anxious thoughts about her conversion can be compared to Descartes's *Meditations on First Philosophy*. Although one explored spiritual temptation and the other intellectual truisms, both did so through solitary mental exercises, believing truth to be attainable through reason.

Religion explains the natural world, how humans are supposed to use it, and how much responsibility we have toward it. Organic and mechanistic religious practices continue to coexist in the modern world, interacting and reacting to the social, environmental, and geographical changes. They are defined largely by priorities: social maintenance or individual growth; continuity with the past or the potential of the future; and belief in spiritual forces on the earth versus the power of reason and human knowledge to manipulate those forces.

SUGGESTED READINGS

Braude, Ann. *Radical Spirits: Spiritualism and Women's Rights in Nineteenth Century America*. Boston: Beacon Press, 1989.
Brooke, John L. *Refiner's Fire: The Making of Mormon Cosmology, 1644–1844*. Cambridge: Cambridge University Press, 1994.
Gaustad, Edwin Scott. *A Religious History of America*. Rev. ed. San Francisco: HarperCollins, 1990.
Hall, David D. *Worlds of Wonder, Days of Judgment: Popular Religious Belief in Early New England*. New York: Knopf, 1989.
Lovelock, James. *Homage to Gaia: The Life of an Independent Scientist*. New York: Oxford University Press, 2001.
Merchant, Carolyn. *Ecological Revolutions: Nature, Gender, and Science in New England*. Chapel Hill: University of North Carolina Press, 1989.
Monroy, Douglas. *Thrown among Strangers: The Making of Mexican Culture in Frontier California*. Berkeley and Los Angeles: University of California Press, 1990.
Nash, Roderick Frazier. *Wilderness and the American Mind*. 4th ed. New Haven: Yale University Press, 2001.
Pitzer, Donald E., ed. *America's Communal Utopias*. Chapel Hill: University of North Carolina Press, 1997.
Raboteau, Albert J. *Slave Religion: The "Invisible Institution" in the Antebellum South*. New York: Oxford University Press, 1978.
Worster, Donald, and Alfred Crosby. *Nature's Economy: A History of Ecological Ideas*. 2nd ed. Studies in Environment and History. Cambridge: Cambridge University Press, 1998.

Race

It may no longer be the case that textbook narratives of America's religious development begin the story at Plymouth Rock. But most textbook accounts do continue to frame America's religious history almost entirely within what some have called the "Protestant era," a period beginning with the earliest British explorations of the New World in the sixteenth century and ending with the election of the first Roman Catholic president, John F. Kennedy, in 1960. Such accounts typically give prominence to one of two themes: "Puritanism," or the story of how one group of seventeenth-century immigrants to the land they called New England shaped the subsequent religious life of the nation; or "pluralism," the historical processes though which people of different beliefs came to live more or less peacefully together. Often these themes are combined, so that America's vaunted Puritan—or, more broadly, Protestant—heritage is credited with fostering a legacy of tolerance that has enabled people of many different religious backgrounds to live together more successfully in the United States than in, say, Northern Ireland or the Middle East.

When the encounter between races is added to the story of America's religious development, however, then other parts of that story come to seem less inevitable and considerably more complex. Neither the narrative of increasing toleration nor the story of Protestant dominance adequately describes the experiences of black people in the United States, who arrived on the continent before the Puritans did but whose struggle for recognition has shaped their experiences over four centuries. Nor do these narratives account for the history of American Indians, which preceded the European "discovery" of America by perhaps tens of thousands of years. As the religious studies scholar Charles Long suggests, religion in America takes shape not merely as the progress of Protestantism or of increasing pluralism but also as the history of "concealment," of rendering whole populations invisible in order "to enhance, justify, and render sacred the history of European immigrants in this land."

What would it mean to reconsider the history of America's religious development from the standpoint of race? Certainly such a reconsideration risks what historians call "presentism," the reading of the present into the past. Inhabitants of what is now the United States probably saw themselves and others they encountered in terms of nationality, religion, slave status, or kinship groups before they did so in terms of race. Seventeenth- and eighteenth-century conflicts among white, Native American, and black populations, moreover, were never simply about race, at least in the modern sense of the term. But what do we mean by race in the modern sense of the term?

It may be customary to think of race as denoting physical characteristics, such as skin color. But no one's skin, of course, is precisely red, white, or black. Moreover, differences of skin color, together with differences of language, geography, and culture, characterize populations united by race as much as populations divided by race. People are members of different races, it appears, only because they are assigned to them. In colonial Hispanic America, for example, one could become white simply by purchasing a certificate of whiteness. And as late as 1974, an American of ½₂ African ancestry could move from white to black and back again simply by traveling across the southern states. But to acknowledge the arbitrariness of race, its quality as a social construct, is not to say that racial ascriptions, because culturally imposed, can simply be thrown off. The capture and enslavement of American Indian and African peoples, forced removals from their homelands, prohibitions of literacy among them, persecution of their religious beliefs, the refusal to acknowledge family and kinship structures—none of this would have been halted by the acknowledgment of race as a social construct. One could argue, indeed, that insofar as race is socially constructed, it is constructed precisely through these kinds of acts.

The power of racial assignments to oppress, furthermore, resides largely in their arbitrariness, their ability to overrule other markers of difference or affiliation, such as religion, language, social status, and tribal and familial customs. We take note of oppression simply because the terms *race* and *racial* make no sense without it. Racial differences are not neutral and presumably innate differences of biology but rather reflections of unequal distributions of power. The European colonization of America made undifferentiated "Indians" of members of hundreds of independent tribes or nations and undifferentiated black Africans of the members of equally diverse groups from whom slaves were taken. In turn, white, black, and native people developed their consciousness of themselves as races in response to these processes.

Religious history provides a lens through which the emergence of racial thinking and its consequences come into clearer focus. For European colonists, religion was often a primary motivation for conquest. Europeans typically joined divine sanction to the project of racial oppression, making it appear inevitable because ordained by God. Racial thinking animated colonialism, slavery, and westward expansion, all of which were undergirded, and occasionally contested, by religious ideas. In the eighteenth and nineteenth centuries, white congregations debated and frequently divided over slavery, abolition, and Indian policy. At the same time, religious gatherings functioned for black and native people as spaces of self-determination, strategic alliance, and resistance to the dominant culture. In the twentieth century, religious groups have worked both to overcome racial oppression (in the civil rights movement, for example, or the campaign for Native American religious freedoms) and to reinforce it (in the revival of the Ku Klux Klan, for example, or more recently in the so-called Christian Identity movement).

The religious lives of white Americans are likewise bound up in notions of race, their own and others'. To consider the experiences of white people in discussions of race is to keep at least two things in mind: first, that contact is always reciprocal, that white immigrants to America were shaped as much by their interactions with black and native cultures as vice versa; second, that the history of contact is never *merely* reciprocal and that black, white, and Native Americans have rarely met as equal players. If an older "clash of cultures" model for understanding relations between black and white or native and non-native populations has largely been replaced by the view that a "new world" was collectively created in these exchanges, still this new world was created on a field of unequal power. Its history is one of damage as well as of innovation, creativity, and survival.

This chapter looks primarily at interactions among native, white, and black populations in the religious history of the United States. The limitations of such an approach may be stated at the outset. Black and Native Americans are not the only populations whose struggles against racial oppression have shaped America's religious landscape at various moments in U.S. history; immigrants from Ireland, Asia, the Spanish borderlands, and eastern, southern, and central Europe have all been targeted as "racial" threats to a white Protestant America. To focus the discussion of race on Native Americans, African Americans, and white people, moreover, is to exclude the experience of Americans who identity with none of these groups and perhaps to distort the experiences of those who identify with more than one. There are also the dangers of appearing to give a single cultural identity to what is in each case an exceedingly diverse population and of giving race too determinate a role in lives that were shaped by a variety of other factors, including religion, gender, region, and class. Nevertheless, Native and African Americans are the populations who have been most consistently and enduringly racialized in American history; that is, these other markers of their identity were submerged under the presumably more determinate rubrics of Indianness or blackness. The process of racializing Native and African Americans, in turn, requires that whiteness be upheld as the racial norm, even as white people have historically been given much greater scope to define themselves not as white people first but as, for example, Presbyterians, New Yorkers, Republicans, southerners, Gen Xers, Italians, Jews, and so forth.

Instead of a single, continuous narrative, this chapter offers a kind of moving prism, refracting key moments in American religious history through the lens of race and key moments in the development and transformation of racial thinking through the lens of religion. Such an approach yields multiple readings, as a prism fractures perspectives wherever it lights. The frontier, for example, emerges as a space of intercultural contact, where white, black, and native people encountered one another under shifting conditions, yielding new mixtures and precarious freedoms. At the same time, the very concept of the frontier reflects a notion of providential mission that made sense only to whites, empowering them to possess the continent by dispossessing its native inhabitants. Or again, the conversion of large numbers of slaves to Christianity in the eighteenth century represents what some have called a "spiritual holocaust" of indigenous African beliefs. Nevertheless, conversion also enabled involuntary immigrants from different African groups to organize themselves as a common culture, one that could powerfully frame the iniquities of white Christianity in Christian terms.

Precolonial Era

When Spanish and Portuguese ships arrived on the American continent at the end of the fifteenth century, the future United States was home to as many as ten million people who organized themselves into perhaps five thousand different nations or tribes, spoke at least 250 different languages, and had created an enormous variety of cultures whose beginnings extended back over thousands of years. Their religious practices were similarly diverse, often differing as much from one another as "world religions" like Christianity, Hinduism, and Islam differ from one another. At the same time, strands of belief and practice that were common to or at least recognizable among a diversity of native peoples enabled them to negotiate their differences over millennia and have allowed for varying degrees of solidarity among different Indian nations in the centuries since Europeans laid claim to the American continent.

Native Africans, like native peoples in the Americas, represent an enormous variety of cultures. And like native peoples in America, West Africans brought to America as slaves had their former languages, religions, kinship structures, and modes of communal organization submerged in their contact with Europeans. In the "detribalization" process undergone by new arrivals, members of Yoruba, Bakongo, Ibo, and other nations became undifferentiated Africans, just as Pequot, Cree, Muskogee, and Seminole people were becoming undifferentiated Indians. We can draw a composite portrait of precontact religions of America and West Africa by looking to what contemporary practice preserves as traditional knowledge, as well as to the historical accounts of missionaries and traders, bearing in mind that these accounts interpreted African and Native American religion through European lenses.

What unites Native American religious life across a broad spectrum of different theologies, rituals, and modes of sacred knowledge is the belief that spiritual powers animate the world. These powers create and sustain the world and the forms of life within it. For Cherokee people, for example, the Supreme Being and Creator, Yowa, resides as a unity of three Elder Fires Above and, at the same time, permeates all of creation. Navajo people do not name the Supreme Being, whom they regard as incomprehensible to human beings. Instead they approach the Creator through all of created life, which manifests the Creator's power. For the Maya, every element of creation—rocks, plants, animal life—has its own distinct *nahual*, or spiritual energy.

In these and other forms of native religion, spiritual powers also sustain relationships among all created beings and things. Honoring these powers permits individual and communal life to flourish. Illness, for example, might be seen as signaling not so much a physical problem in a particular person as a disruption in that person's relationship with the world and with the sacred processes occurring within it. Among some American Indian peoples, religious specialists (sometimes known as medicine people or shamans) possess expertise in directing spiritual power to cure illness, to make life transitions (for example to adolescence or old age) favorable, or to ensure success in harvesting or hunting. Among other peoples, spiritual expertise is acquired through individual transformation or mediated through councils of elders. Native beliefs and practices are typically all-pervasive in their respective cultures. The Cherokee, for example, have a single word, *eloh'*, to designate religion, history, culture, law, and land. Conflict between native groups seldom takes the form of *religious* strife (in contrast to the conflicts that divided sixteenth-century Europe, for example) because native peoples traditionally define themselves by their spiritual relationship to a particular place and by communal, environmental, and kinship obligations within their respective groups.

Traditional African religions also represent the world as animated by divine powers, which practitioners encounter in different theological forms and experiential contexts. West African traditional religions typically include a number of common features: belief in a transcendent god, belief in a number of lesser divinities who more readily intervene in human lives, belief in spiritual powers who manifest themselves in objects and persons, reverence for deceased ancestors who are accorded spiritual reality by the living, and the practice of sacred medicine, or the healing of mind, body, and community in cooperation with all the divine, spiritual, and ancestral powers.

Divine and human realms continually intersect. In most West African religious systems, the supreme deity remains remote from human affairs. Individuals may nevertheless experience divine knowledge though possession by lesser divinities, who choose their devotees by momentarily inhabiting, guiding, and protecting them. Spiritual forces also infuse certain objects, empowering them to heal or harm those who come into contact with them. Reverence for departed ancestors extends to elders as preservers of sacred knowledge. Elaborate burial rites prepare the dead for entrance into the company of the ancestors, whom they join as custodians of the living.

Precontact African and Native American cultures had no concept we can readily translate as "race." Their encounter with Europeans created New World Africans and Indians as "races" rather than as diverse peoples who were both linked and separated by language, religion, geography, and political organization within their respective groups. If racial thinking is never inevitably present whenever and wherever human beings encounter one another (as it was not when Africans encountered other Africans, or Indian peoples other Indians), neither, however, did it emerge ex nihilo when Europeans encountered native peoples or held Africans in slavery. If we think of race as the category that results when a more powerful group submerges the communal, political, tribal, and other affinities and distinctions of a less powerful group in the interest of social control, we can see that Europeans were acting in ways that made the creation of "race" in America possible even before they set out to claim possession of American lands.

For nearly five centuries before the founding of the Massachusetts Bay Colony, for example, England maintained a colonial presence in Ireland, Scotland, and Wales. English documents from the twelfth century describe the native inhabitants of these lands as "a most filthy race, a race sunk in vice," who required the presence of English Christians among them in order to be brought to civilization. Somewhat like the native peoples of Africa or America, peasants in the British Isles and in continental Europe worshiped local deities, whose powers were grounded in particular places and addressed to particular kinship and communal groups. (The words *peasant* and *pagan*, in fact, share a common Latin etymology.)

Thus differences of religion became an acceptable justification for conquest, not only of peasants and "pagans" in western Europe but also of non-Christians in remote lands. The 1455 papal bull of Nicholas V, for example, granted to King Alphonso of Portugal "free and ample facility . . . to invade, search out, capture, vanquish, and subdue all Saracens and pagans whatsoever, and all enemies of Christ wheresoever placed . . . and to reduce their persons to perpetual slavery, and . . . [to seize their] dominions, possessions, and goods, and to convert them to their [own] use and profit." One result of this "free and ample facility" granted to Portugal by the Catholic pontiff was the Portuguese slave trade in Africa, which established a system of plantation slavery reproduced by Spanish and Portuguese settlers in America.

The Protestant Reformation divided groups of Christians—Catholic and Protestant—against one another and their respective nations, but it did not significantly alter either group's perspective of non-Christians. In the late sixteenth century, for example, the Protestant monarch of England, Queen Elizabeth I, authorized Sir Walter Raleigh and later voyagers to America to "seize remote heathen and barbarous lands." The Protestant English ambassador Charles Cornwallis asserted that the Irish were "so savage a people" that they deserved the same treatment "used by the [Catholic] King of Spain in the Indies, or those employed with the Moors . . . scattering them into other parts." Despite attempts to distinguish themselves from the conquistadors of Catholic Spain in their proposed dealings with native peoples in America, the English would categorize natives and, later, Africans in the New World in the same way that they had categorized the Irish. They dealt with these new "savage peoples" similarly, refusing to recognize their laws or religions, exploiting their labor, expropriating their lands, and, in varying measure, incorporating without integrating them into the national community.

Colonial North America

European expeditions to the New World extended and reconstituted the Catholic-Protestant religious conflicts that had divided the Old World in the sixteenth century. The first successful French colony in the future United States, Fort Caroline near present-day Jacksonville, Florida, was founded as a haven for Protestant refugees from Catholic France. Spanish and other French expeditions, meanwhile, sought to claim the New World for Catholics, and Puritans founded the Massachusetts Bay Colony as a haven from what they saw as the "popish" forms of worship and church organization that corrupted the Church of England. Their religious exclusiveness shaped many of the ways European settlers perceived native peoples. Describing the religious rites of the Algonquin Indians, for example, the English Protestant Thomas Herriot wrote that the Algonquins' carved posts resembled "the faces of nonnes [i.e., nuns] covered with their vayles." But European Protestant immigrants treated American Indians very differently than they treated other Europeans —Catholics, Jews, Quakers, or "heretics"—who were persecuted for their religious beliefs. Offending Europeans were occasionally exiled; both groups were tortured and sometimes put to death; but Native Americans were murdered in far greater numbers, and only Native Americans could be sold into perpetual slavery. From the early seventeenth century to the early eighteenth, the native population of New England declined dramatically as a result of European-borne disease, warfare, and the export of American Indian prisoners of war as slaves to Bermuda and the West Indies.

Native peoples in contact with Catholic invaders fared no better. Beginning in the late sixteenth century, Spanish expeditions in what is now the southeastern and southwestern United States spread disease, incited (and bloodily suppressed) rebellion, and altered native forms of economic and political organization with the result that native cultures collapsed or were reorganized on hybridized Indian-Catholic lines. Conversion, in turn, often deprived natives of many of the protections of their indigenous familial, political, and spiritual networks, leaving them even more vulnerable to the institutional power of the colonizers' religion.

Encounters with others who looked, worshiped, governed, and communicated differently had long been a feature of native experience in the Americas prior to the arrival of Christopher Columbus in 1492. The encounter between native peoples and Europeans was unevenly weighted, however, as Europeans expected the Native Americans to accommodate them materially in exchange for the alleged spiritual benefit of the colonizers' religion. The goal of converting American Indians to Christianity enabled Europeans to express their relationship to native peoples as one of benevolence and to ignore the assault on native religions, kinship structures, and land tenure that made the exercise of such benevolence possible. The Puritan minister John Cotton counseled the first members of the Massachusetts Bay Company departing for New England in 1630 to "offend not the poore natives, but as you partake in their land, so make them partakers of your precious faith: as you reap their temporalls, so feed them with your spirituals: winne them to the love of Christ, for whom Christ died."

In both Catholic and Protestant colonies, conversion could represent a survival strategy for Native Americans whose communities had declined precipitously in numbers. Although some Native Americans whose communities had been weakened by war and disease banded with members of other tribes in similar circumstances, others chose conversion to Christianity as a calculated alternative to the loss of cultural and kinship identity that resulted from fusions with other tribes. By reinterpreting Christian symbols and narratives in light of their own traditions, some Native Americans enabled their distinctive cultures to survive beneath what one scholar calls "the protective coloration of the invaders' religion."

Such a strategy could easily backfire, however. Following King Philip's War (1675), in which thousands of Massachusetts inhabitants, native and English, were killed, Native Americans who had subjected themselves to English rule were resettled in places from which the colonists could monitor them. Native Americans found outside these locales could be murdered on site. "For security of the English and Indians in unity with us," a 1676 Massachusetts ordinance ran, "it shall be lawful for any person, whether English or Indian, that shall find any Indian traveling in any of our towns or woods . . . to command them under our guard and examination, or to kill or destroy them." Although the category of "Indians in unity with us" nominally included the native inhabitants of the "praying Indian" settlements who had remained loyal to the Puritan cause, the ruling effectively gave all English colonists power over any Native American, Christian or not. Indeed Christian Indians were especially vulnerable, since conversion required them to sever ties with their unconverted Native American kin without guaranteeing their protection by the English. One English colonist suggested that even "praying Indians" were in reality "preying Indians" who had "made preys of much English blood," adding that the English faced constant danger from Native Americans as a group "because they cannot tell a Heathen from a Christian [Indian] by his Visage, nor apparel." In any event, King Philip's War put an end to most missionary activity among Native Americans in New England.

Unlike native people in the Americas, Africans brought to this continent in bondage lacked even the option of responding to European colonial power from within their tribal communities. Columbus's "discovery" of America was preceded by an expedition to West Africa, where trade in slaves and other wealth inspired his designs on the East. African slaves bound for Spanish and Portuguese colonies in the New World were baptized en masse by Catholic priests as they were crowded onto departing ships, and slaves accompanied Spanish missionaries to their settlements in the southeastern and southwestern parts of the future United States.

The first Africans to arrive in a British colony came aboard a Dutch ship that landed at Jamestown, Virginia, in 1619, a year before the Pilgrims landed at Plymouth, Massachusetts. Like those Europeans who arrived in the New World without resources, these twenty African immigrants were indentured to landowners who paid their passage in exchange for their labor. Thus they joined a pool of workers that included Native Americans taken prisoner in war and indentured English and Irish servants.

Despite the de facto enslavement of Native Americans, "slave" was not an official legal category in the Virginia colony until its statutes of 1660 defined slavery as a permanent condition of servitude. Some Africans in Virginia had converted to Christianity, and British law forbid the enslavement of Christians. Like Native Americans, however, for whom conversion to Christianity offered only marginal protections, Africans in Virginia encountered forms of prejudice that greatly facilitated their eventual enslavement, including prohibitions of marriage between Africans and Europeans. In 1670, Virginia legislators declared that baptism into Christianity "did not alter the condition of a person as to his bondage or his freedom."

Puritans in Massachusetts, meanwhile, had held Africans in bondage since at least 1638. Puritans also owned Native American slaves and kept white indentured servants. That only black and Native American people could be held in perpetual slavery, according to the Congregationalist minister Samuel Willars, was "so ordained in the providence of God." Some Puritans defended slavery as having taken Africans out of a condition of servitude and introduced them to Christianity. Baptism did not change the status of slaves; indeed, said the Puritan minister Cotton Mather, Christian slaves would know "that it is

GOD who has caused them to be *Servants*, and that they serve JESUS CHRIST, while they are at work for their Masters."

African slaves fared somewhat better in the largely Quaker Pennsylvania colony. The Quaker George Fox appealed to slaveholding Quakers to free their slaves ("after a considerable term of years") and to educate them as Christians on the grounds that "Christ died for all . . . for the tawneys and the blacks as well as for you that are called white." Even so, until the American Revolution, more prosperous Quakers owned slaves; William Penn was still a slave owner at the time of his death in 1718, and Quaker merchants participated in the slave trade well into midcentury. Although free black people lived in Philadelphia in the early eighteenth century, they were forbidden to trade with slaves, to bury their dead within corporate limits, or, on penalty of enslavement, to marry or cohabit with white people.

To the south, where the majority of slaves were concentrated on plantations, slaves and slave owners alike resisted slave conversion to Christianity, for different reasons. Among slaves, indifference to Christianity belonged to broader patterns of resistance to slave owners' institutions, and whites for their part appeared to fear that extending Christianity to slaves would undermine the slave system. The majority of slaves who became Christians in the eighteenth century did so in the context of the evangelical revivals that swept the colonies beginning in the mid-1730s. The support of slave converts was in turn critical to the survival of "new method" evangelism, and the incipient religious antislavery movement was in large part a product of their participation. Indeed, what was "new" about the evangelicalism brought to the mainland colonies by John and Charles Wesley and George Whitefield, unleashing the Great Awakenings, included lay preaching, open-air religious meetings, and sudden, spontaneous conversions, often accompanied by full-body "shouts," all of which became staples of eighteenth-century Anglo-American revivalism. Baptist and Methodist movements, particularly, were strengthened considerably by the presence of slave and free black converts. Both Baptists and Methodists opened their doors to all who had experienced "new birth" in Christ, a feature that found a parallel in West African rites of initiation, in which joining a believing community was ritualized as symbolic death and rebirth.

The evangelical revivals of the eighteenth century were facilitated by contact not only between white and black Christians but also between white Christians and Native Americans. The Puritan dissenter Roger Williams, who later became a Baptist, wrote of Narragansett shamans in 1643: "These doe begin and order their service, and Invocation of their Gods, and all the people follow, and joyne interchangeably in a laborious bodily service, unto sweatings, especially of the priest, who spends himself in strange antick gestures, and actions even unto fainting." Eighteenth-century accounts of the styles of white itinerant preachers in the Great Awakening strongly recall Williams's description of Native American shamans, including full-body preaching, spontaneous shouts, and trance behavior. Into the nineteenth century the similarity between Native American religious practices and those of revivalist Christian sects like the Baptists and Methodists was explicitly cited by some of revivalism's detractors. One anti-Methodist pamphlet, *Camp-meetings Described and Exposed*, contained the account of an erstwhile "heathen youth" who "went one evening to a Methodist prayer meeting, but directly left it affrighted, and, by signs, and broken English, described it at his boarding house: 'They act just as they do in me own country.'"

Revolutionary and Early Republican America

A century and a half after Africans had been brought to the American continent and thousands of years after native peoples had settled there, both black and Native American people were again forced into an involuntary relationship with whites, who deprived them of the very rights that the founding documents of the United States claimed to be self-evident. Slaves and Native Americans resided in the new nation not by consent but by white force and were deprived of the civil rights that a government-by-consent ("of the people, by the people, and for the people") supposedly conferred.

To be sure, revolutionary fervor did bring ringing indictments of racial slavery from some white Christians. In 1774, the white preacher Nathaniel Niles of Newburyport, Massachusetts, compared the British government's injuries to colonists' liberties to those of American slaveholders: "God gave us liberty, and we have enslaved our fellow-men . . . for shame, let us either cease to enslave our fellow men, or else let us cease to complain of those who would enslave us." Even those revolutionary statesmen who condemned slavery tended, however, to keep their slaves, to free them only in token numbers, or to urge that, once freed, they be removed from the United States.

By this time, however, most black people in America were generations removed from their African origins and, if they could not claim political membership in the United States, nevertheless played as formative a role in the nation's cultural life as slave labor did in its economics. African American religion, in particular, emerged as a distinctly New World phenomenon in the latter part of the eighteenth century and the nineteenth.

By 1780, a sizable group of black preachers, most of them Baptist, had emerged to minister to black people, interpreting the Bible in light of African American experience and in ways that whites could not fully control. In the South, black congregations affiliated with mainstream religious bodies, though nominally overseen by whites, often outnumbered white congregations and were occasionally led by slave preachers. Slave Christianity emerged as an "invisible institution" of often clandestine religious meetings where slaves interpreted Christianity by their own lights and in full awareness of the fact that although the slave owners' religion might be compatible with slavery, their own was not.

Slavery was very gradually abolished in the North following the Revolution, fostering the development of independent black Episcopal, Methodist, Baptist, and Presbyterian churches. The largest of these, the African Methodist Episcopal Church, was established in 1816 by black Christians who found themselves segregated in mainly white denominations. In preaching and in hymns, black worshipers, free and slave, fashioned the symbols and narratives of Christianity into messages of freedom that, strategically, could remain in varying measure acceptable to and hidden from white authorities. Slave and free black Christians also made use of the "black Jeremiad"—a form of preaching by reproach—to exhort their white Christian counterparts to confront the moral claims of their faith. Maria Stewart, for example, used her status as an African American Christian to address "the great and mighty men of America." Stewart asked, "Are not [black men's] wives, their sons, and their daughters, as dear to them as the white man's? Certainly, God has not deprived them of the divine influences of his Holy Spirit, which are the greatest of all blessings, if they ask him. Then why should man any longer deprive his fellow man of equal rights and privileges?"

Native American religions also became "invisible institutions" in the eighteenth and nineteenth centuries. Unlike black slaves, Native Americans in the southern states did not convert to Christianity in significant numbers. Many devoted themselves instead to nurturing their own "cultural undergrounds," keeping their spiritual lives hidden from the white plantation owners and slaves who inhabited lands formerly theirs and checking the spread of Christianity in their communities. For other Native Americans, however, evangelical Christianity offered a context for the expression of a distinctly Native American identity and for protesting the racial entitlement of a white Christian elite. William Apess, for example, a Pequot Indian who had converted to Methodism, wrote in his 1836 *Eulogy on King Philip*: "I do not hesitate to say that through the prayers, preaching, and examples of those pretended pious has been the foundation of all the slavery and degradation in the American colonies toward colored people." Apess added: "We might suppose that . . . Dr. [Cotton] Mather, so well versed in Scripture, would have known his work better than to have cursed any of God's creatures."

For white Protestants, the removal of government support for any single church (in the Constitution's First Amendment) promoted interdenominational efforts among Baptists, Methodists, Episcopalians, Presbyterians, and Congregationalists, who jointly founded missionary and tract societies to bring the nation to the cause of Christ. The visibility of such cooperative efforts allowed the white Protestant theologian Charles Hodge to claim in 1829 that America had become a single people, "having one language, one literature, essentially one religion, and one common soul." In fact, however, America was becoming more rather than less fragmented along religious, racial, and regional lines. As black and native people increasingly used religious forums to call white racism to account, Catholic immigrants were arriving in numbers that eventually would make their church the largest single religious body in America, and southern Protestants were poised to secede from their national religious communities over the question of slavery.

Numbers of white Methodists, Baptists, Presbyterians, and Quakers had preached against slavery in the eighteenth century, but only Quakers had, by the beginning of the nineteenth century, excluded slaveholders from their churches. In 1784, Methodist leaders voted to expel all slaveholders from their nascent organization, but they repealed the law within six months. Early Methodist antislavery efforts were compromised by the fact that the Methodist Church remained open to slaveholders in the years of its greatest growth. Over the next several decades, white Methodist leaders agreed that the effort to save black souls would take precedence over efforts to liberate slaves from bondage.

Black Christians discerned in their faith a different set of directives. For example, Denmark Vesey, a free black carpenter in Charleston, South Carolina, was charged with plotting a slave insurrection in 1822. Vesey belonged to the African Methodist Episcopal Church in Charleston, where he preached prophetic sermons likening American slaves to the ancient Israelites whom God had freed from captivity. The slave-Israelite analogy had long been a staple of evangelical antislavery preaching, black and white, but the court that sentenced Vesey charged instead that he had been "totally insensible to the divine influence of scripture," which was "to reconcile us to our destinies on earth." Vesey and scores of his followers were hanged or deported, and their house of worship was destroyed.

If predominantly white Christian churches were increasingly divided on slavery in the early decades of the nineteenth century, most remained united on the need to extend the blessings of civilization and Christianity to Native Americans. They did, however, debate the ends of such a policy: Was it to secure the flourishing of Native American nations or to dissolve them as obstacles to white Christian dominance? In either case, white Christian mission boards set themselves up in a proprietary relationship to the Native Americans they claimed to serve, a relationship that mirrored that of the federal government to Native American nations.

Prior to the Revolutionary War, Native American nations had dealt politically with the separate governments of each British colony, which were reconstituted as states following independence. The new federal government claimed to recognize treaties made between colonial governments and Native American nations that gave the latter limited sovereignty. At the same time, the federal government promised the new state governments that it would abolish Native American sovereignty in favor of the states as soon as it was practical. Native Americans thus fell under the "protection" of a federal government that had begun to contemplate their removal beyond the nation's borders as early as 1802.

The degree to which American Christian missionaries constituted native peoples as strangers in their own lands is suggested by the inclusion of the word *foreign* in the names of certain missionary societies. One example is the United Foreign Missionary Society, founded in 1819, which operated within the United States and its territories to bring Native American nations to the cause of Christ. Similarly, the American Board of Commissioners for Foreign Missions (ABCFM), a Protestant society originally founded to minister to "the heathen in Asia," eventually voted to include native peoples in America in its definition of inhabitants of "foreign" and "heathen" lands. Both societies worked closely with the federal government in the early decades of the nineteenth century to set up English-language schools for natives, give them new Christian names supplied by white benefactors, and otherwise absorb them into American life. The ABCFM rejected all plans for evangelization that retained Native American languages. "Assimilated in language," an 1816 report argued, "[Indians] will more readily become assimilated in habits and manners to their white neighbors, intercourse will be easy and the advantages to them incalculable." Such a policy also conferred incalculable advantages on white settlers moving westward.

There were limits, however, to the degree of assimilation the ABCFM was willing to countenance. For example, when a Cherokee convert to Christianity, Elias Boudinot, so excelled in his studies at a mission school in Cornwall, Connecticut, that he won a scholarship to Andover Seminary, the board in charge of the school, headed by Lyman Beecher, praised Boudinot as living proof of the wisdom of the policy of Christianizing Native Americans. But when Boudinot announced his impending marriage to a white woman, the board denounced the match as "an outrage upon public feeling" and promptly exiled the newlyweds to a mission station in the Cherokee nation in Georgia.

Georgia state authorities, meanwhile, were pressing for a removal of Cherokee to lands west of the Mississippi. In 1831, white missionaries to the Cherokee were jailed for refusing to recognize Georgia's jurisdiction over Cherokee land, but they withdrew their objection in exchange for a government pardon and followed the exiled Cherokee westward. Elsewhere, the Jacksonian policy of moving natives farther and farther westward into "Indian territory" broke up missions from year to year, and the ABCFM eventually resigned its work among native peoples in America to focus on the spread of evangelical Christianity abroad. Some white missionaries argued futilely against the policy of removal as fatal both to the cause of Christianization and to Native Americans themselves. Others, however, argued that moving Native Americans beyond the reach of hostile whites offered their only salvation from extinction.

Similarly, many of the white Christians who wished to see slavery abolished considered the removal of emancipated slaves to Africa to be the best means of protecting them and, at the same time, of healing the growing rift between white northern and southern Christians. White Presbyterian and Congregationalist clergy—the first white Christians, apart from Quakers, to organize opposition to slavery in their churches—proposed that the removal of black slaves to Africa begin with the removal of *free* blacks. Such a plan, antislavery proponents argued, would hasten abolition by enlisting slaveholders in the colonization effort and provide a precedent for the liberation of slaves as their "liberation" from the nation's borders. With like-minded clergy, Presbyterian Robert Finley organized the American Colonization Society in 1817. The national bodies of the major white Protestant denominations—Presbyterian, Methodist, Baptist, Episcopal, Dutch Reformed, and Congregationalist—all officially endorsed the society by 1825. By 1831, however, white churches in the southern states had renounced the colonization effort, paving the way for the division of Protestant churches into pro- and antislavery factions.

Between 1830 and 1860, the policy of the U.S. government was to empty the states of their native inhabitants through the compulsory removal of Native American nations to territory west of Arkansas and Missouri. Thus, in what is now Kansas, for example, Native American nations from other parts of the Midwest—Shawnee and Munsee from Ohio, Miami from Indiana, Ottawas and Chippewa from Michigan—were relocated alongside indigenous nations like the Kansa and the Osage. Nations in the southern states—for example, Creeks, Cherokee, Choctaw, and Chickasaw—were removed to territory just south, in present-day Oklahoma. Although the Six Nations of the Iroquois in New York resisted removal, every other Native American nation east of the Mississippi and south of Lake Michigan, with the exception of small remnants in Ohio, Indiana, and the South, came under federal removal programs by 1844.

Some white missionaries who followed native peoples westward maintained, though with evidently lessening conviction, that Native Americans could better find their salvation away from white settlements, but Andrew Jackson, the architect of the removal policy, more forthrightly proclaimed its real aim. As Jackson wrote in his Fifth Annual Message in 1833, "Established in the midst of another and a superior race, and without appreciating the causes of their inferiority or seeking to control them, the [Indians] must necessarily yield to the force of circumstances and ere long disappear." Certainly Jackson was wrong in predicting that removal would mean Native American extinction. But forced removal from their lands did result in the deaths of thousands of native people through disease, exposure, and federal retaliation for acts of violent resistance. More generally, removal represented a form of social death for people who regarded the earth as sacred and themselves as rooted to a particular part of it. As a Seminole chief explained to John Quincy Adams, "Here our navel strings were first cut and the blood from them sunk into the earth, and made the country dear to us."

Free black preachers in the antebellum United States, particularly in the South, needed to be shrewd in their dealings both with white church leaders, who typically expected black preachers to keep their congregations in line, and with black worshipers, who looked to their preachers for charismatic leadership in the struggle for black freedom. Slave preachers sometimes felt that they had less to lose than their free black counterparts in interpreting the Christian message. According to the black leader W. E. B. Du Bois, the slave minister "early appeared on the plantation and found his function as the healer of the sick, the interpreter of the unknown, the comforter of the sorrowing, the supernatural avenger of wrong, and the one who rudely but picturesquely expressed the longing, disappointment, and resentment of a stolen and oppressed people." The slave preacher Nat Turner, for example, believed that he was doing the will of the Christian god in leading an insurrection of slaves in Southampton County, Virginia, in August 1831. Turner's rebellion resulted in the deaths of seventy white people and, soon after, the retaliatory murder of scores of innocent slaves and free blacks. Before being hanged in November of that year, Turner faced those who condemned him to death and asked, "Was not Christ crucified?"

As slaves and free black people increasingly found Christianity on their side of the struggle for freedom, white Christian churches grew more sharply divided on the question of slavery. Proslavery Christians in the South insisted that slavery was ordained by God and part of the natural order of human relations. Pressing for a stronger segregation between church and state, they cast antislavery Christians as political opportunists who tarnished religion with secular concerns.

As white-led Protestant denominations divided into pro- and antislavery camps, so the abolitionist movement also divided into "gradualist" and "immediatist" factions, with the former eventually losing ground to the latter. Those who favored gradual abolition believed it would be impractical to end slavery all at once; they also felt that public sentiment would eventually move to free the slaves as soon as they were thoroughly Christianized and colonization policies were in place to remove them to Africa once emancipated. Immediatist abolitionists roundly rejected colonization and ridiculed continued efforts to promote Bible literacy among slaves, arguing for nothing short of immediate emancipation. Whereas the spokespeople for gradualism were almost to a person white and Protestant, the movement for immediate abolitionism brought together white and black activists, including deeply religious Protestants like Sojourner Truth, Theodore Dwight Weld, and Angelina Grimké, critics of institutional Christianity like Frederick Douglass and William Lloyd Garrison, and non-Protestants like the Irish Catholic Daniel O'Connell.

Even as white Protestants experienced widening regional and political divisions, the influx of more than three million non-Protestant immigrants during the middle decades of the nineteenth century provided an occasion for assertions of a tenuous unity. During this period, a number of white Protestant organizations, including the Organization of United Americans, the

Organization of the Star Spangled Banner, and, most prominent, the Know-Nothing Party, emerged to combat the influence of foreign immigrants, primarily Catholics, whom they perceived as threats to American institutions. Southern proslavery Protestants could exalt slavery as the bulwark of civilization and Christian morality against the perceived decay of Christian morality associated with new immigrants. Antislavery Protestants, for their part, often used anti-Catholic sentiment to galvanize fellow Protestants to the abolitionist cause. According to Charles Beecher, for example, "*Any* system . . . which darkens the mind, and tends to prevent repentance, and faith, and holy living, must in the highest degrees incur the wrath of God"; since "all Protestants admit to this principle as applied to Roman [Catholic]ism, consistency requires them to admit it as applied to slavery."

Prior to the waves of Catholic immigration beginning in the 1840s, the South was home not only to the majority of the nation's black inhabitants but also to the majority of its Catholics. Whether to protect Catholic immigrants from further political ill will or to guard itself from becoming divided as Protestant churches were being divided over slavery, the Catholic Church never involved itself as a body in the antislavery cause, despite the fact that a hundred thousand black Catholics were enslaved in 1860. Most Catholic slaves resided in Maryland, Louisiana, or smaller Catholic outposts along the coasts of Mississippi, Florida, and Alabama. As slave converts to Protestant Christianity combined elements of their new faith with traditional African religion, so also did Catholic slaves find in the ritual and sacramental practices of Catholicism resources for the continuation of some traditional African elements as well as for covert protest. This was especially true in New Orleans, where black practitioners of Vodun (or voodoo), like the celebrated priestess Marie Laveau, created an Afro-Catholic synthesis that provided a context for healing and divining practices, the veneration of gods and spirits, and the transmission of coded information necessary for the slaves' survival.

Postbellum and Industrial Nineteenth Century

If the Civil War sharpened regional tensions and cast racial divisions into new configurations, it also brought a resurgence of evangelical Protestantism: as many as three hundred thousand Union and Confederate soldiers, or 10 percent of the total, experienced conversion to Protestantism or deepened their Protestant faith during wartime revivals. Strengthened white Protestant churches, together with the intensely religious meanings given to the war by both sides, paved the way for the reconstitution of the Union, less through the extension of political and social equality to nonwhite persons than through a renewal of loyalties between northern and southern white Christians.

With slavery abolished, the southern states moved rapidly to establish Jim Crow laws to limit the potential of emancipation to produce a system of social equality. By the end of the nineteenth century, however, the entire nation joined the South in romanticizing its pre–Civil War past, and white supremacy was on its way to becoming a national, not just a southern, cause. National reunification, understood in racial and religious terms, also paved the way for the expansion of Manifest Destiny—the view that the American continent had been providentially given to white settlers for the taking—to include overseas territories. The white Congregationalist minister Josiah Strong, for example, saw the "Anglo-Saxon race" as "more vigorous, more spiritual, more Christian than any other" and poised at century's end "to dispossess many weaker races, assimilate others, and mold the remainder, until, in a very important sense, it has Anglo-Saxonized mankind." Jewish and Irish Catholic immigrants to the United States, meanwhile, found some respite from the forms of prejudice they encountered in Europe insofar as the white Americans' preoccupation with distinguishing white from nonwhite put these new arrivals on the white side of the divide, though both anti-Semitism and anti-Catholicism would take on racist overtones by the end of the century.

Educational institutions founded specifically for black students emerged after the Civil War, as southerners set up segregated schools and northern churches, Catholic and Protestant, white and black, sent missionaries to the South to teach freed slaves. The Hampton Institute in Virginia, for example, was founded under white Protestant auspices to equip black students with manual skills, a respect for property, and Christian values through what its early administration called a system of "tender violence." One of Hampton's most famous alumni was Booker T. Washington, who, like many graduates, went on to become a prominent educator, instructing other black southerners in the moral and economic principles of what he called "racial uplift." Whatever his successes, Washington was accused by other black leaders, notably W. E. B. Du Bois, of continuing the white-run missionary schools' program of fitting black persons only for manual labor, political quietism, and second-class citizenship.

After emancipation, African Americans moved en masse to black churches, primarily Methodist and Baptist in name but differing in theology and practice from white denominations. The creation of separate churches enabled black Christians to institutionalize forms of community that largely escaped white surveillance. Black Christians formed splinter churches more frequently than whites did, in part because opportunities for black leadership outside churches were so few. In an effort to foster greater unity among them, separate black Baptist churches combined in 1895 to form the National Baptist Convention, which today remains the largest black denomination in the United States.

In both black and white churches, men were outnumbered by women, many of whom found in church membership political, spiritual, and organizational resources for women's advancement. As white Christian women assumed leadership in the women's rights movement and black Christian men assumed leadership of black churches, black Christian women needed to negotiate gender and racial inequality simultaneously. Even when black and white Christian women were united in causes such as temperance, black women needed to articulate their positions shrewdly, so that they represented the concerns not only of women but specifically of black women and, with them, black men. For example, Frances Willard, the white president of the Woman's Christian Temperance Union, openly preached that alcohol exacerbated what she saw as the sexual threat that black men inevitably posed to white women's "purity." Willard's views on African American men outraged the black Christian antilynching activist Ida B. Wells. Exposing the double standard of antimiscegenation laws in her antilynching pamphlet *Southern Horrors*, Wells wrote that these laws not only "operate against the legitimate union of the races, they free the white man to seduce all the colored girls he can, but it is death to the colored man who yields to the force and advances of a similar attraction in white women. White men lynch the offending Afro-American, not because he is a despoiler of virtue, but because he succumbs to the smiles of white women."

Although Josiah Strong's vision of "Anglo-Saxonizing" humankind was not directed explicitly at black people or Native Americans in the United States, its implications were not lost on those who were then formulating racial policy. Under the so-called peace policy launched by President Ulysses S. Grant, Native Americans were to be educated in white-run boarding schools, where they would learn to speak, dress, worship, and otherwise conduct themselves as white Christians did. Native Americans were often brought from western reservations to "training schools" in the East, including the formerly all-black Hampton Institute, where they were educated for American citizenship. Increasingly, the citizenship for which Native Americans were being fitted appeared to be the narrowly circumscribed citizenship of the black former slave. In 1886, for example, Native American graduates of the Hampton Institute sang a song written for them by a white teacher, which included the lines:

"[I] do the work I once despised / I've thrown away my bow and arrow / I've taken up the plough and harrow / I'm willing to be civilized." The majority of Hampton's Native American graduates worked as subsistence farmers, often returning to find their lands further diminished. In 1887, Congress passed the Dawes Severalty Act, which broke up parcels of land held in common by Native Americans, allotting portions to individual owners and selling the "surplus" land created by this division to non–Native American homesteaders, oil companies, and railroads.

As white southerners stung by the Confederacy's collapse created shared rituals to give meaning to the defeat of their way of life, so Native Americans innovated new rituals to signal spiritual unity across tribal difference and to bring traditional sacred knowledge to bear on continuing conflicts with nonnative Americans. Whereas the southern white "religion of the lost cause" was centered on the past, however, Native American religious movements of the later nineteenth century were devoted to transforming past defeat into future hope. One such movement was the Ghost Dance, which takes its form from the Round Dance ritual of the Paiute Indians. In 1889, a Paiute prophet, Wovoka, experienced a vision in which the desert bloomed, the dead were raised, and conflict ceased between different Indian nations and between Indians and non-Indians. In this vision, Wovoka felt himself divinely commissioned to spread the Round Dance ritual, which had been practiced as a way of opening participants to spiritual influence. In its new form, the dance, performed monthly, would hasten the renewal of the world and bring participants into contact with the dead (as well as with the depleted animal life) in anticipation of their promised return.

The Ghost Dance quickly spread among other Native American nations to the east and west, many of which sent representatives to Wovoka's home in Nevada to meet with him and be initiated into the new way of life his vision represented. In this way, elements of Wovoka's prophecy were mixed with the spiritual traditions of other tribes (which, after generations of contact with missionaries, often contained elements of Christianity as well). Although the Ghost Dance combined elements that were important in both native and Christian culture—notions of end time and resurrection, a continuum between living and dead, and the transformation of history through spiritual means—many white Christians found the presence of these elements in the Ghost Dance to be incomprehensible or threatening. White administrators of Indian policy attempted to prohibit the Ghost Dance from the time of its earliest performances. Wovoka himself urged Native Americans to stop the dance after the federal army massacre of more than two hundred Lakota Sioux at Wounded Knee, South Dakota, at the end of 1890. But many Native American nations retained the practice, which was revived most vividly in the American Indian Movement of the 1970s.

The population of Native Americans in the United States reached its lowest point in 1890. A year later, the United States for the first time stretched continuously from coast to coast, extending the "frontier" (and the concept of Manifest Destiny) to lands that could be colonized beyond the nation's borders. The Spanish–American War of 1898 nurtured feelings of Anglo-Saxon superiority among white Protestant Americans and, by bringing territories in the Caribbean and the Pacific under American jurisdiction, made missionary subjects of these territories' inhabitants, who were figured as different, both racially and religiously, from "true" Americans.

At the same time, the need to combat white stereotypes of black life led some black church leaders to promote an ideology of racial uplift that unwittingly played into imperialist formulations of America's civilizing mission abroad. The genuine piety of many black Christians at the turn of the century often kept them from questioning the white imperialist dogma that the forces of Christianity and civilization together would rescue so-called heathen peoples from "savagery." Thus W. E. B. Du Bois addressed both black and white Christians when he urged in 1900 that "the cloak of Christian missionary enterprise [not] be allowed in the future, as so often in the past, to hide the ruthless economic exploitation and political downfall of less developed nations."

Early Twentieth Century

Du Bois's critique of missionary imperialism amplified and extended the protests of those American slaves who had rejected Christianity as a white religion, a "sham religion" that united white masters and preachers in a conspiracy against black advancement. In the early twentieth century, many black Americans found their spiritual flourishing not in new interpretations of Christianity, still perceived by some as the religion of slaveholders, but in new interpretations of Judaism, Islam, and the African past.

In 1005 a black congregation describing its members as Jews was established in Belleville, Virginia. Its founder, William S. Crowdy, contended that the Jews of the Bible were black, and he emphasized (as many slaves had) the shared experiences of Jews in bondage to Egypt and Africans enslaved in the New World. Recognizing the Jewishness of Jesus, however, Crowdy's congregation also made use of the New Testament and stressed faith in Christ.

Members of the Church of God, an African American congregation established in Philadelphia in 1915, also described themselves as Jews and celebrated only Jewish holidays. Its founder, F. S. Cheney, insisted not only that the original Jews were black but that black people were the only authentic Jews. Reversing many white Christian interpretations of the curse of Ham in Genesis, which figured black and other dark-skinned populations as the cursed descendants of Noah's banished son, Cheney preached instead that *white* skin was a punishment from God and that white Jews were impostors.

Some leaders of black Jewish congregations were inspired by the work of Marcus Garvey, a black Jamaican immigrant who founded the Universal Negro Improvement Association (UNIA) in 1916. Garvey's UNIA originally drew most of its members from Harlem's black population, although it soon attracted followers from all over the United States, Latin America, the Caribbean, and Africa. The UNIA was not an explicitly religious organization, but Garvey, nominally a Catholic, drew support for it by speaking in black Christian churches. In 1921 Garvey appointed a UNIA chaplain and Episcopal priest, George Alexander McGuire, to head the new Africa Orthodox Church. Both Garvey's UNIA and the new Africa Orthodox Church preached that God and Jesus were black and were united with African peoples throughout the world in their struggle for independence from European domination.

Although some black churches, notably the African Methodist Episcopal Church, had undertaken missionary work in Africa in the late nineteenth century, they and other black churches had roundly rejected the colonization schemes of the gradualist abolitionists. Garvey was the first black leader to win large-scale black support for a back-to-Africa movement of black people from all over the world. Although the effort collapsed in 1924 and Garvey's leadership declined precipitously thereafter, his views gave rise to new black religions and nationalist movements for the remainder of the century,

During this period other black Americans chose to identify religiously with Islam. Although some African-born slaves had been influenced by Islam in their own countries, under slavery their Islamic practices mingled with other religious elements and were eventually submerged in the creation of a distinctive black Christianity. Among those who continued into the twentieth century to condemn even black Christianity as the oppressive religion of white masters was Timothy Drew, known to his followers as Noble Drew Ali. In contrast to those who found their spiritual roots in Africa, Ali contended that black Americans were not really Africans at all but instead Asiatic Muslims whom white Christians had robbed of their identity. Ali's Moorish Science Temple, founded in 1915 in Newark, New Jersey, was followed by others in

Detroit, Pittsburgh, and Chicago, all of which drew their adherents largely from recent black immigrants from the rural South.

After Ali's death in 1929, many of his followers joined the movement of W. D. Fard, the Nation of Islam. Fard preached that African Americans had been stripped of their true religion, Islam, by "white devils" who imposed Christianity on them in order to make them docile. In the tradition of W. E. B. Du Bois's anti-imperialism, Fard's successor, Elijah Muhammad, was imprisoned in 1942 for declaring that black Americans had no obligation to join American forces in an imperial war against another "colored" race, the Japanese. (In the 1960s and 1970s, Muhammad's call would be taken up by many black Americans within and outside the Nation of Islam, among them the boxer Muhammad Ali, who protested the U.S. war in Vietnam on similar grounds.)

As many black Americans found religious contexts outside Christianity for the cultivation of black solidarity, some new black Christian movements were attracting interracial followings. For example, the Peace Mission movement of the black spiritual leader Father Divine (born George Baker) drew black and white followers to its Harlem headquarters during the period of the Great Depression. Father Divine's Peace Mission combined elements of traditional black Christianity, Pentecostalism, Catholicism, and New Thought in a gospel of hope and human flourishing. Members of the Peace Mission movement believed in Father Divine's divinity and sought to channel his blessings into positive thoughts of a world free of poverty, hunger, and racism. Like many black religious movements, the religion of the Peace Mission was this-worldly as well as spiritual: adherents opened a network of relief shelters as well as successful businesses, campaigned avidly for civil rights, and feasted together on elaborate banquets whose endless courses, mysteriously provided by Father Divine, made his gospel of abundance real.

During this period white Jews and Christians also joined African Americans in the work of the National Association for the Advancement of Colored People (NAACP). The NAACP was founded in 1909 in response to deadly race riots in Springfield, Illinois, which killed scores of black people. Signers of the call to action that launched the NAACP included black leaders like Du Bois and the black Catholic lawyer Frederick McGhee, white Protestant New Englanders (including some of the descendants of the Garrisonian abolitionists), and a number of urban Jews, including the jurist Felix Frankfurter and the anthropologist Franz Boas. Though not a religious organization, the NAACP was vigorously supported by the National Baptist Convention, to which one-third of black churchgoers in the United States belonged.

The social dislocations of the early twentieth century also contributed to the rebirth of the Ku Klux Klan, the southern vigilante organization founded during Reconstruction, which was revived as a massive national movement claiming three million members by 1923. The new Ku Klux Klan was primarily a rural and suburban movement, and its members championed the values of white, Protestant agrarian culture against what they perceived as the corrupt morals of northern cities like New York, where both Catholic and Jewish immigrants and black arrivals from the South were clustered. As one Klansman put it, the Klan represented the "return of the Puritans in this corrupt and jazz-mad age." The automobile magnate Henry Ford won enormous support from the Klan in the 1920s for his theory that jazz was the product of a black-Jewish conspiracy, a "Jewish invention" for seducing "gentile girls" with "monkey talk" and "jungle squeals." The Klan also played a prominent role in the 1924 Democratic convention, where it wrested the party's nomination from the Catholic presidential candidate, Al Smith. As Du Bois had predicted in 1900 when he wrote that "the problem of the twentieth century is the problem of the color line," antiblack prejudice was increasingly being conflated with broader forms of American imperialism. Best-selling books from this period included Lothrop Stoddard's *The Rising Tide of Color against White World Supremacy* and Madison Bell Grant's *The Passing of the Great Race*, according to which only Anglo-Saxons were truly "white"; people of African, Asian, central European, and Mediterranean ancestry all fell under the rubric of "colored." Nevertheless, African Americans remained the primary victims of racial hatred: of the 455 documented lynchings in America between 1918 and 1927, 416 were black.

In 1924 Congress passed the Johnson-Reed Act, which put sharply restrictive quotas on all but Anglo-Saxon immigrants. In the same year, ironically, it passed the Indian Citizenship Act, which automatically conferred U.S. citizenship on all American Indians. Although viewed as a victory by some Native Americans and the non-natives who wished to see them assimilated, the Indian Citizenship Act was seen by many Native Americans as the culmination of a centuries-long effort to deny Native American sovereignty over their own lands. Federal limitations placed on the political and economic agency of Native Americans made religion one of the few venues for their struggle. In 1918, a year after the federal government had begun anew to liquidate Indian lands, Native Americans from various tribal nations came together to form the Native American Church. Its leaders institutionalized the ceremonial use of peyote, which had been used by native tribes in present-day Mexico since before the Spanish conquest. Peyote, an ingested substance used in healing and making contact with spirits, had been given different meanings in various tribal contexts. With the emergence of the Native American Church, peyote now became, in addition, the centerpiece of a pan-Indian movement that encouraged Native Americans of different tribal nations to see themselves as part of a common political and spiritual culture. Like the pan-Indian Ghost Dance, however, or like certain religious rituals of various tribes that had been outlawed by white "guardians," peyote religion also eventually came under attack by the federal government.

Modern America

The years following World War II were marked by the most dramatic growth in white church membership in U.S. history. This growth was largely fueled by the renewal of American Christian triumphalism attendant on the nation's military victories over totalitarian regimes in Europe and Asia. At the same time, however, many religious Americans came to question America's alleged moral superiority over other nations in light of continuing injustices perpetrated at home. In 1952 the National Council of Churches, an organization of different Protestant denominations, condemned racial segregation as un-Christian. Six years later, the Catholic bishops of the United States likewise affirmed as a body that "discrimination based on the accidental fact of race or color . . . cannot be reconciled with the truth that God has created all men with equal rights and equal dignity." It was predominantly through the work of black churches, however, and not the largely white leadership of mainstream churches, that the struggle for racial justice took center stage.

The civil rights movement of the 1950s and 1960s continued the freedom struggle that had informed both Christianity and the new religious movements of African Americans since the late eighteenth century. Although the movement relied on the contributions of many thousands of civil rights activists who worked within and outside Christian churches, it has come largely to be associated with the preaching and organizational leadership of Martin Luther King Jr. King had been recently appointed minister of the black Dexter Avenue Baptist Church in Montgomery, Alabama, when the U.S. Supreme Court's 1954 decision in *Brown v. Board of Education* declared segregation in public schools unconstitutional. In December 1955 Rosa Parks, a black woman returning home from the white Montgomery neighborhood where she worked as a maid, was arrested for refusing to give up her seat to a white man and move to the back of a segregated bus. King led the ensuing bus boycott by black Montgomery residents, which lasted for nearly a year before the U.S. Supreme Court declared that Alabama's segregation laws were unconstitutional. The boycott's success gave rise to the Southern Christian Leadership Conference (SCLC) in 1957, which brought black clergy together from all over the South to further nonviolent opposition to racial segregation. The SCLC organized demonstrations in which black men, women, and children responded to beatings and taunting with displays of prayerful dignity, solidarity, and strength.

In 1965, King called all the nation's clergy to Selma, Alabama, for the freedom march to Montgomery. In the same year, the United States escalated its involvement in the Vietnam War, a move accompanied by the kinds of imperialist rhetoric rehearsed in the Spanish-American War and in nineteenth-century campaigns for Indian removal. At about the same time, a change in U.S. immigration laws opened the nation to greater numbers of Asian and Latino immigrants, whose presence further altered a religious landscape already fractured by disagreement over national policy in Vietnam and the struggles for civil rights. In the last several years of his life, King, like Du Bois and other black leaders before him, increasingly turned his attention to the links between overseas imperialism, domestic poverty, and racial injustice. He spoke out fervently against the war in Vietnam and was in the midst of organizing an interracial "poor people's campaign" when he was assassinated in 1968.

Although King was influenced by the ideas of the Hindu resistance leader Mohandas Gandhi and, later, by those of the exiled Vietnamese Buddhist Thich Nhat Hanh, he relied primarily on Christian symbols and narratives in his public speeches. King preached a vision of racial unity in which the children of former slaves and former slaveholders would sit at the same table, study at the same schools, and work side by side for justice. This element of King's vision appealed to the many thousands of white people who took part in the civil rights movement. But King also preached a religion of blackness, which drew on the tradition, nurtured in black Christian spirituals and in the black Jewish movement, of black people as the chosen people led out of bondage. The religion of blackness drew also on the image of a black Jesus that figured both in rural black Christian churches and in the secular ministry of Garvey and Du Bois and, albeit indirectly, on the black nationalism of the Garveyites and the Black Muslim movement.

The Black Muslim movement produced another of this period's most important civil rights leaders, Malcolm X. Born Malcolm Little, he discarded his last name and signified by "X" both the loss of his ancestral community under slavery and his protests against white privilege, including the privilege of slave owners to own, breed, and name their slaves. For much of his public career, Malcolm X had been a member of the Nation of Islam and a trusted ally of Elijah Muhammad. In 1964, a year before his death, Malcolm X broke with the Nation of Islam to form the Organization of Afro-American Unity. A pilgrimage to Mecca had brought him closer to orthodox Islam and, at the same time, to a vision of black unity that transcended religious affiliation. After his 1965 assassination by members of the Black Muslims, from which he had broken, Malcolm X's ideas survived to inspire the black power movement of the later 1960s as well as changes in the Nation of Islam. As Malcolm X had, the Nation of Islam gradually ceased to promote a message of black separatism and moved closer to organized Islam, changing its name to the World Community of Al-Islam in the West. The older Nation of Islam was eventually reconstituted by Louis Farrakhan, and other splinter movements of African American Muslims appeared. Today, however, most black Americans who are Muslim—approximately one million out of a total Muslim population in the United States of six million—identify with orthodox Islam and not with Farrakhan's Nation of Islam.

Native Americans were also waging the struggle for civil rights and against internal colonization during these years. In 1962, members of different tribal nations formed the American Indian Movement (AIM) as a pan-Indian civil rights organization devoted to ending poverty and discrimination against Native Americans in urban areas as well as to securing sovereignty for Native Americans on reservations. Like members of the black power movement, AIM activists frequently became targets of federal violence, including a long siege at Wounded Knee, South Dakota, in 1973 that left several AIM members dead.

Native American activists working in a variety of venues increasingly focused their efforts on defending the right to free exercise of religion for native people. As a result of these efforts, Congress in 1977 passed the American Indian Religious Freedom Act (AIRFA). Under AIRFA's provisions, many Indian remains and tribal objects that had been housed in museums were returned to Indian nations, Native American prisoners were granted the same freedom-of-worship rights as other prisoners, and the ceremonial use of some protected animal species was granted to Native American practitioners. But AIRFA was compromised by a series of U.S. Supreme Court decisions that sacrificed the interests of Native American religious practices to those of environmental protection campaigns; tourism, logging, and mining industries; and the touted "war on drugs," which sought further restrictions on the use of peyote.

Ironically, at the same time that Native American religious freedoms came under sharpened legal attack, non-natives drawn to the New Age movement increasingly constructed a religion of "Indianness" by taking new Native American names, participating in allegedly Native American modes of healing and personal transformation, and casting Native Americans as symbols of ecological harmony. Such practices provided non-natives unmoored from traditional sources of value within their own cultures a vehicle for recovering the "authenticity" they projected onto Native Americans. The view of American Indians as mystically connected with nature, a Native American scholar points out, "denies Indian personhood" and turns native peoples into nothing more than guardians of the land for the benefit of generations of European invaders, including those non-natives who would find their own spiritual redemption in "Indianness."

Nevertheless, in the past several years, American Indians of different tribal nations *have* turned increasingly to promoting environmental justice, largely because land rights are central to the struggle for Native American spiritual and political sovereignty. Native American environmental activists recognize that both Native American people *and* the earth have suffered from environmental devastation, including fallout from nuclear weapons testing and atomic power plants that dispose of toxic wastes on Indian lands, degradation from mineral mining that leaves Indian lands uninhabitable, and massive irrigation projects that divert water flowing through Indian lands to urban and suburban areas. Environmental destruction is particularly devastating to Native Americans who live on tribal lands, since their links to specific places make it very difficult simply to pack up and move elsewhere, yet to remain is to risk extinction.

As black religious leaders of the 1960s and 1970s increasingly reaffirmed a theology of blackness, so Native American religious thinkers began publicly to affirm a theology of Indianness. Vine Deloria Jr., for example, titled a 1973 manifesto *God Is Red*. Theologians of blackness and "redness" made claims on those who were not black and not Native American, declaring that God sided with the oppressed and that the cause of theology was the cause of freedom from racial injustice. According to the black theologian James Cone, the appearance of theologies of blackness and redness on the American scene "is due exclusively to the failure of white [Christian] religionists to relate the gospel of Jesus to the pain of being [nonwhite] in white racist society." As had enslaved Christians before them, Deloria, Cone, and other nonwhite religious thinkers refashioned potentially oppressive Christian traditions into critiques of racial injustice and powerful resources for change.

Conclusion

A century and half ago, religious historians defined the United States as a white and Protestant country, even as millions of black Americans, most of them Christian, struggled for freedom and recognition, Catholics and Jews began arriving in ever greater numbers, and the federal government took up arms against Native Americans to keep them confined to an ever shrinking Indian territory.

America is even less white and less Protestant today than it was then. Approximately 30 million Americans are black. From a low point of 250,000 in the late nineteenth century, the Native American population now numbers more than 2 million. Six million Americans are Muslim. More than 1 million Asian immigrants practice Buddhism, although the majority of new converts to Buddhism in America are from European backgrounds. In the past several decades, black immigrants from South America and the Caribbean—practitioners of voodoo from Haiti, Rastafarianism from Jamaica, Santeria from Cuba, Shango from Trinidad, and Condomblé from Brazil, among others—have formed vibrant religious communities in Miami, New York, Los Angeles, and other cities. In large cities, the Nation of Islam, black Jewish congregations, and black spiritual churches, which blend elements of Pentecostalism, Roman Catholicism, and voodoo, claim significant members.

With increasing religious and racial diversity have come new alignments. Many African American Christians continue their struggle for racial justice even as they find themselves allied politically on such issues as abortion and school prayer with conservative white churches that had in their past stood with slave owners and segregationists. Large numbers of Asian immigrants have converted to Catholicism or Protestantism, and those Asian immigrants who continue to practice different varieties of Buddhism and Hinduism have seen their traditions rapidly "Americanized" once established in the United States. Adherents of New Age spirituality, who come predominantly out of European Christian and Jewish contexts, borrow liberally from traditions they associate with Native American, African, and Asian religions.

More and more Americans whose ancestors come from all parts of the world find themselves at a loss when asked to indicate their race. Caribbean immigrants, for example, do not always readily identify as African American. Some Irish Americans, Jews, and others whose ancestors were victims of discrimination in Europe and America have proudly reasserted their own historical status as not-quite-white. In many parts of the West and Southwest,

Asian and Latino Americans—typically classed as ethnic, not racial, groups—outnumber people of European or African descent and tend to identify racially with neither. Some Americans have called for an end to "race" altogether, arguing that its continued use as a descriptive category tends to naturalize harmful social constructions as though they were needful and inevitable.

Eliminating "race" in the interest of asserting and valuing a common humanity, however, seems uncomfortably close to the nineteenth-century Protestant historian's project of erasing racial (and religious) conflict in the interest of asserting a unified America. "How is it possible," Charles Long asks, "to do justice to the facts of American religious history and at the same time overcome the concealment of peoples? How might it be possible to make visible those who have been rendered invisible religiously and historically?" The challenge is to restore race to American religious history without advancing a history of racism. This requires a focus not only on "invisible" groups of people but also on the forces that made them invisible, even as the groups under discussion take on new configurations and "race" comes increasingly to be understood as a fiction that obscures power.

SUGGESTED READINGS

Ahlstrom, Sydney E. *A Religious History of the American People*. New Haven: Yale University Press, 1972.

Albanese, Catherine. *America: Religion and Religions*. 3rd ed. Belmont, Calif.: Wadsworth Publishing, 1999.

Allen, Theodore W. *The Invention of the White Race*. Vols. 1 and 2. London: Verso, 1994.

Axtell, James. *The Invasion Within: The Contest of Cultures in Colonial North America*. New York: Oxford University Press, 1985.

Chireau, Yvonne, and Nathaniel Deutsch, eds. *Black Zion: African American Religious Encounters with Judaism*. New York: Oxford University Press, 1999.

Deloria, Philip J. *Playing Indian*. New Haven: Yale University Press, 1998.

Engs, Robert F. "Red, Black, and White: A Study in Intellectual Inequality." In *Region, Race, and Reconstruction: Essays in Honor of C. Vann Woodward*, edited by J. Morgan Kousser and James M. McPherson, 241–66. New York: Oxford University Press, 1982.

Fields, Barbara. "Ideology and Race in American History." In *Region, Race, and Reconstruction: Essays in Honor of C. Vann Woodward*, edited by J. Morgan Kousser and James M. McPherson, 143–77. New York: Oxford University Press, 1982.

Gossett, Thomas F. *Race: The History of an Idea in America*. New York: Oxford University Press, 1997.

Lepore, Jill. *The Name of War: King Philip's War and the Origins of American Identity*. New York: Knopf, 1998.

Lincoln, C. Eric, and Lawrence H. Mamiya. *The Black Church and the African American Experience*. Durham, N.C.: Duke University Press, 1990.

Long, Charles. *Significations: Signs, Symbols, and Images in the Interpretation of Religion*. Philadelphia: Fortress, 1986.

Martin, Joel W. "Indians, Contact, and Colonialism in the Deep South: Themes for a Postcolonial History of American Religion." In *Retelling U.S. Religious History*, edited by Thomas A. Tweed, 149–80. Berkeley and Los Angeles: University of California Press, 1997.

Moore, R. Laurence. *Religious Outsiders and the Making of Americans*. New York: Oxford University Press, 1986.

Newman, Louise M. *White Women's Rights: The Racial Origins of Feminism in the United States*. New York: Oxford University Press, 1999.

Raboteau, Albert. *Slave Religion: The "Invisible Institution" in the Antebellum South*. New York: Oxford University Press, 1978.

Smith, H. Shelton. *In His Image, but . . . Racism and Southern Religion, 1780–1910*. Durham, N.C.: Duke University Press, 1972.

Thomas, G. E. "Puritans, Indians, and the Concept of Race." *New England Quarterly* 48 (March 1975): 3–27.

Tiro, Karim. "Denominated SAVAGE: Methodism, Writing, and Identity in the Works of William Apess, a Pequot." *American Quarterly* 48, no. 4 (1996): 653–79.

Tweed, Thomas A., ed. *Retelling U.S. Religious History*. Berkeley: University of California Press, 1997.

Weaver, Jace. *Defending Mother Earth: Native American Perspectives on Environmental Justice*. Maryknoll, N.Y.: Orbis Books, 1996.

Wills, David W. "The Central Themes of American Religious History: Pluralism, Puritanism, and the Encounter of Black and White." *Religion and Intellectual Life* 5 (Fall 1987): 30–41.

Ethnicity

"Catholic-Protestant Violence Claims More Victims," a headline in the 1990s screamed about Northern Ireland. Tragically, it is possible that Americans who read this news story also might have seen an ad splashed on the next page, announcing: "*Wild* Time Tonite! Don't Miss Our *Awesome* St. Patty's Day Celebration! 2-fer-1 Green Beer All Nite! Be There!!!" How can we make sense of these jarring images? One reflects the tortured history of the Irish homeland, and the other plays on an unsavory stereotype tagged to the Irish experience in the United States. But both are part of what many of us typically think at the mention of the word *Irish*. On the one hand, by the 1990s Americans had been so used to hearing about violence in Northern Ireland that they could not help but conjure bloody images when they thought of Ireland and its ethnoreligious conflict. On the other hand, Americans of Irish descent for so long have been caricatured as "unruly" and "happy-go-lucky" that beer distributors and pubs still rely on the power of that stereotype to try to outdo one another's profits every Saint Patrick's Day.

Irony and contradictions abound. One of the fatalities in the news report was a woman who was targeted because she was Catholic and had married a Protestant, this in a land where Irish Catholics and the descendants of English Protestants have been killing each other for centuries. But we Americans loudly proclaim that *anyone* can be Irish on St. Patty's Day, presumably even folks of English-Protestant ancestry; and who even notices when English Americans and Irish Americans intermarry? How can ethnicity and religion be a matter of life and death among a people in one place but seemingly irrelevant for their descendants in an adopted land?

Ethnicity and religion have always mattered, and they continue to be vital today. *E pluribus unum*, the Great Seal of the United States proclaims, "out of many, one." Although this phrase originally symbolized the forging of a single nation from the thirteen separate British colonies, after the early twentieth century it became the basis of the myth of the American "melting pot," which claims that one unified culture emerged from the many ethnicities and faiths immigrants brought to these shores. But that notion has always been more of a dream than a reality; our nation has always been more *pluribus* than *unum*, and the undying importance of ethnicity and religion is largely responsible for that. Ethnicity and religion have been the basis for inclusion or exclusion in our society, rendering some Americans "insiders" and others "outsiders," yet they have also promoted unity by giving both insiders and outsiders a sense of community and thereby a role in forging their own destinies and the nation's. Ethnicity and religion have profoundly affected the history of the United States and made conflict and accommodation integral and permanent features of the American experience.

Americans have always been keenly aware of ethnic differences. To the Europeans who began arriving in North America in the fifteenth century, an "ethnic" was a heathen, someone who was not Jewish or Christian. The word *ethnic* comes from the Greek *ethnos*, meaning "nation" or "people." Thus today we often think of ethnic groups according to nationality, and we assume they share a sense of peoplehood, a sort of tribalism bonded by a fundamental cultural, linguistic, and racial kinship. But history shows that ethnic identity does not necessarily derive from political nationhood. When the first Germans arrived in America, for instance, they shared a sense of ethnicity, a "Germanness," even though their various homelands had not yet become "Germany." Sicilians, Calabrians, and other immigrants from southern Italy became "Italians" only after they discovered their common language, customs, and interests in the United States. Many sociologists, moreover, argue that religion is second only to language as an "ethnic carrier." Southern Italian immigrants, for example, shared a kind of Catholicism (with its own saints, prayers, rituals, and other traditions) that was directly tied to Italian language and cultures. These specifically Italian traditions were alien to the Irish who dominated the church hierarchy, setting the stage for ethnocultural conflict even within the Catholic Church, to say nothing of conflict between religious Protestants and Catholic groups or between Christian and non-Christian immigrants.

Similarly, "Africans" in fact were Mandingos, Yorubas, Ibos, and other ethnics—a point recognized by slave traders, who sometimes advertised the particular "quality" of various African ethnicities (some were thought to be more docile than others, some more prone to running away) in order to increase sale prices of enslaved persons. On these shores, Native Americans comprised an array of more than five hundred ethnic, language, and cultural groups, a fact that proved to be advantageous to whites who used tribal enmities to further English, French, or Spanish territorial aims. There was, then, no such thing as "the Indian" or "the Negro," despite the propensity of white settlers to lump different ethnicities into a single pseudogroup—essentially inventing a "race" (an important point discussed further in chapter 5 in this volume).

It is important to distinguish between the slippery terms *race* and *ethnicity*. *Ethnicity* is a term and a concept that came into existence only recently as a new understanding of the nature of race began to evolve in the early to mid-twentieth century. Before that time people understood race largely in terms of supposedly unchanging biological as well as intellectual and moral traits. Guided by the notion that their white skin color and Christian religion made them inherently superior, "white" (meaning, basically, Anglo-American but not necessarily meaning southern or eastern Europeans) peoples generally categorized the rest of humanity as "black" (African), "yellow" (Asian), and other "colored" races that were assumed to be inferior by most measures. What we might now call "white ethnics" did that as well, claiming the category of "white" precisely by differentiating themselves from other "races"—even when those races might be phenotypically more "white"-skinned than they were. This process has been described in a number of recent works whose arguments are summarized in titles such as *How the Irish Became White*. For some Euro-Americans, in other words, learning how to be white—learning what it meant to be a "white American"—was part of the process of acculturation.

It also, of course, involved enacting racism. White Californians thus justified their violence and discrimination against Chinese and other Asian immigrants in the late nineteenth and early twentieth centuries. Claiming the Chinese were docile workers who threatened American ("white") labor, they persuaded Congress in 1882 to stop Chinese immigration through a series of Chinese Exclusion Acts. But there was more than just labor competition behind the "Chinese Question." Many Americans argued that Chinese Taoism, Confucianism, and other non-Christian religions polluted the American Christian landscape—were they not "the Heathen Chinee"? In much the same spirit, American Christians railed and rallied against the "Yellow Peril" they perceived in the arrival of Japanese and Asian Indians who introduced Buddhism, Hinduism, Sikhism, and other faith traditions into a nation where many people claimed superiority over others by virtue of their Christianity and whiteness; historically Americans of European heritage set themselves apart and above "colored" peoples at least partly because of their religion and "race."

Into the early twentieth century, however, the distinctions between white and nonwhite and between race and ethnicity were far from clear and raised the important question of who could expect to become full-fledged Americans. In the early 1920s two Supreme Court decisions dashed Asians' hopes for citizenship by declaring that they were not white and therefore ineligible for naturalization. In *Ozawa v. United States* (1922), Japanese-born Takao Ozawa had argued that his skin was "white," indeed "whiter than the average Italian, Spaniard or Portuguese." But the Court insisted that "white" meant "Caucasian" and that Ozawa belonged to the "Mongolian" (or "yellow") race. The very next year the Court rejected its own equation of "Caucasian" and "white." In *United States v. Thind* (1923), the Court denied citizenship to Bhagat Singh Thind, an Indian immigrant, ignoring the scientific community's classification of Indians as Caucasians and opting for a definition of whiteness based on what was "popularly known." In other words, the Court sided with what "the average man knows perfectly well," that a Caucasian was a northern or western European, not an Indian from the Punjab.

Other immigrants and even some native-born Americans found that the blurred line between race and ethnicity burdened their lives. For example, southern Italians, Mexicans, and Mexican Americans, although not denied citizenship, suffered widespread social ostracism and discrimination because of their racial "in-betweenness." As implied in the words of Takao Ozawa, Americans were suspicious about claims to whiteness made by southern Italians and Spaniards. Historically, northern and western Europeans and their American descendants looked down their nose at these southern Europeans, the so-called Mediterranean races, because of their proximity to Africa and their Catholicism. By extension, well into the twentieth century many Americans accepted the conventional wisdom that Mexicans and Mexican Americans, the descendants of Spaniards, Native Americans, and Africans in the New World, were a "mongrel" people who deserved segregated schools and public facilities largely because of the ambiguity of their ethnic identity.

Significantly, throughout history there have been peoples whose ethnic identity has fused with their religious beliefs and traditions. For these groups, their understanding of the cosmos and their place in it (their worldview) is so thoroughly enmeshed in religious beliefs and customs that they find it impossible to understand who they are apart from their faith; religion permeates their everyday life and outlook, making it an inextricable ingredient of a way of life and sense of peoplehood. Jewish immigrants are examples of this "ethnoreligion." Others have come close to this melding of ethnic and religious identity. For example, Americans of French Canadian, Irish, Polish, Mexican, and Italian backgrounds continue their historical ties to Roman Catholicism. Similarly, Serbs and Greeks in the United States have almost always been Greek Orthodox, and Episcopalians and Quakers have tended to be of British ancestry. Ethnic and religious differences and conflicts were present from the outset, even before the multiplicity of Americans-to-be landed on these shores.

Precolonial Era

In order to appreciate the importance of ethnicity and religion in U.S. history, we must understand some of the divisions and conflicts that were deeply rooted among Europeans and other peoples long before they reached the Americas. Even before Spain, England, and France were locked in their struggles for control of the New World, ethnic and religious conflict had already shaped their peoples' attitudes toward one another. Europeans crossed the Atlantic with these bitter memories and rivalries intact. The emphasis here on ethnoreligious conflict is not meant to downplay other sources of conflict, for certainly political and economic motives overlapped with religious ones. Still, religious intolerance and ethnic hatreds helped to mold attitudes, and that legacy played itself out in the Americas.

In some cases, to refer to ethnoreligious "tensions" or "differences" between these groups is to put it too mildly; some of them despised one another —and with good reason. Take, for example, the tragic history of relations between the Irish and the English. Today's ongoing "troubles" in Northern Ireland stem from conflict rooted far back in time. The efforts of Saint Patrick and others to establish Christianity in Ireland in the fifth century were partly undone by the Viking invasions that began in the late eighth century. The Norsemen spurred a rebirth of paganism, and thus there were many Gaelic-speaking "natives" to reach in 1155, when Pope Adrian IV issued his bull empowering King Henry II of England (1154–89) to conquer Ireland and convert its inhabitants to Christianity. Pope Adrian would have the Christian king extend "the right faith" to the Irish, whom he felt needed it "for the restraint of vice, for the correction of morals and the introduction of virtues." In return the pope expected Irish gratitude and pliancy. "And may the people of that land receive thee with honour, and venerate thee as their master," he wrote to Henry.

We know that the Irish indeed embraced Christianity, becoming among the most fervent of devotees of the Catholic faith. But despite a shared religion, relations between the Irish and English were hardly built on honor and veneration. Instead, the brutal treatment the British meted out to their subjects over the next five centuries ensured the rooting of abiding hatreds and fed the fire of Irish resistance to political and economic enslavement. Eventually even the balm of a common religion was lost when England became Protestant and Ireland remained Catholic. From that point on, whatever restraint a common religion might have imposed on master and subject was forever lost, and the Irish added religious persecution to their woes as British subjects. Historian James Olson perfectly captured these developments and their impact:

> In Ireland, after centuries of Anglo-Protestant persecution, religion and nationality fused. Indeed, the Gaelic word *Sassenach* meant both "Protestant" and "English." The attempt to anglicize Ireland created a dualism in Irish life: a deep, personal reverence for Roman Catholicism and a proud consciousness of Irish nationality. Members of the Irish Catholic clergy, like most of their parishioners, were poor, landless, and politically impotent. A siege mentality possessed both priests and peasants, and the Irish identified with the church as the central institution of their lives.

The die was cast for future relations between English Protestant and Irish Catholic settlers in the British North American colonies.

There were also long-standing conflicts in southern Europe. In the early eighth century, Muslim armies from North Africa conquered most of the Iberian Peninsula, overrunning Christian kingdoms that later became the nations of Portugal and Spain. To the routed Iberians, the "Moors" were "enemies of God," "infidels" (or unbelievers) who dared to deny Christianity's authority, claiming theirs' was the final truth revealed by God. Christians portrayed Islam as a religion of the sword, and they attributed the most vicious traits to its followers. "Unclean" they were called, wicked men with an unbridled lust for Christian lands and women. Those attitudes propelled Christians into the furious holy wars against the hated Muslims. By the end of the twelfth century the Iberians had recovered half of the peninsula, and in 1492 they defeated the last Arab stronghold, Granada. Flush with victory and confident of the righteousness of their cause, the Spanish soon revealed their obsession with *limpieza de sangre*, or purity of blood, moving immediately to cleanse their lands of those who had defiled their corner of Christendom for eight centuries. The Catholic monarchs, Ferdinand and Isabella, first "encouraged" Muslims to convert to Christianity, but in 1502 Isabella ordered their expulsion. Victory over the Muslims steeled the Spanish for future encounters with dark-skinned "others" in the Americas. It also fortified their ardent Catholicism, which, much like Irish Catholicism, had melded with their growing sense of nationhood in the cauldron of religious and political warfare.

During the High Middle Ages European Christians despised Muslims, but they showed particular contempt for Jews. Before Isabella expelled the Muslims, she drove out most of Spain's two hundred thousand professed Jews in 1492. But she was actually late to the game; for at least two centuries other Europeans had been zealously persecuting and spreading malicious lies about the so-called Christ-killers. It had not always been so. Generally, Christians had tolerated the Jews' presence throughout Europe until the eleventh and twelfth centuries. But the thirteenth century saw intolerance escalate into fanatical hatred and violence. Eventually, Christians' desire for ethnic purity led them into ethnic cleansing. Crusaders on their way to fight the infidel in the Holy Land took time to drive out Jews from towns along the way.

Age-old hatreds among Christians, Muslims, and Jews are somewhat easier to understand than the violence unleashed by the Protestant Reformation. The Reformation ripped apart Western Christendom's unity after Martin Luther rejected the teachings and practices of the Holy Roman Church in 1517. Catholic monarchs countered Luther's efforts to reform Christianity with fierce repression of his movement, Lutheranism, and the splinter movements to which it gave birth. Consequently, throughout Europe untold numbers of Christians died imposing or resisting one another's interpretation of God's will. And so ethnic and religious conflict deeply etched itself in the collective memories of Europeans. At times the brutality of the religious wars made some wonder where their religious zeal had taken them. A German writer remarked in 1650: "Lutheran, popish [Catholic], and Calvinistic, we've got all these beliefs here; but there is some doubt about where Christianity has got to." Newcomers to America would also wonder.

Colonial North America

The Spanish were the first permanent European colonizers in the New World, but they never had a free hand in exploiting the fact that they were the first on the scene. The New World's riches quickly attracted colonists from Spain's rivals, and with that the whole gamut of European ethnic and religious conflict spilled onto American shores.

As early as the 1530s the French began to prey on Spanish galleons making their way through the Florida Straits bound for Spain with silver and gold. "Corsarios luteranos!" railed the Spaniards—Lutheran pirates! Not surprisingly, the Spanish had a special contempt for these Huguenots (as French Protestants were known) who sometimes killed priests and defiled churches. In all likelihood these Caribbean marauders probably thought little about religion as they went about their business of plundering. But in the eyes of the Spanish these particular pirates were doubly cursed because they were *Protestant* pirates; they not only attacked the Spaniards' ships and outposts but also threatened to infect "their" American Eden with the cancer of Protestantism. For Spain's King Philip II, Protestantism was treason, punishable by death. His orders were clear: show no mercy to the "Protestant devils."

By the 1560s, Huguenots were looking for places in the Americas to escape from the prejudice and violence they faced in France. Some had tried but failed to establish colonies in Brazil and Canada. In Florida they finally succeeded. In 1564 an initial group of 150 Huguenots built Fort Caroline near present-day Jacksonville. Later some three hundred more hopefuls arrived. The colony settled into a routine, and the future seemed promising. But Spanish steel quickly put an end to the Huguenots' dreams of a haven in Florida. Forty miles south of Fort Caroline, the veteran soldier Pedro Menéndez de Avilés founded St. Augustine on September 8, 1565, and then quickly set out in pursuit of the Huguenots, eager to strike a blow against the "evil Lutheran sect." His army surprised the French colony at dawn on September 20. The Catholic avengers spared women and children, but not so more than 130 Huguenot men, who awakened to a fate worse than any nightmare. A survivor later wrote that "awful outcries and groans arose from those who were being slaughtered." The Spaniards had struck when the Huguenots' main fighting force was away chasing Spanish ships. Again, luck eluded the French Protestants. Shipwrecked near St. Augustine, the survivors surrendered to Menéndez, who promised to do as God instructed him. Menéndez ordered the remaining 150 or more men "put to the knife," and, with that, the Spanish rubbed out Protestantism in Florida. "I do this, not as to Frenchmen, but as to Lutherans," Menéndez later stated. Like his king, the hard-bitten captain believed it was his duty to annihilate the heretic. In Spanish eyes, such bloody but righteous blows were justified against an evil people whose beliefs were "probably Satanic in origin."

Indeed, as Europeans of different ethnic and religious backgrounds began to cross paths in North America, the ugly ghost of intolerance haunted them. In some places, unwanted groups were hounded by discriminatory laws and practices, but in some cases individuals paid much more dearly for being too "different" and uncompromising about their identity and way of life. The earliest British colony, Virginia, wasted little time in legislating against "popery," or Roman Catholicism. A law of 1641 barred Catholics from holding public office there, and any "popish priest" who might find himself in Virginia would be given five days to leave. Anxious to keep Quakers away, too, Virginians passed a law in 1660 to prohibit sea captains from bringing Quakers to their shores. Quakers had a hard time of it in New England, also, where Puritans mercilessly persecuted them as well as anyone else who dared to express different religious views. Massachusetts Puritans believed that Quakers were leading people into damnation, so they took serious steps to quiet them —encouraging them to leave by branding them, boring holes in their tongues, cutting off their ears, and hanging at least four of them.

Of course, prejudice was an equal opportunity disease in the New World, not a monopoly of the British colonists. Authorities in Dutch-controlled New Amsterdam, for instance, tried to bar Jews. In the 1650s, the Dutch Reformed minister Johannes Megapolensis railed against "these godless rascals," who he claimed had "no other God than the unrighteous Mammon, and no other aim than to get possession of christian property." Meanwhile, Governor Peter Stuyvesant, who found the Jews "very repugnant," did everything he could to make their lives miserable. Stuyvesant made it hard for Jews to buy homes or even find a place to bury their dead, despite orders from his superiors to tolerate the Jews' presence. The Dutch in New Amsterdam also chafed at the presence of Puritans, Lutherans, Mennonites, and, of course, Catholics, the most despised group of all. In this intolerant climate, Catholics carved out their own religious space when they established the colony of Maryland in 1634. Significantly, they did something no other colony was willing to do, guarantee religious freedom to others. But even theirs was a qualified tolerance; Maryland's Toleration Act of 1649 extended freedom of religion only to those who believed in the divinity of Christ, not to Jews.

Feelings of cultural superiority also fed the tensions and prejudice that characterized life in the colonies. Some seventeenth- and eighteenth-century Europeans were becoming strongly nationalistic; that is, they were developing a fiercely patriotic identification with emerging nation-states such as England and Spain. Their nationalism and ethnocentrism, or deep preference for "their own kind," largely explains why, for example, Britons loathed Spaniards and vice versa. In 1753, Benjamin Franklin worried that too many non-English people were coming to America. The large influx of Germans particularly disturbed Franklin, who considered them "the most ignorant Stupid Sort of their own Nation." Why, he asked, should they "be suffered to swarm into our settlements, and by herding together establish their languages and manners to the exclusion of ours?" Franklin feared that his beloved Pennsylvania would "become a colony of *Aliens*, who will shortly be so numerous as to Germanize us instead of our Anglifying them." In a similar vein, Scots-Irish Presbyterians found no welcome mat when they migrated to the frontier regions of Pennsylvania, Virginia, and the Carolinas. The Church of England had long lorded it over the Scottish Presbyterians of Ulster Province, in Northern Ireland, making their lives so difficult that huge numbers began migrating to America in the early 1700s. There the established British Anglicans looked down their nose at them. Charles Lee, for example, ridiculed the Virginia frontier where the Ulster immigrants were clustered as a "Macocracy," a place overrun with "banditti of low Scotch-Irish whose names usually begin with Mac."

Charles Woodmason echoed these attitudes. A Church of England missionary in the Carolina backcountry in the mid-1700s, Woodmason found the Scots-Irish Presbyterians thoroughly disgusting. The feeling was mutual, Woodmason discovered. The Anglican missionary complained that the Scots-Irish Presbyterians constantly harassed him and interfered with his missionary work any way they could. At various times, Woodmason claimed, they purposely misdirected people who asked for directions to his services; stole his keys; herded dozens of howling dogs around his windows during services; or yelled and howled outside his meetinghouse themselves. The frustrated preacher reported that the Scottish Presbyterians even hired some local goons to "invite" him to leave, "telling him they wanted no 'Damned Black Gown Sons of Bitches' among them."

Clearly, many colonists linked ethnicity and religion, and this had explosive implications, for just as emerging nations vied for dominance in Europe, so too their colonists fought for political and economic control in the New World. And nowhere was this struggle more clearly drawn along religious and ethnic lines than between European Protestants and Spanish Catholics who claimed a strip of territory that stretched from Florida to California. At this point we should note a very important development, the rise of *la leyenda negra*, or the Black Legend, in order to appreciate more fully the experiences of U.S. Latino Catholics.

In a nutshell, the Black Legend was the belief among Anglo-Americans that Spaniards were, in historian David Weber's words, "unusually cruel, avaricious, treacherous, fanatical, superstitious, cowardly, corrupt, decadent, indolent, and authoritarian," the key word here being "unusually." Like so much that colored North American colonists' perceptions and attitudes, this anti-Spanish myth was rooted in their strife-ridden European heritage. It was a product of the European, especially British, propaganda mills, an expression of the Protestants' intense hatred of the militantly Catholic Spanish, and part of the Europeans' cultural baggage. *La leyenda negra*, like other myths, contained some truth. Spanish soldiers *did* commit atrocities in the wars against Europe's Protestant heretics, and indeed they savagely subjugated the Indians of the New World. But, ironically, it was a Spaniard, Bartolomé de las Casas, who provided so much of the grist for the propaganda mills. His impassioned pleas in defense of the Indians found a wide audience all over Europe and gave the British and others plenty of ammunition with which to snipe self-righteously at the Spanish. Ignoring their own savagery—hangings and burnings of religious dissenters and their vicious repression of the Irish, for example—the English had a field day promoting Hispanophobia among people in Europe and the colonies, most of whom had never even seen a Spaniard. Take Cotton Mather, the prominent Congregationalist minister, for instance. Foreshadowing the attitudes of many who later would come into contact with the Spaniards' descendants in Texas and the Southwest, Mather wrote a religious tract hoping to "open their eyes and be converted . . . away from Satan and to God."

In the meantime, Spaniards were consolidating an empire to the south and west of the emerging thirteen British colonies. In the area that later became Texas and the American Southwest (as throughout Latin America), the Spanish mixed with the indigenous peoples to create a new mestizo, or mixed-race, society. Northern Europeans usually cringed at the mere thought of miscegenation, or the biological mixing of the races. Actually, in their eyes the Spanish were already suspect because of their long coexistence with the Muslims in the Iberian Peninsula. When Americans later encountered mestizo Catholics in the early nineteenth century, their ethnic ambiguity complicated the story of ethnicity and religion in America. Meanwhile, ethnoreligious diversity in the thirteen British colonies continued to play important roles as the colonists edged toward an "American" identity and nationhood.

Revolutionary and Early Republican America

In the years leading to the American Revolution, the colonists saw themselves locked in a struggle between good and evil. King George III's representatives in America—the American tax collectors, governors, and other enforcers of British power—were the devil's pawns. Significantly, the colonists drew on their old anti-Catholic sentiments to define and express their emerging Anglo-*American* Protestant identity.

The most telling custom that evolved in the 1760s and 1770s to promote Anglo-American ethno-Protestantism was the annual Pope's Day celebrations, which the colonists staged on November 5 to affirm their loyalty to the Protestant Reformation and their hatred of all things Catholic. On Pope's Day thousands of people would pour into the streets of Boston, Newport, and other cities for a day of elaborate processions and gleeful burnings and hangings of effigies of the twin "evils" (the pope and the devil). But it would be a mistake to see the Pope's Day celebrations as simply a reflection of religious bigotry. In the 1760s and 1770s the familiar Catholic pope of the celebrations became a British "pope" that symbolized the "devilish" King George. The Pope's Day effigies clearly linked the devil, the pope, and such "evils" as the Sugar Act, Stamp Act, and Quebec Act. Increasingly estranged from continental Britons, the American colonists began to see themselves as a separate people. Religion was at the center of this shifting ethnic consciousness and nation building. The colonists appropriated the anti-Catholic Pope's Day celebrations to vent their political frustrations and define themselves as American Protestants. In turn, this sharpened their emerging sense of peoplehood as they began to form their own nation.

While these colonists of English descent were reshaping their identity, other European settlers in British North America were trying to hold on to their distinct cultures. Throughout the late 1700s and early 1800s, ethnicity and religion entwined to produce a sense of separateness among non-English peoples who wanted to preserve little pockets of Europe in America. Germans, for example, tended to stay to themselves, trying to avoid all but the most necessary contact with English-speaking colonists and their institutions. Germans simply wanted to be left alone to farm their lands and live a life rooted in their own language and religion. But in Pennsylvania some Germans' religious beliefs rubbed their English-speaking neighbors the wrong way. In addition to large numbers of Reformed and Lutheran Germans, some pacifist groups, Mennonites, Amish, Moravians, and others, had settled in Pennsylvania. English-speaking Pennsylvanians took a dim view of anyone who refused to take up arms. Colonists who lived on the ever dangerous frontier during the French and Indian War (1756–63) and later when war with England loomed were especially suspicious of the pacifists and questioned Germans' loyalty to the British Crown. The Germans' refusal to learn English and their large numbers—by the 1760s they constituted about one-third of Pennsylvania's population—made Benjamin Franklin and other Anglo-Americans a bit nervous.

In this context of distrust of "outsiders," some influential English churchmen devised a scheme to Anglicize the "Palatine Boors." The plan actually evolved from efforts among German Reformed ministers to provide more pastors and teachers for their co-religionists in Pennsylvania. Unable to raise the needed funds, the German ministers appealed to prominent British Anglicans and Presbyterians, who took up the campaign but added an assimilationist twist to it: Why not use the opportunity to mold German children into good, loyal British subjects? Under the guidance of a London group called the Society for the Propagating of Christian Knowledge among the Germans, the plan called for setting up twenty-five charity schools in German communities. Even though the free schools intended to use a bilingual approach, it was obvious that the ultimate aim was to have the German children adopt the English language and English ways. German critics saw in the plan no humanitarian concern for the religious needs in their communities; rather, they charged that the whole idea was a "purely political matter" driven by nativist fears. The English "care very little either for the religion or for the cultivation of the Germans," a German asserted, adding that "this was done out of fear, so that the multitude of Germans do not make themselves into a separate people and in a war with France join them to the damage of the English nation." The charity schools never really got off the ground, and the project was abandoned in 1763—to some degree because of resistance by the Germans and lack of funds but more so because nativist sentiment abated somewhat after the Germans proved their loyalty to the British in the just-ended French and Indian War.

Given their neighbors' distrust of them, it was not unnatural for Germans to keep to themselves. But other reasons help to explain why Germans resisted Americanization and clung to their Germanness well into the nineteenth century. Many English-speaking colonists saw the Germans as dull-witted "country bumpkins." As one German complained, "The 'superior nations' look upon the Germans as nothing but wig-blocks, which are thick and hard, to be sure, but wanting brains." But more important, Germans, like most other people, simply preferred their own culture and ways over those of others. In an environment that was physically demanding and often hostile, Germans found strength in the familiar, in a tight-knit culture based on a rural way of life with language and religion at its center. And so Germans clustered, primarily in Pennsylvania, western Maryland, upstate New York, and New Jersey. Their communities solidified around family farms envied as the most productive in America. In these rural enclaves they built schools and churches to pass on their cultural values and religious beliefs in their own language; kept their children close by helping them buy nearby farmlands; and almost always married among themselves.

Germans spoke numerous dialects from their homelands, the High German dialects of Alsace, Bavaria, Austria, and Switzerland as well as Low German dialects such as Dutch, Flemish, Friesian, and Prussian. They also professed different (mostly) Protestant faiths. The largest traditions were the Lutheran and Reformed, and about 10 percent of Pennsylvania's Germans on the eve of the American Revolution were Amish, Mennonites, Dunkers (German Baptists), Moravians, Schwenkfelders, and other pietists. Yet the differences between them did not prevent them from banding together. In fact, their "outsider" status reminded them of the common elements of their Germanness; they did, after all, share a common language for church services— High German—and they were mostly Protestant (Catholics in significant numbers would arrive later in the nineteenth century).

In Pennsylvania and other colonies Germans tried hard to replicate the world they had left behind. By the early 1800s, however, the pressures of assimilation began to show—Germans began to marry non-Germans, and church records and services in English became more common. But just as this trend began, the first wave of a flood of German immigration appeared, a great migration that would bring more than five million Germans to the United States over the course of the next century. For the time being, however, Germans would continue to be a distinct thread in the ethnic and religious fiber of the young nation.

Antebellum Nineteenth Century

The United States changed significantly in the decades before the Civil War. For one thing, the rising tide of immigration in the 1820s became a virtual flood in the 1840s and 1850s, when some 4.2 million newcomers arrived. About 75 percent of these immigrants were from Ireland and various German provinces, and the majority of them were Catholics. In Ireland a catastrophic potato famine in the latter half of the 1840s killed a million people and forced another million to flee, penniless. In contrast, most of the Germans were fairly prosperous farmers and craftsmen. Another factor responsible for change was the wars with Mexico, which added another one million square miles of land as the nation's borders reached the Pacific Ocean, fulfilling in some minds a God-given destiny. Americans cheered as the young nation flexed its muscles, but many found the shifting ethnic and religious landscape troubling. Catholics became the largest denomination by 1850, and by 1865 they numbered some 3.5 million. Native-born Protestants feared this change and tried desperately to keep the United States an English-speaking Protestant nation.

As more Catholic immigrants arrived, religious newspapers issued dire warnings. Protestants began organizing societies, such as the New York Protestant Association (1832) and the American Society to Promote the Principles of the Protestant Reformation (1840), to "educate" Americans about the nature of Catholicism, at least as they saw it. The American Society's constitution did not mince words. Catholicism was "totally irreconcilable with the gospel of Christ; liberty of conscience; the rights of man; and with the constitution and laws of the United States," the preamble stated, adding that "Romanism" was "endangering the peace and freedom of our country." To allay any doubts about who the "real" Christians were, the society pledged "to convert the Papists to Christianity."

Newspaper articles, religious tracts, flyers, cartoons, and novels spread the venomous message that Catholics could never be good citizens because of their loyalty to the pope. The pope (who many Protestants believed was really Satan's emissary) was conspiring with Europe's "Despotic States" to subvert the American Republic, the nativists screamed. And the pope's "legions," his loyal parishioners and their priests and nuns, would do his bidding to bring about America's demise. The influential clergyman Lyman Beecher warned, "A tenth part of the suffrage of the nation, thus condensed and wielded by the Catholic powers of Europe, might decide our elections, perplex our policy, inflame and divide the nation, break the bond of our union, and throw down our free institutions." Various images reflected these insecurities. Political cartoons depicted drunken Irish and German immigrants rioting at the polls during elections. Similarly, a flyer captioned "The Aim of Pope Pius IX" presented a menacing pontiff defiantly trampling the American flag, one hand holding a crumpled American Constitution while the other plunged his pastoral staff-turned-sword into the breast of a lifeless American eagle at his feet. That flyer was an advertisement for the Reverend Isaac

Kelso's anti-Catholic novel *Danger in the Dark*. Kelso's novel was typical nativist reading fare in the mid-1800s.

In 1836, however, Maria Monk's *Awful Disclosures of the Hotel Dieu Nunnery of Montreal* gave Americans what they wanted—a titillating peek at the "awful" goings-on in convents. In the style of the time, the author intimated more than she explicitly described. But she left no doubt about what she *claimed* was going on. Behind the cloistered walls priests and nuns shamelessly violated their vows of celibacy, Monk wrote. Worse yet, nuns who resisted "usage" by the priests were killed, along with infants born from those perverted unions. (Of course, babies were properly baptized before their quick burial!) Purportedly written by an escaped nun, *Awful Disclosures* was pure fantasy and shown to be so at the time. Still, it was a blockbuster, selling more than three hundred thousand copies before the Civil War. But more important, the book fanned the fire of religious bigotry, helping to create a climate ripe for violence.

And indeed violence against immigrants erupted periodically in the 1830s, 1840s, and 1850s. Most of it was aimed at the Irish, since not all Germans were Catholics and few were as desperately bedraggled as the majority of the Irish, who had arrived "looking almost like skeletons." The Irish, then, bore the brunt of violence largely because of who they were—their Irishness and their Catholicism marked them as outsiders and made them easy targets. In 1834 a mob in Charlestown, Massachusetts, evicted the Ursuline nuns and their schoolchildren and then ransacked and burned down their convent. The climate turned even uglier in the 1840s and 1850s as political nativism combined with ethnic and religious bigotry to create a deadly mix. Anti-immigrant "American" political parties began forming in the 1840s, and by the mid-1850s the powerful Know-Nothing Party seemed poised to crush the influence of "foreigners." In 1844 rumors that Catholics refused to read the required Protestant version of the Bible in public schools touched off several days of rioting in Philadelphia, leaving thirteen dead and more than fifty wounded. In 1855 a Louisville newspaper exhorted Know-Nothings to keep Catholics from voting in local elections: "Rally to put down an organization of Jesuit Bishops, Priests, and other Papists, who aim . . . to sap the foundations of all our political edifices," the writer raved. "So go ahead Know-Nothings, and raise just as big a storm as you please." And indeed they did. "Bloody Monday" claimed more than twenty lives, most of them immigrants, and hundreds were injured in rioting at the polls.

Of course, deadly violence and full-blown riots were not daily occurrences. More common was a low-intensity warfare. "Native" Americans conducted economic war through ethnically restrictive hiring policies, exemplified by the appearance of "Irish Need Not Apply" signs at business establishments. In myriad ways—minor altercations, disparaging remarks, hateful looks— nativists reminded immigrants that they were a despised people. Their outsider status set them apart, no doubt, but it is important to understand that there was also a conscious side to the immigrants' separateness. Immigrants did not want to give up their identity, so they clung to those things that most deeply defined them, especially religion and language. Thus, despite the tensions with native-born Americans, and indeed because of them, immigrants were able to carve a space for themselves. In other words, they used their outsider status to preserve an identity of their own choosing. Separateness proclaimed to immigrants and others who they were and what they believed; it was an assertion of a sense of peoplehood and a way to make a place for themselves in their new environment.

The Irish, for example, settled primarily in the cities and began to try to re-create the way of life they had left behind. By pooling their meager resources, families and even entire villages chain-migrated and settled together in American cities. They then built their own churches, schools, confraternities, aid societies, orphanages, hospitals, and other institutions to guard against Protestant influences and preserve their ethnoreligious identity. At the center of it all was the Catholic Church. The Irish quickly became a major influence in the church through their loyalty to their clergy, their willingness to provide sons and daughters for religious training, and their sheer numbers. At midcentury they approached the near-monopoly control with which they would shape the future of Catholicism in the United States.

Far from the Irish urban villages, expansionism brought Americans increasingly into contact with Mexican Catholics in the Southwest. In the Mexicans' case, however, the border crossed *them*—three times—as a result of the Texas Rebellion (1836), the Mexican War (1848), and the Gadsden Purchase (1853). The first encounters took place in the 1820s in Mexican Texas, where Americans accepted generous land grants in exchange for their sworn loyalty to Mexico and Catholicism. But Americans were loath to live under foreign rule, especially Catholic, and soon a flood of American "illegal aliens" wrested control of Texas from Mexico. Often they used religious imagery in revealing their intentions. Stephen F. Austin, who brought the first legal Americans into Texas, declared that he immediately became obsessed with "redeeming" Texas from the "wilderness," thus rhetorically equating himself with Moses. Many Americans equated Texas with savagery, a wild place inhabited by primitive people—Native Americans and Mexicans. But its bountiful lands made it a wilderness that could be "saved" for Christianity and civilization, expansionists contended, if only the right people controlled it. Thus Secretary of State Henry Clay asked, "By what race should Texas be peopled?" Certainly it should not remain a place where "the Inquisition and superstition" reigned, he urged. Religious and ethnic animosity went hand in glove with American nation building.

Americans brought to Texas and the Southwest attitudes tainted by the Black Legend. Mexicans embodied the most repugnant traits many Americans mistakenly attributed to nonwhite peoples—the licentiousness of the African, the bloodthirstiness of the Native American, and the cold-bloodedness of that "questionable" European, the Spaniard. The Mexicans' Catholicism further compounded their stigma as a "mongrel" people. Americans in Texas railed against "Popish superstition and despotism." Recalling the claim that Catholics could not be good Americans, Austin decried, "Rome! Rome! Until the Mexican people shake off thy superstitions & wicked sects, they can neither be a republican, nor a moral people." This boded ill not only for *tejanos* (Texas Mexicans) but also for Mexican Americans throughout the Southwest. Hispanophobia echoed as Americans moved westward after 1848. Missionaries favored the word *benighted* to describe the religious world of the *hispanos* (Mexican Americans in New Mexico). Appalled, missionaries denounced as "barbarities" the whipping and other self-mortification practices they found among some Catholics. In California, meanwhile, nativists replaced church crosses with American flags, and newspapers dripped with disdain for Catholicism. One editorial implied that building a new Catholic church was not a sign of progress but "a retrogression toward the medieval age."

The editor's choice of words here is significant, for indeed, what Mexicans practiced was medieval Catholicism, or western Christianity, the faith western Europeans shared before they split into Protestants and Catholics. The Spanish planted this age-old faith tradition in the New World, and in the Southwest it became Mexican American Catholicism. Meanwhile, the Council of Trent (1545–63) gave rise to a new form of Catholicism in western Europe, Tridentine Catholicism (from the Latin *Tridentum*, for the city of Trent, Italy), which was destined to become the style of the overwhelming majority of Catholics in the United States. These two traditions differed fundamentally. Tridentine Catholicism was a modernized and intellectualized Catholicism. It emphasized doctrinal knowledge; required strict church attendance and adherence to church-approved practices; and separated the sacred from the secular, "real" religion from superstition, and "important" religious expression from "quaint" customs. In contrast, pre-Tridentine Catholicism did not compartmentalize the sacred and the secular; daily life, religion, superstition, and magic all overlapped; its followers worried little about theology; and there was an emphasis on emotional expression and celebration through pilgrimages, saint veneration, and feasts.

Mexican Americans clung to their pre-Tridentine Catholicism just as tenaciously as the Irish did to their more "modern" version. It was their anchor in a hostile world, and it defined and sustained their communities, so they were not about to abandon it easily. Thus American society splintered further over ethnic and religious differences as the nation grew, revealing tensions both among and within faith traditions.

Postbellum and Industrial Nineteenth Century

Immigration reached unprecedented levels between the Civil War and World War I, bringing dramatic changes in its wake. Most newcomers were eastern and southern Europeans, quite different in language and religion from old-stock Americans. Between 1880 and 1910, 8.4 million Russians, Poles, Slovaks, Greeks, Hungarians, Lithuanians, Italians, and many other groups came from the Mediterranean and Slavic regions. Besides these "new" immigrants, large numbers of Asians and Mexicans arrived in the second half of the 1800s and early 1900s. Asians—represented in 1880 by some 100,000 Chinese and, by the early 1920s, 180,000 Japanese and 6,400 Indians—brought such distinctive non-Christian religions as Confucianism, Taoism, Shinto, Buddhism, Hinduism, Sikhism, and, to a lesser degree, Islam. Mexicans were Catholics, but their style did not fit the American mold, making them a problem in the eyes of the church leaders. As immigrants and native-born Americans confronted and accommodated each other, ethnicity and religion revealed the cleavages inherent in America's manyness as well as the basis for community building among the outsiders.

The Jewish experience illustrates the complexity of ethnic and religious pluralism in postbellum and industrial America. By the late nineteenth century, American Jewry was mostly of German background, English-speaking, and prosperous. Jews had successfully blended into society partly because anti-Semitism, or prejudice against Jews, had not yet surfaced in a major way. But equally important was their acceptance of a "modernizing" and "Americanizing" mentality, an outlook that prized material *and* religious progress, materialism itself, individuality, and strong patriotism. Established Jews revealed some of this outlook in their preference for Reform Judaism, a radical new interpretation of the ancient Jewish religion. Leaders of the Reform movement insisted that Reform Judaism was a "progressive religion, ever striving to be in accord with the postulates of reason," and not tied to the "primitive ideas" of traditional Judaism. Reform Jews altered or discarded centuries-old beliefs and practices: they abandoned segregation of men and women in worship; replaced Hebrew with English; ignored dietary laws; added organ music and choirs; and strove for "decorum" in worship. They began to act very much like America's Christian majority.

A flood of Orthodox Jews from eastern Europe, however, challenged all of this. Freed from the terror of Europe's pogroms (bloody massacres), these traditional Jews saw in America's freedom a chance to continue—not abandon—their ancient faith. Poverty-stricken, Yiddish-speaking, and easy to spot, they seemed the very embodiment of Europe's "wretched refuse" and "huddled masses" immortalized by poet Emma Lazarus. They embarrassed established status-conscious Jewish Americans, who ridiculed their "Medieval" and "half-civilized orthodoxy." Reform leader Isaac Mayer Wise prodded Orthodox Jews to become modern Americans. Rather than "gnaw the dead bones of past centuries," it was "high time for them to understand that they live in America." But Orthodox Jews wanted only to obey the ancient laws (or Torah) and preserve the old ways; Americanization could be fatal, they feared.

The novel *The Rise of David Levinsky* (1917) revealed those fears. When the novel's central character announces he will immigrate to the United States, a fellow Russian Jew is dismayed: "To America! Lord of the World! But one becomes a Gentile there." Levinsky comes to the United States to become a rabbi, but he abandons his dream and his religion for material success instead. "The striking thing was that it was not a world of piety," Levinsky noted about the United States. In America, Orthodox dress, decorum, and diet went out the window as America's freedom transformed the émigré. "If you are a Jew of the [Orthodox] type to which I belonged when I came to New York and you attempt to bend your religion to the spirit of your new surroundings, it breaks. It falls to pieces. The very clothes I wore and the very food I ate had a fatal effect on my religious habits." Reform Jews daily reminded the Orthodox of what they might become; thus they resented Americanizers and fought Americanization. In turn, they often felt the sting of rabid anti-Semitism, particularly at the hands of a revived Ku Klux Klan in the early twentieth century.

Out of these two polar visions arose Conservative Judaism, a compromise. Conservative Judaism aimed to keep the essentials of Judaism but alter some practices to be more in line with prevailing attitudes about religion in a modern society. Conservative Jews, in other words, were anxious to fit into American society, but they were unwilling to surrender what was unique about their Jewishness. Rabbi Solomon Schechter declared, "There is nothing in American citizenship which is incompatible with our observing the dietary laws, our sanctifying the Sabbath, our fixing a Mezuzah (a small Hebrew prayer) on our doorposts, our refraining from unleavened bread on Passover, or our perpetuating any other law essential to the preservation of Judaism." Not "a single iota of our Torah" needed to be sacrificed for inclusion in American society, Conservative Jews insisted. Thus American Jews, Orthodox, Reformed, and Conservative, contested the meaning of Judaism and being Jewish in the United States. Freedom of worship could unite, but it could also create division and conflict, both among themselves and with others.

Catholics also fought among themselves. Immigrants so closely associated language, religion, and ethnic identity that their demands threatened to tear apart the church. In the late nineteenth and early twentieth centuries, the numerous Catholic immigrant groups all clamored to worship exclusively with people and clergy of their own kind and in their own languages. This created a major headache for the church leadership, given that between 1820 and 1920 the languages used in the church grew from three to twenty-eight. For most immigrants the parish was the center of their lives, and they wanted it to reflect those things they associated with their own identity—*their* language, *their* saints, *their* liturgy. Rather than risk losing them, the Catholic leadership relented and established nationality-based rather than territorial parishes, that is, parishes in which membership was determined by language rather than by the usual geographical boundaries, which mixed ethnicities. Normally, there were several immigrant groups in the same neighborhood, and each Little Italy or Little Poland had its own parish. Thus one could find an Irish church only a few blocks away from a German one, which was near a Czech one, and so forth. At the same time, the bishops who ruled over the parishes were nearly always Irish, leading to conflicts and misunderstandings about which practices constituted "true" Catholicism. In the eyes of Irish American church officials, the elaborate public festas of Italian Catholics smacked of paganism. The immigrants linked ethnic identity and parish so strongly that, when asked where they were from, they would answer not with a neighborhood name but with the name of their parish, a typical Old World practice. Some groups did not yield on their demand for separateness. A significant number of Poles eventually split from the American Roman Catholic Church and formed their own Polish National Catholic Church in 1904; in 1906 Lithuanians established their national church, and Slovaks formed a few independent parishes in the early twentieth century.

Eastern-rite Catholics represented a deeper division among Catholics. In the year 1054 the Christian church had split into two separate churches, the Western Church (under Rome) and the Eastern Orthodox Church (under Constantinople, or modern-day Istanbul). As their name indicates, Orthodox Christians (also generally referred to as Greek Orthodox) claimed theirs was the "correct" form of Christianity. Influenced for centuries by Muslim culture, they followed a "less legalistic and more mystical" form of Christianity and were under the spiritual guidance of one of several "patriarchs" often located in the capital city of their former homelands. Orthodox Christians came to the United States by the tens of thousands in the late nineteenth and early twentieth centuries and in seemingly endless variety—Russians, Greeks, Albanians, Ukrainians, Serbians, Syrians, Bulgarians, Romanians, and others. They settled mostly in the coal-mining regions and industrial centers of the Northeast, where the Roman Catholic Church tried to incorporate them. But the differences—not only religious customs but also the presence of married clergy and disagreements over ownership of parish property—were just too great. In 1891 some 225,000 Ukrainians left the Roman Church and joined the Russian Orthodox Church. By the start of World War I the distinctive onion-shaped domes of Orthodox churches graced many cityscapes. Like Orthodox Jews, Eastern-rite Catholics found community and sustenance in their struggles to remain distinct.

Americanization and modernization also tore at Protestants. As with Catholics, the language issue proved divisive. "Language saves the faith," immigrants insisted, so rather than form a single American Lutheran Church, Lutherans from Germany, Sweden, Norway, Denmark, Iceland, and Finland all went their separate ways. Some Danish congregants reflected the depth of their feelings when they referred to their church's shift to English as "the English disease." Again, American freedom and the individualistic nature of the society tended to erode Old World standards of hierarchical male authority in churches and families. For example, the audacity of parishioners often shocked European pastors. When a minister sternly reminded his congregants that the Almighty had commanded him to take the helm at their church, a congregant remarked, "We are the ones who are paying him, not the Almighty." Despite their shared ethnicity, Americans pointedly reminded their immigrant clergy "to understand that they were in a new country and a new environment." Used to unquestioned authority, European clergy bemoaned the "bad habits" American freedom fostered, sometimes comparing their outspoken American congregations to disrespectful children. Lutheranism in the United States was like a "vivacious daughter . . . not as demure and considerate as her [European] mother." Feeling "so free" but "not yet used to her freedom," the daughter had formed bad habits, a clergyman lamented.

For the German Lutheran immigrants who formed the Missouri Synod, the basis of a good society was the belief that theirs' was the one true church and a strong patriarchal family, one in which a father's authority was supreme and the submission of wives and children was accepted as divinely ordained. Missouri Synod Lutherans believed that Lutherans who had arrived earlier and immersed themselves in American society had lost sight of these "corporatist" ideals and become victims of Americanization; they had all but lost their distinctiveness and become just "generic" Protestants, no longer members of the one true faith. To avoid the same fate, Missouri Synod Lutherans separated themselves from other people—people of other faiths and even non–Missouri Synod Lutherans—and from American institutions. They settled as much as possible among their own, setting up an extensive parochial school system, seminaries, and other church-related organizations to shield their faith, language, and corporatist way of life.

Thus Missouri Synod Lutherans both embraced and rejected America, most obviously by making it their home but resisting some of its "modern" values and the English language. Their efforts succeeded well into the twentieth century, but, like immigrant Jews, they paid a price. Their cocooned lives aroused suspicion. Preservation of the German language particularly invited the wrath of old-stock Americans who were beginning to form anti-immigration groups like the American Protective Association (1887). With America's entry into World War I against the German-led Axis Powers, violence flared against the Missouri Synod Lutherans. In late 1918, mobs burned down three Lutheran schools, in Kansas, Ohio, and Missouri. In the early twentieth century Americans still contested the nature of their society and who fully "belonged" to it and who did not. The German Lutheran, a critic wrote in the early twentieth century, was among those who had "never quite become a modern American."

Early Twentieth Century

In the early to mid-twentieth century, Americans of Mexican, Italian, and Japanese origin faced the challenge of being different in a nation that demanded cultural unity. The experiences of southern Italian Catholics and people of Mexican origin were remarkably similar; the Japanese American experience revealed the extreme hostility religious and ethnic differences could elicit from American "insiders," even as those differences strengthened the "outsiders."

Mexican American Catholics held to the basic tenets of Roman Catholicism, but most ignored strict churchgoing, mastery of doctrine, and other requirements that the church leadership demanded as measures of "true" Catholics. Mexican Catholics preferred their home- and community-based religious life. Their way of being Catholic included time-honored beliefs and practices, such as saint veneration, processions and pilgrimages, miracles, and magic, as well as selective participation in "formal" church activities and requirements. But their Catholicism drew constant criticism. A missionary reported: "If you ask a Mexican, 'Are you a Catholic?' he will answer: '*Sí, señor, yo soy muy católico,*' ('Yes, sir, I am a good Catholic'), and as proof he will show you a medal that he wears, or point to the brightly-colored pictures [of saints] which decorate the walls of his cottage." Clerics were dismayed at hearing Mexican parents say about their children: "O, sometimes they say a few prayers or light a candle before the picture of our favorite saint. So, you see, *Padrecito*, though they do miss Mass or Sunday-school, they are still good Catholics at home." A priest was understandably distressed when a religious picture he was asked to bless turned out to be of Martin Luther! Before "Luther was cast into the devouring flames of the stove," the picture's owner insisted that the image was that of not only a saint but one who was *muy milagrero* (a great miracle worker)!

Despite their failings in the church leaders' eyes, Mexican Americans saw themselves as good Catholics and kept to their ways. Throughout the early twentieth century (and to this day), they maintained their distinctiveness through many traditions that mixed religion with socializing and socialization. For example, parish fund-raising projects such as the *jamaicas* (church bazaars) involved whole neighborhoods and cemented the values and relationships that undergirded Mexican American ethno-Catholic culture. The *jamaicas* enveloped parishioners in cooperative work and cultural celebration, creating a sacred-secular space in which they enjoyed traditional Mexican foods and entertainment, carried out courting customs, acknowledged godparentage ties, and otherwise affirmed a sense of dignity and community. The *jamaicas* formed part of a large repertoire of traditions that were equally expressive of ethnic as religious identity—*posadas* and *pastorelas* (Christmas-time neighborhood processions and nativity plays), *quinceañeras* (fifteen-year-old girls' rites of passage), baptism parties, and other social-religious customs. Choosing to be a different kind of Catholic this way was a form of cultural resistance against those in the church who held Mexican Americans at arm's length while trying to "Christianize and civilize" them.

In strikingly similar ways, Italian immigrants invited vicious criticism because they remained steeped in their Old World Catholicism. Theirs was a festive Catholicism, rich in emotional displays of an intertwined sense of religion, family, and community. Many Italians were openly hostile to the church and its clergy and generally they kept their distance from them. They preferred to express their understanding of being a good person—of being religious, being a Christian—through selective church attendance and their age-old *festas*, great celebrations complete with processions, fireworks, brass bands, hearty meals and partying, penance, and other fervent expressions of their spirituality. From the late 1800s to the mid-1900s, for example, New York's Italian Catholics choked the streets for several days in mid-July celebrating the great *festa* of the Madonna of Mount Carmel. Church leaders often looked on in dismay and disgust, especially at the more unusual forms of penance—crawling in processions or *lingua strascinuni*, the practice of women honoring a patron saint by crawling or being carried toward a saint statue while their tongue dragged along the church floor. For the more straitlaced, this was just too much. "The Italian people," many clergy agreed, "are in a state little better than Paganism." Real religion, they charged, "does not consist in processions or carrying candles, [or] in prostrations before a statue of the Madonna," and so they constantly pressured the Italians to conform to the Irish American model of Catholicism.

Despite condemnation from the pulpit, however, the Italians held on to many of their unique ethnoreligious customs into the mid-twentieth century. Like Mexican American Catholics, immigrants from southern Italy and their descendants found in their way of being Catholic the sustenance for understanding themselves and the often hostile world around them. In particular, as religion scholar Robert Orsi has shown, the *festa* "cleansed" and "healed" Italian Catholics, fortifying them "to live another year." And that fortification was useful in a color-conscious society that often denigrated them. Because southern Italian immigrants came from the *mezzogiorno* (meaning "midday"), the hottest part of Italy and that closest to Africa, they were stigmatized as "swarthy," "kinky-haired" "Africans" and "Turks." Americans' attitudes toward southern Italians recalled their earlier encounter with Mexican Americans, who were also seen as "tainted" by African blood. And, like many Mexican Americans who strove to claim whiteness to avoid racial discrimination, the Italians immigrants "learned that achievement in their new environment meant successfully differentiating themselves from the dark-skinned other." And again, in society's eyes both peoples' "exotic" and "pagan" religiosity was another mark against them, even as it nurtured unity and spiritual well-being within their communities.

As Catholics of Italian and Mexican origin relied on their distinctive faith traditions to forge their communities in the early to mid-twentieth century, so too did Japanese Americans. By 1924 immigration restrictions had virtually ended the migration of Japanese to the United States, but viable communities had taken root nonetheless, particularly in California. Second-generation Japanese (Nisei) who came of age during the 1920s and 1930s found ways through their church- and temple-based organizations to resist the racism that pervaded their lives and claim a place for themselves in American society. Particularly useful to Nisei Christians (who were mostly Protestants) were such organizations as the Young Men's/Young Women's Christian Organizations (YM/YWCAs), the Young People's Christian Conference, and others modeled after white Protestant associations. Japanese American Buddhists (most of them "Shin" or Jodo Shinsu Buddhists) similarly formed Young Women's and Young Men's Buddhist Associations and leagues. But the organizations were not way stations to total assimilation or the abandonment of Japanese ethnicity. Rather, they actually strengthened Japanese ethnicity by deflecting some of society's animosity and providing the Nisei a "safe" place in which they could create community and form a bicultural identity. As a Japanese American Buddhist from Los Angeles stated, "Just because I don't happen to be a Christian, can you say that I am not a true American? We may be referred to the Constitution of the United States, and find written there, the guarantee that an American citizen may worship whatever religion he chooses."

At the many conferences these organizations sponsored, the Nisei socialized and networked, sharpened their leadership skills, heard provocative speakers, discussed what it meant to be a Japanese American, and learned to negotiate the often hostile American terrain. Similarly, the magazines and newsletters these organizations and conferences generated took up the difficult issues of the day and offered advice and support. This became increasingly important as the clouds of war formed in the late 1930s. In 1938 a participant at a Christian conference in California stated: "Faith is a necessity in our everyday Christian living. For with faith, we, as Christians, are able to face the huge obstacles of our chaotic life with an optimistic attitude. It gives us the strength, the power, and the hope in the face of un-Christian forces at work in the world today." Stated in reference to the rise of Hitler and Mussolini and the coming of World War II, the remarks applied equally to the difficulties Japanese Americans faced, especially as the United States edged closer to war with Japan in 1941. Of course, neither their American citizenship nor their efforts to be more like other Americans saved the Japanese from confinement in internment camps during World War II. But undoubtedly their strong dignity and ethnic solidarity nurtured by their religious traditions held them in good stead in that critical time, as they had before.

Modern America

In the second half of the twentieth century, the nation's ethnic and religious makeup changed at a dizzying pace. The intersection of two major developments in particular, large-scale immigration from Asia and Latin America and ethnic civil rights movements, revealed more vividly than ever the vitality, importance, and permanence of ethnicity and religion.

The post–World War II years (1945–60) were the lull before the storm, giving no hint of the massive changes to come. The absence of heavy immigration since the mid-1920s seemed to indicate that ethnicity was dead and that the country would yet achieve cultural unity. Will Herberg's influential book *Protestant, Catholic, Jew* (1955) described American society as "one great community divided into three big sub-communities religiously defined [Protestantism, Catholicism, Judaism], all equally American." The "triple melting pot" had worked its magic on Catholics and Jews so that they were now part of mainstream society, and ethnicity no longer mattered. That view was mistaken in two important ways. First, it failed to see the multiplicity of well-rooted, viable faith traditions in America and misjudged the continuing importance of ethnicity. Well before the 1950s "America had become a Catholic-Jewish-Orthodox-Protestant-Pentecostalist-Mormon-New Thought-Humanist nation, to list only some of the major options," historian Robert Handy observed; and we should add the varieties of the well-established Buddhist and Hindu traditions as well as other numerically smaller but viable faith expressions that flourished among Asian Americans. Second, many Americans belonged to the so-called mainstream religions but were still treated as religious outsiders and social pariahs. For example, African Americans had Americanized, but they clearly remained shut out of America's promise. The nation's "race problem" had never been simply black and white, however. And in the 1960s and 1970s Latinos (those of Mexican origin or other Latin American heritage) also pressed for equal opportunity and first-class membership in church and society.

Labor organizer César Chávez first riveted national attention on the Mexican American quest for social justice, or the Chicano movement. In organizing California farm workers to fight against their miserable working conditions, Chávez drew inspiration from his own Catholic heritage as well as from two great spiritual leaders, Mohandas Gandhi of India and the Reverend Martin Luther King Jr. A spirituality clearly imbued Chávez's struggle. The farm workers marched under the banner of Our Lady of Guadalupe, the central figure in Mexican American Catholicism, and through rigorous fasting and other forms of personal sacrifice he gave his all to the workers' cause. "When we are really honest with ourselves we must admit that our lives are all that really belong to us," he once reflected. "So, it is how we use our lives that determines what kind of men we are. It is my deepest belief that only by giving our lives do we find life. I am convinced that the truest act of courage, the strongest act of manliness is to sacrifice ourselves for others in totally non-violent struggle for justice. *To be a man is to suffer for others*. God help us to be men." Unlike many Chicano activists who bitterly attacked the Catholic Church, Chávez patiently prodded the institution: "What do we want the Church to do? We don't ask for more cathedrals. . . . We ask for its presence with us, beside us, as Christ among us. We ask the Church to *sacrifice with the people* for social change, for justice."

With some individual exceptions, the response from the Catholic Church was mostly cautious and sometimes hostile, spurring lay and clerical activists all over the country to pressure the institution to support the Chicano movement. In Texas the Chicano movement was sparked by *la marcha*, a widely publicized and dramatic 490-mile trek staged by striking farm workers and co-led by two Chicano clerics, Father Antonio Gonzales and Baptist minister James Novarro, both of Houston. In 1969 Católicos por la Raza (Catholics for the People), a lay organization, militantly confronted church officials in Los Angeles for spending millions on a new cathedral while closing down a barrio Catholic girls' school for "lack of funds," and members of the organization took to the streets to demand the appointment of a Chicano bishop for San Diego. Some Protestants also supported church involvement in social change. Notable efforts included the Migrant Ministry's aid for farm workers and the eloquent advocacy of Presbyterian minister and theologian Jorge Lara-Braud. By the early 1970s even priests and nuns were organizing for social justice. A group of activist Chicano priests organized Priests Associated for Religious, Educational, and Social Rights (PADRES) in San Antonio in 1969, and in 1971 Chicana nuns formed a similar organization for social change called Las Hermanas (Sisters) in Houston. This activism began to yield fruit in 1970 when Father Patricio Flores, a Houston priest and founding member of PADRES, became the first Mexican American bishop in the American Catholic Church. The ensuing decades saw a handful of Mexican Americans and several other Spanish-surnamed priests rise to the office of bishop, as the church responded to internal and external calls for attention to its often neglected Latino parishioners. The church convened three *encuentros* (national conferences) to discuss the needs of Latino Catholics—in 1972, 1979, and 1985—and it began allocating more funding for its Spanish-speaking ministry as well as to address the material needs of Latinos.

Since the 1970s a huge wave of immigration from the Caribbean and Central and South America has been augmenting the U.S. Latino population. Actually, Puerto Ricans and Cubans began coming to the United States shortly after the Spanish-American War (1898), but in the post–World War II years their numbers increased noticeably. The Puerto Rican Great Migration (mostly to New York City) began around 1945, and Cubans started arriving in southern Florida in large numbers immediately after the Castro revolution of 1959. As with Mexican Americans, saint veneration, pilgrimages, and socioreligious celebrations held profound meanings for these Latinos. They held tightly to their "island" identities and their own way of being Catholic even as the American Catholic Church tried to Americanize them. They brought different styles of Catholicism but also new (to most Americans) Afro-Latino religions, such as Cuban Santeria and Puerto Rican Spiritism. In addition, many Puerto Ricans and other Latinos adopted evangelical Protestantism, particularly Pentecostalism. A growing phenomenon in Latin America and the United States, evangelical Protestantism continued to make inroads among Latinos a century and a half after mainline Protestants first gained a foothold among Mexican Americans in the Southwest. In the late twentieth century the old mainline Mexican American churches, like their Anglo counterparts, were shrinking drastically, overshadowed by the evangelical storefront churches so popular with recent Latino immigrants. As the twentieth century ended, the "browning of America" was well under way. In the early 1990s Latinos already accounted for about one-third of the U.S. Catholic population, were the fastest-growing Protestant group, and were expected to become the largest ethnic group in the country early in the twenty-first century.

At the same time, new immigration laws, including the Immigration Act of 1965, the Indochina Migration and Refugee Act of 1975, the Refugee Act of 1980, and the Amerasian Homecoming Act of 1987, have spurred heavy migration particularly from the Philippines, Vietnam, Cambodia, Laos, Sri Lanka, Thailand, and Korea. Peoples from these countries have added substantial ethnic flavor to such established religions as Catholicism, Protestantism, Buddhism, and Hinduism. By 1990 Thai Americans numbered slightly more than 91,000. Mostly followers of Theravada Buddhism, they have established 55 temples in cities in California, New York, Texas, Florida, and Illinois. The number of temples of all Buddhists approaches 150. Asian Indians (who numbered more than half a million by 1985) have also prospered, as indicated by the 50 or so temples Hindus have erected in such diverse places as New York, Atlanta, Chicago, Houston, Los Angeles, Washington, D.C., San Francisco, and Philadelphia. Today some 75,000 Asian Indians in the United States follow Jainism, mostly around Boston and Chicago. There are signs of permanence everywhere. Outside Los Angeles sits the largest Buddhist temple in the Western Hemisphere, Hsi Lai Temple. Built in 1988 at a cost of $30 million in the well-to-do suburb of Hacienda Heights, the temple is home to 20,000 members, mostly Chinese immigrants from Taiwan. In 1987 the U.S. Armed Forces recognized their growing number of Buddhist personnel and began assigning Buddhist chaplains for the first time. Among the Vietnamese, who numbered about 593,000 in 1990, estimates put the number of Buddhists at 60–80 percent and Catholics at 30–40 percent.

These latest immigrants have not met with the warmest of receptions, even when they have religion in common with other Americans and their experiences recall those of earlier groups. Among Catholic Vietnamese, elements of Confucianism mixed with Catholicism, conflicting with what had become the American Catholic style. Non-Christian Asians have met even more resistance, leading some to suggest that it will take considerable time for Buddhism and Hinduism to be acculturated. For example, Thai Buddhists found strong opposition to their plans to build a temple in Miami in 1989. "They've gotten their foot in the door," a resident complained, "and now they want to build this huge edifice." He opposed building the temple at least partly because it was "a church that's not even in the mainstream of American life." The Thais eventually won the right to build their temple, but over the past thirty years Buddhists, Sikhs, Hindus, and others have found themselves in many similar disputes and have not always felt free to practice their religions. But although the incident in Miami revealed the ethnic and religious divisions so prevalent in the nation's history, it also was significantly different. Miami's Thai Buddhists, for one thing, did not suffer the violence that commonly afflicted Asians and other immigrants in the nineteenth and early twentieth centuries. And not only did cooler heads prevail, but the Buddhist community found allies among local religious leaders. The intervention by a Catholic priest, a rabbi, and other clergy on behalf of the Thais helped them gain permission to build their temple—and it revealed, perhaps, a model for future ethnic and religious community building among Americans.

Conclusion

The importance of ethnicity and religion in the United States has endured throughout our history. Since the nation's inception Americans have developed an abiding pattern of contestation over what kind of place America should be and what it means to be an American. Ethnicity and religion have persistently played a part in that contention precisely because of the rich ethnic and religious diversity of the American people themselves. From the very start Americans fought over who belonged in America and who should fully share in its opportunities. Attempts to make the United States a Christian nation modeled after England failed in the face of early and sustained immigration by the "wrong" kinds of Christians, non-Christians, and non-Europeans. That part of the struggle to define America was often violent, especially in our early history. And even after the failure of the "melting pot" to reshape everyone into "standard" Americans, tensions have continued to divide our society along ethnic and religious lines, though not with the violence that marked earlier years.

Significantly, despite all this divisiveness, ethnicity and religion have often interacted in ways that have diffused much of their destructive potential. Historically, Americans have linked ethnicity and religion in powerfully constructive ways—to develop identity, build community, and struggle for a better life. For example, both insiders and outsiders developed a healthy sense of identity in opposition to each other, and in this way they were important to each other despite their ethnic and religious conflicts. Separate identities were the building blocks of community solidarity among the distinct groups that came to these shores. And from that strong sense of ethnoreligious community flowed an array of goals. Ethno-Protestantism, for example, helped the British colonists break away from England. And immigrants facing a bewildering new environment clustered among their own kind, working together to build schools, preserve traditions, and otherwise form the ethnoreligious cocoons that helped them adjust to life in America. Of course, ethno-Protestantism also helped to promote imperialism, as in the taking of the Mexican territories in the Southwest. But in response Mexican Americans found in their own ethnoreligiosity the wherewithal to weather conquest and marginality and, later, to launch a civil rights movement that improved their lives. Thus, even though ethnic and religious differences have caused strife throughout our history, at the same time they have given people ways to deal with it constructively.

As the twenty-first century dawns, we continue to debate the meaning of

America. Buddhists and Muslims already outnumber some mainline Protestants and are soon expected to eclipse other, larger denominations. Demographically, America is more ethnic than ever. Yet many deny these realities, insisting that America is a "Christian" nation and analyzing it as a "postethnic" society. What accounts for such myopia? Clearly, ethnicity and religion still matter. If they did not matter, would neighborhood associations across the country continue to file lawsuits to prevent Muslims and Buddhists from building temples and mosques? Would there be such hoopla over the Jewishness of Senator Joe Lieberman, the Democratic vice presidential candidate in the 2000 election? America cannot yet claim to be a paradise of tolerance. Following the appalling attacks by the Islamic fundamentalist organization Al Qaeda on the World Trade Center and the Pentagon on September 11, 2001, mosques across the United States came under threats, with some being defaced. Nonetheless, it is important to recognize that despite the bigotry and violence that has marred its history, the United States has not become a Northern Ireland or a Yugoslavia. For example, despite the horrific terrorist attacks and some threats of violence to mosques that followed, numerous religious leaders immediately spoke out against religious bigotry. Meanwhile, American Islamic leaders made the case that true Islam in no way supported the mass murder perpetrated on that day. Despite some examples of intolerance and bigotry, in other words, Americans seemed determined not to replay the violence that often characterized relations between the nation's ethno-religious groups in the past. Yes, ethnicity and religion remain vital, and potentially disruptive, in the culture. But that is as "normal" for America today as it has been throughout the past. Ours is a perpetually contested society in which ethnicity and religion often bring divisiveness but also the means to channel and contain it.

SUGGESTED READINGS

Albanese, Catherine L. *America: Religions and Religion*. 2nd ed. Belmont, Calif.: Wadsworth Publishing, 1992.

Dolan, Jay P. *The American Catholic Experience*. Garden City, N.Y.: Doubleday, 1985.

Dolan, Jay P., and Gilberto M. Hinojosa, eds. *Mexican Americans and the Catholic Church, 1900–1965*. Notre Dame, Ind.: University of Notre Dame Press, 1994.

Dolan, Jay P., and Jaime R. Vidal, eds. *Puerto Rican and Cuban Catholics in the U.S., 1900–1965*. Notre Dame, Ind.: University of Notre Dame Press, 1994.

Gaustad, Edwin Scott. *A Documentary History of Religion in America*. 2 vols. Grand Rapids, Mich.: Eerdmans, 1982–83.

————. *A Religious History of America*. Rev. ed. San Francisco: HarperCollins, 1990.

Gjerde, Jon. *The Minds of the West: Ethnocultural Evolution in the Rural Middle West, 1830–1917*. Chapel Hill: University of North Carolina Press, 1997.

Handy, Robert. *A Christian America: Protestant Hopes and Historical Realities*. 2nd ed. New York: Oxford University Press, 1984.

Marty, Martin. *Pilgrims in Their Own Land*. New York: Penguin, 1984.

Matovina, Timothy M. *Tejano Religion and Ethnicity: San Antonio, 1821–1860*. Austin: University of Texas Press, 1995.

Moore, R. Laurence. *Religious Outsiders and the Making of Americans*. New York: Oxford University Press, 1986.

Olson, James S. *Catholic Immigrants in America*. Chicago: Nelson-Hall, 1987.

Orsi, Robert A. *The Madonna of 115th Street: Faith and Community in Italian Harlem, 1880–1950*. New Haven: Yale University Press, 1985.

————. "The Religious Boundaries of an Inbetween People: Street *Feste* and the Problem of the Dark-Skinned Other in Italian Harlem, 1920–1990." *American Quarterly* 44 (September 1992): 313–47.

Sarna, Jonathan D. *Minority Faiths and the American Protestant Mainstream*. Urbana: University of Illinois Press, 1998.

Schwartz, Sally. *"A Mixed Multitude": The Struggle for Toleration in Pennsylvania*. New York: New York University Press, 1987.

Stevens Arroyo, Antonio M. *Prophets Denied Honor: An Anthology on the Hispanic Church in the United States*. Maryknoll, N.Y.: Orbis, 1980.

Tweed, Thomas A., and Stephen Prothero. *Asian Religions in America: A Documentary History*. New York: Oxford University Press, 1999.

Walker, Randi Jones. *Protestantism in the Sangre de Cristos, 1850–1920*. Albuquerque: University of New Mexico Press, 1991.

Yoo, David K. *Growing Up Nisei: Race, Generation, and Culture among Japanese Americans of California, 1924–1949*. Urbana: University of Illinois Press, 2000.

Gender

In jam-packed sports megaplexes and quiet church basement fellowship halls, for almost a decade Christian men have joined together singing, praying, holding hands, hugging, and tearfully begging Christ's and one another's forgiveness for their sins. The men gathered at these emotive meetings are Promise Keepers, participants in an evangelical revival movement that encourages men to surrender to Christ and reclaim their "godly manhood." The Promise Keepers movement was founded by former University of Colorado head football coach Bill McCartney; its adherents range in age, ethnicity, and culture but unite around their belief that they are facing a spiritual crisis because they have lost control of their God-given authority in their families. Promise Keepers affirm that the spiritual makeup of men differs radically from that of women and that they require a "masculine context" to understand and express their spiritual longings. The Promise Keepers have attracted considerable media attention because of their insistence on the theological and biological underpinnings for male authority, a gospel they proclaim with tearful resolve. Even the most casual observer is struck by the unusual mixing of masculine identity rhetoric and such culturally recognized feminine behaviors as crying and surrender that characterize the Promise Keepers' religious beliefs and practices.

The Promise Keepers remind us that religious identity is intimately linked to gender identity. Masculinity, for the Promise Keepers, is both an identification with the father God and a set of "masculine" behaviors and characteristics that serve as a religious witness. It is their actions, what some scholars call "performances," that illuminate the complexity of their beliefs. To identify as a Christian man, a Promise Keeper must act like a Christian man. Finally, the Promise Keepers alert us that sometimes religious renewal requires acts of gender transgression: in this case, "manly" Christians cry and hug. However, more often than not, as is the case with the Promise Keepers, these seemingly transgressive moments ultimately reinforce a gender hierarchy already in place.

How do we know a person's gender? Or, for that matter, how do we know a person's religion? Is there one essential quality that constitutes all males, females? Hindus, Jews, or Christians? Must we ask a person to declare his or her gender or religion, or is it possible to know simply by observation? Asking these questions together illustrates that our understandings of gender identity and religious identity might be closer than we think.

Most people who attempt to define gender begin with the category of sex, explaining that humans are divided into two biological categories, male and female. One is categorized male or female based on one's anatomy, specifically the reproductive organs. Gender, then, is defined as the rules that each culture provides for biological males and females. But if anatomical differences define males and females, then logically we would need to see every person naked before we could determine his or her gender. But we know (or think we know) in one glance a person's gender, for gender is not in the end about anatomical difference but about how individuals perform their male and female identities. Gender is created and sustained by what people do, how they act, what they wear, how they speak, all of which signify "maleness" or "femaleness." To understand gender, one needs to know the cultural and religious rules that determine how males and females behave.

Why is it that the distinction between male and female remains primary? Many scholars have concluded that there are social and economic reasons for dividing humanity into these two classes. Some have argued that this division not only allows for one group of people (non–child bearers) to oppress another (child bearers) but also enforces one type of sexual behavior (heterosexuality) as "normal." Any other sexual behavior, such as homosexuality or celibacy, is labeled "unnatural" and "abnormal" because it does not play a part in reproduction. The Western division between two sexes is explained not simply as a scientific fact of "nature" but also as a divine truth.

To say that society creates a false "natural" binary opposition between males and females so that one group might oppress another is not to claim that gender hierarchy and oppression are figments of a culture's imagination. On the contrary, the success of gender distinction and discrimination is dependent on the belief of the "truth" of the opposition between males and females, a difference so obvious it need not be questioned. This fundamental distinction, then, becomes a primary distinguishing characteristic, more basic and often more important than other identity markers including family affiliation, language, nationality, and culture. Think about the first question that was asked about you when you were born, Is it a boy or is it a girl? Gender is so important that we set up a system of internal hierarchies that subordinates all other identity categories to gender, and we use this system of hierarchies to further delineate power relationships. This sounds complicated (and in fact it is), but we have so thoroughly embraced such systems that we have become unaware of their power. In what we might think of as a gender pyramid, men are generally superior to women. When other hierarchies, such as race and economic status, are added to the mix, however, the gender hierarchy becomes more complex, and sometimes certain women are superior to men. For example, in the slaveholding South, a white woman, although considered inferior to a white man, would have considerably more power than an African American man (either slave or free). Individuals thus move up and down the gender pyramid depending on these other identity markers. Another of these markers is religion, to which we now turn.

As we asked earlier, how do we know a person's religion? It might seem that religious categories are different from gender categories because generally our culture allows people to move in and out of religions but resists people switching genders. Religion in many cases is a matter of individual choice. But, as with gender, we know someone's religious identity by "performative" acts. A Christian will wear a cross, a Jew will hang a mezuzah on the portal, a Muslim will pray facing Mecca. These are visible practices we can observe. Of course, religious identity also includes statements of beliefs, but it is the practices—even if it is the act of professing a belief—that shape religious identity. As observers of religion and gender, we look first to the performative acts to discern one's identity.

When we view American religious history with an eye focused on gender, we find that theologically distinct groups share common religious concerns. For example, in the twentieth century, Jews, Christians, Buddhists, and Muslims have all struggled to reconcile women's desire for leadership roles in traditionally male clerical offices. Recent writings by feminist theologians attest to the continuing attempt to provide female models of the sacred in rituals, texts, and religious practices. Jews, Christians, and Muslims are also united by their monotheistic vision of a sovereign, male deity. The association between masculinity and divinity creates theological and social challenges for men and women that cross all three traditions. Women within these traditions will always be defined as cosmically "other," whereas men will know that they are in the image of God, though they will never live up to that ultimate male model. But attention to gender also highlights divisions among religious groups. Religious intolerance and persecution are often born of conflicting conceptions of gender that seem to threaten basic religious beliefs and practices.

We cannot identify an essential experience across cultures that indicates maleness or femaleness and compare how religious groups respond to that universal experience. What we can examine is the way in which the dominant European religion and culture divided humans into two sex categories and the impact that division had on these Europeans' encounters with other religious groups in the United States. There are many ways to approach this task. In some instances, we will examine how different religious groups' conceptions of the divine reflect and reproduce ideal notions of masculinity and femininity. In other instances, we will consider how the gendered symbols and practices of the dominant religious groups serve to legitimate power and oppression. We will also explore how religious understandings of what it means to be male or female justify and sometimes reinvent the social order. And we will see how gender "truths" of the dominant religious groups in America affected the ways in which they understood the beliefs and practices of all the groups they encountered.

We must keep in mind that gender does not simply signify "woman"; rather, it is a complex system that operates on all people. Although this chapter examines conceptions of both masculinity and femininity, one should not assume that men and women have held equal power in religious traditions or an equal place in the way American religious history has usually been narrated. An attention to gender does not balance the interpretive scales, but it does expose the power of gender ideology to constitute order and authority within and between religious groups.

Precolonial Era

The Europeans who "discovered" the New World in the fifteenth century carried with them not only maps, compasses, swords, and provisions but also Bibles that directed them in their proper roles as Christian men and women. Beginning with the two creation stories of the first man and woman found in the Book of Genesis, Jewish and Christian scriptures provided a divine blueprint for how Christian men and women should act in this world. There is a significant difference between the two accounts of creation that has theological as well as social ramifications for the Christian West. The first story (Gen. 1:1–2:4) tells of God's simultaneous creation of the first man and the first woman with the command to be fruitful and multiply. In the second, more elaborate creation account (Gen. 2:4–25), God creates the first woman, "Eve," from the body of the first man, "Adam." The story continues as a snake challenges the woman and tricks the couple into disobeying God, with the ensuing punishments that man and his descendants will forever toil and the woman and her descendants will have pain in childbirth.

Later Jewish and Christian interpreters deemed Eve the true villain of this tale in seducing Adam, thus causing humanity to fall into sin. The sign of this state of sin is the knowledge and shame of their nakedness. Although some interpreters would look to the first creation story to justify religious and social egalitarianism between men and women, most Christians tended to remember the lessons of the second story. They knew that a virtuous Christian man should not "succumb" to "womanly" ways and that a virtuous Christian woman should not act like Eve. The mythical story of the first couple—their creation, fall, and punishment—helped to explain the social, sexual, political, and economic differences between European men and women. In fact, challenging these gendered "truths" constituted a direct challenge not just to society but also to the faith. Both Adam and Eve were prototypes for all men and women, demonstrating both their original characteristics and an original relation of authority between men and women.

Christian men and women also drew on New Testament scriptures to understand their proper relationship to one another and the world. In I Corinthians 11:3–12 the apostle Paul reminds Christians of the divinely sanctioned social order. "Christ is the head of every man, and the husband is the head of his wife, and God is the head of Christ." He continues his exhortation by stating that men should pray with their heads uncovered and women should pray with their heads covered. This is because of the order of creation: "he is the image and reflection of God; but woman is the reflection of man." Other Christian scriptures are more detailed about proper Christian gendered behavior. In 1 Timothy 2:8–15, the writer commands that in places where men pray "women should dress themselves modestly and decently in suitable clothing, not with their hair braided, or with gold, pearls or expensive clothes, but with good works as is proper for women who profess reverence for God." In the next sentence, a verse that would codify Christian ecclesiastical roles and power for almost two millennia, the writer states, "Let a woman learn in silence with full submission. I permit no woman to teach or to have authority over a man; she is to keep silent. For Adam was formed first, then Eve; and Adam was not deceived, but the woman was deceived and became a transgressor. Yet she will be saved through childbearing."

Scholars have pointed out how gender norms have changed dramatically throughout the history of Christianity. For example, early Christians promoted sexuality within marriage for procreation; it was not until the thirteenth century that the Catholic Church declared marriage a sacrament. In fact, prior to that, many Christians believed that the true route to salvation was through celibacy. At the same time that marriage became a sacrament, canon law codified "natural" and "unnatural" sexual behavior. "Sins against nature" (nonprocreative sex, including homosexuality) and sexual activity outside heterosexual marriage were concluded to be in the first category, "unnatural," and the second category, criminal, respectively. Despite the elevation of marriage in Christian belief and practice, celibacy remained a spiritual ideal. Catholic Church fathers connected celibacy to clerical office, maleness, and spiritual maturity. Women, always connected to Eve's transgression and sexuality, could choose a celibate life, but they could not hold male-defined clerical roles (such as priest, bishop, or pope) outside the convent's walls. The sixteenth-century Protestant Reformers continued the Catholic Church's position on "natural" and "unnatural" sexual activity but rejected celibacy as a prerequisite for clerical office. Instead, the Reformers emphasized the divinely ordained role of procreative sex within heterosexual marriage.

Europeans did not rely solely on the Bible for their knowledge of gender. By the fifteenth century, scientific texts passed down from the ancients, such as the physician Galen of Pergamum and Aristotle, explained the differences between males and females. The male and female body, according to these writers, was basically the same, except the female body was inferior because it was turned "outside in." Both males and females had the same genitalia, but the female body was reversed and therefore imperfect. Males also were believed to be internally hot, whereas females were internally cool. Men's warm body temperatures made them active and strong; colder females were passive and weak. Later elaboration on this basic theory would suggest that because males have the ability to spark life through insemination, they were associated with the soul, whereas women, who sustained life through pregnancy, were more closely associated with the body. These scientific "facts" that maintained that males and females were united around one body but divided by internal temperature were not seriously challenged until the late eighteenth century.

Beyond the notions of gender that the Europeans brought to their religious contact with other people, the earliest explorers imagined the land itself in highly gendered terms. Christopher Columbus believed that the earth was not simply round but pear-shaped like a woman's breast. The "Other World" (which later would be termed "New World") was located at the nipple, a place he described as "virgin" territory, with exotic fruits and people ready to be taken and conquered. Indeed, after considering astrological charts and the landscape's natural topography, including the four rivers that he determined flowed from the nipple like milk, Columbus became convinced that he had discovered the Garden of Eden, an earthly paradise, with himself a new Adam. Quoting scripture, Columbus believed that his "discovery" fulfilled God's New Testament promise for a New Heaven on earth. Although Columbus placed his actions within the course of Christian history, he legitimated the conquest of the land and people by characterizing both as "feminine": the land, like a womb, needed to be cultivated with seeds; the people, like women, required mastery and eventually subjugation. Thus, the story of Columbus's first encounter with the continent and the people blends both religious and gendered imperatives to justify conquest.

Prior to Columbus's arrival the land was populated by more than ten million people who were organized into thousands of different language groups and cultures. There were, however, some shared characteristics that united Native American religious traditions and shed light on their understandings of what it means to be male and female. As with the Europeans, Native American conceptions of what it means to be male and female were connected to religious beliefs and reflected in religious practices.

Unlike with the Europeans, among many of the Native American cultures in North America a third alternative to the "two-gender" system existed. The people who constituted this third option were called "berdaches" by European onlookers, an anthropological term originally used to described young, male Arab sex slaves. Like so many misapplied terms, the label "berdache," which today is deeply offensive to most Native Americans (who prefer the term "two spirit"), tells us more about the European observers' misconceptions than it does about the Native Americans. These men-women and women-men, according to anthropologist Walter Williams, were typically biological males (although there were also females) who determined through the help of the spiritual world and through their community that they were of "non-male" (or "non-female") character. Many different Native American cultures acknowledged and accepted this third group. Although some, like the Pimas of the Southwest, did not, most honored the men-women and women-men as having special spiritual qualities and ceremonial responsibilities. Many Native Americans understood that the "two-spirits" were present at the creation of the world and were important sources of contact between this world and the true world of the spirits. Dressing as women and adopting their social, economic, and sexual roles, men-women were valued as powerful figures who dually mediated between men and women and the physical and spiritual world. Much of the evidence for this practice comes from European onlookers. Although many Europeans were appalled by the practice, calling men-women "sodomites," most observers were baffled, like French Jesuit missionary Joseph François Lafitau, who admitted in 1724 that that they were honored within their own culture. Few outsiders understood the theological precedents for the two-spirits' existence found in creation stories; nor did they understand their spiritual importance within tribal culture. Predictably, men-women were condemned by Europeans as being "unnatural" men for assuming female habits and behaviors.

Those Native American cultures that accepted two-spirits had theological justifications for the social order embedded in their creation stories. The Navajo, for example, tell of a first man, a first woman, and twins—Turquoise Boy and White-Shell Girl—who were the first *nàdle* ("changing ones"). In the Navajo creation story the *nadle* are known for their inventiveness because they created the first implements and tools for cooking, weaving, and farming. The Plains Arapaho call the men-women and women-men *haxu'xan* and believe them to be a sacred gift from the birds and animals. In the Arapaho creation myth the *haxu'xan* are bestowed with supernatural power. The Mohave of the Colorado River valley tell of an original time when people were sexually undifferentiated, and the *alyha* represent those first beings.

Because the men-women and women-men were guided by the spiritual world to accept their distinct character, they often performed sacred rites and held a position of honor within their communities. Among the Navajo, for example, they were responsible for preparing sacred food. The Plains tribes had them bless the tree used in the sacred Sun Dance. The Cheyenne believed that they were great healers and brought them along during battles. Two-spirits were also respected for their position as mediators between the sexes: possessing both male and female elements, they had an ability to view the world from both perspectives.

In both Native American and European societies, differences between men and women were necessary to maintain social order and were deeply embedded in religious beliefs. But in the Native American cultures that accepted the two-spirits, the relationship between males and females could be characterized as complementary rather than hierarchical. Therefore, the volatile religious encounter between these cultures often began with observations of distinct gender practices. One scholar has shown that much of the strife between Virginia Algonquians and the English colonists emerged around conflicting notions of gender identity. According to the English social rules, proper men owned property and produced agricultural goods, whereas proper women, known as "good wives," did not own property and worked primarily inside the household. The Algonquian women, in contrast, produced and maintained property, and the Algonquian men hunted. The Algonquians' manners and dress also conflicted with those of the English. Algonquian men shaved their faces (rendering them to English eyes as immature boys), and Algonquian women painted their bodies and dressed in ways the English deemed immodest. The Algonquian men's apparent failure to take dominion over the land (unlike Adam) and the Algonquian women's sexualized bodies (like Eve) proved that the Native Americans were not simply uncivilized but also irreligious. To the English the divinely ordained rules for men and women were turned upside down and could be righted only through Christianization. In the end, the gender differences led to a much larger task than conquering the land. It ultimately required colonizing the body and soul of Native Americans.

Colonial North America

The Puritan settlements in New England exemplify how conceptions of proper male and female roles served to clarify theological differences within a fairly homogeneous religious community. Puritans, like most Protestant Europeans, believed that within marriage women and men had complementary family roles with the husband at the head of the household. The male clergy, called by the community of believers, preached Calvinist tenets of salvation of the elect and left the individual congregants to scrutinize their own souls for signs of God's grace. Theologically, Puritan male and female souls were equal before God, but socially, Puritan men and women held divinely ordained stations on earth that placed men above women. Gender trouble arose precisely because of the Puritans' insistence that each individual—both male and female —should read the scriptures for him- or herself and contemplate its meaning for his or her life, leading some people to conclude that they should act apart from their prescribed gendered roles.

The story of Anne Hutchinson (1591–1643) offers a well-known example of a Puritan woman who, following her religious beliefs, overstepped her prescribed social station. Goodwife Hutchinson, a midwife and devoted parishioner in the congregation of the prominent Puritan clergyman John Cotton, in 1637 spoke out against theological errors she believed Cotton's assistant preached from his Boston pulpit. Both women and men gathered at the Hutchinson home to hear her condemn the clergyman and expound on the gospel. Hutchinson was called to civil court for preaching falsely and violating church order because she stepped outside her "natural" station by speaking publicly to men, "a thing not tolerable or comely in the sight of God nor fitting for [her] sex." After a twenty-four-day trial in which both sides referred to scripture to justify their positions, Hutchinson revealed to her accusers that her authority came directly from God and that the Spirit had on many occasions spoken to her. Rather than deeming her a prophet, the court returned a guilty verdict, determining that she was unfit theologically and socially for Puritan society. She was banished from the colony in 1638.

Governor John Winthrop was so unnerved that he accused Hutchinson and two of her close followers, Mary Dyer and Jane Hawkins, of being witches. Hutchinson's infamy spread across the Atlantic as the "notorious Mastris Hutchinson" became a negative model of womanhood in John Brinsley's 1645 sermon, "A Looking Glass for Good Women." Brinsley exhorted his English female parishioners to subject themselves to their husbands and never to preach the gospel like Hutchinson, reminding them that Eve's discontent with her God-given position led her to taste the apple. But Protestant women throughout American history would continue to read scriptures for themselves and sometimes interpret them in ways that directly challenged their gender roles in the religious and social order.

The accusation that Anne Hutchinson and her companions were witches, although a serious offense, was not that uncommon in Puritan New England. Puritans believed that saints and sinners were both male and female, but a disproportionate number of women were believed to be the worst kind of sinner, one who had signed a pact with the devil. Scholars debate the reasons that fear of witchcraft escalated into the Salem witch trials of 1692, but all agree that the predominance of women as accusers and accused deserves special attention. Puritans conceived of the soul as female and passive and the body as male and active. God and Satan, so the Puritans believed, were vying for their souls; but whereas God spoke to their hearts, Satan entered through their bodies to reach their souls. Because females were viewed as "weaker vessels," they were more vulnerable to Satan's attacks on their bodies. Male souls, also conceived of as feminine, were well protected by stronger male bodies and therefore less likely to submit to the devil. Significantly, most of the "proof" of witchcraft was determined by marks on accused witches' bodies, evidence of physical (often sexual) contact with evil inscribed on the female body.

The connections among female bodies, sin, and witchcraft did not originate with the Puritans but were articulated as early as 1496 in Heinrich Kraemer and James Sprenger's *Malleus Maleficarum* (the "Hammer against Witches"), used during the Inquisition in Europe. The text explains that because of Eve's carnal lust, women were sexually insatiable and therefore more likely than men to accept Satan for sexual pleasures. Once in league with Satan, women would ravage men sexually (thus providing an explanation that male impotence was caused by a witch's spell) and overthrow society. Accusations of witchcraft reveal much about Puritan views of female identity but also suggest the contours of Puritan male identity. Puritan men, unlike Puritan women, were portrayed as physically strong, able to resist evil, and sexually controlled. Hutchinson was neither tried nor convicted as a witch, but calling her one brought to mind all these gender anxieties of female sexual insatiability, sin, evil, and social disorder.

Although acts of religious and social insubordination in the colonial period were often performed by women, men also were accused of this type of behavior. When men challenged the religious and social order, they were "feminized" to demean and discredit their efforts. George Whitefield, the popular eighteenth-century evangelist, was routinely characterized as "womanly" by his opponents. The Anglican revivalist preacher challenged the established clerical authority by stressing a direct personal experience of God's grace and the leveling of social distinction among the converted. Whitefield's colorful preaching style blended dramatic interpretation of biblical characters with tearful pleas to listeners to ask for God's forgiveness and experience a "new birth" in Christ. An editorial in the Anglican *Weekly Miscellany* satirized Whitefield's theological beliefs and his preaching style by characterizing him as a woman. "Hark he talks about a sensible new birth — then belike he is in labour, and the good women around him are come to his assistance. He dilates himself, cries out, and is at last delivered." Among Protestant white women, the revival experience would transform into a growing sense of women's spiritual authority over men that gave them more authority to evangelize inside of their households, but fewer reasons to leave their domestic sphere.

Converted slaves who looked to scripture for guidance would have a difficult time following the basic gender prescriptions outlined in the Bible. For example, how might a male slave be a good Christian man if he was not the head of his own household? How could a Christian slave woman dress modestly and obey her husband when marriage between slaves was illegal and they were both their master's property, leaving them vulnerable to their masters' needs and whims? Some slave owners encouraged their slaves to convert to Christianity, believing that slaves would follow the same scripture that commands women to "obey their husbands" and to "obey their masters." But most slaveholders resisted missionary efforts because they understood that baptism signified that slaves were more than chattel and that through this Christian ritual slaves were recognized as men and women who had souls.

Revolutionary and Early Republican America

The building of a new republic out of thirteen colonies required not only economic and political power but also an articulation of what it meant to be a citizen of the United States. The "self-evident" truth proclaimed in the Constitution "that all men are created equal" referred to white, propertied men in the new Republic and no others. Despite egalitarian rhetoric, women, free African Americans, slaves, and Native Americans were all excluded from citizenship. Gender and racial identity, therefore, were intimately linked to the construction of national identity. The American man was portrayed as brave, moderate, rational, clearly exemplary in contrast to other men and women, who were fearful, excessive, and irrational. Two hundred years after Columbus envisioned the New World as a woman's breast, John Adams imagined the new Republic as a male political body representing "all great, manly, and warlike virtues."

Not only were women excluded from the political process and "manly" citizenship, but they also remained absent from the ranks of religious leadership. With the exception of the Quakers, no Protestant denominations officially allowed women to speak in public, Catholic nuns took religious leadership roles only among other women within convents, and Jewish women's religious practices were confined to the home. Women who felt the call to preach had to overcome both biblically based objections and now national constructions of gender that constitutionally denied women's capabilities to govern themselves or anyone else. For the same reasons that the Founding Fathers could not imagine women as full citizens, most post–Revolutionary War men and women could not conceive of a female religious leader. The handful of women who did preach openly were harassed, sometimes beaten, accused of sexual promiscuity, and ridiculed for acting "manly" or contrary to their sex.

Like Anne Hutchinson in the seventeenth century, a few extraordinary women claimed authority based on a direct revelation from God. Jemima Wilkinson (1752–1819), the radical leader of the Universal Friends, declared that she had died and had been resurrected into a genderless body or "tabernacle." Although she still appeared female, Wilkinson claimed to be a new body inhabiting God's pure spirit. To emphasize this genderless state, she renamed herself the Public Universal Friend, donned robes that resembled men's clothing, and remained celibate throughout the rest of her life. Wilkinson's intention was to transcend her sex, becoming "neither male nor female." She was chastised by her enemies for trying to become male through her dress, her rejection of childbearing and domesticity, and her dominant position within her religious group. Opponents characterized Wilkinson as an irrational woman lusting for power, and her male followers, not surprisingly, were described as "weak" and "effeminate."

In contrast to Wilkinson, "Mother" Ann Lee (1736–84), the founder and leader of the Shakers (the Society of Universal Believers in Christ's Second Coming), did not try to erase her sex but based her religious authority on her unique position as a woman who could spiritually nurture her children. After experiencing a life-transforming revelation in which she saw that the root of evil began with lust in the Garden of Eden, this illiterate Quaker formed a religious community and, with seven followers, moved from England to western New York, heralding the arrival of Christ and the new millennium. Mother Ann described herself as "mother to all living" and "lover of Christ," but testimonies written after her death by community members claimed that she *was* the Second Coming of Christ in female flesh, completing the unity of God as both male and female. Lee and her followers remained celibate and lived together in extended families practicing their religion based on Lee's visions and ecstatic rituals including joyous dancing. Although the communities prospered in the nineteenth century, the Shakers were attacked continually by outsiders and especially apostates who accused them of drunken debauchery, sexual licentiousness, and heresy. With a strong female founder, a theology that confirmed the female as well as male aspects of God, and the vigorous rejection of the body as "lustful," Shakers were not just hated, they were demonized. As one critic wrote, in Shaker communities, "women become monsters, and men worse than infidels."

A few decades after Ann Lee's death, while the Shaker communities were growing, a series of Protestant revivals swept the Northeast and the frontier regions of Kentucky, western New York, and Pennsylvania. People living in the western settlements traveled for miles and pitched tents to attend enormous, week-long camp meetings. Methodist, Baptist, Presbyterian, and Disciples of Christ preachers, along with many others, exhorted listeners to confess their sins before the crowds. At one famous meeting at Cane Ridge, Kentucky, in 1801, eyewitnesses reported that men and women were intermixing freely and were so overcome that they expressed religious agony and joy through crying, fainting, trancelike states, jerking, dancing, and even barking. The strong emotions expressed at camp meetings created an arena in which evangelical Protestant men and women could act outside their gender roles. It was not unusual in the camp meetings, for example, for men to cry and beg forgiveness of sins, participating in distinctly "feminine" acts of surrendering to Christ. Women, for their part, testified, exhorted, and prayed to "mixed" assemblies, exerting "masculine" authority to speak in public. This was not just the case in frontier camp meetings. Revivals throughout the North and South, in rural and urban areas, opened up a religious space for anyone (men, women, children, and slaves) to speak freely and authoritatively. Thus the strict social order of post–Revolutionary War America that demanded particular gender practices was being renegotiated in these religious settings.

While men were acting like women and women like men in camp meetings and revivals, the Protestant itinerant missionaries who inspired much of this behavior were masculinizing their profession. Unlike their eighteenth-century predecessors, who depended on spiritual maturity and deliberate theological explications to aid them in conversion, these male missionaries found that charisma as well as "manly" physical stamina and strength were essential ingredients for spiritual success on the frontier. Peter Cartwright, a rough-and-tumble Methodist preacher (who himself was converted at a camp meeting), ridiculed other timid and "effeminate" missionaries who exaggerated their hardships on the frontier and sent "doleful tidings" back home filled with "wailings and lamentations." Soft, "bookish" missionaries spoke a language the settlers could not understand, and their learned sermons fell mostly on deaf ears. Frontier people, Cartwright explained, "wanted a preacher who could mount a stump, a block, or an old log, or stand in the bed of a wagon, and without note or manuscript, quote, expound, and apply the word of God to the hearts and consciences of the people." Other missionaries, recognizing the success of brawny preachers like Cartwright, begged their sponsoring societies to stop sending "missionary boys" whose "timidity, humility and meekness" rendered them unfit for frontier labor. No longer simply a matter of piety and preaching, home missionary work became a particular type of masculine performance. On the nineteenth-century American frontier the strongest man won the most souls.

Antebellum Nineteenth Century

Although Christianity had a long tradition of associating the female with the carnal and the male with the spiritual, by the nineteenth century Protestant Americans had reversed that thinking. Women came to be described as "naturally" more spiritual than "naturally" more carnal men. No longer the sexual temptress like their foremother Eve, American Protestant white women became chaste and vulnerable to sexually aggressive men. Nonwhite, non-Protestant, and poor women did not enjoy the luxury of being considered chaste and vulnerable, but they were defined against this new ideal. At the same time, male and female bodies were now viewed as distinct entities. Unlike in the "one-sex" model of the same body inverted, men and women were imagined to be completely separate from each other, thus creating a "two-sex" model that is still with us today. Female bodies were posited as weaker than male bodies and more prone to disease, but women's moral backbone was stronger.

Many scholars have noted that this ideological shift occurred simultaneously with social and economic changes in the United States. As the nation became increasingly industrialized, women's domestic role inside the household was elevated in direct relation to men's economic role outside the household. Masculine identity revolved around notions of economic competition and sexual aggression, and feminine identity derived from an ideology of "True Womanhood," as one scholar has termed it, which portrayed women as sexually restrained moral custodians for their families, the nation, and the world. Sermons and advice literature informed women that they had enormous influence within their own home to instill morality in the family, a cornerstone for building a moral nation. Jonathan Stearns's 1837 discourse *Female Influence and the True Christian Mode of its Exercise* advised, "If she makes [the home] delightful and salutory—the abode of order and piety, though she may herself never step beyond the threshold, she may yet send forth from her humble dwelling a power that will be felt around the world."

Many female Protestant preachers were encouraged by the implications of the shifting gender ideology that viewed them as "naturally" more virtuous than men. Unlike earlier female preachers, they did not need to transcend their gender but justified their right to preach as women. Critics of preaching by women (and later ordination of women) would continue to condemn women for stealing the "masculine" space of the pulpit and speaking immodestly before mixed assemblies. But some women understood that the ideology that sought to restrict them to homes opened doors to larger arenas. Moral reformers like Angelina and Sarah Grimké of South Carolina, for example, felt compelled to move beyond their "proper sphere" of female influence to speak out against the "sinfulness" of American slavery. Jeering crowds constantly followed the Quaker sisters, accusing them of acting against their "nature." What began for the Grimkés as a crusade for immediate emancipation soon became inextricably linked with the rights of women to speak in public. In a 1837 letter to abolitionist Theodore Weld, Angelina wrote, "We are gravely told that we are out of our sphere even when we circulate petitions, out of our 'appropriate sphere' even when we speak to women only. . . . What can a woman do for the slave when she is herself under the feet of man and shamed into silence?"

Some women neither faced mobs nor suffered being called "manly" when addressing religious gatherings. Spiritualists, who believed that the souls of the dead communicated with those of the living, often relied on female "mediums" to bridge the gap between this world and the next. Female mediums were prevalent in part because women were believed to be "naturally" receptive to the spirit world and because Spiritualism affirmed the authority of the direct experience of spiritual contact, allowing women to assume leadership roles. All mediums operated in trancelike states and transmitted messages from the spirit world by relinquishing control of their minds and bodies and allowing the spirits to communicate through them. Spirits worked through the mediums' bodies by means of rappings, voices, "automatic writings," spelling out words on a Ouija board, tilting tables, moving furniture, and other physical "evidences" of the existence of souls beyond death. Because the medium was perceived to be only a vehicle of a spirit's voice and guidance, female mediums were able to speak in the voice from beyond this world on pressing social issues such as abolition, woman suffrage, and moral reform. Female mediums held both public and private séances, and some earned a considerable income without ever leaving their sitting room. Although many observers doubted the veracity of these encounters with the spirit world, few people attacked the women personally because, in essence, they themselves were not challenging gender norms. Rather, they remained in their parlors as voices from the dead transmitted through their seemingly passive bodies.

At the same time that Protestant women were being told that female piety was best expressed through domesticity, there was a dramatic increase in non-Protestant immigrants to the United States. Defenders of a Protestant America accused Catholics of drunkenness, laziness, poverty, and antidemocratic "popery." The most vicious attacks against Catholics, however, arose from what Protestants deemed to be the "perverse" gender practices of Catholic priests and nuns. Priests were characterized routinely as "unmanly" because they remained celibate, and nuns were considered "unwomanly" because they exercised "manly" authority within the convent. The Protestant anti-Catholic anxiety hit fever pitch in 1834 when a convent school in Charlestown, Massachusetts, was burned to the ground. Graphic anti-Catholic literature, replete with gender anxiety, quickly circulated, serving to incite mobs to further violence.

Maria Monk's 1836 *Awful Disclosures of the Hotel Dieu Nunnery of Montreal* was one such publication. Written as a first-person account of an escaped nun from a Montreal convent, it became an overnight success, selling twenty thousand copies within its first weeks of publication. Later discredited as a work of Protestant nativist fantasy, Monk's *Awful Disclosures* remains an important example of anti-Catholic literature that was widely available in antebellum America. This fabricated text illuminates the gendered nature of anti-Catholicism. Monk tells a salacious story of a gullible young nun who falls prey to licentious priests; a domineering, "manly" mother superior; and the horrors the nun experienced as a result of the moral and sexual indignities she suffered while held captive within seemingly impenetrable convent walls. The convent, in Monk's account, represents a secret brothel, with the mother superior acting as the madam, priests as clients, and nuns as prostitutes. As one scholar has noted, the attacks against the convent and Catholicism seen in this and other anticonvent literature were ultimately about protecting Protestant gender roles and the family. The mother superior was described as unwomanly because she cared little for her children (prostituting them to priests). She demonstrated manlike authority over the nuns (torturing them if they disobeyed) and wielded masculine power by running the convent (amassing wealth and luxury).

New utopian movements within Protestantism caused even greater concerns about gender roles, sexuality, and families. Communal and utopian ventures such as Brook Farm and Fruitlands sprang up in the mid-nineteenth century, restructuring basic social arrangements of property, gender roles, sexuality, and family. The people who joined these communities hoped to perfect themselves and society, often expressing these goals in specifically religious terms. The Oneida Perfectionists, led by John Humphrey Noyes (1811–86), moved as an extended "family" to Sherrill, New York, in 1848 to regenerate themselves and society by instituting Noyes's principles of Bible Communism. Based on his reading of the Book of Acts, Noyes believed that, like the early Christians who held all things in common, his "family" was to do the same. Noyes's radical theology and the social vision that he and his "family" practiced for almost forty years included (among many other things) the assertion that a sinless existence was possible on earth and that he himself had achieved that state. The social and sexual implications of Noyes's theology of Bible Communism and "sinlessness" challenged gender norms in dramatic ways. In his 1848 "Bible Argument Defining the Relation between the Sexes," Noyes reasoned that the "restoration of true relations between the sexes" could occur only by abolishing the unholy practice of marriage, an institution he believed "assigns the exclusive possession of one woman to one man." Noyes contended that marriage was in fact a threat to society because it encouraged "special love" rather than social harmony. In its place, he set up a system of "complex marriage" in which each man and each woman in the community could enjoy—with the approval of Father Noyes—a sexual relationship with one another.

Noyes's family, which at its height numbered almost three hundred people, reorganized not only marriage but also gender roles. Men and women worked together in most aspects of community life. Besides traditional female domestic work, women also engaged in "manly" tasks of manufacturing, industry, farmwork, and administration. In some instances, women held positions of authority over men. Likewise, men participated in "womanly" tasks including cooking, cleaning, child rearing, and sewing. Men practiced "male continence," a form of birth control, so that women were not disadvantaged by unplanned pregnancy. Even clothing had to change. Women cut their hair and shortened their skirts in order to move and work as freely as men. Noyes even challenged the nineteenth-century gender notion that women were more "naturally" spiritual than men. At Oneida, the social and sexual hierarchy was based on "ascending" and "descending" fellowship. Although Noyes reworked sex and gender roles to restore proper relations between men and women, he always maintained that males were "naturally" spiritually superior to females. As in all gender pyramids, some more spiritual women were superior to less spiritual men. Not surprisingly, the person who sat at the very top was John Humphrey Noyes himself.

For nineteenth-century Mormons (the Church of Jesus Christ of Latter-day Saints), as for other utopian groups, the family was the primary arena in which gender roles were defined. Basing their beliefs on the direct revelations of their founder, Joseph Smith, Mormons held that no marriages would be performed in Heaven but that those properly sealed by the Mormon priesthood on earth would last eternally. Early on the Mormons adopted the practice of polygamy (many wives), replicating the Hebrew prophets to institute a patriarchal order on earth and in heaven. Mormons were roundly attacked for this practice as "un-Christian" and immoral. In a published pamphlet, *The Peace Maker, or, The Doctrines of the Millennium* (1842), the Mormons defended their practice as the only way to restore proper relations between the sexes and avoid social chaos. The writer argued that nineteenth-century women had assumed "unnatural" power in the family and that monogamy allowed women to control their husbands sexually. Polygamy lasted until 1890, providing a system that Mormons believed reinstituted proper gender roles and relations between men and women.

Postbellum and Industrial Nineteenth Century

Between 1880 and 1912, almost two million Jews from eastern Europe immigrated to the United States. Jews, of course, had lived in North America prior to this time, many having moved into middle- and upper-class American society. Like all immigrant groups, Jews struggled with the question of assimilation —how much should they modify their religious and cultural practices to fit in with the dominant culture? Here again, conceptions of gender played a crucial role in this religious and cultural negotiation.

Historians have pointed out that anti-Semitic European intellectuals at the turn of the twentieth century were developing elaborate theories to prove that Jews were moral and physical degenerates, setting the stage for the Holocaust. In this literature, Jewish men were portrayed as "womanly," sometimes compared to menstruating women, who, these writers claimed, smelled bad, were weak, and dirty. Jewish men were accused of cowardliness, stinginess, and even hysteria, a quintessential negative female trait, at that time directly associated with the female body. Jewish women were painted as loud, vulgar, immodest, and, unlike their male counterparts, physically strong. One of the "proofs" given for these negative images came from religious practices. Because Jewish men are primarily responsible for religious observance and thus devoted a large portion of their time to Torah study and contemplation, they were criticized for appearing to be weak and unwilling to work. Jewish women supported men in this task, often working so that their husbands could fulfill their religious obligations. Thus, anti-Semitism depicted the religious order of male piety and authority within Judaism, which in fact resembled male piety and authority in Christianity, as "feminine."

Jews who had lived in the United States for some time and joined the middle and upper classes were sensitive to the negative images. Some Jewish philanthropists responded by establishing programs to "Americanize" newcomers. Many of these efforts were geared toward Jewish youth. Girls were taught etiquette, domestic skills, and the arts to "feminize" them, and boys' programs focused on athletics to overcome the stereotype that Jewish young men were weak and fearful. Advice literature and domestic magazines such as Chaim Malitz's *The Home and the Woman* (1918) advised women to make their homes clean, moral spaces, a haven for their husbands to retire to after a long day's hard work. Some Zionist literature promoted "muscular Judaism," calling for the construction of Jewish gymnasiums to build Jewish bodies while constructing a new Jewish nation.

By the last decades of the nineteenth century, Protestant women had so thoroughly dominated the laity through congregational membership and activity in social reform and missionary organizations that they were gaining power to direct those labors. Among liberal Protestants, such as Congregationalists, Unitarians, and northern Methodists, some women were being ordained to the ministry, although few congregations were willing to hire them. The first Protestant woman ordained, in 1853, was Congregationalist Antoinette Brown Blackwell. Female religious leaders took charge of new religious movements, most notably in this period Mary Baker Eddy (1821–1910), who founded the Church of Christ, Scientist (1879), and Madame Helena P. Blavatsky (1831–91), who, with Henry S. Olcott (1832–1907), began the Theosophical Society in 1875. The "Woman Warriors" of the Salvation Army, wearing army uniforms and evangelizing in slums and saloons and on street corners, reinterpreted "womanly" behavior and fashion to advance their spiritual cause. In her weekly column in the Salvationist publication *War Cry*, Salvation Army commander Maud Booth dispelled the notion that proselytizing was immodest or unwomanly. Other, even more radical Protestant women publicly condemned the Christian Bible for being adulterated by the hands of men to demean women. Suffragist Elizabeth Cady Stanton (1815–1902) edited the scandalous *Woman's Bible* (1895, 1898), an interpretation of scripture that rejected all passages that she found oppressive toward women and, in her mind, "un-Christian." Although her work was discredited by most Protestant men and women of her time, she set the stage for future feminist interpretations of the Bible.

Unlike Jewish and Protestant men, who were implored to build their bodies to "masculinize" themselves and their religion, Irish Catholic men were urged to moderate their bodies to realize full Catholic and American manhood. Although the Catholic clergy continued to be feared and ridiculed as "womanly" men, in the last decades of the nineteenth century Irish Catholic laymen were stereotyped as exaggerated men—rowdy, physically strong, irresponsible, single, and sometimes menacing. Clearly these images directly reflected middle-class anxiety about the working poor in the cities where many young Irish American men lived. Nonetheless, Catholic clergy, fiction writers, and social reformers responded to these gender stereotypes as uniquely Catholic problems. The negative images of boisterous Catholic men inspired sermons, speeches, and essays calling for Irish Catholic men to give up their boyish, immature ways and become "true" men. Manliness, in this case, meant moderation, reliability, and a concern for family and religion. Catholic women, at the same time, were told in periodicals such as *Ave Maria* that a True Catholic Woman resembled the True Protestant Woman of a few decades earlier. Domesticity, a religious and social ideal preached from many pulpits and printed in Catholic devotional and family magazines, remained elusive for many Irish Catholic women who worked long hours outside the home to make ends meet.

Early Twentieth Century

Protestant men, fearful of losing their religious leadership roles, fought to reclaim Christianity as a "manly" religion. Former professional baseball player Billy Sunday (1862–1935) responded by waving an American flag in one hand and a Bible in the other while preaching the gospel of muscular Christianity to crowds of men. Called the "most advertised man in the religious world," Sunday spoke plainly and aggressively, urging his mostly northern white listeners that salvation would come through moral reform and manliness. Blending patriotism, masculinity, and morality, Sunday called on every Christian man to have the courage to fight for the gospel. Defining his "manly" Protestantism against a more liberal and, in his mind, "effeminate" Protestantism, Sunday prayed, "Lord save us from off-handed, flabby-cheeked, brittle-boned, weak-kneed, thin-skinned, pliable, plastic, spineless, effeminate, sissified, three-carat Christianity." Sunday's blending of physical and spiritual strength was echoed in Protestant youth movements in the United States, such as the Young Men's Christian Association and the Boy Scouts, that linked strong bodies with strong souls.

Billy Sunday (and the countless evangelists who followed in his footsteps) was not simply preaching his gospel of Protestant manliness to the choir. He was preaching to the culture. By the early twentieth century, many Americans were struggling to understand men's and women's roles in a rapidly changing country. The social and economic structure that had upheld a gender ideology separating American men and women into distinct realms was shifting as women entered the public sphere through the workforce and voluntary organizations formed to rid the cities of moral vices (such as poverty, prostitution, and intemperance). The "New Woman" of the new century was in the public working, volunteering, shopping, participating in clubs—in short, acting outside her domestic sphere. Of course, lower-class women and upper-class women had always been in the public sphere; the liberation that the New Woman found was a middle-class freedom. By 1921, the debate over women's place in public life was resolved constitutionally with the passing of the Nineteenth Amendment, giving women the right to vote. But caricatures of public women as "mannish" or acting against their nature would follow American women up to the present day.

Women still numerically dominated Protestant churches across theological lines. Despite the rallying cry of "muscular Christianity," men continued to be noticeably absent from church life. Many Protestants, swayed by new biblical scholarship and evolutionary theory, promoted a Christianity that accommodated modern culture. To combat this "liberal" approach, fundamentalists (called so because they stressed what they believed were the fundamentals of Christianity) condemned modern society and new scientific claims as irreligious. Fundamentalists believed that they provided a corrective for Christianity and American culture by returning to a literal reading of biblical texts to understand male and female roles. Although fundamentalists divided over women's authority to speak in lay settings as "naturally" spiritual beings, they united in their condemnation of women's ordination as contrary to biblical commands. In the words of one vocal opponent, a woman who sought ordination should be considered an "unscriptural monstrosity." Fundamentalist rhetoric proclaimed that it was "manly" to fight for Christ (against a secular culture) and that Jesus himself was "the most manly man." Denouncing feminized and watered-down Christianity, fundamentalists called for "virile" men to join the ministry to put the "unscriptural monstrosities" back in their homes and win the religious war against effeminate Christian men.

One woman, claiming the inspiration of the Holy Spirit, did not simply enter the public sphere, she dominated it. Aimee Semple McPherson (1890–1944), or "Everybody's Sister," as she portrayed herself, a charismatic Pentecostal, built her own temple in Los Angeles, performed dramatic faith healings, promoted herself brilliantly through radio and the print press, and preached a simple "Foursquare Gospel." McPherson's theatrical preaching style, which included costumes and props (she once rode down the aisle on a motorcycle dressed as a policeman), not only entertained her listeners and built her notoriety but also allowed her to transcend gender expectations in her world of religious spectacle. Although outsiders questioned her preaching techniques and wondered about her indiscretions "off stage," she masterfully balanced "feminine" emotive qualities with "masculine" aggressiveness to create her larger-than-life image.

Meanwhile, a broader cultural battle between men's definitions of religion and religious women's practices was taking place outside the pulpit. The movement to legalize contraception went to the heart of the legal and religious claims that connected married sex to reproduction. For centuries churches and governments had tethered sex to marriage and marriage to procreation. With technological advances and the growing political power of women, however, at least the latter of those two connections received a long second look from various religious traditions. Whereas some, namely, the Roman Catholic Church, remained solidly opposed to contraception as contrary to biblical instruction, the mouthpiece of moderate to liberal Protestantism, the Federal Council of Churches, endorsed the legalization of contraceptives. In all, it was a moment of definition for women's religious lives, as millions—with the blessings of their home denomination—broke from centuries of tradition that had kept women from reproductive control of their bodies.

Modern America

The years after World War II saw growth in families, advancements in higher education, and increases in religious participation. As Will Herberg said in *Protestant-Catholic-Jew*, it was American to have religion as long as it was within the mainstream. The "Beat" writers Jack Kerouac, Gary Snyder, and Allen Ginsberg, just to name a few, rejected mainstream religion and culture and pursued the teachings of Eastern religions, particularly Zen Buddhism. As illustrated in Jack Kerouac's *The Dharma Bums*, the Beats sought spiritual enlightenment through complete freedom from society's expectations of adult men. A largely male phenomenon, the Beats glorified masculinity through hard drinking, smoking, hitchhiking, fighting, philosophizing, and unemotional sexual intercourse. In their quest for enlightenment they reveled in male companionship while disdaining women (or, as Kerouac called them, "chicks"), marriage, mainstream religion, domesticity, anything confining—in short, anything "effeminate."

The "sexual revolution" of the 1960s convinced many Americans that pleasure was an essential component of sexual activity, distinct from reproduction. The celebration of sexual pleasure became evident in the popularity of such secular sex manuals as Alex Comfort's *The Joy of Sex* (1972). Some liberal religious groups (such as mainline Protestants and Reform Jews) followed this cultural trend toward celebrating sexual pleasure and in the past few decades have tended to accommodate sexual relationships that do not produce offspring or that occur outside marriage. Although always affirming the importance of marriage, liberal religious Americans are less likely to condemn unmarried sex; some even reject scripture that prohibits nonprocreative sexual activity.

The majority of religious Americans, both clergy and laity, favor contraceptives and family planning within marriage, but they remain deeply divided over the permissibility of electing to terminate a pregnancy. Since *Roe v. Wade* (1973), when the Supreme Court ruled that women have a constitutional right to abortion, religious groups have mobilized both in protest and in support of this decision. The underlying question is whether morality is a public or private matter. In the case of abortion, should the matter be an individual decision, or should it be part of collective societal values? Like the majority of Americans, most religious groups affirm that abortions should be available in cases of rape or incest or when the mother's life is in jeopardy. Most liberal religious Americans believe that abortion is an individual moral choice and appeal for the human rights and liberties of the mother as the proper moral agent to determine whether to end a pregnancy. Conservative religious groups, on the other hand, generally focus on the human rights and liberties of the fetus and view abortion as a moral evil that will bring danger to the well-being of the entire society. Many conservative Christians and Jews point to scripture—"Thou shalt not kill"—as the final authority. Unlike religious liberals who argue that biblical injunctions should be interpreted within changing historical circumstances, religious conservatives contend that scripture mandates timeless, universal standards.

By the 1970s it became apparent to many people that religion played an important part in sanctioning gender roles and reinforcing gender identity. Some theologians and religious activists advocated expanding gender roles or reinterpreting gender identity by reformulating or "uncovering" religious traditions. Others, who saw the value in religiously defined gender roles, affirmed these religious "truths" with renewed vigor.

The heated debates about the relationship between religion and gender occurred in religious settings, in classrooms, in "consciousness-raising" groups, among friends and family, and in the avalanche of books that began to be published on this highly contested topic. Catholic feminist theologian Mary Daly set the tone for the discussion in her classic text *Beyond God the Father* (1973). She urged women to give up the idea of a cosmic father-God as a fictional symbol created by men to legitimate their social power and oppress women. Maleness, according to Daly, became deified as an outgrowth of patriarchy (the rule of the fathers). This cosmic order allowed for the systematic devaluing of women and their religious rituals and ultimately led to the complete erasure of female sacredness. In her next major work, entitled *Gyn/Ecology*, Daly, who was always evolving and self-critiquing, moved beyond her previous notions of transforming the theological project. She now saw herself as a "Postchristian." She could no longer use words such as *God*, since there was no way to remove masculine imagery from it; nor could she employ terms such as *androgyny* and *homosexuality*, which by their very notions of "inclusion" were exclusive of women who wanted to break from old patriarchal patterns. She discarded old theological semantic baggage "so that Journeyers will be unencumbered by malfunctioning (male-functioning) equipment." Daly wrote for "the Hag/Crone/Spinster in every *living* woman," not for any mythical, broader theological community. Daly employed a self-invented vocabulary that both exasperates and excites readers to this day. Her work provided a theoretical and theological context for women who sought to explore a spirituality not defined by church fathers.

Although Daly offended many by challenging the gendered basis of Judaism and Christianity, she struck a chord with some women seeking to come to terms with what they perceived as their "secondary" status within their religious traditions. Judith Plaskow, in *Standing Again at Sinai* (1991), for example, argued that the central categories of Judaism (God, Torah, and Israel) needed to be reexamined in light of women's experiences. Sacred text, language, history, and rituals (including the sign of the covenant being inscribed on the male body through circumcision) all needed to be reformed not only to include but also to celebrate Jewish women. Fatima Mernissi, in *The Veil and the Male Elite* (1987), called for a reclaiming of the Koran as a liberating text for Muslim women, one that had been adulterated by male scholars for the benefit of Muslim men. Scores of other feminist theologians joined the conversation, some focusing on "inclusive language" in sacred text, others seeking liturgical reform, and still others probing the past to find authentic female voices within their religious traditions. In general this cross-tradition religious reform movement united around the belief that divine masculinity reinforced male domination and, reciprocally, that a patriarchal social order created a male divinity.

For some women, it was not enough to reform Christianity, Judaism, or Islam. They sought to create new religious traditions or uncover forgotten ones. Perhaps the most notable and culturally mainstream of these efforts involves goddess worshipers, a broad spectrum of people who believe in a time before patriarchy when women were powerful and everyone worshiped a female deity (such as Diana, an ancient Greek goddess). As Merlin Stone explained in *When God was a Woman* (1976), all aspects of women's lives and bodies were sanctified when the earth goddess was worshiped. Gender roles changed dramatically when men established patriarchal rule and created a male sky god. Goddess worshipers claim that life under the goddesses' rule was peaceful, and they believe that society was structured around sanctifying the earth, female bodies, and sexuality. The goddess, they contend, was revered as a creator mother. Women were priestesses, and religious rites revolved around the female life cycle. Some goddess worshipers (such as those associated with Wicca) incorporate men into their rituals as symbolic of lovers or sons of the goddess. Goddess worshipers today insist that if female deities were worshiped and women ran the world, society would be peaceful because, as biologically determined mothers, women will always be nurturers. Put simply, women's religious and social value in the goddess tradition is elevated but ultimately dependent on their reproductive capacity.

In the 1970s, in addition to political activism through support for the equal rights amendment and pro-choice abortion policies, feminists and others in the women's movement engaged in "consciousness-raising" sessions. Designed to encourage women to explore alternate ways of thinking and being, such practices spread to religious groups that increasingly encouraged alternative therapies to replace coldly rational techniques of modern medicine that tended to the body and not to the soul. In the 1980s, a number of male writers and cultural figures initiated a "men's movement," modeled on consciousness-raising among women and also mimicking the kinds of "invented traditions" used by goddess worshipers. The urtext for many in the fledgling men's consciousness-raising sessions was Robert Bly's *Iron John*. Bly noted that the feminist movement had inspired men to develop their "feminine" (i.e., soft and nurturing) side, yet he also sensed that something was wrong. If men had become "more thoughtful, more gentle," Bly remarked, by this process they had not necessarily "become more free." Bly called men to the mythological traditions of ceremonies of initiation, in which a man would find "lying at the bottom of his psyche, a large, primitive being covered with hair down to his feet. Making contact with this Wild Man is the step the Eighties male or the Nineties male has yet to take." Bly led men's seminars and group therapy sessions through the 1980s, promoting his notion of setting the wild man free.

Essential male and female characteristics (such as warlike or peaceful), based on biological categories (those who inseminate and those who give birth) writ large in the cosmic order (a male deity has "fatherly" and warrior qualities, and a female deity has "motherly" and nurturing qualities), are neither new nor unique to goddess worship or the men's movement. In fact, at the same time that goddess worshipers were uncovering these "truths" from a buried religious history, conservative religious groups were also reaffirming the biological and religious "truths" of masculine and feminine identity. Both sides of the religious spectrum were responding to their perception of feminism and its influence—for better or for worse—on religion and American culture. In 1987 the Council on Biblical Manhood and Womanhood outlined the biblically based differences between men and women. This nondenominational conservative Protestant group proclaimed that the "distinctions in masculine and feminine roles are ordained by God" and that husbands must assume "loving, humble headship" of wives, who in turn must practice "intelligent, willing submission." Evangelical same-sex support groups such as the Promise Keepers and the woman's group Women's Aglow help men and women realize these goals. Jewish and Muslim orthodox communities also have seen an increase in the encouragement of women. Dressing modestly and finding meaning in scripturally defined roles and status have been appealing to women disenchanted with what they perceive to be the materialism of secular society and the sexual promiscuity (not freedom) that they believe is tied to feminism. Across traditions, the dramatic growth in female orthodoxy in the United States is directly related to the rejection of "secular" feminism and a desire to return to religious communities that afford women respect within their divinely sanctioned roles.

While religious people across the United States are affirming their gender identity and gender roles through a spectrum of beliefs and practices that ranges from new religious movements to a return to orthodoxy, perhaps the most pressing gender question facing all religious groups today is homosexuality. There is deep disagreement among and between religious groups about the rights of homosexuals, same-sex marriage, and the ordination of gay men and lesbians. Although there is little consensus around this volatile issue, most religious responses tend to be based on sacred text, religious tradition, and the notion of "natural" or "unnatural" sexual orientation. Advocates of gay men and lesbians argue that biblical writings and traditions on homosexuality were formed in a different cultural context, no longer relevant to today's world. Opponents of accepting homosexuality contend that religious truths written and practiced transcend time and place. Some religious groups seek to convert homosexuals, some accept homosexuals if they remain celibate, many promote civil rights (speaking out against discrimination) but not religious rites (such as performing same-sex marriage), and a few embrace homosexuals as equal participants in the laity and clergy.

Conclusion

Although the contemporary debate about homosexuality and religion is usually argued in terms of sexual orientation, the central issues bring us back to the topic of how gender identity shapes religious identity. As religious groups and individuals wrestle with concerns about homosexuality, their religious identity is clarified through their response to this question of gender identity. Religious traditions teach us what it means to be male and female. The majority of religious traditions practiced in the United States affirm through sacred texts and rituals that heterosexuality is divinely ordained. Therefore, to challenge religiously prescribed gender identity through homosexuality potentially destabilizes religious identity. In other words, religious men and women who transgress the traditional gender roles become vulnerable to attacks against not only their sexual identity but also their religious identity. Furthermore, religious groups that accept homosexuality but demand celibacy or withhold religious rites such as same-sex marriages illustrate again that religious and gender identity is ultimately about performance. These groups do not denounce or deny homosexuality, but they will not allow it to be practiced alongside religious performances. In other words, what you do (remain celibate) or how you act (get married) is equally or more important than what you profess.

Throughout this chapter we have looked at specific examples of religious renewal that have allowed for acts of gender transgression, but we have discovered that these radical moments have often reinforced a strict gender standard and hierarchy already in place. One wonders if acts of gender transgression apart from intense moments of religious renewal, but still performed by religious people, might ultimately lead to new religious understandings of what it means to be male and female.

SUGGESTED READINGS

Axtell, James. *The Invasion Within: The Contest of Cultures in Colonial North America*. New York: Oxford University Press, 1985.

Bartowski, John. "Breaking Walls, Raising Fences: Masculinity, Intimacy and Accountability among the Promise Keepers." *Sociology of Religion* 61 (Spring 2000): 33–53.

Boyarin, Daniel. "Gender." In *Critical Terms for Religious Studies*, edited by Mark C. Taylor, 117–35. Chicago: University of Chicago Press, 1998.

Braude, Ann. *Radical Spirits: Spiritualism and Women's Rights in Nineteenth-Century America*. Boston: Beacon Press, 1989.

———. "Women's History *Is* American Religious History." In *Retelling U.S. Religious History*, edited by Thomas A. Tweed, 87–107. Berkeley and Los Angeles: University of California Press, 1997.

Brekus, Catherine A. *Strangers and Pilgrims: Female Preaching in America, 1740–1845*. Chapel Hill: University of North Carolina Press, 1998.

Brown, Kathleen. "The Anglo-Algonquian Gender Frontier." In *Negotiators of Change: Historical Perspectives on Native American Women*, edited by Nancy Shoemaker, 26–48. New York: Routledge Press, 1995.

Butler, Judith. *Gender Trouble: Feminism and the Subversion of Identity*. New York: Routledge Press, 1990.

Bynum, Caroline Walker. "Introduction: The Complexity of Symbols." In *Gender and Religion: On the Complexity of Symbols*, edited by Caroline Walker Bynum, Stevan Harrell, and Paula Richman, 1–20. Boston: Beacon Press, 1986.

Coakley, Sarah, ed. *Religion and the Body*. Cambridge: Cambridge University Press, 1997.

Deberg, Betty A. *Ungodly Women: Gender and the First Wave of American Fundamentalism*. Minneapolis: Fortress Press, 1990.

Foster, Lawrence. *Religion and Sexuality: The Shakers, The Mormons and the Oneida Community*. Urbana: University of Illinois Press, 1984.

Franchot, Jenny. *Roads to Rome: The Antebellum Protestant Encounter with Catholicism*. Berkeley and Los Angeles: University of California Press, 1994.

Hyman, Paula. *Gender and Assimilation in Modern Jewish History: The Roles and Representation of Women*. Seattle: University of Washington Press, 1995.

Keller, Catherine. "Place: De/Colon/izing Spaces." In *Apocalypse Now and Then: A Feminist Guide to the End of the World*, 140–80. Boston: Beacon Press, 1996.

Kvam, Kristen E., Linda S. Schearing, and Valerie H. Ziegler, eds. *Eve and Adam: Jewish, Christian, and Muslim Readings on Genesis and Gender*. Bloomington: Indiana University Press, 1999.

Lang, Sabine. *Men as Women, Women as Men: Changing Gender in Native American Cultures*. Translated by John L. Vantine. Austin: University of Texas Press, 1998.

Laqueur, Thomas. *Making Sex: Body and Gender from the Greeks to Freud*. Cambridge: Harvard University Press, 1990.

McDannell, Colleen. "'True Men As We Need Them': Catholicism and the Irish-American Male." *American Studies* 27, no. 2 (1986): 19–36.

Prell, Riv-Ellen. *Fighting to Become Americans: Jews, Gender, and the Anxiety of Assimilation*. Boston: Beacon Press, 1999.

Reis, Elizabeth. *Damned Women: Sinners and Witches in Puritan New England*. Ithaca, N.Y.: Cornell University Press, 1997.

Scott, Joan Wallach. "Gender as a Useful Category of Historical Analysis." *American Historical Review* 91 (December 1986): 1053–75.

Taves, Ann. "Sexuality in American Religious History." In *Retelling U.S. Religious History*, edited by Thomas A. Tweed, 27–56. Berkeley and Los Angeles: University of California Press, 1997.

Welter, Barbara. "The Cult of True Womanhood, 1820–1860." *American Quarterly* 18 (Summer 1966): 151–74.

Williams, Walter L. *The Spirit and the Flesh: Sexual Diversity in American Indian Culture*. Boston: Beacon Press, 1986.

Winston, Diane. *Red-Hot and Righteous: The Urban Religion of the Salvation Army*. Cambridge: Harvard University Press, 1999.

The State

The First Amendment to the U.S. Constitution provides, in part, that "Congress shall make no law respecting an establishment of religion or prohibiting the free exercise thereof." In December 1980, Daniel Donnelly of Pawtucket, Rhode Island, brought an action in federal court to prevent the erection of a nativity scene as a part of a city-funded Christmas display. Donnelly claimed that its presence would violate the "establishment clause" of the First Amendment to the U.S. Constitution. In 1986, Alfred Smith and Galen Black, Native American employees of an Oregon state drug rehabilitation program, were fired because they had used peyote in a Native American Church ritual. Ingestion of peyote, the hallucinogenic fruit of a cactus that grows in Texas and Mexico, was prohibited by Oregon narcotics law. Smith and Black were later denied unemployment compensation because they had been fired "for work-related misconduct." The two brought an action against the state of Oregon, claiming that their constitutional right to the free exercise of religion had been denied. The Supreme Court of the United States held against the plaintiffs in both these cases. According to the Court, the First Amendment both permits government to fund and display historically significant religious symbols to honor a public holiday and gives full protection only to religious opinions, not to religious acts, which remain subject to neutral laws of general application.

The First Amendment, which was ratified with the rest of the Bill of

Rights in 1791, was written by representatives of an overwhelmingly Protestant United States who were members of a government with very limited federal power. Today, more than two centuries later, the United States has a powerful national government and is a formidable world power—and its citizens come from every religious tradition in the world. The First Amendment remains a powerful symbol of American freedom. What did it mean to those who wrote and passed it? And what does it mean for us today? Should historical changes influence how the First Amendment is interpreted?

In *Democracy in America*, a portrait of the early American Republic based on travels in the United States in 1831–32, Alexis de Tocqueville commented, concerning religion in America, that "all thought that the main reason for the quiet sway of religion over their country was the complete separation of church and state." Subsequent history has largely confirmed Tocqueville's astute observations about the distinctive characteristics of the relationship of religion, law, and politics in America and the importance of that relationship in defining American identity. Americans have taken pride in their seemingly paradoxical commitment both to the separation of church and state and to the importance of religion in American public life. This chapter considers how, on the one hand, the religious lives of Americans can be said to happen in a private space largely defined and set apart by secular law and politics, while, on the other, legal and political discourses and institutions have been profoundly influenced by religion and, likewise, religion by politics and law. The shared life of the American political community is at once highly secular and highly sacralized. Furthermore, unlike in Europe and to the astonishment of many Europeans, with whom the vast majority of Americans share a religious tradition, disestablishment of religion in America has meant that religion has flourished rather than withered.

The marvels of American religious freedom and vitality have been somewhat exaggerated, of course. There have been times and places throughout American history in which certain religious communities have enjoyed a cultural power and even legal protection that supported real political domination. The American government, along with its founding documents, its heroes, and its defining events, has even taken on certain sacred qualities. At times government has interfered with or persecuted religious communities. Because of increasing religious diversity and a growing commitment to equality, however, religion, law, and politics have moved gradually, over the course of American history, toward less and less interdependence.

The subject of this chapter is *church–state* relations, a term inherited from medieval Europe, when kings vied for power with popes. Today *church* has come to be understood to include all religion and *state* to refer to a broad range of governmental and political functions beyond the central coercive power of a national government. The effort at rhetorical inclusiveness produces difficulties, though. It turns out that defining *religion* is much more difficult than defining *church* because not all religion is institutional. Enforcing the legal separation of religion and law and protecting legally the free exercise of religion demand a definition that sees religion as autonomous and divorced from culture. But religion is protean and incredibly varied, blending often into other aspects of human life and culture. Consider the cases mentioned at the beginning of this chapter. Is the crèche in the Pawtucket case a religious symbol or part of a secular national holiday? Is the use of peyote religious or cultural for Native Americans? What is gained (or lost) by calling each religious? Or not? Can we call religion free if only religious *opinion* is constitutionally protected? These are the kinds of hard questions that American courts face every day.

Much of the writing on religion, law, and politics in the United States is highly partisan, even rancorous. Moreover, as always with important themes in history, present concerns shape our understanding of the past. Political actors, as well as historians, participate actively in and influence the interpretation of America's religious past. Persistent questions include: What role have religious people, institutions, and ideas played in shaping American law and politics? What level of interdependence between religion, law, and politics amounts to an establishment of religion? To what extent should religion be "free"? Does religious freedom belong to the individual alone or also to religious communities? In a country without an established religion, who will decide and how will they decide what counts as religion for legal and political purposes? Why does the separation of church and state seem both necessary and impossible? Answers to these questions have changed over the course of American history. The meaning of the key words of the First Amendment provisions with respect to religion—"establishment," "religion," and "free exercise"—remains highly contested. But Americans have an opportunity in a time of increased global interdependence, as constitutions are being created and amended around the world and as international human rights law develops, to review their history honestly and to consider these issues.

Precolonial Era

Before Europeans came to America in the fifteenth century, the existing societies of both Europe and America were what might be termed "premodern" or "traditional" societies, in which religion, law, and politics were highly integrated. Although not lacking all distinction, and although they changed over time, the social institutions in premodern societies often shared personnel, language, rituals, cosmologies, mythologies, and public space.

Europe had been Christian—with various local orthodoxies, vestiges of pre-Christian religions, and diverse folk practices—for almost a thousand years by the time some of its countries began colonizing the New World. Established Christian institutions, ideas, and images defined the nature of the person, of society, and of the natural world. Churches were often privileged actors in European countries in the early modern period, sometime playing roles of "king maker" and providing courts for legal disputes. At other times churches were forced to recognize the political power of the sword, as princes forced acceptance of corrupt friends and new political ideas into positions of power in the ecclesiastical hierarchy. In all, the Christian church partnered with the most powerful people of the continent—sometimes leading and sometimes following the lead of a more powerful rival. Those Europeans who traveled to the New World interpreted the religious lives of those they discovered there using the models they knew.

One of the first indigenous American societies encountered by Europeans was the powerful and extensive Aztec Empire. We know about the Aztecs from their own writings, the writings of the Spanish conquistadors and priests who knew them, and archaeological evidence, including the impressive remains of many great ceremonial buildings and artifacts. When the Spanish arrived, the Aztecs, having recently conquered, through both war and intermarriage, a large territory of what is now Mexico, governed by means of a complex set of political institutions and a large bureaucracy through which they ruled over a conglomeration of city-states. This centralized administration collected taxes, regulated agriculture and business, and oversaw the administration of law and the performance of religious ceremonies.

Aztec society was divided between a noble and a peasant class whose respective positions were defined by sumptuary laws that limited luxury goods to the upper classes. Only nobles, for example, were permitted to own land, have two-story houses, wear certain kinds of jewelry, hold certain public offices, practice polygamy, wear cotton, and go to certain schools. The religious mythology and ideology of the nobility functioned to give legitimacy to the Aztec state and provided an understanding of the origin and purpose of human life that permeated all activities. As in many urban cultures, religion, law, and politics were centered in the capital city, in the central Temple Mayor of Tenochtitlán. There the natural order of the cosmos and the created order of

Aztec society were linked and maintained by a cycle of ceremonies, including a continuing process of human sacrifice in imitation of the original sacrifices of the gods in the creation of human society.

Meanwhile, to the north, some five hundred nations lived in the geographical area of what are now the lower forty-eight states. A wide range of legal and political institutions governed them. Several of these nations, making up the League of the Iroquois—the Seneca, the Cayuga, the Onondaga, the Oneida, and the Mohawk—a group numbering about twenty thousand, lived near the lower Great Lakes around 1600. Twentieth-century members of these tribes inherited a rich traditional history of the political genius of their forebears who founded the Iroquois Confederacy. An epic narrative known as the Great Law is still enacted at the Condolence Council of the Iroquois people for the mourning and installation of chiefs. The Great Law tells of Deganawi:dah, the peacemaker, a prophet who founded the League of the Longhouse, an alliance of tribes that were previously enemies. Although smaller than the nations of Europe or the Aztec Empire, these nations, too, were traditional societies in which law and politics presumed a religious cosmology and anthropology.

European settlers left many writings about American Indian culture. One early European account comes from Roger Williams, a Puritan minister who eventually settled what is now Rhode Island. Williams lived among and studied the Narragansett, near present-day Providence. In 1643 he published a book describing their language, daily lives, and religious beliefs, *A Key into the Language of America*. The book is naive and incomplete by contemporary standards; nonetheless, it records research based on careful and sympathetic observation. Williams wrote: "They have an exact forme of King, Priest, and Prophet, as was in Israel typicall of old in that holy Land of *Canaan*, and as the Lord Jesus ordained in his spirituall Land of *Canaan* his church throughout the whole World: their Kings or Governours called *Sachimaüog*, Kings, and Atauskowag Rulers doe govern: Their Priests, performe and manage their Worship; Their wise men and old men of which number the priests are also, whome they call *Taupowaüog* they make solemne speeches and Orations, or Lectures to them concerning Religion, Peace, or Warre and all things." For both the Narragansett and the Iroquois, as for the Aztec (and the English), religion, law, and politics were closely intertwined. Each of those societies had an understanding of the world peculiar to its own religion and culture. Williams used the Hebrew Bible as a model to describe the political forms of the Narragansett, the same model he used to assess the political and legal order of the colonists. Williams struggled to understand and to describe Narragansett society on its own terms, yet he was bound by the strong religio-political ideal in front of him. Williams (as we do) understood new things by comparison with what he knew.

The indigenous societies of North America were deprived of most of their political power and virtually all their political and legal institutions as a result of the European conquest. The religious lives of Native Americans continued, however, and continue today, within a context many of them would regard as political occupation by a hostile, often aggressively Christian state. Native Americans resist this occupation today, in part, by making constitutional claims under the Mexican Constitution, the religion provisions of the First Amendment to the U.S. Constitution, and the provisions of international treaties.

Beginning in the early modern period (fifteenth and sixteenth centuries) and stimulated in part by the Protestant Reformation, Christian churches in the West began a gradual, still ongoing process of disentanglement from law and politics. As the modern nation-state and market economy developed and Europeans "discovered" the world, so also eventually grew a commitment to religious tolerance and to the separation of church and state. These emerging modern ideas, ideas with deep roots in the Western tradition, classical and Christian, traveled to the New World with the European immigrants. In this sense, the United States was from the beginning a modern country. Religion was never successfully legally established in a European sense, and law and politics developed separately, on the whole, from particular religious communities.

Colonial North America

Christianity, in a seemingly infinite number of incarnations, has been the dominant, but never the exclusive, religious expression of North Americans, including most Native Americans, since the conquest. Indeed, North American culture might accurately be described as Christian, in the broadest sense of the word. In contrast to both Native Americans and European Christians, though, North American Christians have not known the close official identification of religion, law, and politics characteristic of traditional societies. One result of this absence has been that there is virtually no widely shared memory in the United States, as there is in Europe, of the oppression, conflict, and corruption created by state control of religious matters or by religious control of the state. American atheism, secularism, humanism, and agnosticism are, on the whole, less anticlerical and hostile to the churches than their European counterparts.

The specific religious communities and political histories of each European settlement in the New World combined to make each colony's "church-state" history distinctive. Each colony, however, made a contribution to the eventual and peculiarly American consensus embodied in the First Amendment to the U.S. Constitution of 1788 (and in the various state constitutions) to guarantee religious freedom while prohibiting established religion. The rich and complex conversation about "church-state" relations that resulted in this consensus took place first against the backdrop of radical and sometimes violent changes in the Protestant and Catholic churches of Europe and their places in the emerging European nations. It continued against a global backdrop.

The distinctive American commitment to religious liberty finds its origins in three characteristics of colonial society at the end of the eighteenth century. First, religious opinions and religious communities in the colonies were incredibly diverse, particularly after 1740, making an imposed uniformity seem, practically speaking, impossible, however theologically desirable it might have seemed to some. Second, the seemingly limitless physical space and weak colonial governments allowed dissenters simply to move down the road if they did not feel welcome. Third, a growing number of colonists espoused political and philosophical ideas that supported religious disestablishment. All three characteristics seem to have been necessary. The combination was new in human history.

Seventeenth-century New England is often cited as the place where Americans most successfully attempted a coercive religious establishment. Puritans, particularly those of the Massachusetts Bay Colony, were religious reformers. Influenced by such continental religious innovators as Martin Luther and John Calvin and believing the Church of England to have been corrupted by "popish" innovations, they sought to return to the purity of the early church and establish a holy commonwealth. Puritans understood themselves to be founding a new society governed by the Bible and purged of medieval error, one that would serve as an example to the world. They had many disagreements about exactly what it meant to govern according to the Bible, but Puritans like John Cotton and Roger Williams shared a commitment to working out a new kind of Christian society.

What did religious establishment look like in New England? It was not like the English establishment, in which the king was the head of the church and bishops sat in Parliament. The church and the state in the New England colonies were understood to be separate in the sense that ministers held no political positions. Civil authorities, however, were responsible for maintaining religious orthodoxy. In some places church membership was necessary as a condition of voting in civil elections. Religious dissenters found themselves jailed, whipped, exiled, and even occasionally executed by the civil authorities for challenging the Puritan ministers' understanding of God's purpose.

Law was one area in which Puritans argued about how religion and society should be combined in the new world they were creating. Rejecting English common law, Puritans looked to the Bible as a source of law. Yet they disagreed about how to interpret the Bible and the extent to which civil magistrates ought to enforce religious prescriptions: Should the magistrate enforce both tables of the Ten Commandments, for example, the first four commandments concerning religious observance, as well as the six commandments containing general moral proscriptions? Should a person's religious conscience, if based in a different interpretation of the Bible or based on a direct revelation from God, exempt her or him from civil laws? Because Puritans had rejected an ecclesiastical hierarchy above the level of the congregation as nonbiblical, there was no way to decide these questions for the whole church. All legal authority was located in the colonial government.

An early trial in the Massachusetts Bay Colony concerned the colony's flag. The flag included the cross of Saint George, as does the flag of the United Kingdom today. John Endecott, a former colonial governor, cut the cross out of the colony's flag, arguing that its presence invited the worship of a physical object, rather than God, contrary to the first of the Ten Commandments. Some colonial leaders argued that Endecott's act was treasonous because it attacked the sovereignty of the Crown. Others defended his views. A complicated debate ensued about the appropriate scope of human reason in interpreting scripture. As in the Pawtucket crèche case there was an ambiguity about what the cross signified. Did the cross of Saint George symbolize the colony's connection to England? Or was it a religious symbol? If it was a religious symbol, how did it work? Did it invite worship (making it an idol), or did it simply memorialize a historical event? The Massachusetts General Court tried to have it both ways. In the end Endecott was reprimanded—and the flag was changed.

One of the most interesting participants in the debate over law and authority in seventeenth-century New England was Roger Williams, the author of *A Key into the Language of America*, mentioned earlier. Williams had arrived in the Massachusetts Bay Colony in 1631. A Cambridge-educated Puritan minister who had been a protégé of the famed English jurist Sir Edward Coke, Williams was soon banished from Massachusetts because he insisted, first, that the colony's land—legal title to which was given to the Puritans in a royal charter—belonged to the Native Americans, not to the king; second, that unsaved persons should not swear political oaths, as doing so constituted worship of God, which was to be kept separate from civil government; third, that the Puritan churches should separate themselves entirely from the Church of England; and, fourth, that the civil magistrate could punish only secular offenses. A passionate and tireless proponent of these views, he debated all comers, finally moving with other dissenters to establish Providence Plantations (later Rhode Island) on land purchased from the Narragansett Indians, a colony that guaranteed freedom of religion and the separation of church and state from its inception.

From Providence, Williams published *The Bloudy Tenent of Persecution, for Cause of Conscience, Discussed in a Conference between Truth and Peace*, explaining why he opposed an established church, whether of the English or the Massachusetts kind. Williams believed that the medieval church—what he sneeringly called "Christendome"—had so corrupted Christianity that there was no modern church that could trace continuity with the early church. Furthermore, he argued, Christian churches, unlike the Jewish kingdoms of the Old Testament, were intended by God to consist only of truly converted Christians gathered together, separate from civil society. Peace would better be achieved if civil life was entirely separate from religion. Williams was answered by John Cotton, another Puritan minister, in *The Bloudy Tenent, of Persecution, for Cause of Conscience, Washed, and Made White in the Bloud of the Lamb*. Williams, in turn, responded with *The Bloudy Tenent Yet More Bloudy by Master Cottons Attempting to Wash It with the Blood of the Lambe*. Williams convinced few in his time but has been celebrated in the twentieth century for his early insistence on the separation of church and state. Massachusetts maintained a religious establishment in various forms for two hundred more years, decades past the American Revolution.

By the eighteenth century, the southern colonies, for the most part, had Anglican (Church of England) establishments. This meant that the Church of England was financially supported by the colonial governments; outward conformity to its strictures was a requirement for public office. Membership also was necessary to maintain one's position as a gentleman. Beginning with the first charter in 1606, Virginia stipulated that all ministers should preach Christianity according to the "doctrines, rites, and religion now professed and established within the realm of England." Dale's Laws in 1611 required everyone to be a churchgoer and observe the Sabbath, and they punished blasphemy, sacrilege, and criticism of the doctrine of the Trinity. Anglican ministers were publicly maintained, and only ordained clergymen were permitted to perform the marriage ceremony. As there were no Anglican bishops in the colonies before the Revolution and only sporadic efforts were made to police conformity, a rather weak and lax regime in fact prevailed in most of the southern colonies. The Carolinas also had and largely tolerated large populations of religious dissenters, which further weakened the Anglican establishment: in North Carolina, Quakers and Presbyterians; in South Carolina, Baptists, Presbyterians, and Huguenots.

Maryland had a somewhat different beginning, although it, too, had an Anglican establishment by the end of the colonial period. Issued a royal charter in 1634, Cecil Calvert, Lord Baltimore, and his son, who were among the few English Catholics, founded Maryland as a proprietary colony, meaning that they were given absolute rule. By the Act of 1649, the principle of toleration, articulated by the Calverts at the founding of the colony, was expressed: "noe person . . . professing to believe in Jesus Christ, shall from henceforth bee any waies troubled . . . for . . . his or her religion nor in the free exercise thereof . . . nor in any way compelled to the beleife or exercise of any other Religion against his or her consent." Toleration was short-lived. In 1692 Maryland became a royal colony, and in 1702 the Church of England was established and Catholics legally disabled.

Maryland Catholics, however, continued to nurture a rather un-Roman interest in the separation of church and state. John Carroll, consecrated the first Roman Catholic bishop in the United States in 1790, eagerly embraced American-style religious freedom. Carroll wanted to create "A National American Church," staffed with native clergy educated in American seminaries, democratically run, using English in the liturgy, and embracing religious pluralism and the separation of church and state. This vision of a reformed Catholic Church proved to be far ahead of its time, but it shows American Catholics to have been full participants in the heady revolutionary spirit of the late eighteenth century.

The Middle Colonies were more mixed in population than either New England or the South, making enforced religious conformity much more difficult. A policy of toleration often was as much a matter of pragmatic calculation as it was a considered ideology of religious pluralism. New York had a nominal English establishment in the eighteenth century, but the presence from the beginning of Dutch Reformed, French Huguenots, Presbyterians, Quakers, Catholics, and Jews made enforcement impractical. New Jersey and Pennsylvania espoused religious toleration from their inception, Pennsylvania because of the Quaker commitment of its founder, William Penn, to freedom of conscience. These colonies were not without occasional religious conflict, however, and laws still disadvantaged some religious outsiders.

The Spanish and French colonies of North America shared a world defined in large part by the newly refurbished theology of the Catholic Reformation. The Council of Trent (1545–63) assumed the exclusive possession of religious truth by the Roman Catholic Church and, on that basis, insisted on the need for state enforcement of that truth. In the Catholic colonial regimes in California, the Southwest, and the Northeast, church and state went hand in hand. The pope's grant of *real patronato* gave Spanish imperial authorities virtually complete authority in appointing the officials of the church in the colonies.

The Roman Catholic Church of the Spanish and French colonies was not without internal diversity, however. New Spain, for example, had both secular clergy, appointed by the Catholic bishops to care for the Spanish parishes, and regular clergy (those belonging to religious orders), who often acted independently with respect to Rome. Churchmen disagreed about the legal and moral status of the indigenous peoples, for example. A public debate between two Catholic priests before Charles V of Spain in 1550 considered this question. Juan Ginés de Sepúlveda, a Spanish legal scholar, argued with Aristotle that the American Indians were less than human, being natural slaves. In opposition was Bartolomé de las Casas, a Dominican missionary who had been living in Mexico for thirty years, who argued that the Native Americans were fully human and practiced a religion entitled to respect. The pope and the kings of Spain responded by prohibiting forced conversion and enslavement of Native American peoples. But the prohibitions were largely ineffectual. In California, for example, Spanish soldiers and Franciscan friars together established a series of missions in which Native Americans often worked and lived as slaves in all but name.

The traditional integration of religion, law, and politics in the Catholic colonies left its stamp in the distinctive cultures of New Orleans, New Mexico, and Quebec. The state of Louisiana is divided into parishes, not counties, for example. Louisiana law is a civil law, not a common-law, jurisdiction. It derives its law, as does France, from the Napoleonic Code. But the Catholic colonies, like the Protestant colonies, were a long way from Europe. They, too, worked out new church-state arrangements that were to change the world's understanding of religious freedom.

Revolutionary and Early Republican America

When the Second Continental Congress declared the independence of the "united states of America" in 1776, it appealed to "the Laws of Nature and of Nature's God." "Nature's God" was different from the other colonial gods, the gods of the Puritans and the Roman Catholic Church. The law of Nature's God was not revealed in the Bible or in the work of the Holy Spirit through the history of the church but discovered through the use of human reason. Nature's God, the Deists' God, was a *deus otiosus*, a creator god who does his work, withdraws, and then leaves humans to administer it. The Declaration of Independence made a strong claim for the sufficiency of human reason for human governance.

Christianity in its various forms had powerful rivals in the colonies at the end of the eighteenth century. Deism was both the expressed religious philosophy of an educated few and an important influence on many more. The Revolution itself, moreover, was in some ways a religious event. Although the end of the eighteenth century was a time of the lowest church attendance in American history, "religion" was everywhere—in the mouths of politicians, in the ritual celebrations of revolutionary fervor, and in the language ordinary people used to describe what was happening to them. The language spoken by the revolutionaries was a curious mix of Enlightenment rationalism and Calvinist providentialism. The Protestant clergy largely supported the Revolution, saturating the country with patriotic sermons evoking images of a covenanted people protected by the special hand of Providence. For these preachers, revolutionary republicanism and Protestant Christianity went hand in hand. The Revolution, as religion, had its own myths, saints, dogmas, and rituals. A sacred aura was constructed around the life and person of George Washington, for example. Many throughout the colonies participated in dances around the liberty tree.

Among those who did not support the Revolution were many American Anglicans. After more than a hundred years of religious establishment throughout the colonies, the Anglicans still had no bishops in the colonies. The church was ruled from England. Bishops were therefore regarded by many colonists as associated with royalist politics and as a symbol of the English establishment. Passage of the Quebec Act by Parliament in 1774—granting religious freedom to the Roman Catholic Church in Canada and creating, in effect, a dual religious establishment—only intensified American fears of Anglican power. Non-Anglican Protestants and Deists in the colonies were often united against the Crown.

The unamended Constitution, ratified in 1788, lacks even a reference to Nature's God. The only mention of religion in the Constitution is the provision in Article VI that "no religious test shall ever be required as a qualification to any Office or public Trust under the United States." The new federal government was a government of express and limited powers, none of which included the power to establish religion. Some states expressed concern nevertheless that the new government might usurp the rights of the people with respect to religion, as well as other matters. The states ratified the Bill of Rights in 1791 to alleviate this concern and to make explicit certain rights of the people as against the federal government. Today the religion clauses of the first of the Ten Amendments included in the Bill of Rights are understood to be the governing statement of the relationship of religion to government for all Americans. At the time they had a somewhat more limited role. They clarified the federal government's lack of power to legislate about religion. There is much debate today as to exactly what motivated the Framers and what the words of the First Amendment meant to them. But there is no question that, as originally written, the religion clauses principally expressed the disability of "Congress," not of the state legislatures, in the area of religion.

Deists and Protestant dissenters agreed for the most part that church and state should be separate, at least at the federal level. Most states also disestablished religion and guaranteed religious toleration, although religious tests for public office and other privileges for religion continued for some time at the state level. Some of the states continued to have a variety of forms of "establishment" or "quasi establishment" of religion well into the nineteenth century, including tax support for churches and ministers and criminal penalties for blasphemy. Religion was thought to be necessary for society, the way people learned to be good citizens.

Because of the timing, the people involved, and the incisiveness of their debate about religion and the state, Virginia has enjoyed a privileged position among historians and jurists trying to understand the origins of the American system of disestablishment. In 1784, after some ten years of public dispute over state funding of churches in Virginia, Patrick Henry introduced "A Bill establishing a provision for Teachers of the Christian Religion," in effect providing for a general tax. The bill was intended to end the exclusive position of the Anglican Church, mandating instead that assessment funds be allocated among all Christian churches. In proposing the bill, Henry argued that "Christian knowledge hath a natural tendency to correct the morals of men, restrain their vices, and preserve the peace of society, which cannot be effected without a competent provision for learned teachers." Some one hundred petitions were submitted to the Virginia General Assembly, of which only eleven favored the bill.

During this period James Madison circulated his *Memorial and Remonstrance Against Religious Assessments*, a justly celebrated, eloquent, and passionate summary of arguments against government support of religion. The *Memorial* argues several points: as a matter of natural right, religion is a question of individual conscience that cannot be coerced; the proposed bill amounted to an establishment of Christianity over other religions; public funding of religion would result in the bending of religion to serve the uses of the state; Christianity does not need government support to flourish; government does not need religion; and, finally, history shows that establishment destroys true religion and fosters conflict. Henry's bill was defeated.

Two years later the Virginia Assembly passed the Virginia Statute for Religious Freedom (written by Thomas Jefferson in 1777). After a long prologue in which Jefferson described his own understanding of the nature of religion, the Virginia statute provides "that no man shall be compelled to frequent or support any religious worship, place, or ministry whatsoever, nor shall be enforced, restrained, molested, or burthened in his body or goods, nor shall otherwise suffer on account of his religious opinions or belief—, but that all men shall be free to profess, and by argument to maintain, their opinion in matters of religion, and that the same shall in no wise diminish, enlarge, or affect their civil capacities." Jefferson regarded his authorship of this statute as one of his finest accomplishments. In 1802, responding to a letter of support for his presidential candidacy from the Danbury Baptist Association in Connecticut, Jefferson wrote: "Believing with you that religion is a matter which lies solely between man and his God, that he owes account to none other for his faith or his worship, that the legislative powers of government reach actions only, and not opinions, I contemplate with sovereign reverence that act of the whole American people which declared that their legislature should 'make no law respecting an establishment of religion, or prohibiting the free exercise thereof,' thus building *a wall of separation* between Church and State" (emphasis added). Jefferson's metaphor "a wall of separation" has been so often quoted that many Americans believe that those words appear in the Constitution.

Although the Virginia experience is often cited alone to support a Jeffersonian, or "separationist," reading of the First Amendment, historians today would argue that the religion provisions at the time of their passage had a much broader and more diverse base of support both in Virginia and in the other colonies. The alliance that produced the distinctive American dedication to religious liberty was, they would say, the product of a particular historical moment in which a coalition of Enlightenment Deists like Jefferson and religious dissenters from the various state establishments—Baptists, Quakers, and Presbyterians—made common cause on this point, although they may have agreed on very little else. There were people in the eighteenth century who had theological and philosophical reasons for advocating religious freedom. Isaac Backus, an influential early Baptist leader who suffered persecution for his beliefs, was one. Indeed, until the 1980s, Baptists generally have been strong supporters of the separation of church and state. But the sheer fact of religious diversity made apparent to most the need for disestablishment. The religion clauses on this reading were "articles of peace," not "articles of faith." The disestablishment of religion created a new kind of society, one that regarded government as secular and religion as entirely voluntary.

Antebellum Nineteenth Century

Although religion was *legally* disestablished by the constitutions of all the states by 1833, when Connecticut became the last state to end public support of religion, a peculiarly American brand of Protestant Christianity achieved de facto religious establishment in the antebellum period. Most Americans believed that morality in a civilized society depended on religion. Moreover, the instability and rapid changes of the early republican period provoked enormous anxiety about social norms. Conceding that moral guidance could not constitutionally be provided by an established church, most Americans were convinced that religion was necessary and that the religion that was necessary for Americans was Protestant Christianity. Religious dissenters and religious traditionalists, at odds during the Revolution, made peace. They allied against the Deists to create a "Christian America." The religious saturation that resulted from their enthusiasm and exhortation was far more extensive than establishment had ever been in the colonies. Freed of anticlericalism bred by established religion, American Protestants were enormously successful in the first half of the nineteenth century.

What did this new de facto establishment look like? In many ways it was simply the result of the enthusiastic voluntary efforts of millions of Americans who strove to make their new country into a Christian republic through the spreading of the gospel and the reform of public morality. But in many states it also had support in law: Sabbath laws enforced closing of businesses on Sundays; public schools provided religious instruction, including Bible reading; missions for the conversion of Native Americans were paid for by federal funds; presidents proclaimed days of Thanksgiving, fasting, and prayer; churches were tax exempt; land was set aside in the new territories for churches; and legislative chaplaincies were funded. American evangelicals energetically worked to provide a religious culture for this Christian America.

The de facto establishment in the antebellum period could be oppressive to minorities and dissenters. Jews and Sabbatarians objected to being forced to observe Sunday rather than Saturday as a day off. Catholics and others objected to reading the Protestant Bible and reciting Protestant prayers in the schools. Episcopally organized churches objected to the courts enforcing the wishes of a majority of a local congregation over the wishes of the bishops. Native Americans objected to being proselytized by federally funded missions that persecuted native religions. In many ways, though, the religious freedom promised by the revolutionaries was real and liberating. Unconstrained by a religious establishment and a uniform national religious past, the social and religious ferment of the antebellum period saw the founding of new religious movements, some with radical social ideas that challenged reformed theology, Victorian social mores, laissez-faire capitalism, and even the separation of church and state. The most successful numerically of these new groups and one that challenged social norms in all these ways was the Church of Jesus Christ of Latter-day Saints: the Mormons.

Mormons began to found a church in 1830. Early Mormonism, under the leadership of Joseph Smith, sought, like the Puritans, to create a new kind of faithful society. Among other doctrines, the new church espoused economic communitarianism and polygamy modeled on the lives of the patriarchs of the Hebrew Bible. In Nauvoo, Illinois, and then in Utah, despite considerable hostility from the state and federal governments and from their neighbors, Mormons established a theocratic society—a society run entirely by a church —in the middle of America. Nauvoo was created on land given to the Mormons by the state of Illinois, was governed autocratically by Joseph Smith as king, and had its own militia. Internal and external instability and resentment eventually led to the imprisonment of Smith, who was subsequently lynched by a mob while in jail. Smith's successor, Brigham Young, led the fledgling community on a great trek to what is now Utah, where a new and autonomous state, Deseret, was founded, governed by church leaders inspired by a vision of a just and holy religious community.

The biggest challenge to a de facto Protestant establishment was immigration. A huge influx of mostly Catholics from Ireland and Germany radically changed the religious landscape. The Catholic population increased from

30,000 in 1790 to 600,000 in 1830, becoming by the time of the Civil War the largest single church in the country. Fear of foreigners, many of whom did not speak English, and teaching, by both the Protestant churches and the rationalists, that the Catholic Church was irredeemably corrupt combined to produce an ugly form of American nativism. To many it seemed that being American and being Catholic were incompatible.

During the first half of the nineteenth century, legislatures and courts in all the states were struggling to create new legal forms that would govern the free churches. If churches were to be entirely voluntary, should laws be made for their incorporation? Or was that an establishment? How could the law decide who was in charge if there was a dispute? If a church had been originally founded as a Presbyterian church, what happened if a division occurred in succeeding generations over Presbyterian doctrine? How was the court to decide who were the true Presbyterians and therefore entitled to make decisions for the church and hold title to the property? In the antebellum period, state courts tended toward a congregational system, enforcing the wishes of a majority of the present local church membership. The alternative, they felt, would draw courts into theological disputes that they felt incompetent to assess. Regarding each congregation as a separate legal entity, although convenient in some way for the courts and appropriate for some Protestant congregations, was entirely incompatible with other styles of church governance. Churches with bishops or presbyteries above the level of the individual congregation were forced thereby to defer to the wishes of the local majority, whether or not this accorded with their understanding of Christianity. This issue continues to arise in American courts.

A pervasive evangelical Christian culture did not mean that there were no differences among Protestant evangelicals. Christians divided most significantly over slavery. Slavery was a legal institution. It was not simply permitted. It was thoroughly defined and managed through law, lawyers, and courts. It was also explicitly sanctioned by most churches. Some Christians, in the North and South, argued that slavery was ordained by God; others contended that it was an enormous sin. But law and religion worked hand in hand to construct the evil that was black slavery. In many southern states it was illegal to teach slaves to read. Some slave owners worked to prevent conversion of slaves, for fear that conversion would somehow make them free. Slaves often could not legally assemble for church, and when they did attend white churches, they were segregated and treated as second-class citizens.

Despite these differences between Americans, Lincoln was able to draw on a shared Christian culture in his great speeches interpreting the Civil War.

Speaking as a newly inaugurated president, he addressed people for whom his invocation of God echoed sermons they had heard. He used prophetic biblical language skillfully for political purposes.

It may seem strange that any men should dare to ask a just God's assistance in wringing their bread from the sweat of other men's faces, but let us judge not, that we be not judged. The prayers of both could not be answered. That of neither has been answered fully. The Almighty has His own purposes. "Woe unto the world because of offenses; for it must needs be that offenses come, but woe to that man by whom the offense cometh." If we shall suppose that American slavery is one of those offenses which, in the providence of God, must needs come, but which, having continued through His appointed time, He now wills to remove, and that He gives to both North and South this terrible war as the woe due to those by whom the offense came, shall we discern therein any departure from those divine attributes which the believers in a living God always ascribe to Him?

In his second inaugural address Lincoln said: "Both read the same Bible, and pray to the same God." Trying to bring the two sides together, he appealed to a god recognizable to Americans, in the North and the South—a god at once terrible, inscrutable, and just. Yet at times, both during and after the war, it seemed as if the two sides read a different Bible and prayed to different gods. Preservation of the Union had become a sacred duty for many in the North, whereas for many in the South the Confederacy, the "state," was itself sacred.

Postbellum and Industrial Nineteenth Century

Politically and legally, federal power increased relative to state power after the war. As far as religion and law today are concerned, the most significant events of this period were the passage of the Reconstruction amendments in 1865, 1868, and 1870, guaranteeing equality before the law for all Americans, although it would be at least a century before legal equality was more than a hope. On their face, the Thirteen, Fourteenth, and Fifteenth Amendments seem to be unrelated to religion. Yet the effect on religion of the Court's interpretation of the Fourteenth Amendment in the twentieth century has been profound. The second sentence of the that amendment provides that "no State shall make or enforce any law which shall abridge the privileges or immunities of citizens of the United States; nor shall any State deprive any person of life, liberty, or property without due process of law; nor deny to any person within its jurisdiction the equal protection of its laws." What are "the privileges and immunities of citizens of the United States"? What is "due process"? What constitutes "equal protection"? Are disestablishment and religious freedom "privileges and immunities of citizens of the United States"? Are they part of the definition of liberty? Does legal recognition of religion constitute a denial of equal protection? In addressing the needs of the new citizens (former slaves), Congress dramatically changed the constitutional framework of all Americans.

Courts continued during the postbellum period to struggle with intra-church disputes. For example, the 1866 General Assembly of the northern Presbyterian Church had declared secession a crime and made rejection of slavery a condition of membership in the church. (Southern Presbyterians had formed the Presbyterian Church of the Confederate States during the war, declaring that "the system of Negro slavery in the South is a divine institution, and that it is the peculiar mission of the Southern church to conserve that institution.") The Walnut Street Church in Louisville, Kentucky, split into two as a result of the 1866 declaration. After the war the General Assembly declared the Union loyalists to be the "true and lawful" Presbyterians entitled to lead the Walnut Street Church. An action was brought in the Kentucky courts challenging the assembly's decision. The southerners won, but the U.S. Supreme Court later reversed the decision. Announcing in *Watson v. Jones* that "the law knows no heresy, and is committed to the support of no dogma, the establishment of no sect," the Court held that judges should defer to the decision-making apparatus of the religious body in question, in this case the General Assembly of the Presbyterian Church, on issues of theology and church discipline. In enforcing the decisions of church tribunals under the *Watson* doctrine, the courts have thus recognized an "institutional" religious freedom—a right of religious bodies to manage, in some degree, their own affairs. This marked a change from the antebellum tendency of courts to favor a congregational church polity.

De facto establishment of Protestant Christianity saw some serious challenges during this period as non-Protestants gained in numbers and influence. Between 1865 and 1915 there were twenty-five million immigrants to the United States, mostly European Catholics and Jews. The continued growth of the Catholic Church in America represented for many Protestants a serious challenge to their idea of America. Catholic Christianity represented everything that Protestants had rejected in the Reformation: a hierarchical church, a fixed liturgy, Latin, secrecy, a celibate priesthood, monasticism, superstitious devotion, and magical practices. Catholics were believed to be obedient to foreign authorities who sought political power in the United States. To many otherwise tolerant and reform-minded American Protestants, the Roman Church seemed a perversion of true Christianity—evangelical Christianity. Catholics themselves were conflicted. Many were intensely patriotic. They wanted to be both Catholic and American. Both lay and clerical Catholics have strongly supported the First Amendment, believing with other Americans that religion is stronger when it is free. But American Catholics were dissenters in the larger Roman Catholic Church. In 1870, threatened in Europe both temporally and spiritually, the Roman Church defined the infallible character of certain papal pronouncements. In *Testem Benevolentiae* (1899) Pope Leo XIII condemned "Americanism," the error of believing in the possible harmony of church and republic.

Anti-Catholicism continued to haunt the political process. After the war the church's growing political presence seemed to threaten legally established American Protestant institutions, especially the Sabbath and the public school. European immigrants brought social practices such as Sunday beer drinking. Catholic bishops argued that the public schools were not neutral, as claimed, but were intended to inculcate Protestant religious principles. In 1887, in reaction to the Haymarket Affair—a brutal confrontation between Chicago police and largely Catholic labor protesters—the American Protective Association was formed, whose members swore never to vote for a Catholic, fanning grassroots anti-Catholicism.

Catholics debated among themselves as to whether separate schools were a desirable response to anti-Catholicism. Some Catholics felt that the common schools were an essential American institution and argued that the public schools should simply provide separate religious instruction for Catholics and Protestants. In 1884, however, the Third Plenary Council of Baltimore, the governing body of the American Catholic Church, made a national commitment to build a parallel school system. Its members voted to require each pastor to build a parochial school within two years, if one did not exist, and to insist that Catholic parents support the parochial schools and send their children to them. No more than a small percentage of Catholic children attended them, but parochial schools represented for many years the most visible part of Catholic efforts to construct a separate culture. Ironically, perhaps, the parochial school effort became most intense when public schools were becoming more secular. Legally, the challenge presented by Catholic demands for public money to fund Catholic education led to stronger political and judicial commitment to church-state separation. If religion in the schools meant public support of Catholic religion, that was too high a price to pay for many Protestants. Neutrality was preferable.

In 1869 the Cincinnati School Board, provoked by criticism from a coalition of Catholic, Jewish, and "freethinking" parents, adopted a resolution ending Bible reading in the Cincinnati public schools. Catholic parents had argued that reading the Bible without comment was not an ecumenical practice because the Bible used was a Protestant one—the King James Version—and because Catholics believe that Bible reading should occur in the context of church interpretation. A group of Protestant parents sued, arguing that the Ohio Constitution required religious instruction in the schools. The Ohio Constitution (ratified in 1851) provided that

> all men have a natural and indefeasible right to worship Almighty God according to the dictates of their own conscience. No person shall be compelled to attend, erect, or support any place of worship, or maintain any form of worship against his consent; and no preference shall be given, by law, to any religious society; nor shall any interference with the rights of conscience be permitted. No religious test shall be required as a qualification for office, nor shall any person be incompetent to be a witness on account of his religious belief; but nothing herein shall be construed to dispense with oaths and affirmations. Religion, morality, and knowledge, *however*, being essential to good government, it shall be the duty of the general assembly to pass suitable laws to protect every religious denomination in the peaceable enjoyment of its own mode of public worship, and to encourage schools and the means of instruction [emphasis added].

In that "however" in the last sentence of the quotation one can see much of the tension about religion and American public life. Before the "however" is a strong statement of disestablishment; after the "however" is a commitment to the importance of religion. The Cincinnati court ruled against the school board, but the decision was reversed on appeal to the Ohio Supreme Court. Ruling that the board had acted within its authority, the court argued that what the plaintiffs and the lower court wished was in fact an establishment of Christianity and an abuse of majority power: "The 'protection' guaranteed by the section in question means protection to the minority. The majority can protect itself. Constitutions are enacted for the very purpose of protecting the weak against the strong; the few against the many."

In contrast to a slowly growing tolerance and willingness among some to accommodate Catholics and Jews legally, two religious minorities that continued to suffer at the hands of the legal authorities were Native Americans and Mormons. Few with political power argued for religious freedom for either. In 1869, in an attempt to end the corruption in the Bureau of Indian Affairs, President Ulysses S. Grant appointed the first Native American to serve as commissioner of Indian Affairs, Richard Ely, and inaugurated a presidential "Peace Policy." Under the Peace Policy, Native American reservations were divided among various religious denominations, each of which was given authority to appoint Native American agents and to set up schools. It was an open partnership between church and state designed to Christianize and Americanize the Native Americans. In the words of one historian, "The Grant Peace Policy replaced the spoils system with church patronage, provided federal support for sectarian missions and worship and, perhaps most serious of its legal transgressions, denied religious liberty as guaranteed by the First Amendment." In 1887, the Peace Policy having failed, a new Indian policy was initiated with the Dawes Act. The Dawes Act granted individual land allotments to Native Americans and was intended to assimilate them into mainstream American practices through ownership of private property. The prophetic Ghost Dance movement arose in resistance to this effort to destroy communal practices and culminated in the massacre at Wounded Knee in 1890. (See chapter 5 for more on this.)

As some within the government worked to "civilize" the Native Americans, other agents of the federal government were struggling to "Americanize and Christianize" the Mormons. The Church of Jesus Christ of Latter-day Saints, born in the ferment of religious experimentation in upper New York State in the 1830s, had expanded and come into increasing conflict with the growing population of non-Mormons in Utah. In 1851 Utah had become a federal territory, and Brigham Young, second president of the new church, became territorial governor. In 1857 President James Buchanan decided to replace Young with a gentile (non-Mormon) governor. From then until Utah was granted statehood in 1896, there were parallel governments in Utah, one church-run and the other federally appointed. Growing tension between federal authorities and the church over the church's practice of plural marriage and its communitarian economic practices led to the passage of the Morrill Act in 1862, outlawing bigamy in the territories.

In 1879, almost one hundred years after the adoption of the First Amendment, the U.S. Supreme Court heard its first case brought under the free exercise clause of that amendment, *Reynolds v. U.S.* (The First Amendment applied in this case because Utah was a territory, not a state.) George Reynolds, a Mormon, had been convicted of bigamy under the Morrill Act. He argued that the law could not be applied against him because he acted as a matter of religious duty. His religion required him to practice plural marriage, he said, and he would literally be damned if he refused. The Court took the opportunity to consider for the first time what was meant by "the religious freedom which has been guaranteed" by the Constitution. Reviewing the history of the Virginia Statute for Religious Freedom and of Jefferson's and Madison's views on the separation of church and state, the Court held that "Congress was deprived of all legislative power over mere opinion, but was left free to reach actions which were in violation of social duties or subversive of good order." It then discussed why "polygamy has always been odious among the northern and western nations of Europe." Reynolds's petition was denied. In 1887 Congress passed the Edmunds-Tucker Act, dissolving the Corporation of the Church of Jesus Christ of Latter-day Saints, declaring its property forfeit, abolishing female suffrage, and disinheriting children of plural marriages. Under growing pressure to conform or be denied statehood, in 1890 the Mormon Church issued a manifesto renouncing the practice of plural marriage. Property was returned to the church in 1894 and Utah statehood granted in 1896.

American ambition to Christianize and "civilize" also extended beyond the borders of the United States. During the Spanish-American War, President William McKinley announced to his fellow Methodists: "I am not ashamed to tell you, gentlemen, that I went down on my knees and prayed Almighty God for light and guidance more than one night. And one night late it came to me this way. . . . There was nothing left for us to do but to take them all and to educate the Filipinos and uplift and civilize and Christianize them and by God's grace do the very best we could by them, as our fellow men for whom Christ also died." And a speaker at the Federal Council of Churches in 1908 echoed his sentiment: "Let it be ours to sustain that flag and to see to it that wherever that flag goes our holy religion goes, in every part of the world." American foreign missions were active and strongly encouraged by the federal government throughout the second half of the nineteenth century.

Early Twentieth Century

American religious historian Martin Marty sees the interwar period as a time when mainstream Protestants began to acknowledge religious pluralism, not always easily. In the introduction to his volume on this period, entitled *The Noise of the Conflict*, he lists the conflicts he sees:

Here are some of the enemies we shall be meeting: original-stock Protestants vs. everyone else; "100 percent Americans" vs. Communists and Slavs in the Red Scare; old-stock Anglo-Saxons vs. Catholics or Jewish or Asian immigrants; the Klu Klux Man vs. the same, plus liberals and blacks; white Christians vs. black Christians; conventional black churches vs. "back to Africa" movements; Zionists vs. Anti-Zionists; pro-labor Catholics vs. anti-labor Catholics; Protestant Fundamentalists vs. Modernists; pro–Peace Pact movements vs. anti–League of Nations sorts; pro-Repeal wets vs. anti-Repeal drys; Protestants against a Catholic president vs. Catholics for a Catholic president; supporters of birth control vs. enemies of birth control; Depression demagogues of the Right vs. left-wing firebrands; Protestant liberals vs. Protestant realists; Catholic workers vs. capitalists; pro–New Deal religionists vs. anti–New Dealers; pacifists vs. "preparedness for war" partisans; and more.

But Marty is also careful to insist that very little actual violence erupted as a result of these conflicts. All these conflicts had legal and political aspects. We will consider only a few.

The by now generations-old debate between Protestant liberals and fundamentalists in response to the new scientific theories of the nineteenth century in biology, geology, and biblical history were dramatically illustrated by the Scopes trial. In 1925 Tennessee passed the Butler Act: "An Act prohibiting the teaching of the Evolution theory in all the Universities, Normals, and all other public schools of Tennessee." In a trial reported all over the country and one almost certainly contrived for maximum effect, a Tennessee high school teacher, John Scopes, was convicted in the same year of illegally teaching evolution. The American Civil Liberties Union took on Scopes's case, and he was represented by Clarence Darrow, one of the greatest trial lawyers in American history. Representing the state was William Jennings Bryan, three times a candidate for president and a great moral crusader.

The Scopes trial was only one vivid and dramatic instance in a long conflict. Beginning in the mid-nineteenth century, Protestants had increasingly divided over modern teachings, particularly those concerning the historical nature of the Bible and Darwin's principle of natural selection. Both seemed to attack the very foundation of American Protestantism, the authority of the Bible. Defending Tennessee, Bryan said, "Power in this country comes from the people; and if the majority of the people believe that evolution breaks down religious faith and threatens Christianity, they have the right to demand that it be suppressed or at least confined to the little group of research men, who may study it as a theory not yet proven." Theological fundamentalists and theological liberals remained sharply divided over these issues throughout the twentieth century, but religion and politics remained closely intertwined. The people of whom Bryan speaks were and are fiercely democratic in religion and politics.

The campaign against "Rum and Romanism" also continued into the twentieth century. One of the last moral crusades of a united Protestantism was the campaign for Prohibition. The Woman's Christian Temperance Union, founded in 1874, worked in tandem with the Anti-Saloon League, leading to passage of the Eighteenth Amendment in 1919, prohibiting the sale of alcohol in the United States. Meanwhile, in 1928 the first Catholic was nominated as a candidate for the presidency by a major political party. Fear of Rome and its ambitions contributed to his defeat. One Protestant minister, summarizing the views of many Protestants, right and left, asked: "Shall we have a man in the White House who acknowledges allegiance to the autocrat on the Tiber, who hates democracy, public schools, Protestant personages, individual right and everything that is essential to independence?"

Catholics and Protestants worked together, however, in the New Deal. Inspired by a renewed commitment to gospel ideals and in response to the social ills created by laissez-faire capitalism and economic depression, Catholic and mainline Protestant leaders joined together to lobby for law reform. Inspired by the "social gospel"—a movement interested in centering Christian practice on social justice—Protestants worked to remedy the social ills created by capitalism and urbanization. Monsignor John Ryan, a Catholic priest who lobbied for workers' rights and wrote a book entitled *A Living Wage*, was known as "the right reverend New-Dealer."

During this period the Supreme Court showed itself reluctant to find First Amendment free exercise violations, tending rather toward affirming constitutional rights that were neutral toward religion. The private schools cases are an example. In 1922 Oregon passed a law requiring all students to attend public schools. The Society of Sisters, a religious order of Catholic nuns, who ran Catholic schools in Oregon, argued that their schools were constitutionally protected. The Supreme Court, in *Pierce v. Society of Sisters*, invalidated the act on the ground that parents have a right to direct the education of their children, rather than on the ground that the act violated the right to the free exercise of religion. In the most important book written on the First Amendment, *The Garden and the Wilderness: Religion and Government in American Constitutional History*, Mark deWolfe Howe argues that during the early twentieth century the Court's preoccupation was with equality and that preoccupation profoundly influenced the Supreme Court's interpretation of the First Amendment: "The constitutional law of church and state which has been forming throughout the last quarter of a century has been shaped as much by collateral doctrines concerning presuppositions of our society as it has by political or theological principle concerning the two societies and their relationship. This century's theory of religious freedom was a byproduct, as it were, of its theory of political liberty. The nation's growing awareness that the gravest brutality of our time is racial inequality had, I believe, important overtones in the evolving church and state." The principle of equality, and its corollary principle of neutrality, would guide the Court in the second half of the century as it mediated among the enemies described by Martin Marty.

Modern America

The year 1940 marks the beginning of modern First Amendment jurisprudence and the ascendancy of the Supreme Court in interpreting the relationship of religion to public life for all Americans. In the second half of the twentieth century a federal policy was worked out with respect to religion, a federal constitutional policy constraining state as well as federal action. The new jurisprudence began with a case out of Connecticut. Newton Cantwell and his two sons, Jehovah's Witnesses, had been convicted under a Connecticut statute that prohibited door-to-door solicitation without a license. The Connecticut Supreme Court upheld the conviction. On appeal, the U.S. Supreme Court declared the Connecticut statute, as applied to the Cantwells, an unconstitutional exercise of state power under the free exercise clause of the First Amendment. The Court argued that the due process clause of the Fourteenth Amendment, in effect, "incorporated" the free exercise provisions of the First Amendment and applied it to the states. The "due process" guaranteed to all citizens by the Fourteenth Amendment was thereby interpreted to include a right to free exercise of religion. *Cantwell* is also significant because of the close association of free speech and the free exercise of religion. The Cantwells' religious practice was arguably protected because it fell under both the free speech and free exercise provisions of the Constitution.

In 1947, in *Everson v. Bd. of Education*, a case concerning state reimbursement of bus fares for public and parochial school students, the Court held that the Fourteenth Amendment due process clause incorporated the establishment provision as well. Henceforth the First Amendment would be understood to begin, in effect: "Neither Congress [nor the states] shall make a law." The *Everson* Court reviewed the history of church–state separation in

America, specifically endorsing the *Reynolds* Court's view that the meaning of the First Amendment was to be found in the Virginia experience. Justice Hugo Black said:

> The "establishment of religion" clause of the First Amendment means at least this: Neither a state nor the Federal Government can set up a church. Neither can pass laws which aid one religion, aid all religions, or prefer one religion over another. Neither can force nor influence a person to go or to remain away from church against his will or force him to profess a belief or disbelief in any religion. No person can be punished for entertaining or professing religious beliefs or disbeliefs, for church attendance or non-attendance. No tax in any amount, large or small, can be levied to support any religious activities or institutions, whatever they may be called, or whatever form they may adopt to teach or practice religion. Neither a state nor the Federal Government can, openly or secretly, participate in the affairs of any religious organizations and *vice versa*. In the words of Jefferson, the clause against establishment of religion by law was intended to erect "a wall of separation between church and state."

Yet, ironically, having said this, Black, in his opinion for the majority, held that it was not a violation of the establishment clause for New Jersey to reimburse parents of parochial school students as well as parents of public school students for bus fare. The statute benefited children, he said, not churches. Parochial school cases that have followed *Everson* have attempted to find the line between educational aid that benefits children and that which benefits churches. The Court's many decisions allowing some forms of aid and striking down others are often ridiculed as being irreconcilable.

Everson also marks the beginning of a constitutional policy of neutrality, not only among churches but neutrality between believers and nonbelievers. Beginning with *Everson*, as can be seen from Black's words just quoted, the First Amendment has been understood by the Court to protect atheists as well as those who identify themselves as religious. This broader neutrality has led to enormous public resentment. The country has divided between those who believe the First Amendment favors religion over nonreligion and those who believe the First Amendment requires that government treat religiously and nonreligiously motivated people equally. The Court's tendency to consider equality and neutrality as guiding principles can be seen in its 1974 *Bob Jones University v. U.S.* decision. The Court affirmed the denial of federal funding to Bob Jones University because it had a discriminatory interracial dating policy. Racial equality as a goal trumped religious freedom, in the opinion of the Court, which denied Bob Jones's claim of constitutional protection under the religion clauses.

While the Supreme Court was working to disestablish Protestant Christianity further, religion of all kinds was enjoying a minor renaissance in the fifties. In 1955, Will Herberg published *Protestant, Catholic, Jew*, arguing that the dominant American religion was what he called the "American Way of Life." It came in three versions, but their similarities were more important than their differences, according to Herberg. The de facto establishment no longer included just mainstream Protestants. It had expanded to include all in the western European traditions. In fact, the second half of the twentieth century marks the "coming of age" of the Catholic Church. Now constituting 25 percent of Americans, and no longer poor foreign immigrants, Catholics entered the mainstream of American life in large numbers. The election of the first Catholic president in 1960, John F. Kennedy, seemed to end a certain kind of Protestant dominance of American political life. The publication by the Second Vatican Council in 1965 of the *Declaration on Religious Freedom*, reversing centuries of Catholic teaching favoring a religious establishment, marked a significant international victory for American Catholics.

Religious believers and the government, however, continued to clash. Since colonial times, conscientious objectors to military service had received special recognition. Historically that recognition had been limited to the "peace churches"—Quakers, Mennonites, and Brethren. The 1917 Selective Service Act had exempted only members of "any well-recognized religious sect." Provision for conscientious objectors was substantially broader, however, in the Selective Service Act of 1940: "Nothing contained in this Act shall be construed to require any person to be subject to combatant training and service in the land or naval forces of the United States who, by reason of religious training and belief, is conscientiously opposed to participation in war in any form. Any such person . . . shall, if he is inducted into the land or naval forces under this Act, be assigned to noncombatant service as defined by the President, or be assigned to work of national importance under civilian direction." Under the 1940 act, between 25,000 and 50,000 men were assigned to noncombatant duty (12,000 of whom were Seventh-Day Adventists) and about 12,000 to the Civilian Public Service (CPS). Some of the CPS camps were run by the peace churches and included religious indoctrination. Local draft boards largely determined who was entitled to an exemption, leaving petitioners subject to the religious philosophy of the board members. More than 5,000 Jehovah's Witnesses, as well as some 300 others, including Black Muslims and

Roman Catholics, all conscientious objectors, were prosecuted for refusing to serve in World War II.

During the Vietnam War the Supreme Court significantly liberalized the exemption for conscientious objectors to military service. In *U.S. v. Seeger* (1965) the Court held that belief in a Supreme Being was not necessary to gain conscientious objector status. In *Welsh v. U.S.* (1970) the Court allowed an exemption for a conscientious objection to war not based in explicitly religious teaching. Welsh had stated on his application form: "I believe that human life is valuable in and of itself, therefore I will not injure or kill another human being." In *Gillette v. U.S.* (1971), however, the Court refused to extend the statute to cover those who objected to a particular war. Note that these cases are not constitutional cases. They involve interpretation of a statute. The court has not recognized a First Amendment right not to serve in the military.

In the second half of the twentieth century, two popular political movements were significantly expressed in religious terms: the civil rights movement of the 1950s and 1960s and the antiabortion movement of the 1980s and 1990s. Both were generated in large part by self-consciously religious groups using explicitly religious rhetoric and actively working to change laws. Martin Luther King and others successfully raised the prophetic voice of the churches to protest discrimination against blacks, particularly in the South. Malcolm X ran a more aggressive campaign in the northern cities, using Black Islam as his foundation. Conservative Protestants and Roman Catholics appealed to biblical and church teaching to protest the liberalization of laws prohibiting abortion, particularly condemning the Supreme Court's decision in *Roe v. Wade* (1973) acknowledging constitutional protection for a woman's right to an abortion.

Most dramatic in the last quarter of the century in terms of the church-state issue was an interesting realignment among politically active religious groups. Before the *Smith* peyote case (described earlier in this chapter), American religious groups had divided along conservative/liberal theological lines with respect to church-state issues. Liberal groups largely supported a separationist agenda, and conservative groups supported more religion in public life. Since *Smith*, and parallel to the realignment after the Revolution, religious groups across the political spectrum have found common ground in resistance to a perceived government promotion of secularism. Together they sponsored the Religious Freedom Restoration Act (RFRA), Congress's attempt to reverse the *Smith* decision. Since the Court's decision declaring the RFRA an unconstitutional usurpation of the Court's power, the coalition has sponsored the Religious Liberty Protection Act, intended to cure the constitutional problems with the RFRA, and the International Religious Freedom Act, requiring the president to take action to protect religious freedom around the world.

The confrontation between federal agents and members of the Branch Davidian community in Waco, Texas, also fed concerns of a united activist religious coalition that the federal government was hostile to religion. In the winter and spring of 1993, a formerly obscure religious millennialist sect known as the Branch Davidians came into national prominence. Led by a man originally named Vernon Howell, renamed David Koresh, the Davidians had built a compound just outside Waco, where they sat awaiting the end days. The Bureau of Alcohol, Tobacco, and Firearms (ATF) became involved with the group because of allegations of child abuse and weapons stockpiling raised by officials of the Justice Department as well as by groups such as the Cult Awareness Network. On February 28, 1993, ATF agents, with assistance from the FBI, attacked the compound, resulting in the deaths of four lawmen and injury of fourteen others. For the next two months, the government laid siege to the area, trying negotiations and psychological tactics to force the Davidians out. Finally, on April 19, 1993, government agents moved in. Soon, the Davidian complex was engulfed in flames. In the fire, nearly all the remaining believers, numbering more than eighty, perished in a horrific scene televised for a national viewing public. Controversy, argument, and recrimination followed this incident for years. Exactly two years later, 169 people were murdered in an explosion at a federal building in Oklahoma City, an act committed by a young man obsessed with avenging the deaths of the Davidians. Reflecting on the events in Waco, a numbers of scholars noted that the government fundamentally failed to follow its own principles of religious freedom. By not taking seriously the Davidians' apocalyptic ideas, government agents almost inevitably forced the group to its tragic denouement. Religion scholars and religious groups across the country saw in the Waco tragedy and in the FBI's and ATF's failure to consult with religious experts evidence of the federal government's ignorance and incompetence in dealing with religious issues.

At the beginning of the twenty-first century, terrorism continues to draw attention to unresolved tensions between religion and the state. The attack on the World Trade Center in New York City in September 2001 caused many Americans to confront for the first time a religion about which most of them knew little: Islam. Many expressed horror at what they saw as a close connection between violence and religion and attributed that connection to something inherent in the Islamic tradition. In looking around them, however, many also became concerned that reaction to the attacks was causing a curtailment of civil liberties for Muslims living in the United States. Meanwhile, President Bush used religious language, including the word "crusade," to describe American counteraction. He also used religious language to discuss domestic policy, as with his "faith-based" initiatives. Religion is very much entwined with law and the state in the United States today.

Conclusion

The religion clauses of the First Amendment remain both a source of enormous pride and a source of constant tension for most Americans. The apparent contradiction between these two responses can be traced to ambiguous wording, an inconclusive legislative history, and radical changes in both religion and government since the amendment's ratification. Two hundred years of experience with legal disestablishment has revealed the inevitable interpenetration of religion, law, and politics in human society and the limits of law as an instrument of social reform: Can law do what it is being asked to do? Can it protect religious values and individual conscience in an unbiased way? Is religion better off if it is privileged or if it is ignored? Should government have a role in creating a virtuous citizenry? Is religion necessary for a moral society? These are questions that Roger Williams asked almost four hundred years ago. For Williams the answer was clear. The civil arena should be entirely secular, and religion should be entirely private. But his is a demanding and, to some, harsh discipline, one that is, for some, destructive of public life.

What have we learned about the legal and political meaning of *religion* from this quick gallop through American history? The traditional American evangelical Protestant definition of religion as chosen, private, individual, and believed is fast mutating into something new. On the one hand, radical religious pluralism is challenging even the most liberal and tolerant of earlier definitions. Many kinds of Protestants, Catholics, Jews, Buddhists, Muslims, Hindus, and practitioners of indigenous religions show us a religion that is given, public, communal, and enacted. On the other hand, American religion divides more readily today into liberal and conservative camps, rather than into denominational camps. Liberal Protestants, Catholics, Jews, Muslims, and humanists may have more in common with one another than with the conservatives in their own religious communities. The differences may be more fundamental than religion. What divides people today is anthropology, their theory of the human person, and their theory of government. What does it mean to say that people are religiously motivated? What happens to religion if people's mental attitudes are explained biologically, chemically, or mathematically? What happens to religion if animals are found to have moral attitudes? What happens to religion if values do not have a clear correlation with behavior? Religion and law, as epistemological systems, make large claims to encompass the realities of the human experience. They will both need to defend those claims against science in the coming yeasrs. There is a tendency in American history for religion to be subsumed by law. Both may in fact be subsumed by science.

SUGGESTED READINGS

Albanese, Catherine. *Sons of the Fathers: The Civil Religion of the American Revolution*. Philadelphia: Temple University Press, 1976.

Berman, Harold. *Faith and Order: The Conciliation of Law and Religion*. Atlanta: Scholars Press, 1993.

————. *The Interaction of Law and Religion*. Nashville: Abington Press, 1974.

Bridenbaugh, Carl. *Mitre and Sceptre: Transatlantic Faiths, Ideas, Personalities, and Politics, 1689–1775*. New York: Oxford University Press, 1962.

Carrasco, David, and Eduardo Mados Moctezurna. *Moctezuma'a Mexico: Visions of the Aztec World*. Niwot: University Press of Colorado, 1992.

Curry, Thomas J. *The First Freedoms: Church and State in America to the Passage of the First Amendment*. New York: Oxford University Press, 1986.

Fenton, William N. *The Great Law and the Longhouse: A Political History of the Iroquois Confederacy*. Norman: University of Oklahoma Press, 1988.

Friedman, Lawrence. *A History of American Law*. 2nd ed. New York: Simon and Schuster, 1985.

Hamburger, Philip. *Separation of Church and State*. Cambridge: Harvard University Press, 2002.

Howe, Mark deWolfe. *The Garden and the Wilderness: Religion and Government in American Constitutional History*. Chicago: University of Chicago Press, 1965.

Kantorowicz, Ernst. *The King's Two Bodies: A Study of Medieval Political Theology*. Princeton, N.J.: Princeton University Press, 1957.

Kurland, Philip, ed. *Church and State: The Supreme Court and the First Amendment*. Chicago: University of Chicago Press, 1975.

Madison, James. "Memorial and Remonstrance." In *The Papers of James Madison*, edited by William T. Hutchinson and William M. E. Rachal. Chicago: University of Chicago Press, 1962.

Marty, Martin. *Modern American Religion*. 3 vols. Chicago: University of Chicago Press, 1986.

Mead, Sidney. *The Lively Experiment: The Shaping of Christianity in America*. New York: Harper and Row, 1963.

Murray, John Courtney. *We Hold These Truths: Catholic Reflection on the American Proposition*. New York: Sheed and Ward, 1960.

Noonan, John. *The Believer and the Powers That Are: Cases, History, and Other Data Bearing on the Relation of Religion and Government*. New York: Macmillan, 1987.

Tocqueville, Alexis de. *Democracy in America*. Edited by Harvey Mansfield and Delba Winthrop. Chicago: University of Chicago Press, 2000.

Williams, Roger. *The Bloudy Tenent of Persecution, for Cause of Conscience*. In *The Complete Writings of Roger Williams*. 7 vols. New York: Russell and Russell, 1963.

Economy

Early in the nineteenth century, the perceptive French observer of American society Alexis de Tocqueville noted that Americans were deeply and equally devoted to the Christian religion and to the acquisition of material goods. Tocqueville was neither the first nor the last to see the peculiar connection between the religious profession and economic action in America. Scholars have spent a great deal of effort striving to understand the character of that relationship.

Religious belief and practice influence virtually every aspect of economic behavior. Religious values shape production by, on the one hand, making labor a sacred obligation and, on the other, demanding periods of leisure for worship. The command that God gave to Adam and Eve, "six days shalt thou labor," is perhaps the most familiar of these. Production is also conditioned by the (often assumed) relationship between human beings and nature, which, in American history, has been generally grounded in religious cosmology. Is the earth, or the nonhuman forms of life that live on it, sacred in the same sense that humans are? Social ethics that grow out of religious beliefs have had a profound effect in both determining and legitimizing the distribution of goods and services. Some Americans have argued that the individual's right to accumulate property is the sacred and inviolable gift of God. Others have emphasized a religious obligation to place the good of others, especially the good of the whole community, ahead of personal gain. The former find religious grounds supporting the unregulated market economy; the latter find religious grounds sometimes for tempering market economics with charity and other times for rejecting them in favor of communalism or socialism. Finally, religious values influence consumption, most often by limiting the use of certain goods or services or prohibiting them altogether. Perhaps this is most obvious in the dietary restrictions—prohibitions on the consumption of all meat or certain kinds of meat at sacred times, for example—that some religions ask of their adherents. Patterns of traffic in other kinds of goods and services, including alcohol, slaves, and sex, have also been limited by religious prohibition.

If religion has shaped economic activity in America, religious beliefs, values, and practices have been conditioned by economic realities. A congregation might wish to worship in a cathedral but, if it lacks the economic means, may find itself in a barn or a storefront. Religious celebrations—Easter and Christmas for Christians, for example—are influenced by the economic means of the celebrants. When the income of a religious people exceeds the costs of their basic needs, the surplus may create a market for religious books, music, art, icons, clothing, and even travel packages. Religion may thus find itself in business.

Students of American culture have often explored the relationship between religion and economics in terms defined by the German sociologist Max Weber in his masterwork, *The Protestant Ethic and the Spirit of Capitalism*. Weber rejected the major models of economic behavior advocated in the early twentieth century. He saw that both Marxist and liberal capitalist theory rely on the assumed natural economic rationality of men and women in history. Defining people as fundamentally driven by their material wants, both Marxists and economic liberals believed that men and women rationally chose (or at least had the capacity to choose) to engage in economic activity that promised the best chance of fulfilling their desires. Weber doubted that economic rationality was in any meaningful sense rooted in human nature. He suspected instead that it was the product of specific historical circumstances. The task he set for himself centered on identifying the circumstances in which men and women came to behave in accordance with liberal capitalist or Marxist notions of economic rationality.

For Weber, the Protestant Reformation of the sixteenth century provided the context that gave rise to this new economic sensibility, which he termed the "spirit of capitalism." In their elimination of sacred orders for the clergy, the churches created under the influence of Martin Luther and, especially, John Calvin made productive labor the sacred obligation, or "calling," of all Christians. The economic effect of this "Protestant work ethic" that demanded incessant production was modified by an ethic of frugality that curtailed consumption. Plain living—austerity in dress, housing, and food, for example—was regarded as morally superior to a life characterized by the conspicuous consumption of goods and services. Reinvesting the profits of honest labor would be more appropriate than consuming them as luxuries. The result, unintended by the reformers, was capitalist accumulation. Protestant ethics created a specific kind of economic rationality most congenial to the development of capitalism.

This inclination toward capitalist accumulation reached its most extreme form, according to Weber, in the followers of Calvin, particularly in those English Puritans, whether Congregationalist, Presbyterian, or Quaker in denomination, who were instrumental in establishing the American colonies. Calvin's theology emphasized the doctrine of predestination, or the belief that each individual's eternal fate in heaven or hell was determined by God in the act of creation. If logical consistency and scriptural authority supported Calvin's notion of predestination, that notion also created severe psychological strains in those who believed in it. They could never know for certain whether they were among the "elect" destined for salvation or the "damned" destined for destruction. Nor could they do anything to alter their fate. At best, they could look for signs of God's grace in their lives. Evidence of self-control and self-denial—ceaseless productive labor and the reinvestment of profits—along with the material prosperity that such behavior often provided figured prominently among the "marks" of grace. The "spirit of capitalism" was thus born in Protestant belief and practice.

The issues that Weber, his followers, and his critics have introduced are broad enough to serve as an organizing theme for thinking about religion and economics in America. The first sections of this chapter thus assess the extent to which Protestantism created, shaped, and tempered American capitalism. After the Civil War, immigration destroyed Protestant hegemony while "modern" ways of thinking undermined those distinctively Protestant beliefs—particularly the doctrine of predestination—that Weber thought played a crucial role in the early culture of capitalism. The later sections of this chapter explore how the Protestant ethic fared in a pluralistic and capitalistic America.

Precolonial Era

Europeans and Native Americans were in contact with each other for more than a century between Christopher Columbus's voyages in the Caribbean and the establishment of the first permanent English settlement at Jamestown. French, Spanish, and English explorers charted the coast of North America and pushed deep into the interior. Fisherman from Great Britain dried their catch, taken from the rich Grand Banks off the coast of Canada, each fall. From this contact, a thriving trade developed. Native Americans exchanged furs, which they had in relative abundance, for cloth, pots and pans, iron and steel tools, weapons, and liquor. On the surface, this mostly amicable exchange appeared to be in the best interests of both parties. Neither Europeans nor Native Americans understood that this simple economic activity was rife with opportunities for misunderstanding and conflict. The mutuality of the exchange was undermined by vastly different understandings about the value of the trade goods, the labor expended to produce them, the appropriateness of accumulating property, and the meaning of the very act of trading. These differences of understanding, meaning, and value were rooted in the different religious cosmologies of the peoples of Europe and America.

Differing religious and economic ways of life do not explain the European conquest of America. By far, the most important factors accounting for that conquest were biological—the microbes that Europeans unknowingly carried in their bodies that caused epidemic diseases—rather than cultural and social. Yet understanding interrelated religious and economic differences helps explain why Native Americans and Europeans behaved as they did. A comparison of the colonizing English and the colonized Native Americans who lived along the East Coast serves to illustrate this point.

England's economic troubles in the 1500s were as difficult as its religious problems. The root of the problem, particularly in the last half of the century, was price inflation. This inflation was caused, on the supply side, by the importation of vast quantities of gold and silver (which passed as money throughout Europe) from Spain's American colonies and, on the demand side, by population growth that outstripped available resources. Landowners, including the Crown and members of the aristocracy, found themselves squeezed between rising costs and a fixed income derived from long-term leases. Increasing numbers of tenant farmers were unable to find land to rent and so became low-skilled and financially insecure day laborers. Skilled workers also found themselves caught between wages that were fixed by law and tradition and costs that rose, despite law and tradition. Underemployment became endemic. The bright spot in this economy was the rise of the joint-stock company, a new form of corporation chartered by the Crown primarily to encourage foreign trade.

The relationship between English Puritanism and the rise of commerce is ambiguous. On the one hand, Puritan theologians, by the end of the Elizabethan era, adopted a way of talking about God's relationship to men and women in terms of covenants or contracts. Similarly, Puritans often described their churches, and even their civil societies, as covenanted communities. This contractual metaphor may have functioned to weld together the Puritan conception of economic and religious life. But, on the other hand, if Puritans adopted the language of the market to talk about theology, they nevertheless expressed a great deal of anxiety about the economic changes of the Elizabethan era, especially about the kinds of behavior those changes produced. Almost everywhere they looked, they saw disorder. Men and women whose lives had been bound by the mutually obligatory terms of traditional hierarchical relationships —master/servant, landlord/tenant, patron/client, for example—sometimes found themselves freed from those obligations. This freedom was feared as much as welcomed. For Puritans, who believed that men and women were naturally inclined to behave wickedly, any decay of social authority was likely to lead to sin and vice. In economic life, Puritans saw evidence aplenty of that wickedness. Covetousness abounded, as people found new ways to take advantage of one another. The Puritans' remedy was twofold. First, they sought to strengthen self-discipline, which, as Weber thought, often meant diligent labor, among those who seemed to be members of God's elect. Second, they demanded "watch and discipline," or strong regulation of moral and economic affairs, in the communities in which they lived.

Certainly not all the English who explored, traded, and eventually colonized North America were Puritans; nor did they all exhibit characteristically Puritan economic attitudes. Puritans did, however, express some of the essential tendencies of Elizabethan economic life, particularly in their concern for the moral value of work (in principle, if not always in practice), their tendency to define human relationships in contractual terms, and their willingness to regard the products of their labor as commodities suitable for exchange. In these regards, Elizabethan English people, whether Puritans or not, differed sharply from the native peoples of North America among whom they would eventually settle.

The Native American peoples who lived along the East Coast exhibited a wide variety of beliefs and practices. With a couple of notable exceptions— the League of the Iroquois and the Powhatan Confederacy—Native American villages were largely autonomous. Most eastern Native Americans were engaged in a mixed economy that combined hunting, fishing, and gathering with the cultivation of corn, beans, squash, and tobacco. They also established an extensive network of trade that circulated certain highly valued goods— obsidian from the Rocky Mountains, copper from the Great Lakes, and shells from Long Island Sound—throughout the eastern third of what is now the United States. As a general rule, the farther south a Native American people lived, the more it relied on agriculture. And, as another general rule, the more dependent a people on agriculture, the more they lived in permanent houses located in fixed village sites. Most employed, to varying degrees, a sexual division of labor in which women farmed and men hunted and fished. The Algonquian-speaking peoples of southern New England—Wampanoag and Narragansett, for example—fished in the spring, gathered and farmed in the summer, and hunted in the fall. Entire villages moved from one semipermanent site to another to take maximum advantage of the seasonal economic activities. To the south and west, the Seneca of western New York also combined hunting and gathering with agriculture. They built permanent villages, however, where women remained whereas men traveled extensively to hunt and trade. Around Chesapeake Bay, Native Americans of the Powhatan Confederacy, male and female, lived in permanent villages that produced a surplus of corn and tobacco. Farther south, among Native American peoples such as the Cherokee, agriculture was so central to the economy that even men participated in preparing the fields, although they devoted themselves primarily to the hunt.

Eastern Native Americans also assessed the value of work and property differently than the English. Preferring leisure to work, they sought to extract what they needed from nature with as little effort as possible. In general, a given Native American people practiced agriculture to the extent that population pressure on the food supply forced it to do so. Gathering the surplus nature produced was easier than clearing fields and cultivating crops. When these peoples farmed, they avoided labor-intensive techniques. In New England, for example, the Wampanoag cleared fields merely by burning underbrush and girdling large trees to prevent them from shading the gardens below. When the soil in a particular field became exhausted, the village simply abandoned it for a new one. The ownership of property was almost always communal—a village or kin group—rather than individual and was linked to its use. Rights to real property were held in usufruct. What was owned was not land itself but the right to use a particular piece of ground for a specific purpose. A village might possess the exclusive right to farm in a particular river valley, for example, but share rights to hunt, fish, and gather in that valley with other groups. These rights could be lost through disuse. If a given people neglected to exercise a particular right, it was considered abandoned and could be claimed by another group. One implication of this Native American notion of property ownership was that no group (and certainly no individual) could claim title to more land that it could reasonably use for its subsistence.

Native American religious systems of belief, value, and ritual show a diversity comparable to their various modes of economic life. Scholars generally classify Native American religions as animistic, meaning that activity in nature is directed by a spiritual power or powers that inhered in nature. This spiritual power, sometimes termed *manitou*, animated everything that Europeans would have recognized as alive (plants, animals, humans) and many things that they might not have recognized as alive, such as storms, bodies of water, pieces of land, and particular implements or tools. Other sorts of spirits, often of the dead, also inhabited the Native American's world. Successful living required securing the cooperation and assistance of the spiritual power that animated nature.

This was especially true in the economic realm. Agricultural Native Americans, such as the Cherokee and Seneca, conducted elaborate rituals at times of planting and harvest, led by shamans, to ensure a bountiful crop. As corn was their staple, its planting and harvest called for special rituals and celebrations. Hunters likewise enlisted the aid of conjurers to help them locate game. According to some scholars, hunters actually sought to contact the spirits that animated their quarry and arrange for its death. This view of hunting and farming as essentially sacred enterprises served to discourage both wastefulness and the accumulation of property. Unnecessary killing, or the failure to use all that one had killed, was a certain means to alienate the hunter from the spiritual power that made his success possible. Ironically, this set of beliefs seems to have produced a surplus of furs. When a hunter killed an animal for food, religious prohibitions against waste encouraged him to preserve its pelt.

The religious beliefs, values, and practices of the English and the Native Americans encouraged them to see economic activity in very different ways. The former saw a religious obligation to labor to turn nature into commodities that it was better to sell than to consume. The latter, who linked rightful ownership with use, took care to consume all they produced and thereby avoid waste. The former saw nature as an object to be acted on and transformed by human exertion. The latter saw nature as a spiritual power with which they must reckon. The former believed that by acting in nature they converted nature into private property that could be bought and sold. The latter saw all property rights as conditional. The very meaning of the goods they traded differed. Native Americans appreciated what they perceived as the spiritual potency of European goods and incorporated them into their culture accordingly.

When English people and Native Americans met, they perceived each other as inexplicably odd. In their point of most common ground and greatest mutual interest, the exchange of American furs for goods of European manufacture, the universes they inhabited, and hence the meaning of the exchange and of the goods exchanged, were incommensurably different. These cultural differences do not in themselves account for English conquest of North America, but in the context of the demographic holocaust that Native Americans suffered, English commodities seemed spiritually potent indeed. The commodification of nature was sure to follow, and with it, the destruction of the spiritual cosmos in which Native Americans had lived.

Colonial North America

The New England colonies of Plymouth, Connecticut, Massachusetts Bay, Rhode Island and Providence Plantations, and New Hampshire were, for the most part, settled by English Puritans in the years between 1620 and 1642. Those Puritans who pressed hardest for religious reform found themselves subjected to prosecution in both civil and religious courts. In this context, migration to what they termed the "American wilderness" looked like a good option. For some, such as the Pilgrims who founded Plymouth Colony in 1620, colonization offered the promise of escaping the perceived corruption of the Old World. For others, such as John Winthrop, a leading figure in the Massachusetts Bay Colony, migration remained part of a grand strategy to bring about the further reformation of England. Whether or not they had larger goals, Puritans shared a commitment to create a pure church and a pure society in America.

In America, Puritan notions of a pure society carried in them the same ambivalence about commercial development evident in England. On the one hand, leaders such as Winthrop, in his private musings, at least, admitted that one of the attractive features of migration was the economic benefits it promised. As an institution, the Massachusetts Bay Colony was first and foremost a joint-stock company in which the principal colonists were shareholders. And surely for many of the colonists, such as the Marblehead, Massachusetts, fisherman who claimed to have migrated solely for "fish," a good society took the economic interests of its members into account. Some New England communities, such as Springfield, Massachusetts, emerged as early, aggressive commercial centers. When historians study places such as Springfield and early Marblehead, they are likely to see a positive relationship between Puritanism and the development of capitalism.

Yet there is also abundant evidence of the persistence of anticapitalist, anticommercial, traditional, and communitarian sentiment in New England. Winthrop's famous sermon, *A Model of Christian Charity*, described a good society as one in which individuals, bound together by love, showed their preference for the public over private good through acts of giving and lending. Many New England towns, such as Dedham, Massachusetts, seem to have been formed in accordance with this communal ethic. The Dedham Town Meeting, at which all inhabitants of the town could attend and speak (but only adult male property holders could vote), closely regulated the economic life of the community. It controlled the resources on lands reserved in common and, as the population grew, eventually distributed these lands to private individuals. It regulated trade, fences, roads, and livestock and had the power to command the labor of town residents for public projects.

The predestinarian Calvinism preached from Puritan pulpits may have created anxiety that found its outlet in work, frugality, and reinvestment. But that very prosperity produced anxieties of its own, as Puritan men and women wrestled in their consciences about the moral implications of their economic behavior. The characteristic mode of production in New England was the family farm. Most farms were subsistence-oriented. Decisions about what to produce were determined mainly in view of what the family needed to consume, rather than by the demands of the market. Yet, remarkably, given the relatively poor soil and climate of New England, many farmers managed to produce surpluses, however small, that they were eager to sell on the market. Many New Englanders also developed skills in various manufacturing crafts, such as shipbuilding and furniture making. Over its first century, New England gradually developed a diversified mercantile economy that, although not especially prosperous, became well integrated into the broader network of Atlantic trade. But New Englanders remained ambivalent about the moral implications of commerce and trade. Puritan ministers developed a new form of sermon, called the jeremiad, that castigated men and women for their self-interested pursuit of worldly goods, called them to return to the pure and charitable religion of New England's founders, and warned them of God's impending judgment.

The revivals of religion in the middle years of the eighteenth century, often termed the Great Awakening, helped to legitimize the economic individualism of the market economy. The revivals, spread by itinerant preachers, taught converts (called New Lights) to challenge many of their established ministers as unfit to preach the gospel. Colonial governments responded by trying to suppress New Light preaching in the name of traditional communal values. New Lights, in turn, learned to challenge traditional authority. The regulation of the economy, no less than the regulation of religion, fell under their criticism, as their conversion experiences made them feel empowered to act, ironically, on behalf of their self-interest. At the same time, however, the explicit economic imperatives in New Light preaching were most often traditional, anticommercial, and anticapitalist. To this extent, the meaning of the revival, in economic terms at least, was a reaffirmation of the subsistence-oriented communalism of the early New Englanders in towns like Dedham. The religion of the New Lights thus reflected the persistent ambivalence of New England culture toward capitalist economic behavior.

The southern colonies present a rather different picture. Virginia, founded in 1607, and the Carolinas, founded in 1660, were settled by Anglicans, who dominated the religious and political establishment through the colonial period. Maryland, established in 1634, is something of a special case, as English Catholics founded it. Its proprietor, Cecil Calvert, Lord Baltimore, (futilely) sought to re-create a feudal economy. Protestant immigrants soon outnumbered Catholic, so that in its religious configuration, like much else, it resembled Virginia. In any case, the dominant religious influence throughout the South in the seventeenth century was the Church of England. In theology, it was not particularly Calvinist. And southern culture did not offer effective inducements to either labor or frugality. Nevertheless, the South developed an economy that, if less diversified, was far more capital-intensive, and far more dependent on foreign markets, than that of New England.

Very early in their development, the southern colonies specialized in the production of commodities for sale in Europe. In the Chesapeake Bay colonies of Virginia and Maryland, the commodity was tobacco. In South Carolina, it was rice. Both crops brought substantial profits, but at the cost of a great deal of labor. From the earliest days of settlement at Jamestown, English migrants showed little inclination to work and a substantial inclination to indulge in whatever creature comforts they could procure. So it is not surprising that, in the Chesapeake, they turned first to indentured servants, usually Englishmen bound by contract to labor for up to seven years in exchange for their passage to America and a promise of fifty acres at their discharge. Carolinians preferred African slavery, with which they had become familiar in the British sugar-producing island of Barbados, from the start. By 1700, Chesapeake colonists, tired of unruly servants and the economic competition freed servants provided, came to share the preference for Africans laborers. Racial slavery served to devalue labor further. The inexorable logic of slavery indicated that work was to be performed by those forced to labor, rather than as a moral response to the sinful condition of humanity. Consumption, likewise, became linked to ethnicity. The supposed mark of superiority in southern society thus became the white consumer who did not work; the mark of inferiority became the black producer who did not consume.

African slavery posed moral, and ultimately religious, problems to the English in America who embraced it. The condition of lifetime, inheritable, bondage had long passed from practice in England. How could it be justified in America? One answer pointed to the service that slave owners performed for the eternal souls of the slaves, if not their bodies, by bringing them from "savagery" to a place where they could hear the Christian gospel, convert, and be saved. This proved to be a satisfying answer, to slave owners at least, until slaves actually converted. Could one Christian legitimately define another Christian as property? The logic of racial slavery demanded no less.

Slavery, of course, posed far greater problems for the slaves. African religious beliefs and practices were ruthlessly suppressed. There were not economic reasons per se for prohibiting African religious practices, but the English justification of slavery as offering conversion demanded it. Until the Great Awakening, however, when revivalists preached a gospel that emphasized human equality that, implicitly, at least, criticized slavery, conversion offered little to attract African American slaves. After the revival, the evangelicalism that became typical in the slave quarters seldom expressed the Protestant economic ethic. The disincentives to labor and frugality inherent in the economy of slavery were more powerful than any incentives that evangelical religion might have provided.

Although southern planters, and the southern economy, were deeply dependent on foreign markets for the commodities they produced, their involvement in trade did not foster the development of a capitalist mentality. Their reliance on slave labor is an indication of a deeper precapitalist culture. Planters valued frugality as little as they valued labor, so that plantations often consumed significantly more than they produced. Thus, the typical Chesapeake planter, for example, was in debt to the English merchants who bought his tobacco. In the colonial South, both Calvinism and capitalism were weaker than in New England. Its history suggests that the links between Calvinism and capitalism were real indeed.

The Middle Colonies—the most important of which were New York and Pennsylvania—developed an economic and religious character quite different from that of New England or the South. New York bore the mark of its origin as the Dutch colony of New Netherlands through (and well beyond) the colonial period. Like English Puritanism, the Dutch Reformed Church was Calvinist. The principal Dutch settlements were decidedly commercial ventures, unmixed with utopian communalism, from the start. New Amsterdam (later New York City) was established as an outpost of the vast commercial empire that the Dutch established throughout the Atlantic world in the seventeenth century. Albany was a fur-trading post. Between these two cities along the Hudson River stretched large estates on which landlords struggled to establish an economy based on raising foodstuffs—grains and livestock—for export. After the Dutch were conquered by the English in 1656, Dutch merchants and landlords competed with English merchants and landlords, mostly members of the Church of England, for both profits and political power.

Pennsylvania, meanwhile, was founded by Quakers, a radical sect of English Protestants, who sought (like Puritans in New England) both a place of refuge from the civil disabilities they suffered at home and an avenue for their entrepreneurial ambitions. With other radical Protestants, Pennsylvania Quakers considered productive labor to be a sacred obligation. Recognizing that African slavery ran counter to their work ethic, as well as to their insistence on equality, Quakers prohibited slave owning among their membership. Further, they insisted on a "plain style" of dress, furnishings, and architecture that severely curtailed consumption. This ethic of productive labor and frugality, combined with their reputation for scrupulous honesty and participation in a Quaker network that stretched throughout the British Empire, gave Philadelphia merchants decided advantages in the Atlantic marketplace.

Although their influence was permanent, Quaker domination in Pennsylvania proved short-lived. Quakers welcomed similarly persecuted Protestants from the European continent as well as from Great Britain. By the end of the colonial period, about a third of Pennsylvania's population consisted of German immigrants, many of them Anabaptists in belief and practice. But the largest groups of immigrants were Scots-Irish, Scottish, and English Presbyterians who shared the Calvinism, but not necessarily the communal impulse, of New Englanders. Quakers and Presbyterians vied for political and economic power with a smaller but highly influential elite composed of members of England's established church.

The Middle Colonies developed a thriving economy based on the export of foodstuffs, principally to the sugar-producing islands of the Caribbean. Agriculture was characterized by family farms that were most often geared, to a greater or lesser degree, to profit-oriented production for the demands of the market. By the American Revolution, Philadelphia and New York City had both surpassed Boston in population and were colonial America's principal commercial centers. From their establishment, New York and Philadelphia both seem to have happily combined Protestant faith with the acquisitive commercial ambitions of their founders. The attitudes and practices of the first settlers of both towns established a commercial ethos that persisted long after immigrants of other Protestant persuasions overwhelmed the founders. In their agricultural hinterlands, competition between ethnic and religious groups created a cultural marketplace that paralleled the development of a commercially oriented economy.

Revolutionary and Early Republican America

The Great Awakening that swept across the American colonies from the 1740s through the 1760s brought about a realignment of the religious patterns of the colonial era. Religion in the revolutionary period can best be understood as stretching along a spectrum that ranged from those groups whose religious life was defined by revivalism to those who rejected it entirely. Regardless of denomination, pro-revivalists sought to foster a vital piety rooted in the experience of conversion. Evangelical piety emphasized how believers felt about God, their neighbors, and themselves and about their duties, sacred and secular, to each. Antirevivalists, in contrast, generally stressed the importance of the rationality in religious matters.

This division in religious sentiments informed the political culture of the revolutionary generation. The patriot movement, in part, was inspired by an ancient political tradition called "civic humanism" or "classical republicanism." The central ethical imperative of this republicanism lay in the demand that individuals exercise civic virtue by subordinating their private interest to the public good. Patriot rhetoric directed against Britain and in favor of independence often claimed that the imperial administration had been "corrupted" by officials in both Britain and America who placed their personal avarice above the good of the nation. Stamp Tax collectors, customs officials, judges, and royally appointed governors and their councils became the immediate targets of this moral critique. But it was also directed against colonial Americans, particularly merchants engaged in transatlantic trade, who both favored and stood to gain from accommodation with imperial policy. In contrast to the corruptible merchant republicans placed the yeoman farmer, who, because theoretically self-sufficient, was regarded as less susceptible to the temptations of personal gain and thus more inclined to champion the public good.

These political concerns emerged in the context of and were heightened by a commercial revolution that saw the proliferation of consumer goods, manufactured in Britain, in American markets. Many of these goods—cloth, liquor, paint—were identified as luxuries. Prosperity, caused in part by the maturation of the colonial economy and furthered by substantial military spending by Britain in America during the Seven Years' War, created rising expectations and made the fulfillment of some of those expectations possible. Lured by the promise of increased creature comfort and by a desire to keep up with their neighbors, Americans of all classes acquired what they could afford. Luxury, in republican ideology, was closely associated with vice. To make matters worse, many Americans went into debt to purchase these things, which undermined their economic independence and hence subverted civic virtue.

Evangelicalism, with its insistence that moral action arose from correct motives—from "hearts" that, after loving God supremely, loved their neighbors as themselves—thus reinforced the patriot insistence on the priority of the public good. As complicity with British policy became identified with self-interest, and hence sin, patriotism, as defined by republican ideology, became a Christian duty. In a similar vein, this evangelical ethic encouraged many Protestants to look askance at the proliferation of British goods made available by the commercial revolution. By resisting the corrupting influence of Britain, some Americans hoped to create a republic characterized by a communal ethic of Christian virtue. Although the correlation is not perfect, evangelical religion was weakest among those groups, located in colonial capitals and principal cities, most closely tied to Britain and strongest in agricultural areas that were less dependent on commercial markets. To the extent that evangelicalism reinforced a traditionalist, precapitalistic or even anticapitalistic economic ethic that infused the patriot movement with moral significance, the evidence from the revolutionary period does not support Weber's thesis.

At the same time, other evidence suggests that the links between Protestantism and capitalism remained strong in the revolutionary era. The transatlantic revivalism of the Great Awakening paralleled and promoted the commercial revolution. Both movements opened Americans to the products, cultural and material, of the broader Atlantic world. Itinerant preachers were as alien to the communities in which they proclaimed the gospel as were British manufactured goods. George Whitefield, the most famous and most successful of the colonial evangelists, was, after all, a British import. American revivalists, such as Jonathan Edwards in New England and Gilbert Tennent in the Middle Colonies, worked with Whitefield to create a transatlantic network designed to promote the revival that paralleled the developing commercial network.

Moreover, the specific policies advocated by New Light patriots were often consistent with the Protestant ethic as Weber defined it. The economic boycotts of the nonimportation movement, calculated to persuade Parliament and the Crown to reverse policies the patriots considered oppressive, were entirely consistent with a Protestant ethic that demanded frugality. Likewise, the rhetoric of resistance, exemplified by the familiar phrase "no taxation without representation," resounded with a liberal defense of individual rights against the claims of the larger political community. The defense of the rights to private property, articulated as clearly by evangelicals as by others, doubtless appealed to the economic self-interest of countless citizens.

In the early Republic, northern evangelical political leaders, such as Connecticut's Roger Sherman and New Jersey's John Witherspoon, strenuously advocated pro-capitalist economic policies that promoted commercial growth, speculative investment, and capital formation. They supported the federal Constitution in part because they thought it would benefit trade, and they argued for the development of a national banking system. By the 1790s, evangelical politicians joined with their fellow Federalists in an effort to create an economic infrastructure conducive to manufacturing. They were far less worried about the proliferation of consumer goods, the concentration of capital, and the development wage labor than they were excited about the incentives to labor, and hence to socially useful behavior, that economic growth promised. Men like Sherman and Witherspoon did not neglect their own financial interests but rather combined vital evangelical faith and leadership in the patriot movement with phenomenally successful speculation in western lands, government securities, and commercial enterprise.

The relationship between Protestantism and capitalism in revolutionary America is thus ambiguous. Although those evangelicals closest to the Calvinist tradition used anticapitalist communitarian rhetoric against their pro-British opponents, they did not allow such rhetoric to determine the policies they advocated. In the course of the revolutionary struggle, they learned how to serve both God and mammon. Perhaps this was their revolution.

Antebellum Nineteenth Century

Whatever the economic vision of the founding generation may have been, America developed a commercially oriented economy in the early nineteenth century and experienced the beginnings of its Industrial Revolution in the North. The development of a market economy was encouraged by improvements in internal transportation, roads, canals, and especially the railroad. By providing inexpensive ways of moving goods from one region to another, the transportation revolution encouraged regional specialization in the production of goods and made urbanization possible. Many farm families reoriented production from commodities they intended to consume to commodities they could profitably sell in the marketplace. According to some estimates, two-thirds of all agricultural produce was consumed by the families that produced in 1800. By the eve of the Civil War, two-thirds of all agricultural produce was sold on the market. This surplus agricultural production was a precondition for urban growth and specialized manufacturing. In the Northeast, where manufacturing and urbanization were most advanced, fully one-third of the population lived in cities and towns by 1860, whereas less than one-tenth had been similarly urban in 1800. Commercialization, urbanization, and the beginnings of industrialization demanded the reorganization of religious institutions, created new ethical problems, and raised new spiritual concerns.

In institutional organization, developments in American religion paralleled those in the broader political and economic culture. The Revolution and its aftermath led to the disestablishment of officially supported churches on a state-by-state basis. The effect was to create a competitive marketplace in religion that allowed men and women to shop for religious institutions that they thought best met their needs. To the extent that the behavior of laypeople is explained by religious consumerism, the clergy became the purveyors of religious products—theologies, ethical systems, ritual patterns—that had to be marketed. Options proliferated. The upstart denominations from the Great Awakening, Baptist and Methodist, enjoyed phenomenal growth. New religious sects, ranging from slight variations on the older Calvinist churches to those based on radically new visions, most notably the Mormons, competed for an audience. New industrial towns also saw the establishment of the oldest of Christian institutions, the Roman Catholic Church, as German and especially Irish immigrants brought their ancestral faith with them to America. In this new religious marketplace, the churches that lost ground were those that had been conceived as state churches on a European model—Episcopal, Presbyterian, and Congregationalist.

More important than denominational realignment, however, was the emergence of new evangelical organizations, or "societies," that crossed denominational lines. Many of these organizations addressed evils that their members perceived in the American economy, such as the production and consumption of alcoholic beverages, poverty, and, most important, slavery. As the commercial revolution created national networks of producers, middlemen, and consumers for a variety of commodities, so these new religious organizations orchestrated the distribution of the Protestant gospel of temperance, industriousness, and free labor to the remote corners of the nation and the world.

The specific relationship between evangelical faith and commercialization and beginnings of industrialization remained ambiguous. Historians who find an anticapitalist ethic in the evangelicalism of the revolutionary era are likely to see it persisting into the nineteenth century. Thus, revivalism, especially in rural areas of the West and South, has been portrayed as a traditionalist mode of resistance to the penetration of the market economy. Yet the individuals who took the lead in reorganizing evangelicalism by developing voluntary societies were very often laypeople, such as financier Arthur Tappan of New York City, who were deeply involved in the development of the market economy. Indeed, studies of revivalism in new industrial towns, such as Rochester, New York, indicate that evangelical religion, sponsored by the respectable commercial middle class, found an audience among factory workers, who quite often were single young men and women outside the sphere of parental authority for the first time in their lives. Evangelical religion, with its insistence on rigorous moral discipline, may have instilled, as Weber suggested, a habit of punctuality and diligence that was necessary for the particular demands of factory work.

Unitarianism, a rationalistic offshoot of New England Congregationalism, itself produced an interesting response to the revolutions in manufacturing and commerce in the transcendentalist movement. After resigning from the Unitarian ministry because of its allegiance to what he termed the "dead weight of the past," Ralph Waldo Emerson developed an important critique of the acquisitive materialism made possible by economic development. In essays and public lectures, Emerson argued that Americans ignored the spiritual dimensions of life in their penchant for valuing nature as mere commodity, rather than as an emblem or ideal that pointed to a transcendent God who was immanently present in the world. The pursuit of material goods made men and women become merely the "dwarfs" of the "gods" they were created to become. Ironically, the consumers of Emerson's transcendentalist literature were most often the very same middle-class individuals who created the new commercial and manufacturing order in the North.

Perhaps the most important point at which religion and economics intersected, however, in the antebellum period concerned the southern labor system of racial slavery. In the North, evangelicalism and transcendentalism combined to infuse the emergent abolitionist movement with religious significance. For some, slavery became identified as the national sin that would provoke the judgment of a righteous God. The evil they saw in slavery lay not merely in the denial of the rights of the slave but in the ways in which the power of the master and the subjugation of the slave worked to corrupt the morals of both. According to abolitionists such as the former slave Frederick Douglass, slavery taught the most Christian masters to become cruel tyrants and cultivated an ethic of laziness rather than work among all classes of southern whites. Other writers stressed the way the economic system in which they found themselves encouraged slaves to disregard Christian morality. Sometimes abolitionist writers emphasized the direct pressure that masters put on slaves to behave immorally, as in the sexual exploitation of slave women. But they also criticized the southern labor system for providing few incentives for honest labor and creating a society in which theft and insubordination to authority were the reasonable reactions of slaves.

Some southerners, most notably the Virginia planter George Fitzhugh, responded with a Christian defense of slavery. Assuming that human beings were in fact unequal in strength, health, and intelligence, Fitzhugh argued that it was the Christian obligation of those who were blessed by God to assume responsibility for those less able to care for themselves. In his view, slavery was a paternalistic social system in which masters, like dutiful fathers, looked out for the well-being of those who lacked the wisdom, foresight, and ability to look out for themselves. Racial slavery, Fitzhugh argued, was vastly more moral than what he called the "wage slavery" of the North, where workers were paid simply for their time, without respect to their needs, the needs of their families, or their ability to work. Simply put, masters loved and cared for their slaves, whereas northern employers reduced their wageworkers to the status of mere commodities. Not surprisingly, southern slaves did not share Fitzhugh's views about the benign paternalism of the institution in which they were legally property as well as persons. Evangelical religion, however, became a vital way of helping them cope with the oppression they experienced.

Weber's analysis of the affinities between Protestantism and capitalism works to some extent in the antebellum North, where new modes of marketing the Protestant gospel sometimes combined with an explicit articulation of the work ethic. It does not work so well in the South, where the evangelical Protestantism of neither masters nor slaves did much to cultivate an entrepreneurial ethic.

Postbellum and Industrial Nineteenth Century

The victory of the North in the Civil War ensured not only the end of racial slavery but also the triumph of industrial capitalism. The war itself, with its demands for iron, steel, and textiles, did much to promote the development of northern industry. Led by the railroad industry and banking, American businesses developed new forms of corporate organization that allowed for exponential growth. By the beginning of the twentieth century, giant corporations, such as Standard Oil and U.S. Steel, dominated the U.S. economy. Industrialization transformed the lives of all classes of Americans. The men who made the Industrial Revolution—including Cornelius Vanderbilt, J. P. Morgan, Andrew Carnegie, and John D. Rockefeller—became new cultural heroes of mythic proportions. Industrial production accelerated the growth of cities and further encouraged immigration. For most urban Americans, wage labor became typical. But the new forms of corporate organization also gave rise to the development of a salaried middle class of managers and professionals, whose prosperity and confidence fostered a new set of cultural and social values. The social and economic distance between the richest and poorest urban Americans increased dramatically as a result of these changes. Nevertheless, in real dollars, wages rose throughout the century for most workers. Industrialization brought not merely new social distinctions but an increased abundance of goods for consumers to purchase. The division of labor, mechanization, the development of new sources of power, and the centralization of production decreased the relative cost of goods, tempting consumers, particularly those of the middle and upper classes, with a level of material comfort undreamed of by their parents and grandparents in 1800.

The changes wrought by industrialization, combined with related developments in scientific knowledge, created what some historians characterize as a "spiritual crisis" of this Gilded Age. In part, this crisis was precipitated by the sheer power of technology that brought about apparently miraculous transformations that most men and women could fathom no easier than those phenomena that their ancestors accounted for by reference to divine providence. Writing near the end of his life in 1907, Henry Adams—the great grandson of President John Adams—captured this transformation in his brilliant autobiography. The dynamo—the electrical generator—had replaced the Virgin as the most powerful symbol in Western culture. Rapidly accelerating technological progress seemed to meet the material needs of human beings. Whereas both Christianity and Enlightenment rationalism had linked social and material progress to morality, technological progress seemed amoral to Adams. This disassociation of progress and morality was accentuated by the new evolutionary science of Darwinism, which suggested that development was the product of a natural struggle of one species against others. Sociologists, most famously William Graham Sumner, developed a "social Darwinism" that applied the law of competition and struggle to individual human beings within society. Social progress, understood as material progress, came about not because of the application of the religious, specifically Christian, ethic of caring for the poor and unfortunate, which simply rewarded the least adapted and least fit at the expense of the most adapted and most fit. Social Darwinism seemed to explain the success of America's new "captains of industry" and to suggest an ethic whereby the winners in the new industrial order owed little or nothing to the losers. Naturalism in literature, produced by writers such as Jack London and Theodore Dreiser, similarly suggested that individuals thrived best when their natural instincts were unclouded by "delusions" of the supernatural or by the notion that moral behavior was rewarded in this life or the next. The power of technology, the proliferation of consumer goods, and new scientific understandings served to excise the spiritual dimensions from the world.

The philosophy of pragmatism, particularly as developed by the Harvard psychologist William James, can be understood in part as a response to this spiritual crisis. James defined truth as nothing more than a belief that helps the human organism to negotiate successfully through the challenges posed by its environment. Religion and morality thus become true insofar as they contribute to the psychological and social well-being of believers. James assured Americans that however amoral the natural and technological engines that drove industrial progress seemed to be, they could nevertheless exercise their "will to believe" in ultimate meaning and order.

Although social Darwinism and pragmatism both exercised considerable influence in political and intellectual life, they do not seem to have transformed the religious sensibilities of either the new industrialists or their working-class employees. Carnegie, for instance, articulated a "gospel of wealth" that stressed the moral obligation of men and women to maximize their economic potential as a means of doing good to their fellow human beings as well as to themselves. Like Rockefeller, who remained a devout Protestant, Carnegie devoted the last years of his life to giving away much of the fortune he accumulated. Philanthropic contributions to worthy causes, particularly those that facilitated the improvement of those less fortunate people with ambition to help themselves, in their view, were the moral obligation of the self-made millionaire.

With regard to the industrial workers of the late nineteenth century, two religious phenomena are worthy of note. First, stories of economic opportunity brought a new wave of immigration that contributed to religious diversity, challenging the plausibility of America as a Protestant nation. These new immigrants migrated primarily from southern and eastern Europe (and, to a lesser extent, Asia), bringing their Roman Catholicism, Eastern Orthodoxy, Judaism, and Buddhism with them. Despite the earnest wishes of Protestant clergymen such as Josiah Strong, who (like his Puritan ancestors) feared that the relative decline of Protestantism would bring national ruin, immigrants found a crucial source of ethnic identity in their religious communities. Second, evangelical revivalism remained an important characteristic of nineteenth-century urban life. Mass revivalists such as Dwight L. Moody sought to bring the Protestant gospel to the unchurched. New religious organizations, most notably the Salvation Army, developed administrative structures modeled on the large-scale organization of economic life to bring the gospel to urban workers. Like the revivalists earlier in the century, along with the gospel, they preached a moral discipline centering on work, frugality, and temperance that served to empower converts for a measure of economic success in the industrial order. Revivalism, with its emphasis on personal salvation, its work ethic, and its legitimization of property relationships, undermined attempts of those who wished to organize workers along class lines in order to advance their material well-being in this world.

At the beginning of the twentieth century, the religious culture of America could by no means be described in terms of the Protestantism of the Puritans. Industrialization, technology, materialism, and science had undermined confidence in the Calvinist God who providentially governed the world. Immigration presented Americans with a plethora of non-Protestant ways to practice religion. Nevertheless, in the vestiges of Protestantism that remained in men like Carnegie and Rockefeller, the work ethic, with its promise of material blessing in this world, remained strong. Evangelical Protestants who took the industrial city as their special mission similarly cultivated that ethic. Although those revivalists enjoyed limited success in converting the new immigrants, their fracturing of working-class solidarity contributed to the hegemony of the culture of capitalism in the American Republic.

Early Twentieth Century

Serious criticism of American capitalism as it developed through the Industrial Revolution emerged in both Protestant and Catholic circles in the early twentieth century. This criticism was consistent with broader trends in political economy. According to capitalist economic theory, reinforced by social Darwinism, an unrestrained economy should produce healthy competition that serves to decrease costs and improve the quality of goods and services. But the actual history of American capitalism moved in a different direction. Monopolies, organized as "trusts," that stifled competition emerged in crucial sectors of the economy, particularly in rail transportation, steel, and oil industries. In the last decades of the nineteenth century, especially in the South and West, farmers created populism, a major political movement that pointed to tensions between political democracy, with its stress on liberty and equality, and the economic power of industrial organizations. Populists such as Nebraska senator and presidential candidate William Jennings Bryan, often deeply devoted to evangelical Protestantism, sought to utilize the power of government to restore a greater measure of equality by checking the power of corporations. Although populists failed to attain national power, reformers who took the name Progressives, mostly from the Northeast and Midwest, adopted substantial parts of their programs. These reformers sought to enact policies that enlisted the power of government—city, state, and federal—to make the economy both fairer and more efficient. They supported reforms that gave governments the power to break up or regulate monopolies, reformed the money and banking systems, mediated between capital and labor in industrial conflicts, and alleviated some of the poor living and working conditions created by the industrial order.

Progressive reformers found supporters and allies among many of the Protestant clergy in American cities, particularly in the industrial Northeast and Midwest. No single individual was more important in articulating a new relationship between Christian faith and economic action than clergyman and seminary professor Walter Rauschenbusch, who developed a social gospel that addressed the problems created by the industrial order. Central to Rauschenbusch's theology was the notion that the redemptive act of Christ was social as well as personal. Evil resided in social, political, and economic institutions as well as in individuals. Just as Christians were obligated to struggle to eradicate the evil in themselves, so too were they obligated to strive to create a social order consistent with the ethics of Jesus. Capitalism, particularly when shaped by a social Darwinist ethic that encouraged economic individualism, ran counter to the Christian obligation to love one's neighbor as oneself. The tendency of men and women in capitalist societies toward self-aggrandizement needed to be checked not merely through the cultivation of personal morality but by institutional reform. Thus, proponents of this social gospel joined with Progressive reformers in their effort to use the power of government to make the economy more rational and more just. They entertained the hope that this effort might contribute to the creation of the Kingdom of God in this world. This millenarian hope linked them to evangelicals of the revolutionary and early national periods.

Two fictional works served to popularize the social gospel by illustrating its principles. *In His Steps*, by Wichita clergyman Charles Sheldon, tells the story of a minister who confronts the evils in his city—liquor, poverty, industrial conflict, and the like—with a simple question: "What would Jesus do?" If Jesus lived in an industrial democracy, thought Sheldon, he would get involved in local politics to suppress the liquor trade and promote temperance, to ensure adequate living conditions for the poor, and to ameliorate conflict between workers and their employers. *Looking Backward*, by Edward Bellamy, a Springfield, Massachusetts, newspaper editor, is a utopian novel set in the year 2000. Its protagonist found himself transported to a future in which cooperation had replaced the irrationality and exploitation inherent in competitive capitalism. Nineteenth-century America, according to Bellamy, had been organized on the assumption that men and women would follow their worst instincts—that they would spend their lives striving against their fellow human beings for their personal material well-being. In Bellamy's future, this assumption was reversed. If men and women were assured of the material well-being of themselves and their families, they would follow the instincts of their higher social and spiritual natures. Unlike Sheldon, whose social gospel contained an imperative to ameliorate the adverse conditions caused by industrial capitalism, Bellamy envisioned an economic order transformed. For Bellamy, socialism, not capitalism, was the logical outcome of Christian ethics.

At bottom, however, the social gospel was about action more than vision. No single individual better embodied its principles applied to social evils than Chicago settlement house worker Jane Addams. The settlement house movement, in which Addams played a leading role, originated in the desire to facilitate the adaptation of new immigrant workers to American urban and industrial life. Settlement houses sought not merely to help the immigrant find appropriate work and adequate food, clothing, and shelter but also to teach the social skills and inculcate the habits that would facilitate immigrant success. Instruction in the English language, food preparation, and urban hygiene was thus essential to their program. Inevitably, settlement house workers became politically involved in issues vital to the well-being of immigrant workers. They urged cities and states to establish codes to ensure safe housing, clean water, and adequate waste disposal. Poor wages and unsafe working conditions also came to figure on their agenda. Thus, the settlement house sought both to alleviate the suffering of individuals and to achieve institutional reform. For Addams, settlement house work was the natural activity of men and women who followed both their own best instincts and Christian ethics to build a better world than the one created by industrial capitalism in America.

American Catholics also embraced a social gospel in the early twentieth century. As working-class immigrants constituted a large portion of the church in America, Catholic attention quite naturally centered on the contest between labor and capital. Throughout most of the nineteenth century, the Catholic hierarchy officially discouraged working Catholics from joining unions and their priests from lending them support. This stance changed with the papal encyclical *Rerum Novarum*, issued in 1891, which criticized both socialism and capitalism and affirmed the rights of owners to private property and the rights of workers to form unions. Minnesota priest and seminary professor John Ryan applied the ethics of *Rerum Novarum* to the condition of American workers. The publication of his two major books, *A Living Wage* and *Distributive Justice*, established Ryan as the foremost spokesperson for a Catholic vision of economic justice. In 1919, he penned the "Bishop's Program of Social Reconstruction," a document that endorsed many of the Progressive reforms—a minimum wage; the right of workers to organize; public insurance against old age, sickness, and unemployment; the government regulation of corporations—championed by Protestant spokespeople for the social gospel. At the end of the Progressive era, it appeared that Christian ethics, Protestant and Catholic, were allied against the spirit of capitalism.

But if Christianity could provide a powerful critique of capitalism, it could also accommodate to its demands and succumb to its seductions. Industrialization provided a wide array of consumer goods that an increasingly prosperous middle class demanded for its comfort and desired as a demonstration of its affluence. Religious holidays became marketing opportunities for merchants. For Christians of nearly every denomination, they became occasions for lavish consumption. At Easter, Christians not only marked the resurrection of Jesus; they also, as their means permitted, adorned their churches with extravagant floral displays and paraded their bodies bedecked with fine new clothes. Ritual gift giving at Christmas was transformed by material abundance. The holiest of the Christian holidays thus sacralized the culture of the consumer. These trends accelerated during the 1920s, as the fortunes of the social gospel waned along with the broader Progressive impulse of which it was a part. The mass production of consumer goods, particularly electrical appliances and the automobile, brought increasing prosperity and unprecedented comfort to urban and industrial America. In a decade that enjoyed easy credit and consumption, materialism was christened. Bruce Barton's *The Man Nobody Knew* retold the life of Jesus, casting him as the world's greatest salesman. In the wildly popular novels of Grace Livingston Hill, conspicuous consumption and evangelical Christian virtue went hand in hand. If Protestants continued to celebrate the productive power of capitalism, as Weber had argued, they did so under rather different terms than the ones he outlined. Consumption, rather than frugality, became the mark and measure of virtue.

Although American Christians celebrated consumption in general, they became increasingly critical of the consumption of alcohol. Ranging across the spectrum from fundamentalist preachers of the "old-time religion" like Billy Sunday, to proponents of the social gospel like Charles Sheldon, to Catholic activists like Henry J. Anderson, president of the charitable society of St. Vincent de Paul, many Christians agreed that intemperance was the moral cause that lay at the root of poverty and want. Drink not only threatened the souls of inveterate imbibers but also impinged on their ability to purchase the material goods industrial capitalism offered. The Prohibition movement, with its roots deep in nineteenth-century social reform, culminated with the passage of the Twentieth Amendment in 1920. Religious impulse shut down an entire industry, as brewers, wine makers, and distillers, along with their networks of suppliers and distributors, were legislated out of legal existence. Prohibition proved notoriously difficult to enforce, and the economic collapse of 1929 to 1932 demonstrated that the ills of the American economy could not be blamed on drink. The repeal of Prohibition marked the end of American Christianity's most energetic effort to shape economic behavior by proscribing the consumption of specific goods.

The Great Depression and World War II forced a measure of austerity on most Americans, compelling them to reconsider the relationship between their material and spiritual lives. Although leading Protestant social thinkers derived their perception that American capitalism had produced social injustice from their precursors in the social gospel movement, they exhibited far less optimism about the possibility of creating a just society, let alone ushering in the Kingdom of God. Led by clergyman and seminary professor Reinhold Niebuhr, Protestant thinkers developed a "Christian realism" that, in the tradition of the Puritans, emphasized the irreducible inclination of men and women to sin. Although God's grace might transform the individual, it never redeemed social groups. An individual might behave altruistically, but collectives always acted in their own interest, or the interests of their members, against the interests of other collectives. Selfishness thus became institutionalized in economic and political systems. For Niebuhr and his followers, American Christians were caught in a tragic situation. Their ethic compelled them to struggle for social justice while their theology assured them that all such attempts were doomed to failure. Like Weber's seventeenth-century Puritans, twentieth-century Christian realists could not escape the logic of capitalism, even as they denied themselves the full enjoyment of the material benefits it provided.

Depression-era Catholics, for the most part, similarly reconciled their religious ethic to the realities of the American economy. For leading thinkers and activists such as Father Ryan, the demand for social justice found its outlet in support for the reform measures of the New Deal that protected the rights of both labor and capital. Other Catholics, however, rejected capitalism altogether. On the right, the suburban Detroit priest Charles Coughlin used his national radio broadcast to condemn communism, capitalism, and the New Deal, preferring instead his own version of national socialism. On the left, the lay-led Catholic Worker movement, founded by Dorothy Day, rejected political solutions to economic problems. Rather than organizing in support of reform programs, Catholic Workers sought to create communities characterized by voluntary poverty that lived by Christian principles of love and justice.

Modern America

For Americans, World War II ushered in a period of economic growth that continued into the early 1970s. The United States emerged from the war as the single industrial power whose economic infrastructure had not suffered serious damage. Higher wages won during the war made workers better consumers. Veterans received subsidized college educations that increased their earning power and home loans that extended their spending power. A high birth rate guaranteed increasing demand. As never before, postwar Americans were a people of plenty.

Material prosperity, in the minds of many Americans, was the natural product of political freedom and economic individualism, which in turn were rooted in essentially religious conceptions of the human person. The specter of international communism seemed to make this constellation of values plausible. Communism, according to Whitaker Chambers, the famous witness against Alger Hiss, a State Department official convicted of spying for the

Soviet Union, was the logical result of atheism. If, as the Marxists claimed, there was no God, then material well-being was quite reasonably the highest goal of human beings. In their quest for prosperity, human collectives, unrestrained by divinely sanctioned morals, would surely use their power of the state to take property from those individuals who possessed it. The denial of property rights would inevitably lead to the destruction of other human rights, and the individual would fall helpless before the power of the state. The pairing of the terms *godless* and *communism* implied its opposite: the pairing of religion and capitalism.

Thus, during the 1950s, a broad consensus emerged that saw religious belief and practice as an essential bulwark in the struggle to preserve capitalist values against the threat of communism. As the Weber thesis predicted, Protestants of self-consciously Calvinist heritage were among the most outspoken anti-Communists. Carl McIntire, a fundamentalist Presbyterian, used his weekly radio broadcast to castigate liberal theology, the social gospel, and socialism. Neo-orthodox theologian Reinhold Niebuhr, although not abandoning his position that all human societies tend to immorality, increasingly focused his attention on the failures of socialist societies. Religiously inspired anticommunism, however, was by no means limited to Protestants but rather cut across the entire religious spectrum. The former Marxist Will Herberg, a secular Jew, contended that the essential message of American Protestants, Catholics, and Jews had converged on the sacralization of what he termed the "American Way of Life." Economic individualism, the work ethic, consumerism, and the belief in limitless prosperity were values shared by all Americans. They found sanction in all the American varieties of religious faith.

Accordingly, religion came to be celebrated not as an end in itself but as a means to preserve a particular economic and social system. President Dwight Eisenhower, for instance, praised the general religiousness of Americans, confident that it did not matter what specific form religion took. God's enlistment in the service of mammon found symbolic expression as the U.S. Mint began to stamp the phrase "In God We Trust" on the front of American coins.

The complacent belief that religion generally validated the American economic order was severely tested in the course of the 1960s and early 1970s. For one thing, it became apparent that not all Americans shared in the postwar prosperity. In 1960, Michael Harrington, a veteran of the Catholic Worker movement, published *The Other America*, revealing the persistence of poverty in inner cities and rural hamlets and among the aged and people of color. This poverty could not be attributed to failure of the poor to live by the work ethic but rather to structural inequities that excluded as much as a fifth of the population from the material rewards that American prosperity afforded. Harrington's work played a crucial role in raising consciousness and prompting the presidential administrations of John F. Kennedy and Lyndon Johnson to launch a "War on Poverty."

The interrelated struggles for civil rights and for "Black Power" also called the sanctity of the American economy into question. The Baptist minister Martin Luther King, leader of the Southern Christian Leadership Conference and architect of its strategy of nonviolent protest, came to understand the theological and ethical dimensions of social injustice in part through his reading of the chief luminaries of the social gospel. By the mid-1960s, it had become apparent to King that civil and political rights alone would not bring full equality to African Americans. So long as economic power—that is, capital —was in the hands of whites, people of color could never hope to achieve equal rights or equal opportunity, let alone economic equality. Theologians such as James Cone and Joseph Johnson developed a "black theology" that defined economic individualism and the private ownership of capital as cultural values that served the interests of rich whites by legitimizing economic and racial inequality. In this version of the social gospel, Jesus was cast as the "Liberator" whose redemptive mission centered on freeing men and women from the most distressing injustices that beset them.

Other African Americans turned away from Christianity altogether. The Nation of Islam, an American variant of the Muslim faith, enjoyed substantial growth and, under the articulate rhetoric of Malcolm X, significant visibility. Much like seventeenth-century Puritanism, the Nation of Islam's economic message centered on hard work, frugality, and self-discipline as the keys to black empowerment. For black Muslims, as for Puritans, religious ethics required rational and acquisitive economic activity.

Finally, America's controversial involvement in Vietnam also raised questions about the moral legitimacy of the "American way of life" and its religious sanctions. The economic prosperity that Americans enjoyed at home seemed to depend on the economic colonization of vast areas of what had come to be called the Third World. The effort to contain communism, central to American foreign policy from the end of World War II through the 1980s, seemed to demand support for regimes that were friendly to American economic and geopolitical interests but systematically denied their own peoples the political and civil rights that Americans held dear. Like the proponents of "black theology" in America, Christian thinkers in the Third World, particularly in Latin America, developed a "theology of liberation" that sought to enlist the gospel on behalf of the material needs of the poor and oppressed.

Many American religious leaders who had been steeped in the civil rights movement found this updated social gospel compelling. The anticommunism of the 1950s, which had justified an interventionist foreign policy, came to be replaced for many mainline Protestant and Roman Catholics by sympathy for men and women involved in anti-imperialist struggles in Asia, Africa, and Latin America. During the 1980s, a number of Christian churches participated in the movement to give sanctuary to refugees from political oppression in United States–supported regimes in Latin America.

Many aspects of the counterculture of the 1960s emerged as an essentially religious reaction against the perceived spiritual poverty of American materialism. Hippies, who forsook (at least temporarily) the comforts of middle-class life, could take their inspiration from any combination of ancient Hindu or Buddhist texts, Native American beliefs and rituals, the experience of psychoactive drugs, or the simple poverty of the early Christians. Each of these systems of belief offered an alternative to the fundamental dualism posited by historical Christianity between the spiritual and material worlds. Accordingly, they suggested different models of religiously appropriate economic activity. Nevertheless, these movements were not immune to the allure of mammon. The quest for self-realization did not run counter to the profit motive. The vast corporate holding of the Unification Church illustrates that the compulsive economic activity religion sometimes generates can be communal as well as individualistic. The boom market for crystals created by New Age spirituality shows that in capitalist societies, at least, the potential for the commodification of religion is ever present.

The resurgence of the Christian Right in the 1980s and 1990s testifies to the enduring power of the postwar consensus about religion and the American way of life. Such televangelists as Jerry Falwell and Pat Robertson defended the marriage between religion and American capitalism with the same fervor as the anti-Communists of the 1950s. Falwell counted support for tax reductions for individuals alongside support for tighter restrictions on drugs, prostitution, and gambling as among the essential political positions of evangelical Christians. Far from being a Christian response to the industrial capitalist order, as partisans of the social gospel had seen it, the welfare state, in the mind of the New Christian Right, undermined the sense of individual responsibility on which public morality rested. Conservative spokespeople such as William Bennett and Robert Bork located much of the cause of what they saw as American decline in the loss of values and virtues rooted in work, individualism, and private property.

An alternative conservative Protestant system, however, arose during the late twentieth century. Itself an outgrowth of the "Seed Faith" theology espoused by televangelist Oral Roberts, by which one gives to a ministry in the hope that God will give it back multiplied, the "Name It and Claim It" theology espoused increasingly by Pentecostal and charismatic preachers taught that God's blessings are not confined to the next life. Indeed, God desires to bless his children materially in this world. By naming what you want (a new car, a better job, good health), claiming it in the name of Jesus, and living in faith that it will come to you, these believers no longer tied private property to the virtue of hard work. This movement reached its apex at the end of the century with the immensely popular ninety-two-page book *The Prayer of Jabez*. Heretofore an unknown character in the Old Testament, Jabez became the hero for many (more than five million books were sold) who daily repeated his simple prayer: "Oh, that You would bless me indeed, and enlarge my territory, that Your hand would be with me, and that You would keep me from evil, that I may not cause pain!" Tying the ancient supplication to modern life, author Bruce Wilkenson claimed, "If Jabez had worked on Wall Street, he might have prayed, 'Lord, increase the value of my investment portfolios.'" Rather than emphasize the virtue of work, Christians were encouraged to merely pray and wait to see how God would spiritually and materially increase their lives.

Still, spokespeople for the Christian Right often position themselves as the bearers of the Puritan tradition in the modern world. Their rhetoric of moral decline, and of the material consequences that must ensue, is indeed appropriated from the Puritans. The jeremiad of the Christian Right, like that of the Puritans, may tell us more about the persistence of America as the most religious and the most capitalist of modern nations. The rapid collapse of Marxism after 1989 left no serious alternatives to capitalist economic organization. American prosperity in the 1990s left relatively few Americans looking for such alternatives. The culture of capitalism remains strong in post-Protestant America. The history of postwar America seems to testify to the power of capitalism to co-opt religion, just as it co-opts so many other forms of cultural expression. American religion remains haunted by the spirit of capitalism.

Conclusion

The relationship between religion and economics in American history cannot be stated simply or definitively. Early America provides a good deal of evidence that supports Weber's argument. There is clearly an affinity between Protestantism and capitalism. Protestantism thrived in a culture of economic rationality—of work, frugality, and investment. And economic rationality thrived in a Protestant culture. Recognizing affinities is relatively unproblematic. Identifying causal linkages is another matter. Did Protestantism, as Weber suggested, create and nurture the "spirit" of capitalism? Perhaps. But it must not be forgotten that Protestantism also carried in it a critique of capitalism. The Boston Puritans and Philadelphia Quakers who created an Atlantic network of commerce were no less (and no more) devoted to their Protestant faith than the subsistence and communally oriented farmers in their hinterlands or the slave-owning tobacco and rice planters to their south. Similarly, the antebellum financiers and factory owners were no more (and no less) committed to their Protestant faith than their employees who celebrated the virtues of work and productive labor. Rather than arguing that Protestantism gave birth to the spirit of capitalism, it may be more accurate to simply acknowledge that Protestantism provided the moral language in which early Americans argued about capitalist economics.

After the Civil War, when Protestant claims to hegemony became more contested and capitalist hegemony became less contested, causal linkages seem to have been reversed. Capitalism seemed to find its religious legitimization in every American form of religion imaginable, from the most ancient and orthodox Judaism to the most recent version of New Age spirituality. It would be tempting to argue, as did the Marxists that Weber opposed, that religion is the product of material reality. In a capitalist culture, religion gives meaning and assigns value to capitalist behavior. Yet such a conclusion ignores the extent to which American religion, Protestant and not, has been a source of rhetoric critical of American economic life. The Protestant realism of Niebuhr, the communalism of the Catholic Workers, and the asceticism of Hare Krishnas evidence a continuing protest, albeit in radically differing ways, to the pervasive notion that God and mammon can be simultaneously served with clear conscience.

SUGGESTED READING

Albanese, Catherine. *Nature Religion in America: From the Algonkian Indians to the New Age*. Chicago: University of Chicago Press, 1990.

Coles, Robert. *Dorothy Day: A Radical Devotion*. Reading, Mass.: Addison-Wesley, 1987.

Innes, Stephen. *Creating the Commonwealth: The Economic Culture of Puritan New England*. New York: Norton, 1995.

Johnson, Paul E. *A Shopkeeper's Millennium: Society and Revivals in Rochester, New York, 1815–1837*. New York: Hill and Wang, 1978.

Lambert, Frank. *"Pedlar in Divinity": George Whitefield and the Transatlantic Revivals, 1737–1770*. Princeton, N.J.: Princeton University Press, 1994.

Lazerow, Jama. *Religion and the Working Class in Antebellum America*. Washington, D.C.: Smithsonian Institution Press, 1995.

Lockridge, Kenneth. *A New England Town: The First Hundred Years: Dedham, Massachusetts, 1636–1736*. Expanded ed. New York: Norton, 1985.

Lovin, Robin W. *Reinhold Niebuhr and Christian Realism*. New York: Cambridge University Press, 1995.

Martin, Calvin. *Keepers of the Game: Indian-Animal Relationships and the Fur Trade*. Berkeley and Los Angeles: University of California Press, 1978.

McDannell, Colleen. *Material Christianity: Religion and Popular Culture in America*. New Haven: Yale University Press, 1995.

Moore, R. Laurence. *Selling God: American Religion in the Marketplace of Culture*. New York: Oxford University Press, 1994.

Weber, Max. *The Protestant Ethic and the Spirit of Capitalism*. Translated by Talcott Parsons. New York: Scribner's, 1950.

Wuthnow, Robert. *God and Mammon in America*. New York: Free Press, 1994.

Science

Extremely popular accounts of science can lend credence to the agnostic or atheistic position and, ironically, simultaneously point to a sense of the religiousness of science. For instance, theoretical physicist Stephen Hawking and astronomer Carl Sagan wondered aloud how there could be room for a creator god in the scientific story that includes a "Theory of Everything"; at the same time they suggest that that story, along with the scientific life, provides an alternative to traditional religious views of human existence and meaning. Sagan, in particular, has written much about the uplifting value, even mystical quality of the scientific cosmology, characterizing space travel, in particular, as an ultimate human adventure. Exploring the final frontier appears as the expression of the highest of human aspirations. This reconciliation of the sciences and the humanities can be seen both in the movie *Contact* and the TV series *Cosmos*. In the latter, Sagan leaves the audience with the hope that meaning and purpose emerge from "the courage of our questions and the depth of our answers." Moreover, it is through this heroic questioning that we humans can discover that we are not alone in the universe and that, in a return to our stardust roots, we may know that "the Cosmos is all that is or ever was or ever will be." What should we make of this irony, this simultaneously scientific and virtually religious stance?

In broadest terms, we can say that science refers to the systematic observation and explanation of events or phenomena according to a logic of cause and effect. Religion, on the other hand, involves expressions of the ultimate meaning of those events or phenomena and the ultimate nature of that logic. A fundamental question, then, in this chapter is: What has been the relationship between science and religion in America? We shall see how the shifting cultural context of America affects both the relationship and the definition of these spheres of culture. At the same time, we shall see how science and religion have played a role in defining an American culture.

In that regard, we can pursue our study with an organizing theme borrowed from Sir Francis Bacon, the English philosopher who himself plays an important role in this history. In describing the significance of the voyages of Christopher Columbus, Bacon referred to the great captain as the "inventor" of America. For Bacon, as for most of his contemporaries, to "invent" meant, first of all, to find; but we can also take it to mean create. It is hoped that, from that point of view, our study may reveal as much about the meaning of America as it does about the relationship of religion and science.

Precolonial Era

The mix of science and religion in the invention of America is plain from the outset. In the age of exploration beginning in the fifteenth century, religious fervor and "New Learning" combined to foster the worldwide expansion of Christendom. The joint incentive was notably expressed by Christopher Columbus (1451–1506), the Genoese sailor whose four voyages from 1492 to 1504 would permanently link the two halves of a hitherto divided world. Imbued with both a crusading spirit and a distinctive understanding of geography, Columbus saw himself as both religiously and scientifically qualified to carry out the task of discovery. His plan of opening trade routes to the East by sailing west—by successfully navigating the "sea of Darkness" and claiming any discovered lands for God and king—entailed a powerful mix of scientific and religious imagination.

At the time, geographical knowledge drew on a variety of sources. The Bible, exotic tales, ancient and medieval cosmology, reports from travelers— all contributed to a developing European picture of the world. There was no real debate about the shape of the earth; its spherical shape had been known for centuries. The problem was how to visualize ocean space so as to allow for navigation and exploration by sea.

Since his particular calculations went against majority opinion (and, in fact, turned out to be wrong), Columbus had to convince his patrons, King Ferdinand and Queen Isabella of Spain, that his idea was not only scientifically sound but religiously significant. In his own eyes, at least, it was the latter argument that won the day. He clearly believed his mission had religious meaning. In his famous *Book of Prophecies*, written in 1500 while effectively under house arrest in Spain for allegedly mismanaging the colony of Hispaniola, he laid out the results of his own systematic study of the Bible. Columbus wished to remind his Catholic sovereigns that his voyages were fulfilling biblical prophecy of the latter-day expansion of Christianity. Here he voiced an early modern link between science and religion by recounting, without too much exaggeration, his multifaceted preparation for a divinely appointed task: "[The Lord] gave me abundant skill in the mariner's arts, an adequate understanding of the stars, and of geometry and arithmetic. He gave me the mental capacity and the manual skill to draft spherical maps. . . . With a hand that could be felt, the Lord opened my mind to the fact that it would be possible to sail from here to the Indies, and he opened my will to desire to accomplish the project. . . . Who can doubt that this fire was not merely mine, but also of the Holy Spirit who encouraged me with a radiance of marvelous illumination from his Sacred Scriptures."

Too much can perhaps be made of Columbus's particular religious and scientific vision. His enterprise was opposed by his contemporaries, who questioned both his science and his theology. Nevertheless, Columbus's self-image as both navigator and seer, as explorer and prophet, suggests the compelling relation of religion and science in the Renaissance that empowered European discovery of "the new world." For good and for ill, the complex mix of crusading spirit, millennial vision, economic interests, and scientific know-how in early modern Europe motivated many a trader, colonist, and missionary to follow in Columbus's wake.

Colonial North America

An important, initial way to view the subsequent interaction between science and religion is through the European encounter with indigenous peoples. Though the missionary goals of the Spanish, French, and English varied to some degree, missionaries generally expected to convert the natives to European life as a whole. This task of cultural conversion required both scientific and religious training.

The combination is suggested in the following account from a traveling companion of the Italian explorer, cartographer, and Jesuit missionary Eusebio Kino (1645–1711). Father Kino spent thirty years in Pimería Alta, the region now comprising the southern part of Arizona and most of the Mexican state of Sonora: "We studied not only astronomy, mathematics, and other interesting fields of knowledge, but we ourselves made all sorts of trinkets and worked at practical things. Some of us made compasses or sun-dials, and others cases for them; this one sewed clothes and furs, that one learned how to make bottles, and others how to solder tin; one busied himself with distilling, a second with the lathe, a third with the art of sculpturing; so that with these goods and skills we might gain the good will of the wild heathen and then more easily give them the truths of the Christian faith."

Such complete preparation—the incorporation of religious and scientific learning into a strategy of evangelization—would come in handy in the European's encounter with his Amerindian counterpart. In order to gain the good will and win the soul of the "savage," the missionary first had to gain the upper hand over his cultural rival, the native shaman. Both men performed many more tasks than what we might regard today as strictly religious. Their personal confrontation embodied a clash between two integrated systems of understanding the cosmos.

The French Jesuits, for example (who set something of a standard for missionary strategy), aimed to replace the Huron, Montagnais, and Algonquian shamans as custodians of native culture. The "Black Robes," as the natives called them, used all available means to undermine the shaman's authority: philosophical argument; early modern medical treatment for diseases (which they themselves had brought), including techniques like bleeding the patient; predicting eclipses; describing lands and peoples unknown to the natives; demonstrating the powers of magnetism or the wonders of the magnifying glass; and praying for rain or a successful hunt. Perhaps most impressive to an oral culture was the Jesuits' ability to convey both human and divine knowledge, across time and space, through the written word.

To the extent that missionaries could win the hearts and minds of the natives in an initial contact, they would then generally gather them into Christian communities to continue the process of conversion. In Catholic New Spain and New France, the institution for this endeavor was the "mission." In Puritan New England, it was the "praying town." In both cases, native converts entered Christian enclaves, segregated from unconverted kin and protected from dangerous Europeans. In these communities, early modern science and religion supported a dual strategy of civilizing and evangelizing—of "reducing" the natives from savagery to civility and radically altering their way of life.

Life in Catholic missions, for example, took on a quasi-monastic routine of prayer and work (*ora et labora*), of instruction and domestication, with natives taught gospel values along with European methods of agriculture. In Puritan New England and Anglican Virginia—to the extent that these colonial enterprises had any interest in missions—the native's vision of nature was severely altered by the demands of English husbandry, summarized by one historian as "the deep-cutting plow harnessed to animal power, fences to enclose the field, or (particularly symbolic) fertilizer in the form of tame animal manure."

The European effort to tame a "wild people" along with a wilderness typically resulted in replacing the sacred and profane economy of the natives while displacing the natives themselves. At the same time, the colonizers, who carved up the landscape into invisible lines of ownership and restructured the cosmos into alternative principalities and powers, would themselves undergo changes in an understanding of God and of nature as a result of living in the New World.

In Anglican Virginia and Puritan New England, basic beliefs about the nature of the universe, about the human being's place in it, and about ways to ensure safe passage through it provided the cosmic framework for colonization. In this larger context, knowledge of God and nature interacted to impose order on the environment. In the seventeenth century and into the early eighteenth, settlement of Virginia (and the southern colonies, generally) proceeded largely according to a vision of right order held by the landed gentry. This vision perceived a hierarchy in nature and society, and in church and state, in which authority was exercised from above and accepted from below. In this worldview, the practical arts and sciences of surveying, agriculture, architecture, and medicine interacted with religious beliefs to give shape to the colony.

At a basic level, even the way the land was carved up and occupied reflected a hierarchical worldview. The "great houses" of great plantations were located near points of commerce on the riverfront; the humbler farmhouses of common planters were constructed farther inland; and slave quarters were clustered together on both greater and lesser estates. Although the pattern of slave settlement expressed, in part, the communal values of the Africans, the layout of colonial land in total displayed the basic organizing principles of genteel society: of rank and privilege, responsibility and deference, and, ultimately, patriarchy. The design of the great manor houses, in particular, with their surrounding complexes of buildings and gardens, expressed social values in carefully calculated proportion and symmetry. Under the patriarchal principle of order, the head of household acted as father-king over his many bond servants. His rule, in turn, reflected the superior fatherhood of king and God. The essence of his authority was expressed in the ideals of leisure and freedom that defined the life of the gentleman. In this cultural framework, formal religion and natural science served the interests of gentility.

Beliefs about the connection between natural, social, and moral orders made visible in the architecture and agriculture are perhaps most clearly seen in the practice of medicine. A close correspondence was believed to exist between the internal "humors" of the body and the external "elements" of nature. The former determined both the physical health and the psychological traits of the individual; the latter affected the climate of a geographical area. Proper diagnosis required a careful reading of both signs. Colonial medical treatment, therefore, entailed a close observation of bodily fluids. Aggressive measures were often taken to restore a proper balance of the internal humors (blood, phlegm, yellow or green bile, and black bile) in keeping with the particular, local mix of the cosmic elements (air, water, fire, and earth).

Authority in genteel society derived from superior command of book learning, and medicine, though it was beginning to change and was also supplemented by English and African folk remedies, still relied on the rather academic humoral theory taught in universities. Education, in general, began with the ability to read and then to write and then to "figure," culminating in familiarity with ancient languages and with the written sources of both sacred and profane knowledge: the Bible, works of classical literature, and the books of law. Such learning defined the "liberal" education of the gentleman. In this context of higher learning, an ideal pastor, for example, was one who combined a sense of propriety with erudition. He was not expected to be overly pious but rather thoroughly acquainted with philosophy, ethics, and economics and able to talk with ease on these subjects as well as preach sensibly on the scriptures. This "liberal" learning could be and was extended through "natural inquiry," and the defining activities of the natural sciences—observing, collecting, describing, and experimenting with the raw materials of nature— were pursued or patronized by the gentlemen and women of the colonies.

The nonconformist Puritans, meanwhile, pushed reform of religion and society further than the civil and ecclesiastical hierarchy in England desired. In times of persecution, they left for America, hoping to pursue their alternative vision of a Bible commonwealth that all of England and Christendom might emulate. The religious sensibilities of these dissenters guided their efforts to understand and control the natural world. As a result, the relation between Puritanism and science exhibits some distinctive qualities important to the historical relation of science and religion in America.

The Puritan "errand in the wilderness" was sustained by various ways of interpreting God's activity in nature. On the one hand, the world seemed alive with divine (and demonic) powers. Popular "wonder books" and ballads, along with scholarly folios and yearly almanacs produced by Harvard graduates, all told of "illustrious providences" and "prodigious signs" indicating God's benevolence or judgment. Natural phenomena like thunderstorms, earthquakes, eclipses, comets, and "monster births" were interpreted as signs of divine displeasure, portents of drastic change or impending disaster. In sixteenth-century New England, these traditional ways of finding meaning in natural events were readily consistent with a covenantal view of God's relation to his creation. Natural signs and wonders were interpreted as warnings of breaches in the covenant, and Puritan divines, in a process not unscientific, compiled lists of God's "special providences" and "deliverances" in the lives of believers, along with instances of judgment in the lives of sinners.

On the other hand, alternative ways of interpreting evidence of divine providence were emerging. These alternatives involved the "new sciences" or natural philosophy, which conceived of divine action indirectly. God's special providences, for example, were understood as secondary or natural causes. This "philosophical" view underwrote the very practical task, often enthusiastically pursued, of meticulously cataloging the natural phenomena of the New World. A noted example of this scientific pursuit appears in the writings of John Winthrop Jr. (1605/6–1676). This well-traveled son of the first governor of the Massachusetts Bay Colony was himself the governor of the colony of Connecticut. He was also an eminent physician and the first colonial to be honored with membership in the Royal Society of London (elected in 1663). In a letter published in the society's influential *Philosophical Transactions* in 1670, Winthrop carefully described the content of his shipment of "natural curiosities." His detailed description, his hint of seeking deeper explanations for his discoveries, and his suggestions for the practical use of these natural resources indicate how systematic observation and collection fit well with the Puritan colonial enterprise. At one point Winthrop thought about the varying abundance or scarcity of acorns throughout the countryside and wondered whether England was experiencing the same thing simultaneously, "and if so, or not so, possibly something not altogether inconsiderable may be thence inferr'd." Such entries suggest how traffic in natural phenomena from the colonies to the home country helped foster the scientific revolution of the seventeenth century.

Indeed, Winthrop wrote at a time of significant transition in higher learning. His approach to natural inquiry presumed the methods and interpretive principles of a new natural philosophy. Aspects of this philosophy were promoted by the Royal Society and had been introduced into the curriculum at Harvard College by the 1650s. The physics of Aristotle and the astronomy of Ptolemy—studied, of course, in Latin or the original Greek—were being supplanted. Alternative subjects that became the bases of modern science included the cosmology of Nicolaus Copernicus (1473–1543), which pictured a sun-centered cosmos as the best way to account for observed phenomena of the heavens; the "mechanics" of Galileo Galilei (1564–1642) and mechanistic philosophy of René Descartes (1596–1650), which pictured the natural world as matter in motion, possessing "primary qualities," like mass and velocity, that could be related mathematically; the "experimental philosophy" of Francis Bacon (1561–1626), which held that the laws governing the material world could be inferred through a process of careful observation, classification, and analysis of natural phenomena; the "corpuscular philosophy" of Robert Boyle (1627–91), who, as the founder of modern chemistry, envisioned matter as made of minute particles that could arrange themselves into specific patterns; and the synthesis of Isaac Newton (1642–1727), who formulated universal laws of nature (like the inverse square law of gravitation) that governed phenomena in both the heavens and the earth and could be expressed in mathematical terms. (Newton's major work, the *Philosophiae Naturalis Prinicipia Mathematica*, appeared in 1687.)

The success of the new *natural philosophy* in providing an interpretive framework for work like Winthrop's generated demand for a new *natural theology*—a theological system of explanation that affirmed the activity of a supernatural creator in a law-abiding, machinelike universe, now apparently devoid of spiritual "qualities." Newton himself insisted that the new "world system" required an image of God as ruler rather than soul of the world. In the late seventeenth century, and for many decades to come, Christian philosophers and theologians shared an interest in developing this new understanding of God, involving a new kind of sermon about creation.

The elements of such a sermon were readily at hand. A long tradition existed of reconciling Greek philosophy with Christian theology by speaking of the Creator in philosophical terms, such as First Cause or Prime Mover. A time-honored analogy also existed between the "Two Books" of divine revelation: the Book of God's Word (the Bible) and the Book of God's Works (nature). It was generally agreed, too, that the reading of one book ought to correspond with the reading of the other. The key to harmonizing these two books of revelation was the time-honored argument from design. This rather effective and popular argument developed, in its seventeenth-century form, in keeping with Newton's "world system" by imagining natural phenomena and processes as marvelous contrivances of an all-wise and benevolent law-giver. In the colonies, the earliest and best example of this influential discourse came from the prolific pen of Puritan divine and scientific enthusiast Cotton Mather (1663–1728).

As a well-educated clergyman in the late seventeenth century, Mather enlisted the range of available ways to depict the sovereignty of God and workings of the spiritual world. On the one hand, he wrote books like *Wonders of the Invisible World*, which described certain events as the handiwork of Satan. Moreover, as a judge in the Salem witchcraft trials of 1692, he initially accepted "spectral" or invisible evidence of the guilt of the accused. On the other hand, he wrote *The Christian Philosopher*, the first comprehensive book on the new sciences produced in North America. He also promoted the innovative technique of inoculating people against smallpox, despite the objections of clergy and physicians alike, preferring to see the cure as a sign of God's mercy rather than the disease as a tool of his judgment.

In *The Christian Philosopher*, Mather integrated ancient and medieval writings with his own scientific observations to produce a thorough survey of the latest "discoveries" in natural philosophy. Throughout the book, he made the argument from design. He drew on other works in this genre to argue for the wisdom and goodness of God made evident in his marvelous works. "The improvement of Knowledge in the Works of Nature," he observed, "is a Thing whereby God, and his Christ is glorified." Mather intended, he said, to demonstrate the harmony between science and religion: the science of Bacon, Boyle, and Newton and the Bible religion of Puritanism. Mather hoped to ensure that natural inquiry would follow the Puritan prime directive: to do all things for the glory of God. He hoped that the curiosity he himself shared with the naturalist remained a *holy* curiosity.

Revolutionary and Early Republican America

Throughout the eighteenth century, an American scientific enterprise gradually organized within the intellectual movement of the Enlightenment and the political movement for independence. The project of inventing America in this context dramatically affected the relation of science to religion.

In the prerevolutionary period, Philadelphia emerged as an important center for natural inquiry. In fact, the Quaker city on the Delaware would "set the pattern of institutional development for the sciences in the urban centers of the new nation." At the heart of the developing community was the American Philosophical Society (APS). Founded in 1743, the APS quickly grew to include members from many colonies/states and several countries. As national independence became a reality, the APS leadership of clergymen, politicians, doctors, and naturalists envisioned a nationwide federation of natural philosophers. The variety of religious convictions represented in the society reflected something of the tolerant climate of Quaker Philadelphia and the range of beliefs congenial to "experimental inquiry."

Members of the APS included, for example, Benjamin Rush (1745–1813) —American statesman, professor of chemistry and medicine at the College of Philadelphia, signer of the Declaration of Independence, surgeon general for the Continental army, and one of the most influential physicians in the early years of the United States. Rush was a devout Christian, deeply affected by the religious revivals of the 1740s. As an evangelical Protestant, he came to reject the Calvinist doctrine of predestination in favor of universal salvation of all people by Christ. Another member of the APS, and its second president, was David Rittenhouse (1732–96), a surveyor, clockmaker, mathematician, and astronomer. Rittenhouse was a lifelong Presbyterian who, it has been said, "talked much of God and not at all of Christian redemption." Like many of his contemporaries, however, he insisted on the basic agreement of the Bible with true science.

The spectrum of beliefs held by eighteenth-century members of the APS actually represented a somewhat narrower range of Enlightenment views toward religion. There seemed to be few, if any, real skeptics in the group. Rather, these particular promoters and practitioners of the empirical sciences ranged from liberal Christians to moderate Deists. Most, if not all, held some form of belief in a creator whose wisdom and benevolence could be demonstrated through natural inquiry. All shared a commitment to science—to observation, classification, and experimentation—as a source of civic pride and enlightenment. They emphasized the practical benefits of "useful science" to a self-governing people and imagined progress to be intended by a divine providence.

From this revolutionary period forward, the ideal of progress tended to link the scientific with the democratic "spirit." In the course of American history, tensions between religious and scientific outlooks often occurred over the idea of progress: over how far improvement in knowledge would lead to improvement in character. To explore this point, it may be helpful to examine more closely the views of the two most prominent members of the APS—

two men who came to embody the link between American political and scientific aspirations. Together they present models of peculiarly American science and religion.

The most famous first-generation member of the American Philosophical Society was its founder and first president, Benjamin Franklin (1706–90). Though noted for his insistence on "useful knowledge," for his inventions and practical advice, Franklin was also one of the few colonists who contributed to developing *theories* of the universe. He was particularly interested in the nature of light and electricity, demonstrating by his famous kite experiments that lightning contained electricity. Basically, though, Franklin abhorred "speculative" thought. His sense of the limits of knowledge expressed the skeptical Enlightenment's aversion to "metaphysical reasoning."

Franklin's skepticism underlay his view of both science and religion. Like many of his contemporaries, he turned away from the strict Protestantism of his youth. He especially rejected the Calvinist doctrine of predestination and the devaluation of good works. Instead, he valued the practical consequences of religious belief and was suspicious of orthodoxy. He stressed the practice of virtue over the preaching of doctrine; ethics over theology; and good deeds over empty piety. At the same time, Franklin exhibited a kind of urbane Quaker tolerance for most forms of religion. And, like the Quakers, Franklin abhorred all forms of dogmatism, including dogmatic forms of *natural* religion. As the archetype of American self-reliance and self-education, he seemed to favor a practical faith for himself and for the nation.

Thomas Jefferson (1743–1826) was the third president of the APS (in 1796). Like Franklin, he was a dedicated empiricist, though perhaps less of a pure experimentalist. Jefferson, too, tended to be practical-minded, wary of metaphysical abstractions. Conservative in scientific matters, he considered contemporary "theories of the earth" to be presumptuous (even though such theories were laying the groundwork for the science of geology). He held to the fixity of species and did not believe in extinctions, famously arguing that, because its bones had been found, the mastodon must exist somewhere in the world. At the same time, he believed wholeheartedly in the progress of knowledge as fundamental to the new Republic. For Jefferson, the religion for the Republic would be based on a rational faith—a faith involving the "assent of the mind to an intelligible proposition" and a mind free of prejudice and "superstitions." He linked the progress of the human mind with the perfectibility of human nature. For him, science and true religion would necessarily serve a republican future—a future of progressive change, continually moving beyond past traditions and present circumstances, resulting in constant improvement in science, government, and ethics.

In the early national period many "friends of revelation" acted as effective promoters and practitioners of the empirical sciences. Consider New England, the focal point of Jefferson's attack on a Christian religion wrapped, as he put it, in the "rags" of orthodoxy and in need of returning to "the original purity and simplicity of its benevolent institutor." In and around eighteenth-century Boston, in particular, a flourishing community of Harvard graduates interested in useful knowledge included a number of rather orthodox clergymen. Joseph Willard, for example, was president of Harvard from 1781 to 1804 and the first vice president of the American Academy of Arts and Sciences (a learned society we shall encounter later, established in 1780 "to cultivate every art and science which may tend to advance the interest, honor, dignity, and happiness of a free, independent and virtuous people"). Willard became an accomplished astronomer who dedicated much time to determining the precise longitude and latitude of various locations in the new United States. John Prince, an amateur astronomer and inventor of an improved air pump, was pastor of the First Church of Salem. Prince became a well-known "experimental lecturer" who used, to great effect, his own "philosophical apparatus" and his collection of specimens to demonstrate, as his biographer put it, "the wonders of Astronomy, Optics, Pneumatics, Botany, Mineralogy, Chemistry and Entomology." In general, Christian attitudes toward natural philosophy were far from antagonistic, and many clergy at the founding of the Republic preached the advancement of science and secular improvement along with an orthodox faith.

Although most agreed about the prospects of a better future brought about by scientific progress, it was in these varying images of the future that tensions emerged. During the Revolution, and in its aftermath, the educated elite expressed competing visions of the "new order for the ages." What mix of reason and philosophy, on the one hand, and of revelation and theology, on the other, would ultimately secure the blessings of liberty and the pursuit of happiness? What should be the relative role of clergyman and naturalist in determining a religion of the Republic? Given the confidence in reason, how would its limits be defined? What would constitute authentic science and true religion?

Illustrations of discord could be seen in many "century sermons" of the time. These special homilies were preached throughout the new nation on the last Sunday of the eighteenth century. In some versions, moderately conservative clergy tried to strike a middle ground between Enlightenment extremes of skepticism and "infidelity" on the one hand and evangelical extremes of egalitarianism and "enthusiasm" on the other. As a widespread public discourse, century sermons laid the groundwork for the "didactic Enlightenment" —a cultural compromise in the early national period accommodating Enlightenment visions of human progress via science and reason with the ongoing need for theology and revelation. As with Jefferson and Franklin, this balancing act involved a conception of the limits of knowledge that could uphold the image of Americans as both a progressive and a moral people.

An influential example of the century sermon came from New York Presbyterian clergyman Samuel Miller. Miller, himself a member of the American Philosophical Society, commemorated the previous century by recounting improvements in the sciences, arts, and literature. The eighteenth century, Miller noted, had witnessed "astonishing" advances in useful knowledge. But, he added, scientific progress had to be distinguished from moral progress. The latter still lagged, he said, as testified to by the variety of "infidel" interpretations of scientific knowledge associated with the French Revolution. Contrary to advocates of natural religion, Miller insisted that "moral science" still required revelation, the wisdom of a divinely inspired Bible and, by implication, the ministrations of the churches and the teaching of a learned ministry. Although Miller shared an American faith in progress, he took to task any pretensions toward human perfectibility. The millennium would certainly come, Miller agreed, but it would be the millennium prophesied in scripture. The "new age" would emerge by "divine illumination and evangelical holiness, already so effective," and not by "the progress of knowledge."

Miller's effort to distinguish true from false progress at the turn of the century foreshadowed a religion-science debate that still exists. The debate involves making a number of important distinctions, especially true science from false science. The latter, according to Miller, overestimated the power of human reason to understand fully the mysteries of creation. False science presumed to explain nature in terms of natural laws and chance alone, without reference to divine providence. Moreover, "science falsely so-called" either ignored or actually contradicted the teachings of scripture. Specifically, certain theories of the origin, history, and end of the world emerging in Miller's day appeared to conflict with biblical stories of creation, complicating a traditional view of creation as a divinely established stage for human redemption.

Antebellum Nineteenth Century

To establish the fragile American Republic on stable foundations required meeting expectations for both freedom and order. In the words of one historian: "Americans wanted to believe at once in social and even scientific progress and in unchanging moral principles." In response, moderate Calvinists (Presbyterians and Congregationalists, principally), along with inheritors of the moderate Enlightenment, attempted to construct some middle ground between the extremes of the revolutionary period.

To accomplish this cultural task, intellectuals relied heavily on a particular brand of Scottish philosophy. This "philosophy of common sense" came to the colonies around the middle of the eighteenth century and eventually formed the intellectual framework for higher education in the United States. Its democratic tenor upheld the beliefs of ordinary folk against the critical reasoning of philosophers, arguing for the trustworthiness of the senses and the reasonableness of human intuitions. The arguments of this philosopy involved assumptions that also maintained the integrity of scientific knowledge: an external world actually existed apart from the mind; ideas actually corresponded to physical objects in this world; and scientific laws of cause and effect actually governed physical processes. Commonsense realism—democratic, pragmatic, and reassuring—thereby justified the *inductive* (reasoning from particulars to generals) method of scientific reasoning.

At the same time, induction took on religious value. Reliable knowledge, it was argued, could emerge only from careful observation and accurate experimentation, comprehensive collection and painstaking classification of "the facts," and cautious, even pious reflection on those facts. Such a patient, humble process ostensibly turned away from illicit "speculation" and "conjecture." This process of inquiry was further associated with Francis Bacon, the seventeenth-century English statesman and philosopher who, in early-nineteenth-century America, was revered as the founding father of modern science.

"Baconianism" and commonsense realism also supported a common method of interpreting both the Bible and nature, the twin sources of revelation. Stress on sticking to the facts recommended a shared humility in the face of the mysterious quality of both "books." This shared standard of virtue grounded what one historian has called the "didactic Enlightenment" in America: a broad educational project in which the vocations of naturalist and theologian seemed united in bringing about intellectual *and* moral progress.

American colleges institutionalized this link between intellect and piety. The education of America's future teachers, lawyers, doctors, ministers, and governors typically began with natural philosophy and natural history along with the study of Christian "Evidences." This last involved a wide variety of "facts" drawn from both nature and scripture testifying to the benevolent rule of God and the divine truth of Christianity. Such facts included the marvelous "contrivances" of nature that revealed the Designer's hand (the core argument of natural theology) as well as the many miracles of the Bible, attested to by reliable witnesses, that upheld the divine authority of Christ and the supernatural character of Christianity.

Yale's president in the early nineteenth century, Timothy Dwight (1752–1817), personified this confident connection between the divine, natural, and moral orders. The grandson of Jonathan Edwards, a Congregationalist pastor himself, as well as chaplain and poet of the Revolution, Dwight led the effort to harmonize orthodoxy and science. As president of Yale, he promoted campus revivals, aiming to eliminate "infidelity" among the young men of the revolutionary generation. At the same time, he promoted the study of nature as both conducive to theology and useful for society. Shortly after becoming president of the college, he convinced the Connecticut legislature to create a new professorship in chemistry and natural history. He himself became a skilled observer of the natural world, and his accounts of the geography, geology, flora and fauna, and native peoples of New England rivaled those of Jefferson's for Virginia. In the critical matter of reconciling the readings of the "Two Books," Dwight believed that any apparent conflicts could be worked out with improvements in interpretation. He himself gave preference to the plain sense of scripture in light of the limits of human reason. In sum, Dwight embodied the effort to blend Enlightenment reason with Christian faith.

The depth of the presumed harmony between Baconian science and evangelical religion can be seen from the evangelist's point of view as well. The life and work of Charles Grandison Finney (1792–1875), in particular, reveal a clear sense of reciprocity between scientific and religious thinking of the time. As a leader of the Second Great Awakening, Finney, in fact, aimed to construct a science of revivalism. In the first place, he held to the antebellum belief in a moral universe ruled by a benevolent creator whose ruling principles could be known. He applied this conception of reasonableness to God's way of salvation. He challenged conventional Calvinist belief that conversion was strictly the work of God, whose ways were simply inscrutable. Instead, he introduced controversial "new measures" into camp revivals by which both penitent and preacher could prepare for God's grace. In his emphasis on "technique," Finney expressed a fundamental sympathy between mainstream religion and science in this age of Jacksonian democracy.

This period of cultural innovation also included unorthodox blends of religion and science. Among the elite, transcendentalism expressed a romantic protest against the rationalism of the Enlightenment. Insight into ultimate reality was gained not through detached observation and cautious reasoning but through creative imagination. Everyone could learn the secrets of nature or the transcendent dimension of everyday life and become, in the (in)famous words of Ralph Waldo Emerson, "a new born bard of the Holy Ghost." At the grass roots, these democratic sensibilities and sense of an intimate relation between the natural and supernatural promised mastery over forces controlling one's world. Popular movements often incorporated techniques of white magic, such as the use of divining rods and seer stones, to gain access to the hidden sources of well-being. The erstwhile religious entrepreneur Joseph Smith Jr. (1805–44), for example, drew on practices of folk magic, the esoteric wisdom of Freemasonry, and early-nineteenth-century views of science, along with Christian sources, to lay the foundations of the distinctively American religion of Mormonism.

Such movements point to traditions of knowledge that sustained these alternative explanations of nature and supernature, explanations that have enjoyed some currency in American history. The intellectual tradition of occultism or harmonialism, in particular, has supported claims of access to realms of unseen reality, knowledge of which is hidden from all but the properly initiated. Social movements based on such alternative metaphysical outlooks offered opportunities for leadership to otherwise marginalized groups in American society. In the antebellum period, with respect for orthodox medicine at a rather low level and with constraints placed on public roles for women, many of these movements involved alternative systems of medical treatment led by women. Ellen G. White (1827–1915), for example, was a prophet and visionary who incorporated popular health regimens of the day, including water cures and vegetarian diets, into the teachings of Seventh-Day Adventism. The Adventists eventually became a significant religious group behind the "creationist" movement of the twentieth century owing partly to the fact that White claimed to have witnessed the creation of the world in a vision. Perhaps the clearest and most lasting example of alternative approaches to health and well-being was Christian Science. Based on her own experiences of sickness and healing, founder Mary Baker Eddy (1821–1910) taught that physical illness resulted from disruptions in the spiritual forces governing life. Restoration of health required understanding these forces, and healers had to be trained in the secret knowledge of these spiritual realities. In addition, the Bible contained spiritual messages hidden from the uninitiated and required a "key" to its real meaning. Eddy provided such an interpretive key in later editions of her principal work, *Science and Health* (1875).

In the antebellum period, drawing precarious boundaries between true and false science involved a collaboration between scientific and religious authorities. In the postbellum period, this boundary work entailed a much clearer conflict of interests between such authorities. Moreover, the apparent strength of the alliance between commonsense science and religion in the didactic Enlightenment suggested reasons for the force of its demise in the Darwinian era.

Postbellum and Industrial Nineteenth Century

In the seventeenth century, the term *naturalist* had been synonymous with *natural philosopher* and denoted a learned person who described the causes of the world's phenomena (including human behavior and morals) without reference to supernatural agencies. This distinction did not completely exclude God from an understanding of nature because most naturalists agreed on the need for a First Cause. By the early part of the nineteenth century, however, the interpretive jurisdiction of the "naturalist" shrank significantly to entail explanations of life (including human life) as part of the natural order. In fact, purely "naturalistic" explanations began to define the content of the natural sciences in general, appearing to be the only way to assure progress in knowledge.

By midcentury, such established disciplines as comparative anatomy and such new ones as experimental physiology stressed the similarities between human and animal natures. Results of research on monkey brains, for example, were applied to human beings, seriously challenging the distinction between humans and beasts. Meanwhile, scientific geologists, as opposed to the "scriptural" or "evangelical" kind, insisted that explanations of past events be restricted to causes that could be observed in the present. This principle of "uniformitarianism" ruled out supernatural causes while, at the same time, greatly expanding the time frame for the formation of the earth far beyond that given by a literal reading of Genesis. In astronomy, the nebular hypothesis had already accounted for the origin of the solar system solely on the basis of natural law. In the words of clergyman–geologist George Frederick Wright: "We are to press known secondary causes as far as they will go in explanation of facts. We are not to resort to an unknown (i.e., supernatural) cause for explanation of phenomena till the power of known causes has been exhausted. If we cease to observe this rule there is an end to all science and all sound sense." Of course, the problem for the believer was when to draw the line, when to say that natural explanations had been exhausted.

At the same time, the term *scientist* itself emerged, replacing *natural phi-*

losopher and denoting the member of a diverse community of scholars dedicated full-time to natural inquiry. The scientist came to rival in social prestige the older professions of lawyer, doctor, and minister. And, because of the close connection between natural inquiry and Christian theology up to this point, the development of an independent profession of science seemed to require, first and foremost, a clear separation from the concerns of the clergy.

Informing this differentiation process was a set of ideas known cumulatively as *scientific naturalism*. These ideas justified the scientific life without reference to any religious role. Indeed, scientific naturalism tended to define authentic science *over against* religion. As a professional ideology, scientific naturalism centered on the positivist criteria for objective knowledge. The scientific profession no longer involved a dual calling of investigating nature as a way to glorify God in his works. Instead, the scientist, as a scientist, operated in a purely secular environment explaining the world in naturalistic terms.

From this point of view, it makes more sense to contrast scientific naturalism and natural theology (or theism) rather than science and religion per se. In fact, we might harken back to a theme that emerged in that initial contact of cultures in the process of colonization and talk about a conflict of cosmic visions. At least one historian proposes such a contrast, calling scientific naturalism and theism "rival cosmologies." Each set of ideas offered a competing interpretation of some aspect of nature (like the earth's origin and its history) to uphold a view of the ultimate meaning of life.

Scientific naturalism also included a substitute humility, an alternative sense of virtue at the time labeled *agnosticism*. The word was coined in 1869 by "Darwin's bulldog," British naturalist Thomas Huxley, and meant the permanent suspension of belief. Huxley insisted that science possessed an "ethical spirit" by which the truth of its claims required "justification, not by faith, by verification." No truths could be accepted as such without empirical evidence. In this way, agnosticism both maintained and inverted something of the old integrity of the scientific vocation that had demanded humble allegiance to the facts. In theologically liberal circles, similar sentiments about the limits and moral integrity of scientific knowledge amounted to an "intellectual gospel." At the same time, the agnostic position rejected the "evidences" of natural theology while intentionally challenging the moral authority of Christianity in modern society. America's "great agnostic" of the period, the "freethinking" lawyer and noted "infidel" Robert Ingersoll (1833–99), succinctly expressed the essence of the new humility. Ingersoll totally rejected the strict Calvinism of his Protestant minister-father and traveled the country giving popular public lectures dubbed "agnostic sermons." He simply and consistently insisted that "beyond nature man cannot go even in thought."

The professionalization of biblical studies paralleled that of the natural sciences, with important consequences for the science-religion relation. Indeed, just as the geologist adopted Charles Lyell's standard for the disinterested study of natural history (i.e., "as if the Scriptures were not in existence"), so the professional exegete came to "interpret the Scriptures like any other book." In this professionalizing context, a critical hermeneutic challenged a commonsense reading of Holy Writ, requiring knowledge of history, archaeology, anthropology, and other sciences to interpret scripture. The new alliance of specialists linked the interests of biblical scholar with those of natural and social scientist in a shared commitment to critical and scientific study. In the terms of the larger question of interpretation, we can say that just as nature became "opaque," obscuring the hand of God, so the Bible became less straightforwardly a divinely revealed book.

The transformation of higher education reflected this cultural shift and provided another context for redefining the science-religion relation. The modern research university emerged in Germany and America in this period shaped by the ideology of science. It became the principal institution for scientific teaching and research and for credentialing the new professions by granting advanced degrees. One leading educator of the time captured the emerging vision of higher education by describing the rationale for his own university founded to serve the state of New York. It was, he said, "an institution for advanced instruction and research, in which science, pure and applied, should have an equal place with literature; in which the study of literature, ancient and modern, should be emancipated as much as possible from pedantry; and which should be free from various useless trammels and vicious methods which at the period hampered many, if not most, of the American universities and colleges." In the eyes of the author of that vision, Andrew Dickson White (1832–1918), "pedantry" characterized the aims of organized religion, and "emancipation" entailed separating higher education from control of the church.

Indeed, White, more than anyone, created the widespread impression that social progress required a "victory" of science over religion. As first president of Cornell University (founded in 1868), White published a series of articles on the history of the science-religion relationship entitled "The Battlefields of Science." His account was instrumental in his own political battle with the New York state legislature and with critics among the clergy and representatives of church-related colleges, who objected to his receiving public funds to promote what they regarded as a thoroughgoing secularism. By 1896, White had synthesized his writings into a very influential two-volume work called *A History of the Warfare of Science and Theology in Christendom*. That work effectively established the persistent "warfare model" of the relation between science and religion.

In his portrayal, White also effectively expressed the liberal-conservative split in the science-religion relation. And here again, the definition of key terms is illuminating. By *science* White chiefly meant an intellectual attitude, a commitment to free and unfettered inquiry and to the value of original research, which would sustain social progress in the modern age. By *religion* he meant one of two things. Whereas "dogmatic theology" meant "outmoded" and rigid thinking "based on biblical texts and ancient modes of thought" that blocked the progress of knowledge, true "Religion" involved a progressive, open-minded, and humble attitude akin to that of science, which cast off dogmatism. True religion, he said, is "seen in the recognition of 'a Power in the universe, not ourselves, which makes for righteousness,' and in the love of God and of our neighbour."

White's point of view on progress and virtue revealed, among other things, the influence of evolutionary thinking in late Victorian America. Such thinking gained scientific status in the postbellum period through the general acceptance by scientists of the theory of organic evolution. Though the "transmutation hypothesis" had been around for some time, it had been given significant naturalistic grounding in Charles Darwin's *On the Origin of Species* (1859). Darwin had specified a mechanism for the historical process by which new life forms could emerge from previous ones. His version of "transformism" pictured a long, gradual, destructive process of "natural selection" in which certain organisms survived while many more became extinct. Survival depended on inheriting the right physical characteristics—"right" in the sense that they conferred an advantage in a "struggle for existence." Inheriting the right characteristics happened by chance and depended on "random mutations" in the invisible, biological bases of life.

Darwinism severely challenged natural theology on several fronts, rendering it not simply irrelevant but implausible for many. In particular, Darwin took the central idea of the adaptation of an organism to its environment and made it not evidence of divine providence but the result of a long, random, wasteful process determined by impersonal forces of nature. His challenge to the fixity of species, in turn, challenged a straightforward reading of Genesis in which God created all living things "according to their kind." Indeed, Darwin developed his theory of evolution principally to counter the theory of "special" or "immediate" creation—a view of the variety and origins of life as resulting from the "will of the deity." At the same time, Darwin's theory reinforced the process of professionalization by laying out a path of research to which many scientific disciplines could contribute. In this case, even the admitted deficiency of supporting evidence for the theory—especially the "missing links" or lack of "transitional forms" in the fossil record—became not so much weaknesses in the theory as areas for research. Darwinism, despite its acknowledged deficiencies, offered the scientific community many things, culminating in a cosmic vision and moral integrity that could exist independently of traditional religion.

The choice for the believing scientist therefore seemed almost apocalyptic. Given the centrality of the theory of evolution to the life sciences, and given its challenges to nineteenth-century faith, the naturalist seemed faced with a stark choice: either modern science or traditional belief. Indeed, historians have long described a "Darwinian revolution" by citing scholars like Charles Graham Sumner (1840–1910), an early proponent of social Darwinism and famous for remarking that one day he put his religious beliefs in a drawer and twenty years later when he opened the drawer his beliefs were gone. In the face of what one scholar at the time called the "blind impartiality, atrocious cruelty and reckless injustice" of the evolutionary process, better to believe in an unknown god and opt for the agnostic position than to believe in a deity who directed such a bloody course of events.

Historians, however, have begun to temper the view of a complete break between "science and religion" caused by Darwinism, emphasizing instead the variety and complexity of responses among American scientists. Examining the views of members of a prominent scientific association in the second half of the nineteenth century, for example, we find a wide variety of religious beliefs represented. Darwinism did not generally have a revolutionary effect on the religious lives of American scientists (most of whom had accepted evolution in some form by the 1870s). Catholic naturalists remained Catholic; Presbyterians remained Presbyterian; agnostics remained agnostic. As an important component of modern thought, Darwinism did, however, contribute to a privatization of religious belief among scientists, if not its elimination.

In response to the challenge of scientific naturalism, the liberal believer and scientist tended to see God acting from within nature. Such a view blurred any stark lines between the natural and the supernatural, the human and the divine, the mundane and the miraculous. And it provided a way to accept the pervasiveness of natural law. Evolution, in particular, could be understood as God's method of creation.

Adjustments to evolutionary biology that characterized a liberal response to the natural sciences were paralleled by similar responses to the social sciences. Generally speaking, religious liberals of the Progressive era envisioned continued collaboration with the "sciences of man" for the purposes of reforming society. Richard Ely (1854–1943), an economist at the Johns Hopkins University, epitomized such a vision. Ely contributed significantly both to the professionalization of his discipline and to efforts to "Christianize the social order." As a social scientist, he introduced German theories of cultural development into the study of economic systems. As a devout Episcopalian, he contributed significantly to the social gospel movement, playing leadership roles in organizations like the Christian Social Union and the American Institute of Christian Sociology. In the context of social unrest caused by industrialization, the Christian economist stressed the ethical function of science.

An illuminating and influential model of rethinking the relation of science to religion is William James (1842–1910). As a philosopher and psychologist, James became a leading advocate of pragmatism—that distinctively American philosophy that rejects absolute truth, teaching that the truth of any idea is determined by its consequences. James's pragmatism was rooted in a deep sense of the uncertainty of human existence, and it included a sense of the limits of knowledge that left room for belief in transcendent reality. James, if not a conventional believer, nevertheless championed "the will to believe." As founder of the field of psychology of religion, he hoped to construct a science of religion based on a systematic analysis of religious experience that could serve religious interests. James himself particularly appreciated the power of mystical experience (or the mystical state of consciousness), which entailed a direct and life-changing encounter with the divine. (His father had been an active Swedenborgian, a nineteenth-century religious movement in the harmonialist tradition.)

As is often the case in American intellectual history, James's position expressed democratic sensibilities in opposition to perceived elitist forms of thought. He bucked the reductionist principles of scientific naturalism, backed the empirical study of paranormal or psychic phenomena, and sympathized with the "crass supernaturalism" of ordinary folks over the "refined" version of liberal thinkers—seeing a reasonableness to the view of a deity effectively intervening in nature and history at particular moments and in concrete ways. William James, then, offered a model of the science-religion relation in which the scientific method might be applied to all forms of experience, allowing the scientist to continue to play a kind of ministerial role—"tenderhearted" as well as "tough-minded"—by acting as moral as well as intellectual guide in unsettled times.

In hindsight, the examples of Ely and James appear as either transitional or minority positions in early-twentieth-century America. Ely embodied the ideals of a liberal Protestantism that gradually lost its dominance in academia; James's science of religion, though pursued in important ways, was effectively overshadowed by John Dewey's more naturalistic approach. In general, by the 1920s, the scientific study of religion moved along reductionist lines, ideally aiming for a value-free or objective vantage point on the subject. As a result, "religion" itself was increasingly analyzed as an artifact of culture like any other, rather than the foundation of culture. In this framework, American Christianity, in particular, could no longer claim special cultural status. Indeed, the particular religious beliefs or ethical convictions of the scholar seemed to be irrelevant to research. Of course, value neutrality is a difficult thing to achieve, and the aggressive reductionism of Freudian psychoanalysis and scientific materialism of Marxist theory, which both perceived traditional religion as pathological, carried their own kind of values.

Liberal Protestants continued their efforts to hold together the marriage of Christianity and the sciences through various strategies of accommodation. Each of these suffered from concessions to methodological naturalism, admitting the need to exclude divine cause from scientific explanations, making it difficult to uphold any transcendent dimension. Roman Catholics self-consciously offered an alternative to both Protestant and secular scholarship, successfully constructing an entire subculture by midcentury. This parallel community included a range of Catholic professional organizations, along with Catholic colleges and universities, unified intellectually by a Thomistic or neo-scholastic philosophy. In the case of both Catholics and Jews, the racist overtones of social Darwinism sparked particular criticism because such thinking supported restrictive immigration policies as well as theories of eugenics that called for sterilization and other forms of birth control. In general, a materialistic-deterministic view of life ran fundamentally counter to widespread religious views of human dignity, free will, and personal responsibility and so elicited religiously based opposition.

The most blatant form of religious protest emerged from conservative evangelicalism and involved the fundamentalist crusade against evolution. At the height of that crusade in the early 1920s, antievolution laws had successfully passed in three southern states, forbidding the teaching of Darwin's theory in public schools. The constitutionality of these laws was to be tested in the summer of 1925 in Dayton, Tennessee. The immediate issue involved the teaching of evolution by substitute biology teacher John Scopes. In the background, however, representatives of opposing sides in that era's culture war maneuvered for control over public education. Chief among the antagonists were the World's Christian Fundamentals Association and the American Civil Liberties Union. In July, the antagonists met in the Dayton courtroom led by Presbyterian layman, three-time presidential nominee, and former secretary of state William Jennings Bryan and renowned trial lawyer and self-proclaimed champion of "innocent, truth-seeking scientists" Clarence Darrow. As "the Great Commoner," Bryan had taken up the antievolutionary cause as central to his populist campaign against the perceived assault on rural and small-town values by the forces of urban America expressed in the language of Darwinism. Darrow, for his part, was prepared to expose the ignorance and prejudice of old-time religion and biblical literalism. The resulting "Trial of the Century" has become part of American folklore, depicted in print and film in terms generally favorable to Darrow's (and Andrew Dickson White's) point of view. In at least one recent account of the case, however, historian and legal scholar Edward Larson has stressed how the trial, and its retelling, have expressed powerful tensions between fundamental principles of democratic society: individual liberty and majority rule; the right of a profession to determine its standards of truth versus the right of parents (and taxpayers) to determine what their children are taught. In this light, "battles" between science and religion, as we have already seen, reflected deep American antipathies toward all forms of elitism.

The subtleties of the science-religion relation are further revealed if we dig deeper into this single year of American history. In a somewhat less celebrated event of 1925, the nation's foremost satirist, Sinclair Lewis (1885–1951), published the first major American novel about scientific research. The book, *Arrowsmith*, won Lewis the Pulitzer Prize (which he refused to accept because, he said, it was given only to defenders of American wholesomeness). In an ingenious inversion of the Puritan way of salvation, the novel recounts the "sanctification" of Martin Arrowsmith, a young medical researcher and "born investigator" whom Lewis presents as a kind of antihero of modern America. In the story, Martin has to struggle free of all temptations of middle-class culture to maintain his integrity and his devotion to "pure science." In a sort of spiritual quest that mirrors the seventeenth-century Puritan classic *Pilgrim's Progress*, Martin forsakes all compromise with conventional values, eventually shunning commercial success, social status, married life, and any sentimental humanitarianism. He must, instead, embrace the specialist's narrow and single-minded pursuit of the truth, seeking the underlying material causes of things by means of the scientific method and the dictates of scientific naturalism, following his hunches wherever they may lead—even though they may lead nowhere. In this "fable," Lewis effectively turned the tables on a Calvinist critique of modernity, suggesting that the secular scientist now embodied a squandered spiritual inheritance; he had recaptured and replaced the moral discipline and integrity of both the early pioneers and the Puritan nonconformists.

Lewis's ironic and profound insight into the relation of science and religion in America could be interpreted as one part of an iconoclasm of the day, also found in the attack on old-time religion in the wake of the Scopes trial. In other words, Lewis could be seen as standing with Darrow in a culture war between modernists and fundamentalists. But delving further into this year of 1925 uncovers even greater richness than such a black-and-white picture suggests. In that same year, British philosopher of mathematics Alfred North Whitehead (1861–1947), then living and teaching in the United States, published his first foray into the developing field of philosophy of science. In *Science and the Modern World*, Whitehead challenged the conflict thesis. He argued, as others had begun to argue, that a fundamental harmony existed between the natural sciences and Western religion. The doctrine of creation, in particular, implied a contingent yet intelligible world, offering a theological framework for the systematic investigation of nature. Whitehead also criticized the "misplaced concreteness" at the heart of scientific naturalism. This "fallacy," he said, assumed that fundamental reality consisted of timeless stuff —of "irreducible brute matter, or material, spread through space in a flux of configurations." On the basis of the new scientific worldview, Whitehead himself proposed a view of reality as "process." His metaphysical system, and his urgent call to his generation to reconcile the two great "forces" of human history, have since provided inspiration to many attempting to integrate religious and scientific understanding.

Modern America

Whitehead's challenge to his generation gained great urgency in the thirties and forties. The Great Depression, the rise of totalitarian states in Europe, the outbreak of World War II, and the start of the Cold War all seriously challenged the survival of democratic capitalism. As a result, a broad discussion of the values necessary to sustain the Republic ensued. In this debate, advocates of science and religion at times squared off and at times sought consensus. This cultural process, which in many ways continues today, laid bare some ambivalent feelings of Americans toward both science and religion and the diverse ways these spheres of society interact.

At the center of this dispute, and making the case for a kind of scientific humanism, was John Dewey. As an educator, philosopher, and public figure, Dewey (like Bacon before him) championed the cultural value of experimental science. Preaching a pragmatic naturalism, he insisted that truth could emerge only from the free and open-ended inquiry characteristic of science. Indeed, the highest value in the intellectual culture, he maintained, was unwavering commitment to such freedom. Moreover, this freedom was a keystone of democracy, amounting, in fact, to an authentic "religious attitude." In 1934, Dewey laid out this link between science, religion, and democracy in a series of lectures published as *A Common Faith*.

At the core of the argument, Dewey distinguished religiousness from religion. In particular, he called for liberating the "religious quality of experience" from "the supernatural load of any particular religion." That genuine religiousness, or "natural piety" and "moral faith," entailed dedication to "ideal ends" pursued in the face of the "actual conditions of life." The process of inquiry was inherently progressive, leading the individual, in Darwinian fashion, to further "possibilities" and a "better, deeper and enduring adjustment to life." In metaphysical terms, Dewey's religion of inquiry entailed a never ending adjustment of one's whole being to the world, a periodic harmonizing of self to the universe. This pragmatic outlook gave up any pretense to knowledge of eternal truths, opting instead for travel down the "one sure road of access to truth—the road of patient, cooperative inquiry operating by means of observation, experiment, recorded and controlled reflection." In this way, Dewey tried to blend fact and value, the interests of the sciences and the humanities, for the sake of democratic culture.

The pervasive influence of Dewey's ideas, especially in education, suggests that he captured something of the core of an American relation of science to religion. In the 1940s, his brand of scientific humanism inspired one of two major responses to the crisis of American democracy. In 1943, the interdisciplinary Conference on the Scientific Spirit and Democratic Faith (CSSDF) met for the first of four successive years aiming to advance Dewey's agenda. Conference organizers touted the moral value of scientific inquiry in a pluralistic society as not only the best hope for but the central faith of democratic civilization. From a Deweyesque point of view, reliance on fixed, transcendent, or revealed truth simply smacked of "authoritarianism"—the kind of authoritarianism then threatening liberty abroad and at home.

However, it was precisely this kind of "return" to the transcendent sources of knowledge and values that had sparked the other major response to America's cultural crisis. Dewey's conference had, in fact, convened specifically to counter the aims of the Conference on Science, Philosophy and Religion in Their Relation to the Democratic Way of Life (CSPR). This interdisciplinary, interfaith gathering enjoyed greater longevity, meeting annually from 1940 until 1960. Its organizers, led by Rabbi Louis Finkelstein of the Conservative Jewish Theological Seminary in New York, also proposed to confront the challenges to democratic civilization posed by totalitarianism, economic depression, and war, but to do so by reasserting the religious foundations of democracy.

Conveners also hoped to overcome the fragmentation of knowledge through interdisciplinary dialogue for the greater good. For some, these hopes translated into a Whiteheadian-type solution, that is, working out an "integrated, articulate philosophy" that might resolve tensions between traditional learning and new knowledge, reconcile "timeless ethical values and our immediate scientific scholarly findings." This aim included aggressively confronting the secularism associated with scientific naturalism. Philosopher Mortimer J. Adler of the University of Chicago, in particular, sparked controversy over his frank opinion that a hierarchy existed among the disciplines with theology and philosophy necessarily setting the agenda for the sciences. Adler expressed the goal of restoring religion in higher learning in stark terms: "Religion cannot be regarded as just another aspect of culture, one among many human occupations. . . . Religion is either the supreme human discipline, because it is God's discipline of man, and as such dominates our culture, or it has no place at all."

In the end, the squaring off of these two groups exposed deep divisions in American intellectual culture. On the one hand, there were those who, in an Enlightenment tradition, tended to see science as an alternative to religion. They aimed to keep scientific research free from a "dogmatism" and "authoritarianism" associated with traditional religion. On the other hand, there were those anxious to reassert the wisdom of traditional religion. From their point of view, the destructive "isms" associated with secular culture culminated in "scientism"—an ideology based on the assumption that empirical knowledge answered all human problems and that anything not scientific was antiquated and irrelevant.

Despite this fundamental division, the desire to reconcile religion and science remained. Tracing the history of two of these groups brings us down to the present day, suggesting how ongoing fissures and bridging operations continue to characterize the relation of religion and science in American society.

The first of these organizations, the American Scientific Affiliation (ASA), formed in 1941 as a professional association of scientists who were evangelical Christians. From the outset, its members have wrestled with a dual allegiance (if not a dual vocation): to their scientific profession and their faith communities. As an organization, the ASA has tried to maintain ties with both constituencies, aiming, in the words of one historian, to reconcile "scientists and scientific theory with Scriptural truth." The group has attempted to retain the respect of mainstream science, principally through the practice and teaching of science, limiting full voting membership to practicing scientists, and the critical acceptance of scientific theory. This criticism has mainly focused on evolution, with members generally acknowledging the evidence for the theory while pointing out its persistent limitations and distinguishing scientific theory from atheistic interpretations. The members of the ASA have also stood firm for a divinely inspired Bible. The group has not insisted on a single ASA standard for interpreting scripture, wishing to retain historical options such as Silliman's day-age theory. It has nevertheless insisted, in familiar terms, on the necessary harmony of true science and sacred scripture. As a mediating institution, then, the ASA has attempted to occupy some middle ground in cultural divisions over science and religion.

It has proved a difficult mediating role to play. In attempting to balance professional and faith commitments, most members generally came to accept the idea of organic development over time. In this regard, two positions seemed possible: "progressive creation," which envisions the process of natural development interrupted at strategic points by divine intervention, or "theistic evolution," which perceives natural history and the "economy of creation" guided by the hand of God without interruption. These positions, however, clashed with a "strict creationist" view, eventually leading to a split in the organization.

The tenets of "flood geology," in particular, were early on deemed both unscientific and an impediment to evangelism. Flood or "deluge" geology had developed in fundamentalist circles in the aftermath of the Scopes trial. Flood geologists held to a young earth and a recent appearance of life in accordance with a rather literal reading of Genesis. They argued that fossil deposits in the various strata of the earth's crust could be explained by the powerful effects of a universal flood, rather than in terms of stages of development over time. As early as 1949, influential members of the ASA criticized this view, rejecting the narrow interpretation of Genesis required and noting that the theory required suspension of scientific laws. The split came in the early 1960s, with strict creationists leaving the group, objecting to a "limited inerrancy" view of the Bible as an unnecessary and dangerous retreat in the face of materialistic science.

The "creation-science" movement emerged from this split. As a continuation of the antievolutionism of the 1920s, the movement crystallized with the formation of the Creation Research Society (CRS) in 1963. At that time, concerns about falling behind the Soviets in the space race (after the launch of *Sputnik* in 1957) resulted in federally funded efforts to improve science education. Such improvements included incorporating the theory of evolution in biology textbooks. At the same time, a series of court rulings outlawed traditional practices of prayer and Bible reading in public schools. In response, the CRS argued that a straightforward reading of Genesis provided a clear-cut basis for a scientific explanation of origins, with no need to accommodate the text to evolutionary science. Led by fundamentalists John C. Whitcomb Jr., an Old Testament scholar, and hydraulic engineer Henry M. Morris, the CRS reformulated flood geology into "scientific creationism." Its principal tenets included a recent creation of the entire universe, a doctrine of the Fall of humanity that explains the second law of thermodynamics, and a worldwide flood that accounts for fossil deposits in layers of rock in the earth's crust. Self-consciously appropriating the authority of science, Morris and others thereby claimed to establish special creation as a scientific theory. The CRS, and its companion organization the Institute for Creation Research, published their own textbooks, supported local challenges to evolution as taught in standard science texts, and insisted that creation science could be taught in public schools as an alternative to Darwinism.

In the early 1980s, a number of school districts debated the wisdom of teaching creation science. Two states, Arkansas and Louisiana, passed legislation requiring "equal time" or "balanced treatment" of "creation-science" and "evolution-science." These statutes were quickly challenged in court, resulting in a "Scopes II" trial in Arkansas in 1982 and a U.S. Supreme Court decision on the Louisiana law in 1987. In both cases, the courts ruled that creation science effectively amounted to religion and therefore teaching it in public schools would violate the establishment clause of the First Amendment. More recently, in 1999, the Kansas State Board of Education decided to remove references to evolution from its standards for science education, leaving to local school districts the decision of whether to teach evolutionary theory. The Kansas action was reversed after local elections, but not before sparking a national debate and becoming the Associated Press's number one story in 1999.

The ASA's constituency seems once again split, this time over the emergence of a new form of progressive creation. Proponents of the Intelligent Design Theory (ID) argue that the "irreducible" or "specified" complexity of living things, made evident in advances in the biological sciences, rule out their being formed by natural processes governed simply by chance and necessity. As professor of biology at San Francisco State University and Roman Catholic layman Dean Kenyon put it in the preface to a pioneering book in the ID movement, *The Mystery of Life's Origins* (1984): "The undirected flow of energy through a primordial atmosphere and ocean is at present a woefully inadequate explanation for the incredible complexity associated with even simple living systems, and is probably wrong." As Kenyon's comment suggests, the ID movement has marshaled a variety of scientific disciplines to argue for "intelligent cause" at work in the world. Proponents of this view, including scientists and philosophers of science, call for expanding our notion of science to encompass the evidence for design. At the same time, they seem to advocate a kind of Baconian view of science, stressing faithfulness to the facts —in this case the facts of designed phenomena. At the same time, they generally avoid talking of God or supernatural cause, holding that such a view requires input from the separate sphere of religion. In the past few years, the theory of Intelligent Design has gained considerable attention in the broader culture. In May 2000, ID proponents brought their message to Congress, presenting scientific evidence for their theory while describing the negative social impact of Darwinism. Almost simultaneously, one could hear a rather sympathetic discussion of Intelligent Design in an episode of the TV series *Touched by an Angel.*

Such is the complexity of antievolutionism in modern America. Taking a different tack, we can trace the parallel history of another sort of mediating institution, the Institute for Religion in an Age of Science (IRAS). Founded in 1954, IRAS has enjoying a longevity similar to that of the ASA but emerged out of the liberal wing of American Christianity. In the tradition of the transcendentalists, the organization grew out of concerns of New England Unitarians. More precisely, it originated out of the millennialist vision of the "Coming Great Church" movement, which, in the late forties, foresaw Christianity surviving only by adapting to "a new world situation." For the religious backers of IRAS, this modernist outlook meant reinstituting the alliance between progressive Protestantism and the new sciences, establishing "a basis of truth [in religion] for which the teachings of science are the guide."

The early and long-standing guiding light for IRAS was Ralph Burhoe (1911–97). Burhoe himself was not an academic but a metallurgist with some theological training and pastoral experience. He was also the first executive director of the venerable American Academy of Arts and Sciences. In that capacity, he stood in the midst of debates over science and values. He brought to IRAS a strong sense of the challenge to "Christian culture" posed by "the logic of scientific ideas." This logic, he observed, tended to "corrode . . . the strength of Christian beliefs as they have been taught." The proper response, in Burhoe's view, was decidedly *not* to insist on traditional dogma as did advocates of neo-orthodoxy. The solution was the reverse: to formulate something like Whitehead's sweeping metaphysical framework for integrating scientific and religious insights.

What needed to be done, said Burhoe, and what he imagined IRAS would do, was to translate traditional theological categories into universal concepts using the terms of science—especially the terms of evolutionary biology. Religion itself, for example, should be understood as a type of survival mechanism, a positive source of attitudes that "allowed men to adapt to the total environment so as to realize values." From this standpoint, God could still be understood as the creator but, given what is known of the universe, could no longer be worshiped as an "anthropomorphic, one-planet Deity" (to quote Harvard astronomer Harlow Shapley). Moreover, the Bible would need revising, since modern times and modern cosmology required a "completely revised library or handbook of human salvation." This new, modernist religion would not only render "the underlying truth" of the Christian tradition "sensible and useful" to the contemporary world but also reverse the apparent decay of religious faith in a scientific and technological age.

But IRAS's liberal strategy, like the ASA's conservative approach, ran into differences of opinion over fundamental goals. In the course of IRAS's long history, Burhoe's founding vision of a new and universal religion from science has failed to materialize. Indeed, Burhoe and Shapley acknowledged that they were prophets of a "minority faith" not shared by many scientists or clergy or, indeed, many Americans. Burhoe also attributed failure of the grand design to the "antiscience revival of primitive forms of religion and 'countercultures'" in the 1960s—of which creation science would presumably be a prominent example. But even at the elite level at which IRAS operated, "missionary" efforts to universities and theological schools failed to win many converts.

Antievolutionism remains strong in America. In the same year as the Kansas Board of Education ruling on evolution, a Gallup Poll found that 68 percent of Americans favored teaching both creationism and evolutionism in public schools. In another survey, half the respondents felt that evolution is "far from being proven scientifically." Other polls, however, could be cited to show majority support for the teaching of evolution, as well as for the compatibility of evolution and the Bible. In light of this apparently perennial struggle over evolution, historian Ronald Numbers has concluded that "as long as the Bible remains the most trusted and widely read text in America and scientists maintain their considerable cultural authority, consensus, even if desirable, seems unlikely."

Conclusion

Perhaps it is no surprise that at the end we return to the beginning. From at least the onset of European colonization, the drive to explore and discover has somehow defined the American character. Closely akin to this drive has been the impetus to investigate and inquire, to understand and tame a frontier, whatever that frontier might be. As a result, science has consistently taken on a spiritual quality or moral value, in some way attesting to that American character.

This spirit and integrity of science have, however, been expressed in various and not wholly compatible ways, encompassing Mather's holy curiosity, Franklin's practical virtue, Dwight's doxological science, White's pursuit of truth for truth's sake, Bryan's democratic science, Dewey's natural piety, and Sagan's courageous questioning. These variations have, in turn, reflected different responses to changing social circumstances, different visions of the greater good, different standards of intellectual authority, different conceptions of the limits of knowledge, and different balances between scientific progress and stable moral principles.

Over the course of American history, then, the spirituality of science has provided a consistent justification for its pursuit while supporting a mix of religious and secular aims. We have encountered the missionary's strategy of evangelism, the Puritan's errand in the wilderness, the gentleman's tangible sense of divine providence, the professional's strict focus on natural cause, the politician's populist cause, the philosopher's "Common Faith," and the astronomer's updated religion.

In the end, perceptions of the spirituality of science have made it both difficult and desirable to reconcile secular and religious purposes, to define and mediate the boundaries between scientific and theological understanding, to balance the pursuit of knowledge with the life of virtue. Herein lies a reason for the powerful, complex, and often contentious engagement of science and religion in the ongoing invention of America.

SUGGESTED READINGS

Axtell, James. *The Invasion Within: The Contest of Cultures in Colonial North America*. New York: Oxford University Press, 1985.

Bozeman, Theodore Dwight. *Protestants in an Age of Science: The Baconian Ideal and Ante-Bellum American Religious Thought*. Chapel Hill: University of North Carolina Press, 1977.

Croce, Paul Jerome. *Science and Religion in the Era of William James: Eclipse of Certainty, 1820–1880*. Chapel Hill: University of North Carolina Press, 1995.

Gilbert, James. *Redeeming Culture: American Religion in an Age of Science*. Chicago: University of Chicago Press, 1997.

Greene, John C. *American Science in the Age of Jefferson*. Ames: Iowa State University Press, 1984.

Hall, David D. *Worlds of Wonder, Days of Judgment: Popular Religious Belief in Early New England*. Cambridge: Harvard University Press, 1990.

Hollinger, David A. "Justification by Verification: The Scientific Challenge to the Moral Authority of Christianity in Modern America." In *Religion and Twentieth Century American Intellectual Life*, edited by Michael J. Lacey, 116–35. New York: Cambridge University Press, 1989.

Hovenkamp, Herbert. *Science and Religion in America, 1800–1860*. Philadelphia: University of Pennsylvania Press, 1978.

Isaac, Rhys. *The Transformation of Virginia, 1740–1790*. Chapel Hill: University of North Carolina Press, 1982.

Larson, Edward J. *Summer for the Gods: The Scopes Trial and America's Continuing Debate over Science and Religion*. Cambridge: Harvard University Press, 1998.

The Libro de las profecías of Christopher Columbus. Translation and commentary by Delno C. West and August Kling. Gainesville: University of Florida Press, 1991.

Marsden, George M. *Religion and American Culture*. San Diego: Harcourt Brace Jovanovich, 1990.

Mather, Cotton. *The Christian Philosopher*. Edited with an introduction and notes by Winton U. Solberg. Urbana: University of Illinois Press, 1994.

Moore, James R. "Geologists and the Interpreters of Genesis in the Nineteenth

Century." In *God and Nature: Historical Essays in the Encounter between Christianity and Science*, edited by David C. Lindberg and Ronald L. Numbers, 322–50. Berkeley and Los Angeles: University of California Press, 1986.

———. *The Post-Darwinian Controversies: A Study of the Protestant Struggle to Come to Terms with Darwin in Great Britain and America, 1870–1900*. New York: Cambridge University Press, 1979.

Numbers, Ronald L. *The Creationists*. New York: Knopf, 1992.

———. *Darwinism Comes to America*. Cambridge: Harvard University Press, 1998.

Proudfoot, Wayne. "Religion and Science." In *Altered Landscapes: Christianity in America, 1935–1985*, edited by David Lotz, Donald Shriver, and John F. Wilson, 268–79. Grand Rapids, Mich.: Eerdman's, 1989.

Purcell, Edward A. *The Crisis of Democratic Theory: Scientific Naturalism and the Problem of Value*. Lexington: University Press of Kentucky, 1973.

Turner, Frank M. "The Victorian Conflict between Science and Religion: A Professional Dimension." *Isis* 49 (1978): 356–76.

Turner, James. *Without God, without Creed: The Origins of Unbelief in America*. Baltimore: Johns Hopkins University Press, 1985.

Williams, Peter W. *America's Religions: From Their Origins to the Twenty-First Century*. Urbana: University of Illinois Press, 2001.

———. *America's Religions: Traditions and Cultures*. New York: Macmillan, 1990.

Wills, Garry. *Inventing America: Jefferson's Declaration of Independence*. Garden City, N.Y.: Doubleday, 1978.

Diversity and Region

Twenty years before the American Revolution, future patriot and president John Adams was entrusted with military papers for the governor of Rhode Island. Leaving his still-Puritan Massachusetts for the first time in his young life, the twenty-two-year-old traveled four days through an unfamiliar colony to complete his mission. Observing the Sabbath Day rituals of the Baptist-dominated region, he concluded that the "manners of Rhode Island [are] much more gay and social than our Sundays in Massachusetts." Nearly two decades later, Adams, then a leader of the American independence movement, left New England to join the First Continental Congress in Philadelphia. His diary reads like a religious travel log. He recorded that religion did not flourish in Rye, New York; that Presbyterians in New York City enjoyed better singing and preaching than he did at home; that the variety of denominations in Brunswick, New Jersey, could be seen in church architecture and different types of pews; and that he could attend Catholic, Episcopal, Presbyterian, Methodist, and Baptist churches in Philadelphia—all in the same day!

If John Adams could visit the modern United States, the interest he showed in regional religious differences in the eighteenth century would quickly turn to complete amazement. Today, the United States enjoys the most religiously diverse population in the world. But one might not realize that fact when standing in one place. Indeed, the religious diversity of the nation can often be appreciated only by car or train, for America's vastly different faiths are often tied to specific regions—sometimes even to specific neighborhoods. Although Americans have become increasingly homogeneous in food, clothing, and styles, they have not exhibited the same trend in religion. Regional differences and religious diversity remain alive and well, despite the blending of tastes and cultures through mass media.

To appreciate fully the role of diversity and region in American religious life, one must understand several aspects of the nation's past—including the importance of place, migration patterns, and cultural isolation and interaction, as well as the intersections of religion, ethnicity, race, and economics. Even though religion's relationships to those latter issues are covered in separate chapters, they appear off and on in this chapter as well, for they are often determinants of where religious groups chose to live. But for now we must focus on the broad contours of diversity and region.

First, there are significant distinctions among diversity, denominations, and pluralism. *Diversity* is a statement of fact, a description of the level of difference—be it ethnic, political, or religious, among a number of possibilities—in a specific time and place. Obviously, the focus of this chapter is religious diversity, that is, the varying amounts of religious homogeneity or heterogeneity among people in American history. Early on in the colonies, Protestant groups recognized that, though they differed somewhat in thought and practice, they shared enough "Christian truths" to coexist peaceably enough in the New World. They acknowledged, in other words, that *denominations* (which means "names") were merely expressions of their differing understandings of the same gospel. Thus, "denominationalism" developed as a philosophy of tolerance first among Protestants and eventually among most forms of Christianity to accept one another as part of the larger, invisible "Christian Church." But over the past half century, as the nation's ethnic and religious diversity went beyond European categories, a superstructure has grown that acknowledges, even enjoys, the diversity of American religion. This is *pluralism*, a philosophical commitment not just to tolerate diversity but to celebrate it.

Second, space, or place, is an important recurring issue in regional religion. Since it appears most often among those faiths tied to nature and natural surroundings, it plays an especially significant role in Native American religions. Rocks, rivers, weather, even the general landscape—all serve to shape understandings of deities, spirits, humans, and animals. But the importance of the natural landscape is not confined to native peoples' religions. It also proved significant to Euro-American faiths on the frontier, as the image of "wilderness" either determined or deeply influenced their self-understanding as

God's new Israel, led here to establish a fresh civilization. The wide-open spaces before westward Protestants fed their imagination as a religiously free people, unfettered to move through the continent they believed was given them by God. Some used ancient biblical names and religious references for their new environs. For instance, the Latter-day Saints entitled their new home "Zion" and referred to the natural landscape in the red rock regions to their south by such names as "Angels Landing," "The Pulpit," and "The Organ."

Since the United States is often referred to as a "nation of immigrants," it is unsurprising that migration also plays an important part in our understandings of religion, region, and diversity. As various cultures settled in different regions, each area had its own religious ethos. Whether we are talking about the Catholic Northeast, the Lutheran upper Midwest, or the Buddhist urban West Coast, we are dealing with a story of emigrants who transported their religious cultures. But just as important as immigration is intra-American migratory patterns. Indeed, one might best understand American immigration as merely part of the larger, global migratory systems that moved people around the world as mass transportation became affordable. Once in North America, religious cultures continued to move about, weaving a colorful tapestry over the religious landscape.

That movement brings to the fore one final element of religious regionalism and diversity: the difference between isolation and intersection. Isolated civilizations through time have retained many of their unique beliefs, self-understandings, and ways of life. Untouched by those who think or behave differently, their lives were unchallenged by difference. As we will see, those with distinct religious ideas and conduct often purposefully removed themselves from those who thought or practiced differently. In doing so, they hoped to remain "pure." What they ultimately created were regions that are distinct in their faith and practice—such as the Latter-day Saints (Mormons) in Utah. Most groups, however, were too dispersed to dominate a region and retained their interaction with the world around them, and in doing so they took on many of the elements of life in the region. When faiths intersect— most often in cities, where large numbers of diverse people reside—there will invariably be a level of disagreement. But in time, syncretism—the act of meeting in the middle whereby ideas and behaviors of others are incorporated into one's own religion—works its way through established religions in each region. Over time, then, regional religion, even different faiths, can take on the look and feel of those in that region, especially in urban settings.

Precolonial Era

Before sixteenth-century advances in sea transportation, continents remained largely isolated. Land travel even within a section of a continent was time-consuming and often dangerous, if not altogether impossible. Not surprisingly, then, differences among regions were very pronounced, as intercultural contact remained minimal. The beliefs and practices of one area could be amazingly distinct from those of another. Other chapters describe how native peoples, Africans, and Europeans differed from one another in belief and practice; however, variations existed within those groups themselves—disparities between regions within individual continents.

The worldviews of North American natives—their stories, tribal myths, community behavior, even their habits—were often determined by the region in which they lived, something pointed out by religious studies scholar Catherine Albanese in her analysis of the Oglala Sioux and the Hopi. The Oglala Sioux—one of the thirty or so American Indian nations who roamed the prairies between the Mississippi River and the Rocky Mountains—understood the world according to their experiences with the natural landscape of that region. Semi-nomadic, they lived in temporary camps and moved with the seasons in pursuit of the buffalo, whose meat offered them food and whose skins provided them with clothing and shelter. That reality shaped their entire cosmology, including their myths, ethics, and rituals.

The Oglala Sioux believed they originated from a once subterranean people. Enjoying the warmth and sustenance the earth provided, they were nonetheless coaxed out to the surface by Inktomi the spider (the trickster in their creation story). Once they realized they could not return to the security they once knew, they cried to Inktomi to save them; he simply laughed and scurried away. Only with the help of Old Man and Old Woman, who taught them how to hunt buffalo and use the animal's meat and skins, did the tribe survive. Oglala Sioux believed that this story told of their origin, but it did not explain everyone else's. Their understanding of the world was insular; it described *their* origin, *their* place in the world, *their* story. It was based on their regional distinctions and the animals that resided alongside them.

Another story that tied them to the buffalo also taught them how to behave toward one another and the rituals they were to follow. According to this sacred story, a beautiful woman dressed in white buckskin with a bundle tied to her back spoke to everyone at the lodge and there presented to the chief a sacred pipe with instructions on how to use it and what it symbolized. "With this sacred pipe you will walk upon the earth," she told them, "for the earth is your grandmother and mother and she is sacred." She then opened the bundle to reveal a round stone with seven inscribed circles, each one representing a ritual for the people to follow. As she left camp, she rolled over and transformed into a white buffalo calf, an image that is still sacred to the tribe.

It is impossible to understand the Oglala Sioux's myths and rituals without keeping in mind the region in which they lived. The ceremonies that brought community commitment and shared, effervescent experiences were predicated on their self-understanding as people tied to the buffalo. Their sweat lodges (constructed of cottonwood and painted with buffalo images) and Sun Dance rituals (warriors circling the central pole in the lodge, symbolically hunting and killing the life-giving buffalo) necessarily brought the bison into their central myth and ritual. Indeed, they drew all their sustenance—physical, material, and spiritual—from the buffalo.

The Hopi provide a good contrast to the Oglala Sioux. The natural surroundings of these desert Indians of Arizona proved far different from those of their Plains counterparts. The Hopi's origin myths taught of a people born of the dark womb of mother earth. An ancient abstract drawing that survives on an Arizona rock shows an ear of maize (corn) growing from the earth's womb, still tied by an umbilical cord. Immediately, we understand that farming meant more to this tribe than it did to the buffalo-hunting Sioux. Indeed, the Hopi's myths provide us with their self-conceptions that arose from their long history in the desert region. Although their origins are sketchy, it appears they arrived in the American Southwest more than two thousand years ago. Once hunter-gatherers, they settled into a life of farming and lived in kivas (pits they dug in the ground). Either because of security or to avoid the flash floods the desert sometimes experienced, the Hopi began around 900 to 1300 C.E. to hew dwellings into the cliff faces that surrounded them. Thus, their origin myth—which taught that they (similar to the Sioux) left their subterranean homes to live on the earth's surface—was literally true. They had, indeed, moved from below the earth's surface (kivas) to above (cliff dwellings).

In all, the feminine symbols of the tribe are unmistakable. The Hopi's understanding of the earth's motherly qualities and an emphasis on vegetables as literally born from the earth led them to understand the world in feminine terms. Despite moving into the impressive terrace apartments, Hopi retained a religious conception of the kiva, which by now represented the sacred womb of the earth. They continued to use these pits for ceremonies, sometimes even pulling back the stone covering from the *sipapu*—a hole dug in the center of the kiva to represent an opening to the world below—during initiations so the dead could participate. Even the creation of the world itself, as they understood it, came about through the work of two women—one made of shell, the other of coral. Although women were excluded from the sacred kivas, the tribe was nonetheless structured along matrilineal lines. This social arrangement underscores the variance with the Sioux, as the Hopi emphasized birth and growth rather than blood and meat.

Just as the natural symbols of the Great Plains appeared in Oglala Sioux rituals, so the southwestern desert life made its way into the Hopi's religious practice. The region's harvest marked the ritual calendar that characterized their lives. Behind these seasonal rites was a singular motivation—the need for water. All these rituals used similar procedures, but the overwhelming aspects of the desert distinguished each in each season. For instance, three ceremonies from December to July marked the presence of kachinas (spiritual beings who lived on local mountain peaks) while the rains came. The first ceremony, occurring during the winter solstice, marked the cessation of the sun's southward journey—a celebration of the symbolic rebirth of the earth as days grew longer and eventually brought corn. The second, in February, marked the rainy season, which brought a fast-growing season for the beans recently planted. The third, in July, bade farewell to the kachinas as they left for home (at the same time the regular rains ended) and celebrated the first harvest of corn. By August, the Hopi again needed rain to help the second planting of corn, so they played haunting music and released captured snakes into the desert in the hope of reconciling themselves to the mythical snake people they had driven out of their camp when they once shared underground homes. September and October saw three ceremonies of fertility for both the ground and humans, as hopes for a harvest of babies corresponded to the desire for corn. In November, while the desert grew cold and dark, the Hopi men crawled into the sacred kivas, removed the *sipapu*, and took part in a ritual of death and rebirth by telling and acting out stories. By the next month, the cycle started again, as rains came to the desert and the sun began its long trek back.

Meanwhile, across the ocean in Europe, a diversity of Christian beliefs and practices along regional lines was apparent. Southern Europe—namely, Italy, France, and Spain—remained closely aligned to the Roman Catholic Church, which exerted both religious and secular power. Northern Europe—Germany, Switzerland, the Netherlands, and England—partly because of Rome's inability to control lands so far away, had broken from the Catholic Church and was a bastion of Protestantism. Again, diversity was the hallmark. German cantons were about equally divided between Catholic (southern Germany) and Lutheran Protestant (northern Germany). Switzerland, meanwhile, retained its Calvinist Protestant character long after the death of John Calvin in 1564. And England created a hybrid church by employing Protestant thought and Catholic ritual.

Of course, in each case, these were "official" faiths sanctioned by the state; but hundreds of thousands of religious dissenters and those who held on to folk traditions lived within the confines of European countries whose state-sponsored churches could not hold their consciences. This held especially true in England, whose political establishment tried to ignore dissenters for more than a century but finally legally recognized them in 1688. Until then, many thousands who did not appreciate the residual aspects of Catholicism in the Anglican Church called instead for a "purified" church that was entirely Protestant. Eventually approximately fifty thousand of the "Puritans" left for the New World. Geographically speaking, more than 60 percent of these Puritans hailed from East Anglia (Suffolk, Essex, Norfolk, and Middlesex counties), where literacy was emphasized among the developing middle class. Thus, not surprisingly, they were extremely well read in the Bible and sought to re-create its moral injunctions in the New World.

One of the debates among English dissenters that would have particular resonance in North America was over the correct church polity. How should church power be structured? Should appointed leaders control the church? Elected officials? The local congregation? That dispute went to the heart of religious power, so it is unsurprising that disagreements over those questions could lead to fissures and ongoing debates among Protestants. Three major options shaped the contours of later American denominations. A top-down structure (whereby appointed bishops held control) characterized the Anglican Church and its offspring, the American Episcopal and the Methodist denominations. Meanwhile, those who believed in a more representative form of church government, such as the Presbyterians (*presbuterios* is the Greek word for "elder"), elected their local leadership, who in turn elected from among themselves a larger governing authority. Finally, some believed the New Testament indicated that the local congregation should control itself in all matters. Thus, the Congregationalists (Puritans), Baptists, and Quakers practiced a more radical, democratic form of church polity. Although they might agree on most other Christian doctrines, the simple question of church structure—a debate going back to the Old World—has continued to separate these historical Protestant traditions.

Colonial North America

Spain's presence in North America was not only Europe's first, but also among the most sustained. From the 1520s, when Spanish explorers, accompanied by Catholic priests, moved through the southern regions of the continent, until the 1840s, when a young republic called the United States pushed its influence outside the region, Spain exerted varying degrees of political, economic, and religious power over North America. Generally speaking, Spanish Catholicism's areas of greatest effect appeared in a sweeping arc from Florida, across Texas and New Mexico, and into California. Unfortunately for both the native peoples and the priests who hoped to convert them, New Spain's Christian concerns accompanied their military interests—and often were overshadowed by the latter. All too often, priests went along with the mistreatment, having used physical pain to bring spiritual purity in Spain during the recent Inquisition. Despite Pope Paul III's 1537 declaration that the enslaved American Indians were indeed people capable of salvation, not animals to be mistreated, the gospel went hand in hand with Spanish guns in the European quest for riches.

Spanish missionaries saw some progress in the West. An impressive mission system was laid out, each about one day's journey from the other. *El camino real*, "the royal road," became a major trading route not only for the Spanish but also for the thirty thousand native converts in New Mexico, whose lives centered around the economic and political, as well as the spiritual, life of the mission system. By the late eighteenth century Spanish missionaries had established a series of missions in California that took Catholicism up the Pacific coast as far north as San Francisco.

Catholicism also moved through the northern and middle regions of North America as French Catholics took the gospel throughout the Great Lakes region and down the Mississippi River valley. Father Jacques Marquette accompanied the first French explorers through the upper Mississippi region, becoming a hero for many young priests after him, risking life and limb in the hope of converting natives. Many Jesuits lost their lives in their efforts to convert tribes along the Great Lakes. In time, they set up churches along the entire Mississippi River to its mouth in New Orleans. Today's maps showing cities with such French names as Baton Rouge, St. Louis, and Des Moines reveal the strongholds of what was once a powerful French Catholic presence.

A variety of Europeans and Africans settled along the eastern seaboard of North America under the aegis of the English, who dominated the region culturally, politically, and religiously. Out of this mixture of religious groups

came a general synthesis of faiths and practices and eventually some tolerance for those who believed or practiced their forms of Christianity differently. The matrix of faiths that settled there resulted from three practices
that the settlers developed early on in their colonization process—religious
dissent, slavery as a labor force, and economic progress.

The northeastern colonies, known early on as "New England" (Massachusetts [including what later became Maine], Connecticut, Rhode Island, New
Hampshire, and Vermont), were initially settled by longtime English dissenters. Often referred to as "Puritans" for their obsession with creating a purely
Protestant church, as opposed to the hybrid Protestant-Catholic church established in England, these religious folk created in the New World the most
democratic form of church polity and state government yet seen. They had
long distinguished themselves from the hierarchy of the Anglican Church,
and now they fulfilled their dream of forging a "congregational" style of church
governance that placed authority in the gathered group of believers rather
than in a sacred bureaucracy. Even though these Puritans sought the freedom
to worship in the purity of their faith without Anglican oversight, they failed
to extend that right to other groups. Many feared that lawlessness would result if they allowed too much diversity in faith and practice. The result was
a society in which Old World religious dissenters became an established New
World faith. Those who disagreed with Puritan tenets either kept their opinions to themselves or were forced to move to Rhode Island, which quickly
became a center for religious freedom. Nonetheless, the spirit of dissent lived
on in Puritan colonies through a more democratic form of secular government and a congregational style of church government—both of which enabled the state and church to be governed more from the bottom up than from
the top down.

In the South, meanwhile, the Anglican Church was the established faith.
But the official Church of England found considerable trouble convincing
the white settlers and black slaves that that was the case. The South differed
from New England in several significant ways that made it a far less "churched"
region. First, those who migrated to the South were not usually religious dissenters; that is, they tended not to put much emphasis on how their faith differed from the Anglican Church. Because of that, fewer southerners wore
their religion on their sleeve. Second, the region itself was too large and dis-
jointed to offer the community spirit necessary to create strong religious bonds.
Impassable rivers, creeks, and swamps throughout the tidewater regions of
Virginia, especially, meandered west and separated potential neighbors from
one another. And since the immigrants moved for economic purposes rather

than religious reasons, they moved inland quickly, settling along the rivers that provided suitable soil for tobacco and transportation for their goods. The established church, then, was left with parishes that at times were more than five hundred square miles in size—an impossibly large piece of spiritual real estate to oversee effectively.

The South also differed from New England in its large African American population. Slave importation grew throughout the 1700s, until by the time of the American Revolution approximately one-half million African descendants lived in the colonies, mostly in the South. The result of this intercultural contact was a southern religious landscape that was quite distinct from that of other areas. Depending on what part of the South one lived in, colonial whites could have witnessed a variety of religious practices among the enslaved Africans. Most had been brought from the west coast of Africa, where nature religions similar to those of Native Americans were dominant. Some items considered powerful amulets in the Old World were secretly transported by those captured in Angola. Excavations of slave quarters in the twentieth century revealed just how long this practice remained in place in America, as historical archaeologists discovered West African stones built into the walls of slave quarters outside Durham, North Carolina. Smaller numbers of enslaved Africans held to Abrahamic traditions, having been converted by Anglican missionaries working among the Kongolese or having embraced or inherited Islam, which moved south from North Africa in the centuries preceding the New World slave trade.

Between New England and the South sat the Middle Colonies—often overlooked because they lacked the social cohesion of their northern neighbors or the racial diversity of their southern counterparts. In reality, the Middle Colonies (New York, New Jersey, Delaware, Pennsylvania, and Maryland) were prototypical of what would eventually characterize religion in the United States: diversity and limited tolerance. From the beginning, these colonies purposefully attracted disparate groups to settle within their borders, all in the hope of guaranteeing economic success while offering religious asylum to those in need.

Maryland, initially founded in 1634 by the Catholic Cecil Calvert, Lord Baltimore, provided a place for English Catholics to settle in the New World. In order to secure freedoms for them, the founder quickly established a policy of religious tolerance; thus, even if Catholics fell into a minority in Maryland, their rights were guaranteed. It was a wise move, for by 1677 three-quarters of the population were dissenting Protestants. The Quakers of New Jersey, Delaware, and Pennsylvania had a similar experience. Given or sold these vast territories, William Penn, previously jailed for his Quaker religious convictions in England, opened these colonies' borders to others willing to join in his "holy experiment" of founding a pacifist society where respect for others was paramount. Penn even made certain to pay the native peoples, who had prior claim to the land, for their rights to the property. In time, word of Penn's colonies spread throughout Europe and North America. Several German religious sects moved to Pennsylvania, Scottish Presbyterians migrated to New Jersey, and several Native American tribes traveled to the western sections of Pennsylvania, seeking solace from the overbearing English settlers in other colonies.

New York's religious landscape, every bit as diverse as that of Penn's colonies, came about quite differently. Initially settled by the Dutch, "New Netherlands" was from the start the most religiously heterogeneous area in North America. German Lutherans, French Calvinists, Puritans, Quakers, English Baptists, Mennonites, even Catholics and Jews settled alongside the numerous Dutch Reformed immigrants in this montage of colonization. After England took control of the region in 1664, its several attempts to establish the Anglican Church failed miserably. By 1688 the colony still contained only one Anglican family for every fifteen English dissenter families and twenty Dutch Reformed families. New York City itself would remain a bastion of religious diversity for the following three centuries.

Throughout the eastern seaboard, most of the colonists lived on farms. In fact, North America remained predominantly rural into the early twentieth century. Still, over time cities grew in importance as cultural and religious meeting places. The population of New York and Philadelphia grew to nearly twenty-five thousand inhabitants by the 1770s, and these cities were marked by increasing ethnic and religious diversity. Although such diverse cities were only a shadow of today's "urban frontier"—where different ethnic and religious groups rub against one another daily—the process of creating cities as "nodal points" of contact among cultures in America began during the eighteenth century. With a slowly developing market economy, those in New England and the Middle Colonies came to cities to trade. In doing so, they ran headlong into those who thought and practiced their faiths differently. In the South, the nodal points were less structured and more intimate, as English and Scottish Protestants interacted more frequently and personally with Africans.

Sometimes religious differences emerged as a result of how particular regions —even neighborhoods—developed. For instance, the seemingly insignificant decision in 1672 by the church in Salem, Massachusetts, to divide the congregation and allow those living in the far northwestern region of its parish to found their own church started in motion the most infamous witch trial in American history. Whereas established Salem Town took advantage of its proximity to the ocean and used its port to trade and interact with other areas, the new Salem Village, to the northwest, was landlocked and its economic growth limited. By the early 1690s, the Puritans in Salem Village began to claim that their constant economic woes were the result of witchcraft—and promptly blamed those Puritans living to their east, those who enjoyed the fruit of living in a port city. Nineteen people, nearly all of whom were from Salem Town, were executed as witches before the Massachusetts court put an end to the trials.

Living in separate towns or villages, then, could cause people to distrust one another, but sometimes those differences could be overcome because of a common cause. In those cases, great strides were made toward tolerance of those of dissimilar belief or behavior. For instance, in the famed Great Awakening of the 1730s to 1750s, revivalists cooperated across denominational and regional lines to evangelize the masses. Anglican George Whitefield of Georgia preached alongside Presbyterian Gilbert Tennent of Pennsylvania and Congregationalist Jonathan Edwards of Massachusetts. To their minds, their differences were only slight compared with the shared belief in the atoning death of Jesus and the need for people to believe in order to be saved from their sins. "Denominationalism," that understanding among Protestant groups that shared many qualities, was under way.

Revolutionary and Early Republican America

In the relatively short period of the American Revolution and the early Republic, religious life in the United States changed dramatically. Those denominations that once dominated the countryside shrank in size and significance as smaller groups took advantage of the states' disestablishment of faith and the religious liberty offered by the Constitution and grew in size. Quite simply, some denominations were better suited to life on the frontier, which began its westward march during this period.

The religious picture at the outbreak of the Revolution looks unfamiliar to us today. The largest faith group was the Congregationalists—the old Puritans —confined mainly to New England, who made up approximately 36 percent of the churches in 1740 but had already fallen off to 27 percent by 1780. Second to them were the Anglicans, the established church in most of the colonies, who constituted about 21 percent of the churches in 1740. Their power dropped significantly during the Revolutionary period, when they accounted for about 15 percent of the churches. But in forty years, neither of these would rank nearly so high. Methodists, Baptists, and Presbyterians, until the war confined to Maryland, Rhode Island and the South, and Pennsylvania/New Jersey, respectively, proved themselves more mobile and moved west with the population to seek greater opportunity.

The Revolutionary War itself was often fought along religious lines of thought. Members of dissenter religions who had fled England the previous century were quick to equate England's desire for political control of the colonies to the mother country's previous attempts at religious control. Congregationalist and Presbyterian ministers relentlessly attacked the Anglican Church's top-down structure and continually sought to increase the people's fears that England would soon send an Anglican bishop to America in order to stamp out their various traditions. By uniting their religious concerns to political concerns, those groups that had cooperated so well during the Great Awakening renewed their ties to one another. Postwar Anglicanism in America, in the guise of the Episcopal Church, had no chance to dominate the scene after such verbal barrage.

But why didn't Congregationalism continue its dominance? After all, it was not only one of the historical dissenter faiths; it was arguably the most significant one. The reason for its decline was its internal struggles. With a radical congregational church structure, in which each individual congregation is autonomous, the tradition was always given over to theological disputes. Postrevolutionary America was rife with them, and each one seemed to show up in New England's established church. By the early 1800s, perhaps as many as one-third of its churches had dropped their historical Trinitarian beliefs for Unitarianism—especially those in the vicinity of Harvard College. Still the stronghold of that faith, the region earned its reputation for believing in the "Fatherhood of God, the brotherhood of Man, and the neighborhood of Boston."

Meanwhile, the three other historical dissenter traditions—Presbyterians, Baptists, and Methodists—rushed headlong into the developing American democracy. Presbyterians, who were concentrated around New York and Philadelphia, began to send missionaries into the Northwest Territories, which had been ceded to the central government by Virginia. Soon these territories would be formed into new states, and the Presbyterians wanted to be there for the droves of people who planned to leave the East Coast for new opportunities. To this day, the greatest concentration of Presbyterians runs from New York across Pennsylvania, Ohio, Indiana, Michigan, Illinois, and Wisconsin, as well as into the Carolinas and southern Virginia, the result of Scottish Presbyterian migrations in the mid-1700s. Baptists, once centered in Rhode Island as non-Puritan congregational outcasts, had moved south during the Great Awakening. After the war they began to move west as well. Employing a congregational style of church government, they were well situated to the westward migration, as local churches could select their own ministers and see to their own affairs, thus avoiding the usual problems of top-down denominations overseeing populations on the move. Baptists became especially powerful in upstate New York and Maine and across the interior South. In fact, by the late nineteenth century they would dominate southern cultural and religious life.

Presbyterians and Baptists certainly grew under America's new circumstances, but no one took greater advantage of the religious free market than the Methodists. A tiny society within the Anglican Church as late as the Revolution, the Methodist Episcopal Church declared its own independence from the English church in 1784. Although it retained the Anglican liturgy, hymns, and church structure, it made itself otherwise thoroughly American. With the leadership of such capable individuals as Francis Asbury and Thomas Coke, the tiny denomination grew with the westward population, employing tireless circuit-riding ministers to found churches in new communities and keep returning there for services every two weeks. The level of their success is astounding. From 65 congregations in 1776, Methodism exploded to 13,300 congregations in 1850. The Methodist Church, like the Baptist Church, was more diffuse in its growth than the Presbyterian Church, but it mirrored the latter in its area of concentration: a "Methodist band" traverses the midsection of the nation to this day, as the faith moved west from its Baltimore base. It even dominated the South until the rapid growth of the Baptists in the late nineteenth century removed it to second place.

It is difficult to overstate the power these three Protestant denominations had in the early Republic. Their practice of joint revivals on the frontier reinforced their image as those churches most closely tied to American democracy, as Baptists, Presbyterians, and Methodists came together to celebrate their form of evangelical religion. First in Kentucky but eventually along the entire frontier, these revivals, often lasting several weeks, brought cohesion to far-flung farming communities whose members otherwise might rarely have seen one another. Featuring perhaps a Baptist evangelist during the day and a Methodist revivalist at night, these camp meetings buttressed Protestants' belief in denominationalism. They had their differences, but their doctrinal similarities and concern to convert sinners helped them overcome most difficulties that might arise.

That general agreement produced a number of transdenominational, or interdenominational, organizations that were national in scope. Cooperating across denominational lines, evangelical Protestants created such long-lasting parachurch institutions as the American Sunday School Union, to teach literacy so that children could read the Bible; the American Bible Society; the American Home Missions Society; the American Tract Society; and eventually the American Temperance Union and the American Antislavery Society. Together, these voluntary agencies formed a cooperative, later referred to as the "Evangelical Empire," that had a combined budget larger than that of the federal government.

Across the Plains and Rocky Mountains, meanwhile, religious settlements continued to flourish along the Pacific coast. Just when the American Founders met in Philadelphia in 1776 to vote for independence, Father Junípero Serra laid the foundation for the Mission San Juan Capistrano—now famous for the annual return of swallows each spring. San Juan Capistrano was one of a series of missions dotting the western coast from Baja California to San Francisco, outposts of Catholicism that also functioned as marketplaces for the local native peoples, schools for children of native and European backgrounds, and often political centers for the Spanish to oversee their New World holdings. Over time, Roman Catholics in the Spanish West saw their once strong institutions falter. With Spain's loss of power in the struggles for control of New World colonies, many of its missions and churches fell into disrepair and were often left without an adequate staff to see to locals' spiritual affairs. In California alone, the missions that once sat as jewels in the crown of American Catholicism were sold off piecemeal to rancheros, Formerly centers of public faith, they became instead hubs of private economic advancement and, often, racial subjugation. Christian natives who once turned to the missions for spiritual sustenance now avoided the privately owned territories for fear of economic exploitation.

Native Americans elsewhere had it no better. As citizens of the new United States pushed ever westward, Native Americans were often forced to leave the lands that tied them to their ancestors and the core of their faith. Cherokee were pushed from their Carolina homelands into reservations in Georgia —where, once they discovered silver, they were forced to leave in the 1830s. Seminoles in the Deep South kept pushing farther into Florida to escape the American soldiers who sought to force a settlement the Native Americans found unacceptable. Once vibrant centers of native culture, homelands inextricably tied to their myths and rituals, were replaced by American villages in which Baptists, Presbyterians, and Methodists tilled the soil.

Antebellum Nineteenth Century

One might be tempted to understand the decades before the Civil War as a copy of the religious scene after the American Revolution. After all, the denominations that came to dominate American culture in the early Republic clearly kept their position well into the nineteenth century. But that fact cannot overshadow the challenges to their power that were developing in the antebellum period. Indeed, while "mainstream" Protestants continued to cooperate and share political as well as religious control, increased diversity and even the regions themselves were setting the stage for a new American religious landscape.

Among the most important of these challenges came from a variety of movements that understood denominationalism as something inherently dangerous. For the most part, this impulse, often referred to as "Restorationism" because of its attempt to get beyond denominational distinctions in order to restore the primitive purity of the New Testament church, never attracted the numbers held by the large Protestant denominations. But the spirit it showed, mostly along the western frontier, represented a powerful voice against the hegemonic position of American mainstream Protestantism.

The most significant representatives of this movement were the "Christians" and the Church of Jesus Christ of Latter-day Saints (Mormons). The "Christian Church" movement, also known as "Disciples of Christ" and "Church of Christ," was a diffuse group led by several charismatic preachers and theologians initially along the Ohio River valley (Ohio, Indiana, Kentucky, and Tennessee) and later in the lower Midwest (Missouri, Kansas, Oklahoma, and Texas). Using the New Testament as their blueprint, members of this movement criticized denominations as contrary to early Christianity. Even the names "Baptist," "Presbyterian," and "Methodist" came under their withering attack, as none of those terms were ever applied to the initial Christian community. They proposed a restoration of the early church—or at least their interpretation of it—in which believers were called simply Christians or disciples and each congregation had considerable autonomy. After nearly twenty years of grassroots revivals and founding of churches, the group began to organize on the state level in 1839 and the national level in 1849. Although small by other standards—in 1850 it had about 170,000 adherents, compared with 580,000 Baptists, 480,000 Presbyterians, and 1.6 million Methodists—the movement became a powerful alternative to mainstream Protestantism in the Midwest and attracted more than a million members by the turn of the century.

The red-hot revivals in upstate New York, which earned the region the nickname "the burned-over district," produced a very different type of Restorationist movement. Joseph Smith Jr., a young man confused by the theological distinctions sometimes highlighted by revivalists of various denominations, claimed to have seen a vision of the angel Moroni, who led him to buried tablets that contained the Book of Mormon in ancient script. Translating it with divine help, he published the document, which was both a severe critique of American denominations and an alternative interpretation of Christianity's role in America. Gathering believers as they moved, these "Latter-day Saints" settled first in Ohio, then in Missouri, and finally in Illinois—all the while finding few mainstream Protestants willing to offer the hand of welcome. After Smith's assassination in 1844, the Mormons split into separate groups over the question of leadership. The largest and most famous faction followed Brigham Young to Utah, then a new American territory where Mormons could practice their faith without fear of martyrdom. Others claimed that Smith's own son was the rightful heir to the line of prophet and finally established a headquarters for their bloc (recently renamed "The Community of Christ") in Independence, Missouri. Still others followed different self-proclaimed prophets to various places in the Midwest. James Strang led a group to Michigan, where he pronounced himself king of Beaver Island and eventually met a fate similar to Joseph Smith's.

The role of region in a faith's self-understanding is perhaps more readily visible in the various Mormon groups than in any other American religion. The members of the Utah-based church under Brigham Young referred to their new surroundings as Zion—the city of God. The story that developed around their trek across the plains and mountains until they reached the Great Salt Lake is reminiscent of the Exodus account of the Jews. But the function of "sacred place" is hardly confined to the Utah Mormons. Indeed, most faith groups that descended from Smith's proclaimed revelations continue to believe that Independence, Missouri, is the site where Jesus will eventually return. Smith himself laid out stones marking the site where the great temple must be built. To this day, many of the various Mormon groups retain buildings surrounding the "temple lot," which is owned by one of the smaller Mormon groups, the Hedrickites. Despite great offers of money from larger Mormon faiths and even foul play to their small building, the members of the tiny church refuse to sell or move. To their mind, they are the pure Latter-day Saints church, and they intend eventually to build the temple on the chosen lot and restore early Christianity to its latter-day place.

Other groups challenged the hold Protestant mainstream denominations held on American culture. In most cases, these movements were tied to specific locales, such as the Oneida Community in upstate New York or New Harmony in southern Indiana. Most of the time they centered around the prophetic personality of a particularly charismatic founder. One notable exception to this was the Shakers, whose tidy villages dotted the landscape from western Massachusetts, across upstate New York, and to Ohio and Kentucky. Although an enduring part of the American religious imagination, the group never exceeded six thousand members at any given time. But their utopian goals were characteristic of a number of nonmainstream Protestants who stood outside the dominant culture.

Without doubt, however, the most lasting challenge to Protestant hegemony came with increased immigration. The thirty years before the Civil War saw a marked increase in European immigrants to the United States. Unlike the colonial period, when 85 percent of European immigrants hailed from England or Scotland, more boats arrived from Germany and Ireland. Those who could afford to continue their westward trek did so, moving alongside Anglo-Americans on the developing frontier. Most, however, had spent what they could on passage and were forced to settle in the cities where they landed. In a matter of two decades, the ethnic and religious composition of Boston, for example, was completely altered. New England ships that had carried timber to the British Isles offered cheap passage back to Boston in order to ensure enough ballast to keep the ship upright in the churning waters of the Atlantic Ocean. Once the stronghold of Congregationalism and Unitarianism, the city now took on an Irish Catholic character that continues to this day.

The process that changed Boston affected most of the East Coast port cities, if not immediately, then during the coming waves of immigration that marked the nineteenth century. New York and Philadelphia, already religiously diverse cities from their earliest colonization, now added Irish Catholics and more German Lutherans to their mix. These changes did not always go so well. Indeed, the differences between the large Protestant denominations and these new arrivals were just too much for longtime residents. Legal, and sometimes physical, fights broke out over such issues as (Protestant) Bible reading in public schools and alcohol served at Sunday Mass. Property was destroyed, a Catholic underclass was created, and long-standing biases were developed. In the end, Catholics separated themselves from their Protestant assailants by creating a parallel school system controlled by their local parish. One might say that Catholics suffered through a "separate and unequal" status for much of the next century.

This era is often studied for the regional differences that led to the American Civil War, but it also proves fruitful to stand back and look at the expansive territory that now made up the United States in order to understand the religious differences that helped to define each area. During the four decades leading up to the devastating war, literally millions of people moved across borders and reshaped the religious landscape.

The North and the South had developed along two separate cultural tracks. It proves difficult to decipher whether religion was a motivating force, a guiding force, or a casualty of other forces. The truth probably lies somewhere in each. Clearly, though, the economic history of each region played an integral role in their differing understandings of what the Bible taught. In the South, which by this point had the largest slave economy in the world, many whites understood in a literal sense those sections of the Bible that mentioned slavery. Throughout the Old Testament, in fact, slavery was a given—with the Jews at one point serving Egyptians and then later enslaving other peoples. Saint Paul's New Testament injunctions regarding slavery were even more direct. He failed to mention a single moral problem with slavery in the Book of Philemon (an epistle written to a slave owner exhorting him to forgive his returning runaway slave) and even warned slaves to "obey their masters" in Ephesians 6. By using a literal interpretation, many southern ministers not only defended slavery but also claimed that it was a commandment of God. For instance, in the story of Noah's family after the flood (Genesis 9), God cursed Noah's son Ham for making light of his father's drunkenness and subsequent nudity. Ham's descendants, now marked by God, were to be universally recognized as cursed by God to slavery. Some southern ministers argued that the dark skin of African Americans was that mark. Obviously, this conclusion went beyond any literal interpretation of the Bible, as there is no description of the "sign" at all. It was instead a myth borrowed to defend the institution of slavery. In all, however, southerners believed in a strict construction of the biblical text—setting a practice that continues to this day, long after slavery ended as an issue.

Ministers in the North, affected by decades of theological development that emphasized larger themes running through the Bible, used metaphoric interpretations to argue for the abolition of slavery. The major idea weaving through scripture, they argued, was a movement from slavery to liberation. First, the Jews in the Old Testament moved from servitude in Egypt to God's chosen nation in Israel. Later, in the New Testament, Jesus taught that people could move from spiritual enslavement to sin to a new life of forgiveness and peace.

The Bible, therefore, was not always to be taken literally; rather, it offered the general story of humanity—a narrative of leaving captivity for a life of liberty. On such a basis, northern abolitionists demanded immediate freedom for African Americans.

The regional differences in biblical interpretation—literal in the South and metaphoric in the North—had been a long time in coming and were the result of many factors. To be sure, the economies of each region fed into the impulse to explicate scripture along certain lines. But the issues ran far deeper than that. Culturally the regions had developed along such vastly different planes that, by the mid-nineteenth century, the national denominations could no longer coexist. The northern regions had, from the start, been settled by those who put more emphasis on reading the Bible, those who dissented against British strictures on religious freedom, those who accentuated (at least to a degree) human rights. The South, on the other hand, never emphasized education of the masses or metaphoric readings of scripture.

These internal denominational issues, so basic that they went to the heart of how one is to interpret the Bible, eventually led to schisms that later were reflected in the South's attempted secession from the Union. Religious division presaged that political break by up to fifteen years, as the Methodist Episcopal Church split into southern and northern wings in 1845. The Baptists did the same. Presbyterians held out until 1857, when they, too, finally divided into separate regional denominations.

Postbellum and Industrial Nineteenth Century

The social effects of the war were plentiful, especially in regard to religion. Immediately after the war, intra-American migrations increased dramatically. Northern Baptists and Methodists moved south not only to develop industry in the economically ruined region but also to carry what they understood as a more civilized approach to life. These white church leaders tried to force southern blacks and whites to adopt a more formal liturgy and reputable hymns rather than give way to freewheeling services where gospel and folk songs mixed easily. In many ways, this only solidified southern Baptists' and Methodists' disdain for their northern brethren. It wasn't enough, they thought, that northerners took away from them a way of life; now they criticized their faith and practice.

Protestants were not the only northerners to move south during Reconstruction. For the first time in more than a century, Roman Catholics exhibited a measurable southern presence. The economic opportunities that European Catholics once saw in New England now appeared in a South that needed rebuilding. Thousands of Catholics moved from the Northeast to areas of the South that had begun an inexorable march toward industrialization and urbanization—Charleston, Atlanta, Richmond, and Raleigh. New Orleans had always retained its French Catholic flavor, but now more cities throughout the South felt the presence of Catholics.

In fact, the entire late nineteenth century must be understood as *the* migratory epoch in a national history based on migrations. Millions of Europeans poured into America's northern cities during this period, changing the face of the region once dominated by evangelical and progressive Protestants. For instance, from 1860 to 1900 some 3.5 million Germans entered the United States—40 percent of them just in the 1880s. Arriving with more money than the Irish immigrants before the war, these German Lutherans and Catholics could afford to travel to the Midwest, where they purchased cheap farmland. Within one generation, the midwestern triangle of Cincinnati, St. Louis, and Milwaukee saw German Lutherans and Catholics come to dominate the region numerically. Still, it was a generally workable, if imperfect, arrangement, for most of these German faithful hoped to protect their ethnic and religious distinctions and thus kept to themselves.

Unlike the antebellum years, European immigration was not confined mainly to Irish Catholics and German Lutherans and Catholics. Italian and Polish Catholic migration exploded in the 1880s and continued through World War I, largely the result of European overpopulation and economic depression along with American industrial expansion. More than a million Italians—mostly Catholics but of varying commitment to the church—arrived before the turn of the century, a number that would triple in the following two decades. Meanwhile, the number of Poles in the United States shot up from 50,000 in 1870 to more than 2 million in 1920. Clearly, the Protestant face of America was changing.

That was most clearly true of American cities—a fact that would grow in significance as the United States became an increasingly urban nation. Northern cities became cramped, dirty industrial centers where first-generation European Catholics provided the bulk of the labor force. From the end of the Civil War until the turn of the century, 14 million people immigrated to the United States as northern industrial cities experienced unheard-of growth: Detroit and Kansas City, 400 percent; Cleveland, 600 percent; Chicago, 1,000 percent; Minneapolis, 5,000 percent. No wonder Josiah Strong wrote in the

1890s, "There is a city of 50,000 added to New York every year." It would be in these bustling cities that modern American life, including religious life, would be born.

In reaction to the loud, crowded, and busy life of the city, several impulses developed in evangelical Protestantism. Some sought the hope of relief from an industrialized life that swept away all memories of quieter days by turning to a belief in the sudden and imminent return of Jesus to set the sinful world right. This doctrine, called "premillennialism" for its belief that Jesus must return before a time of peace can be established, exhibited a great deal of pessimism about all the so-called progress that urbanization and industrialization had wrought. Others sought peace in the assurance that God had made a place for them in heaven. Lacking the guarantee that their sins were forgiven (Catholics could hear a priest declare them forgiven after confession and penance), many evangelical Protestants searched for signs of God's grace in their lives. Some found it in a second experience, beyond the initial conversion experience, called "sanctification." These "Holiness" Protestants represented a number of particularly pious believers across a spectrum of denominations, constantly turning a searchlight on their souls to root out evil and break the power of sin in their lives—sin that was so readily apparent around them in the city. Several new denominations spun out of premillennial and Holiness impulses, including the Church of the Nazarene and the Christian and Missionary Alliance.

Ultimately the issue was not just urbanization; it was also the diversity of those moving to the cities. Although Strong and others used the language of a "melting pot" to describe the mixed neighborhoods that increasingly characterized American cities, what they hoped for was a powerful "Americanizing" process on new immigrants. But most of those arriving found American Protestant culture as foreign to them as the English tongue and tried to avoid both. Streets, neighborhoods, entire blocks of cities became cultural enclaves to Polish Catholics in Chicago, or Italian Catholics in New York, or German Lutherans in Indianapolis. And even though the second generation often learned English in order to move ahead economically, their faith, tied to the homeland and its traditions, kept them separated from culturally Protestant America.

Perhaps this is best seen in the Jewish population, which increased dramatically in the late nineteenth century. Earlier Jewish migration had an altogether different look to it. Arriving largely as middle-class families from Germany (a secular state in which, ironically, many Jews prospered during the nineteenth century), many Jews could afford to move on from their port of entry and settled in the Midwest. In fact, by the 1880s, Cincinnati's religious population was generally split into Jews, Catholics, and Protestants. Relatively unfamiliar with persecution in either Germany or the United States, these Jews liberalized their faith to rid themselves of what they saw as centuries of needless tradition—including dress codes, worship rituals, and kosher food regulations. Reform Judaism was born from this movement. And even those, known as Conservative Jews, who thought Reform went too far were unprepared for the foreignness of those Jews about to arrive from eastern Europe. These Jews practiced an "Orthodox" version of Judaism that found the strength to face persecution through keeping tradition and remaining in isolated communities. Poor, uneducated, and largely unskilled, they arrived in New York and settled there, having no money to move inland to farms like their German Jewish predecessors. Reformed and Conservative Jews found their Orthodox cousins particularly bothersome, with their emphases on tradition and isolationism, and the Orthodox newcomers could hardly recognize the Judaism of their Reformed and Conservative brethren. In all, the situation for Jews in America highlighted the ethnic differences that a single faith tradition could encounter, as well as the "Americanizing" process that older versions of a faith could undergo, thus further differentiating it from more traditional versions.

Early Twentieth Century

While improvements in transportation continued to affect national migration patterns, the needs and desires to take advantage of those developments increased dramatically as the United States moved along the roller coaster of the "Roaring Twenties" and the Great Depression. The ability of Americans to move around grew alongside the economic need to do so and the desire to spread various faiths across regions.

Just as Reconstruction brought Catholics south, opening opportunities in urban America took African Americans north. Literally millions of black Christians moved to northern cities to begin a new life during the 1920s, as new immigration laws adopted during World War I kept down the number of Europeans—until then an easy labor force. Midwestern cities that had long been virtually all white (even if they were religiously mixed) suddenly saw black churches rapidly springing up. Chicago, Detroit, Cincinnati, Pittsburgh, New York, Baltimore, Boston—all experienced vast social change as black Christians constructed African Methodist Episcopal, African Methodist Episcopal-Zion, and National Baptist Convention churches, thus forever altering the religious landscape of the North with a palpable black urban presence.

No group characterizes the transformations of the period as well as the Pentecostal movement, which grew out of the concerns that initially shaped the Holiness movement as some Holiness adherents sought a further sign of God's indwelling Spirit. Although the first appearance of glossalalia—referred to as "speaking in tongues," understood to be a heavenly language—occurred in Topeka, Kansas, in 1901, it fell to an explosive Los Angeles to take it around the world. William Seymour, an African American Holiness preacher at the Azusa Street Mission, began to preach in 1906 about the wondrous "baptism of the Holy Spirit" he had witnessed in Texas by some who had been part of the Topeka experience. Soon his racially mixed congregation began speaking in tongues, a very nontraditional form of worship that earned the ire of mainstream Protestants and Catholics in the city. The local newspaper derided the little church relentlessly, only drawing more attention to it from those who sought a bit of the supernatural in a far too mundane, industrial world. Soon the building was not large enough to hold the crowds. Some of those who had experienced the "blessing" of the Holy Spirit took the message out to others —first throughout the city by way of the trolley system, then throughout the state and country by train, and eventually around the globe by ship. The Pentecostal movement was under way.

Sweeping through both urban and rural Holiness strongholds, Pentecostalism spread into both black and white religious communities. The Church of God in Christ, strongest from the western mountains in North Carolina across to Memphis, Tennessee, followed its leader Charles Mason, himself a most prophetic figure, from Holiness to Pentecostalism. It became a well-trodden trail. The Christian and Missionary Alliance split over the issue of speaking in tongues, with many of its leaders forming the management of the Assemblies of God, now the largest white Pentecostal denomination in the country. In all, the Holiness and Pentecostal movements remained close cousins, with emphases on the deeper Christian life, holy living, separateness from mainstream Protestant culture, and a powerful belief in the indwelling Holy Spirit.

As a result of America's growing industrial power, many rural folk began to move to the city. In fact, during the 1920s the United States officially made the transition to an "urban" nation, as the majority of its citizens now lived in cities and towns rather than on farms. This trend only accelerated in the 1930s, when drought conditions drove many lower midwesterners during the Great

Depression into cities and towns on the east and west coasts. For example, tens of thousands of "Okies"—made famous by the Joads in *The Grapes of Wrath*—packed their belongings and drove to California in the hope of work. This transplantation of Okie culture in California's Central Valley is evident to this day, as the region's radio stations play country and western music alongside gospel. Those denominations once prevalent in the nation's midsection, namely, Church of Christ, Disciples of Christ, and Southern Baptist, were thus carried around the country and into mainstream Protestant- and Catholic-dominated cities.

The western United States, so vast and varied in its geographical landscape, continued to draw many sorts of religious people. Since the discovery of gold at Sutter's Mill in 1848, California had especially attracted a variety of traditions—Russian Orthodox from Canada and Alaska, Japanese Buddhists, Chinese Buddhists and Confucians, Mexican Catholics, and then all forms of Christianity from the East and Midwest. Mainstream Protestant "home missionaries" had planted churches in the nineteenth century that reaped many followers in the early twentieth century. But the region was just too large to be dominated by a single group, as Latino Catholics controlled the Southwest but could not break through the German and Norwegian Lutheran–dominated upper Plains states. And although mainstream Protestants had a powerful presence in the cities, they could not exert social control outside the neighborhoods in which they resided.

The only region in the West—in fact, one of the only regions in the country—where one could find much religious homogeneity was Utah. The Latter-day Saints created a de facto establishment of religion in the inner-mountain West that continues to this day. Peter Williams and Richard Francaviglia have each studied the "Mormon corridor" that extends from Salt Lake City southwest toward San Diego, California, finding a style that marks the area, including

1. wide streets, an amenity called for by Smith himself;
2. roadside irrigation ditches, part of Young's program to make the dessert blossom;
3. barns and granaries located in the town itself;
4. open landscape around each house, with houses located in the town rather than on outlying farmland;
5. the central-hall plan house, a carryover from the Ohio-Illinois days of origin;
6. a high percentage of solidly built brick houses, reflecting communal values of endurance and permanence;

7. the hay derrick, a simple frame device for lifting bales of hay;
8. the "Mormon fence," an unpainted picket fence made up of assorted pieces of leftover lumber;
9. unpainted farm buildings, reflecting communal values of practicality and scorn for unnecessary ornament; and
10. a Latter-day Saints chapel, in recent years usually of simple Georgian revival design, often with a small steeple topped with a needle-shaped spire "resembling an inverted tuning fork," which serves the religious and social needs of a community in which religious pluralism is virtually unknown.

Although Baptists consolidated control of the South, Catholics enjoyed a majority in the Northeast, Lutherans predominated in the upper Midwest, and Methodists were spread throughout, the nation as a whole reflected the West, where diversity reigned. By the 1950s, this hardly mattered to most Americans. Indeed, as sociologist Will Herberg argued in *Protestant, Catholic, Jew*, a best-selling sociological study of religion in America, the three major faiths had coalesced around a set of American values that formed the bedrock of national culture. This "American Way of Life" found expression in each church and synagogue, thus offering a culturally American form of Protestantism (whatever the denomination), Catholicism, and Judaism that acted as a "civil religion" around which all could rally. Regional differences notwithstanding, Americans were united in their belief in faith—faith in God and country. Even the president got in on the act. Dwight Eisenhower pitched the importance of going to religious services—whatever they may be —in public service commercials broadcast on the newest form of mass media, the television. Media could thus serve as a way to offer a message that transcended regional differences, creating a national sense of tolerance that might not exist regionally. The Cold War added significance to those calls for tolerance of national diversity, as different denominations and faiths united behind America's struggle against godless communism.

Modern America

If regional religion had undergone tremendous change before World War II, transitions only came faster and in more obvious ways in the postwar period. By the end of the century, religion in the United States proved as heterogeneous as anywhere on the planet. Indeed, several of the most religiously diverse cities in the world are located in North America. Through continued urbanization, intermarriage, and changes in federal immigration laws, the United States began the new millennium as the most religiously diverse and complex nation on earth.

Nothing during this period changed the face of religion in America as drastically as the Immigration Act of 1965. For more than a century, the federal government had allowed into the country much lower numbers of Asians and Americans from south of the border than Europeans. With increased attention to the growth of communism in Southeast Asia during the 1960s, Congress finally opened the door to Asian immigrants. By the end of the decade, most of the country had become familiar with certain contours of Asian religions through mass media—particularly through the practice of Transcendental Meditation as taught by Maharishi Mashesh Yogi on the "Tonight Show" or sung about by the Beatles. Likewise, the number of Latinos entering the United States rose considerably. At first many thousands moved to farming belts in Florida and the American Southwest as migrant workers, but in time their political power grew as second and third generations (now American citizens) entered universities and then leadership positions. Those from Latino backgrounds now provide powerful voices on national issues. But the changes affected by the new immigrants proved far more significant on local, regional levels.

Los Angeles, which was arguably the archetypal city with regard to these changes, provides a good case in point. What began the twentieth century as the whitest and most Protestant sizable city in the nation ended the century as the most ethnically and religiously diverse city in the world. Long the Xanadu of those seeking health, fame, fortune, or just a new start, Los Angeles became the crossroads of the Pacific rim when immigration laws were changed. Its geographical position on the west coast—where it serves as the north-south axis for U.S., Mexican, and South American (and sometimes Canadian) relations, as well as the east-west axis for U.S. and Asian relations—served to create an urban religious frontier like no other.

Today more than six hundred identified faith groups reside in Los Angeles. Each Saturday the *Los Angeles Times* lists a "Religion Directory" for those seeking a place of worship. It reads like an encyclopedia of religion in America, including, from A to Z, African Methodist Episcopal; Anglican; Apostolic Faith; Ascended Master Teachings—Church Universal and Triumphant; Assembly of God; Avatar Meher Baba Centers; Bahai Faith; Baptist; Buddhism and Zen Meditation; Byzantine Catholic; Roman Catholic; Christian; Christian Church (Disciples of Christ); Christian Community; Christian Non-Denominational; Church of Christ, Scientist; Church of God; Church of God in Christ; Church of Scientology; Church of Jesus Christ of Latter-day Saints (Mormon); Church of the Movement of Spiritual Inner Awareness; Churches of Christ; Congregational; Church of the Nazarene; Eastern Orthodox; Eckankar (Religion of the Light and Sound of God); Episcopal; Episcopal Traditional (1928 prayerbook); Evangelical Bible Church; Foursquare; Full Gospel; Gnostic; Islam; Jewish Traditional; Reform Synagogue; Lutheran (Missouri Synod); Lutheran (Evangelical Lutheran Church in America); Meditation; Messianic-Jewish; Metaphysical; Divine Metaphysical; New Age Bible and Philosophy Center; Pillar of Fire; Presbyterian Church of America; Presbyterian Church U.S.A.; Religious Society of Friends (Quaker) Unprogrammed Meetings; Science of Metaphysics–Religious Psychology; Science of Mind-Religious Science; Self-Realization Fellowship; Seventh-Day Adventist; Soka Gakkai International; Spiritual Psychology Classes; Spiritualists; Theosophy; Unitarian Universalist; United Church of Christ; United Methodist; Unity; and Vedanta Society. One might think that Los Angeles County—with more than half a million Jews, one hundred thousand Mormons, and about 40 percent of all American Buddhists and Muslims—is where truisms about religion in America are turned on their head. Yet a powerful traditional Christian presence continues in the city—one whose character is different from that of other places in the nation. Indeed, with nearly three hundred parishes and 3.7 million adherents, Roman Catholicism dominates the Christian scene with seven of every ten Christians in the county. Only one in four Christians is Protestant, and most of them are members of evangelical or Pentecostal denominations rather than mainline Protestant churches.

While increasing diversity marked urban areas, even America's small towns and suburbs watched their religious landscapes slowly transform. Numerous churches sponsored entire families, sometimes even extended families, who fled to the United States as political refugees toward the end of the Vietnam War. Evangelical congregations often led the way in this movement, characteristic of their desire to offer a gospel of hope. Sizable Vietnamese settlements sprang up in Michigan, Massachusetts, and Florida as thousands of refugees used Christian congregations to take their first tentative steps into American life. Likewise, many thousands of Cubans fled Castro's Communist Cuba, finding economic and spiritual help in both evangelical Protestant and Catholic congregations in southern Florida. These diasporic religious communities offer important insights into the ways migrants relate to their homeland in religious ways. For instance, in 1973 the Cuban Catholic community built in Miami a shrine to Our Lady of Charity. It has since become the sixth most popular shrine in the United States, as Cubans revisit it often to pray for the opportunity to return to their homeland, which has undergone a transformation of memory to become holy in and of itself. Throughout small southern Florida towns, Cuban Catholics continue to pray to "Our Lady of Exile" that the day of return will come soon. Meanwhile, southeastern Michigan has become home to more than a quarter million Arab Americans, mostly Muslim in faith. Early in the twentieth century, Muslims had migrated to the Detroit area to work in Henry Ford's automobile factories (his distrust for Jews led him to view Arab Muslims as a good labor source); as a result of the natural growth of this population and continued migrations, more Arabs are concentrated in that area than anywhere outside the Middle East, except Paris. Today roughly 30 percent of the population in Dearborn, Michigan, is Arab American. Such a large population has, not surprisingly, brought about some changes in the area, including halal (religiously acceptable) chicken McNuggets sold at local McDonalds.

Despite the growing diversity of faiths, a stable regional map of religion marked the late twentieth century. If one looks at the largest religious groups (those with more than a million members) in the United States in 1990, a clear picture develops: eight "national religious families" (to use the terms of scholars William Newman and Peter Halvorson) dominate the three thousand or so counties in the nation, and a second stratum of eight families exhibit regional strengths without the same national force. Table 1 shows the eight "national families" appearing in at least 50 percent of all counties in each region of the country; the other eight are strong in one or two regions but have yet to reach the point of having congregations in 50 percent of the counties in other areas.

Studying the first group of religious families, one can see that Catholics, Southern Baptists, United Methodists, Evangelical Lutherans, Presbyterians (U.S.A.), Episcopalians, Assemblies of God, and Churches of Christ have congregations in at least one-half of the counties in each of the nation's four regions. The clear leaders nationwide are the Roman Catholics, with churches in 100 percent of the counties in the Northeast, 99 percent of those in the Midwest, 91 percent of those in the Southeast, and 98 percent of those in the West, and the United Methodists, with churches in 100 percent of the counties in the Northeast, 97 percent of those in the Midwest, 100 percent of those in the Southeast, and 88 percent of those in the West. Methodists thus earn their reputation as the "official" Protestant faith in the United States despite being far outnumbered by the Southern Baptists, as the latter's strength resides primarily in the Southeast and the West. In fact, outside the Catholics and the United Methodists, the other national religious families are still in the process of growing from a regional base into other areas.

TABLE 1. Largest Religious Groups in the United States, 1990

Name	Adherents	Counties	NE %	MW %	SE %	West %
National religious families						
Catholic Church	53,108,015	2,965	100	99	91	98
Southern Baptist	18,891,633	2,513	71	60	99	91
United Methodist	11,077,728	2,966	100	97	100	88
Evangelical Lutheran	5,226,798	1,709	84	76	51	50
Presbyterian (U.S.A.)	3,553,335	2,381	82	80	77	72
Episcopal	2,427,350	2,089	98	60	67	71
Assemblies of God	2,139,826	2,546	95	82	78	59
Churches of Christ	1,677,711	2,397	76	61	55	62
Multiregional religious families						
Jewish (total population)	5,982,529	748	78	21	28	21
Latter-day Saints (Mormon)	3,540,820	1,671	80	41	49	69
Missouri Synod Lutheran	2,603,725	1,779	60	81	30	64
American Baptist	1,870,923	1,227	87	52	12	28
United Church of Christ	1,993,459	1,270	85	64	17	20
Christian/Churches of Christ	1,210,319	1,300	38	61	45	44
African Methodist Episcopal-Zion	1,142,016	448	42	4	26	4
Christian Church (Disciples)	1,037,757	1,379	27	47	42	52

The eight multiregional religious families display that same process—strength in a particular region with some presence in other areas. The Latter-day Saints are a good example. Although their membership numbers approximately that of the Presbyterian Church (U.S.A.), their strength is largely confined to the West and the Northeast. Still, given their zeal for proselytization and recent growth in the Midwest and Southeast, it is not difficult to imagine they will join the list of national religious families in coming years. Some others among the multiregional list are unlikely to do so. For example, the Jewish population is substantial but tied to particular regions, namely, the Northeast. In fact, there are Jewish synagogues in only one-quarter of the nation's counties. Without evangelistic drive or a need to migrate elsewhere, it is unlikely the Jewish presence will extend into new areas in the coming years.

Of course, such lists can conceal as much as they reveal. First of all, analysts are dependent on the numbers given, or just as bad, not given, by each organization. This method of obtaining statistics tends not to be a problem with larger denominations, but some small religious organizations will offer inflated numbers. On the other hand, some groups are either distrustful of researchers and therefore refuse to give statistics or not prone to keep such statistics in the first place. Lacking strong central authority that keeps track of membership, some important and sizable African American churches remain unrepresented on these lists. The National Baptist Convention (with an estimated 8.7 million members) and the Church of God in Christ are thus kept off lists on which they should clearly be included.

Likewise, there are culturally influential religious groups whose numbers do not grab the eye of researchers or the public. For example, even though the numbers of Hindus and Buddhists in the United States remain small compared with those of the large Christian denominations, many of their practices have entered the vernacular of American life. Often unaware of the roots of such practices, Americans will claim they earned good karma with an act of kindness, or learn to control their blood pressure through meditation, or relax driving home from work to the strains of "New Age" music. Often these traditionally Eastern practices have found their way into Christian forms of worship, as congregations will corporately "wait upon the Lord in silence" using breathing techniques usually taught by Hindu yogis.

Other forms of syncretism have been evident in recent years in the evangelical Protestant churches across the country. Although they do not hold to the practice of "speaking in tongues" like Pentecostal Protestants and charismatic Catholics, they have borrowed an informal worship style that includes repeated choruses and physical expressions of adoration, including lifted hands and closed eyes. This impulse has so affected even Southern Baptist churches —which explicitly reject speaking in tongues—that many now offer separate Sunday services, one listed as "traditional," the other "contemporary." Thus, the influence of Pentecostalism has extended outside its sphere of churches and regional strongholds to affect the worship styles of non-Pentecostal evangelicals across the country.

Alongside these mixings, borrowings, and syntheses on the national level exists a curious "hard-shell" regionalism that continues to characterize religion in America. Sociologists have found signs of cultural penetration among regions on virtually every level—but religion continues to surprise them. Recent studies conclude that those who migrate as, say, Methodists in the Midwest to the South tend not to remain what they once were. Rather, they join a Southern Baptist church and become part of the dominant culture. Is this merely a "When in Rome, do as the Romans do" phenomenon? If so, why does a region transform itself with migrations, change along with the changing population in other ways? Regional religion, unlike cuisine, clothes, and styles, seems immune from outside change. Instead, people change to conform to it when they move to a new area.

Conclusion

Religious diversity and region thus continue to interest scholars. Although we have watched regions change historically, they each now seem embedded with certain cultural symbols and practices that the dominant religion in that region exhibits particularly well. At the same time, the United Methodist Church—which no longer dominates areas as it did in the nineteenth century yet is usually the second largest group in any given county—has a powerful national presence. How can we best understand the regional and national elements of religion in America? One way to get past the conundrum is to look closely at the national denominations for regional variations within them. There is some evidence that Methodist churches in the Deep South are culturally different from those in the urban North. If that is, indeed, the case, then regionalism can trump even denominations when it comes to definition of religious traditions.

Whatever the case, and headway in understanding all the complexities of regional religion is slow but steady, we can state one thing clearly: diversity of religion characterizes the nation as a whole. Certain religious families might dominate the landscape of particular neighborhoods, cities, counties, states, or even regions, but no one faith group holds sway over the country at large. Nor do Americans want such a thing. Tolerance of diversity has given way to an understanding that in our differences lay our strength. All Americans might not universally share this opinion, but it has become the mantra for public officials who must appeal to all types of believers (and nonbelievers) for votes. What began as "denominationalism," that is, tolerance among Protestants in the early American Republic, has now grown to "pluralism," a belief that our national diversity is part of what makes the United States special. The language of Providence is often used to describe it, as many want to believe that America's God led English Puritans, Irish Catholics, Scottish Presbyterians, Japanese Buddhists, Cuban Catholics, and Saudi Muslims here, to live together and practice their faiths in peace.

Albanese, Catherine. *America: Religion and Religions*. 3rd ed. Belmont, Calif.: Wadsworth Publishing, 1999.

Boyer, Paul, and Stephen Nissenbaum. *Salem Possessed: The Social Origins of Witchcraft*. Cambridge: Harvard University Press, 1974.

Carroll, Bret E. *The Routledge Historical Atlas of Religion in America*. New York: Routledge, 2000.

Christiano, Kevin. *Religious Diversity and Social Change: American Cities, 1890–1906*. New York: Cambridge University Press, 1986.

Eck, Diana. *A New Religious America: How a "Christian Country" Has Now Become the World's Most Religiously Diverse Nation*. New York: HarperCollins, 2001.

———. *On Common Ground: World Religions in America*. New York: Columbia University Press, 1997.

Gaustad, Edwin Scott. *Historical Atlas of Religion in America*. New York: Harper and Row, 1962, 1977.

———. *A Religious History of America*. Rev. ed. San Francisco: HarperCollins, 1990.

Gaustad, Edwin Scott, and Philip L. Barlow. *New Historical Atlas of Religion in America*. New York: Oxford University Press, 2001.

Halvorson, Peter, and William Newman. *Atlas of Religious Change in America, 1952–1990*. Atlanta: Glenmary Research Group, 1994.

Hutchison, William R. *Religious Pluralism in America: The Contentious History of a Founding Idea*. New Haven: Yale University Press, 2003.

Lane, Belden. *Landscapes of the Sacred: Geography and Narrative in American Spirituality*. New York: Paulist Press, 1988.

Linenthal, Edward, and David Chidester, eds. *American Sacred Space*. Bloomington: University of Indiana Press, 1995.

Mead, Frank S. *Handbook of Denominations in the United States*. 6th ed. Nashville: Abingdon Press, 1975.

Meinig, D. W. *The Shaping of America: A Geological Perspective of 500 Years of American History*. 2 vols. New Haven: Yale University Press, 1988, 1995.

Newman, William, and Peter Halvorson. *Atlas of American Religion*. Walnut Creek, Calif.: AltaMira Press, 1999.

Porterfield, Amanda. *The Transformation of American Religion: The Story of a Late-Twentieth-Century Awakening*. New York: Oxford University Press, 2001.

Roof, W. Clark, and William McKinney. *American Mainline Religion: Its Changing Shape and Future*. New Brunswick, N.J.: Rutgers University Press, 1987.

Tweed, Thomas A. *Our Lady of the Exile: Diasporic Religion at a Cuban Catholic Shrine in Miami*. New York: Oxford University Press, 1997.

———, ed. *Retelling U.S. Religious History*. Berkeley: University of California Press, 1997.

Wentz, Richard E. *Religion in the New World: Traditions and Cultures.* New York: Fortress Press, 1990.

Williams, Peter. *America's Religions: From Their Origins to the Twenty-first Century.* Urbana: University of Illinois Press, 2001.

———. *Houses of God: Region, Religion and Architecture in the United States.* Chicago: University of Illinois Press, 1997.

Glossary

abolitionism: Antebellum American radical reform movement demanding an immediate and uncompensated end to slavery. Led by figures such as William Lloyd Garrison, abolitionism was at its height from 1831 to 1861.

African Methodist Episcopal (AME) Church: First independent black denomination in the United States, formed by Richard Allen and other black Philadelphians originally in the late 1780s. Officially incorporated as a denomination in 1816, the AME Church became one of the most influential expressions of black Christianity in the United States.

agnostic: A person who does not deny the existence of a personal god but does not think the question can be resolved by human minds. The literal meaning is "not know."

Anglican: Member of the Church of England, a hybrid faith of Protestant beliefs and Roman Catholic worship style.

Arminianism: A Protestant belief system that highlighted human free will. Developed by seventeenth-century Dutch theologian Jacobus Arminius, an ardent foe of Calvinism, the belief was popularized during the nineteenth-century revivals by preachers who taught that humans could play some positive role in their salvation.

atheism: Belief in no God; disbelief in any higher divine power.

Baptist: A religious movement, later a variety of denominations, originating in seventeenth-century England, emphasizing the necessity of baptism by total water immersion and total autonomy of each congregation. Coming to America in the seventeenth century, Baptists spread quickly in both the North and the South and grew to be one of the major evangelical traditions in the United States.

Black Muslims: Adherents of the Nation of Islam, the African American version of Islam.

black theology: Intellectual movement that saw God as identified with African Americans (and, by implication, with all poor and oppressed people). Dating from the nineteenth century and Henry McNeal Turner but blossoming in the 1960s and 1970s with such writers as James Cone, black theology served as a critique of the white supremacist assumptions of American Christianity.

Bryan, William Jennings (1860–1925): Populist orator and perennial presidential candidate, a progressive in politics later best known for his defense of biblical creationism at the 1925 Scopes trial in Tennessee, by which time he served as a caricature of fundamentalism.

Calvinism: The theological system founded by John Calvin, a major leader of Reformation thought, emphasizing the absolute sovereignty of God and human depravity. Election by God, not human action, decided one's eternal fate.

canon law: The corpus of officially established rules governing the beliefs and practices of the members of a Christian church.

Catholic: Literally meaning "universal," the term generally refers to the worldwide Roman Catholic Church, the oldest and largest form of Christianity.

Catholic Worker Movement: Radical Catholic organization based in New York City. Founded by Dorothy Day (1897–1980), the movement emphasizes liberation theology, nonviolence, justice, and radical economics based on a communal vision of sharing.

charismatic: A twentieth-century movement based on the belief that ordinary believers can receive the "gifts" of the Holy Spirit, particularly speaking in tongues. The term is sometimes used to distinguish those outside the historical or "classical" Pentecostal churches, as, for example, a "charismatic Catholic."

Chávez, César (1927–93): Son of Mexican immigrants whose Catholic mysticism and social justice consciousness propelled him to leadership of the United Farm Workers union, which advocated on behalf of the Mexican and Central American migrant farm workers who picked crops throughout California and the American West.

Christian Science: A movement founded by Mary Baker Eddy. The core ideas are found in Eddy's central work, *Science and Health with Key to Scriptures*, first published in 1875. Monistic in nature, this system of metaphysics teaches that physical matter is illusory and unreal. All that is real is Spirit, and salvation/healing lies in the realization of this truth. Disease, sin, and death are illusory and will vanish on the complete assimilation of this truth by the believer.

Church of Jesus Christ of Latter-day Saints: A church founded by Joseph Smith Jr. in 1830. Commmonly known as Mormonism, this faith began with a new set of scriptures (the Book of Mormon) meant to complete the stories in the Old and New Testaments. Members of the church were forced to move on several occasions. After Smith's murder in 1844, the majority followed Brigham Young to Utah, where the church continues to flourish.

civil religion: The interplay between sacred and secular notions of the state, placing religious significance in the nation itself and its leaders. Distinct from mere "religious nationalism," the term instead refers to a "religion of the nation" that transcends sectarian beliefs with ideas of America's divine mission as a "city upon a hill" meant to bring freedom to the rest of the world.

Congregationalism: Denomination that emerged from the original Puritans of seventeenth-century New England, emphasizing the autonomy of local churches and a mild form of Calvinist conversionist theology. Congregationalism became the de facto established church of New England in the eighteenth and early nineteenth centuries. Later it provided the basis for important liberal splinter groups, including the Unitarians and the Universalists.

conjuring, conjuration: African American folk tradition with roots in African practices that invoked the supernatural powers of items such as roots and herbs in healing, harming, and counterharming individuals. Widespread in the slave community, conjuring lived on into the twentieth century and entered the broader streams of American folk culture.

covenant: Usually referring to a kind of contract or promise between two parties, the term was employed by American Calvinists—most prominently the Puritans—to describe a theological system of agreements between humans and God. The Puritans and other types of Calvinists after them taught that people entered into a number of agreements with God related to their own devotion and God's reciprocal blessings.

Dalai Lama: Tibetan religious leader, considered the fourteenth manifestation of the Buddhist Bodhisattva of Compassion. The current Dalai Lama, Tenzin Gyatso (b. 1935), was exiled from China in 1959 and has since served as a spokesperson for repressed and exiled Tibetans and is internationally known as an ecumenical spokesperson for peace and religious freedom.

Darwinism: The scientific explanation for the origins and development of species through natural selection, proposed originally by Charles Darwin in *On the Origin of Species* (1859); Darwin's theory of evolution was challenged since its inception by creationism and other forms of religious thought that insist on divine presence and design in all forms of life on earth.

Dawes Act (1887): A policy of individual land allotments to Native Americans. By this act, Congress gave up the fiction that Indian tribes were independent powers, abolished the treaty system, and recognized that the Indians were wards of the state. The reservation lands were divided among individual Native Americans with a large portion being sold to whites.

Deism: A radical form of unitarian belief that flourished in the Age of Reason. Deism (from the Latin *deus*, god) emphasized a rational deity that created the world and then left it to run according to natural laws. By denying divine intervention in the form of miracles, Deism focused on the present world and the laws governing it. Through recognizing and employing these natural laws in human affairs, most Deists thought, stable governments and societies could be created. This religious philosophy was most associated with American Enlightenment thinkers (including Thomas Jefferson and Benjamin Franklin) of the late eighteenth century.

denomination: A voluntary religious grouping that became the predominant form of religious organization in American history. Denominations (the term literally means "names") include such groups as the Southern Baptist Convention, the Assemblies of God, and the Methodist Episcopal Church.

Disciples of Christ: Denomination founded in the early nineteenth century by Alexander Campbell and Barton Stone emphasizing the doctrine of "no creed but the Bible." It was part of the "Restorationist" movement of the era, which called for a return to the purity of the "primitive" church and the elimination of the excesses and "poperies" of modern denominations.

dispensational premillennialism: Doctrine of the end times originating in the later nineteenth century, most closely associated with conservative and fundamentalist evangelicals, emphasizing the seven periods (or "dispensations") into which God had divided the world's history and the climactic battle of Armageddon that would precede the final establishment of God's kingdom in heaven and the ascension of the saints.

Douglass, Frederick (1818–95): Escaped slave and famous orator, abolitionist, editor, and presidential adviser in the nineteenth century. Douglass's autobiography, updated through several consecutive editions, became one of the classics of American literature. Douglass was a severe and biting critic of proslavery religion and, after the Civil War, of the inadequacies of the black church.

Du Bois, W. E. B. (1868–1963): One of the greatest American intellectuals of the twentieth century, Du Bois is best known for his 1903 classic *Souls of Black Folk*, which memorably portrayed the "double consciousness" of African Americans and poignantly invoked the "sorrow songs" (spirituals) as epigraphs for chapters that explored the spiritual meaning of African American culture.

Edwards, Jonathan (1703–58): Often called America's greatest theologian, Edwards was a minister and theologian in Massachusetts who was a key figure in the First Great Awakening. Edwards's many works of theology married eighteenth-century ideas of knowledge acquired through the senses to the Calvinist and conversionist theology of the colonial Great Awakening.

Emerson, Ralph Waldo (1803–82): Renowned American writer who rejected a ministerial career in the Congregational and Unitarian churches of New England and led the transcendentalist movement of the mid-nineteenth century. Although often seen (and oversimplified) as the prophet of "self-reliance," Emerson was a complex and profound thinker whose works formed a central part of what literary historians refer to as the "American Renaissance."

Enlightenment: An international movement that began in Europe and then took root in the New World. It was a cluster of ideas and emphases that dominated eighteenth-century intellectual life, beginning with the scientific and philosophical issues of the Renaissance and broadening the range of concern, giving it a freer, more secular tone. The core of Enlightenment thought was the question: How do we know things to be true? The leading thinkers argued that human reason, combined with materials obtained through empirical observation, was the path to reliable knowledge.

establishment: A system of public financing for religion that characterized colonial America, modeled on the national church system of Europe. A religious tax was levied on citizens for the support of the official religion of the colony—for example, the local Congregational Church in Massachusetts or the Church of England in Virginia. Most states disestablished religion at the time of the American Revolution (Massachusetts and Connecticut were the exceptions), and the First Amendment to the federal Constitution banned the national government from establishing a religion for the American people.

evangelicalism: A religious movement reflecting the surge of spiritual life after the Great Awakening. The movement has been interpreted as a revolt against rationalism and the notion that the Christian life involved only observing the outward formalities of religion. Emphasizing religious experience, particularly one's conversion or "new birth," evangelicalism came to dominate Protestant culture in the nineteenth century. In the twentieth century the traditional evangelical churches disagreed over issues presented by modernity, with some going the route of fundamentalism. By midcentury some of these conservatives revived their previous social concerns and increased their interaction with culture, trumpeting the "New Evangelicalism" that affected American society and politics over the following decades.

feminist theology: Originating in the nineteenth century (especially with Elizabeth Cady Stanton's *Woman's Bible*), feminist theology reached its apex in the later twentieth century as female religious thinkers began entering and teaching in seminaries. Recasting religious thought to account for the historical sexism of many religious traditions, feminist theology incorporated women's equality into sacred texts, hymns, sermons, and theological treatises.

Finney, Charles (1792–1875): The "father of modern revivalism" was born in Connecticut and raised in New York. Trained as a lawyer, he began a highly successful career as an evangelist after his conversion to Protestant evangelicalism in 1821. He refused formal theological training but still managed to be licensed by the local presbytery. Finney was known for his legal style of preaching, literally "arguing" people into a decision to convert. A strong advocate of social reform, he trained a generation of like-minded college students while president of Oberlin College in Ohio.

First Amendment: Adopted as part of the Bill of Rights in 1791, the First Amendment to the U.S. Constitution prohibits the federal government from establishing a religion or denying the free exercise of religion. In the 1940s this amendment was extended by the U.S. Supreme Court to state and local governments via the Fourteenth Amendment.

Fourteenth Amendment: U.S. constitutional amendment added in 1868, during Reconstruction, guaranteeing the protection of due process of law to all U.S. citizens. This amendment allowed the Supreme Court during the twentieth century to apply other individual rights and government restrictions once reserved for the federal level to all levels of government, including the individual right to free exercise of religion and the restrictions against government-sponsored religious practices.

Freemasonry: Teachings and rituals of a secret society founded on a complex mixture of Renaissance occultism, Enlightenment rationalism, and eventually a claim to wisdom of the stonemasons who had built Solomon's temple. It served as a means to create bonds among men of professional classes. Many evangelicals decried its secret practices in the early to mid-nineteenth century, even founding denominations expressly committed to ending Freemasonry.

free thought: A movement largely tied to Deism in the late eighteenth and early nineteenth centuries that rejected traditional institutional Christianity for a religion based on Enlightenment reason. Thomas Paine and Ethan Allen published two of the more famous free thought documents, arguing against the illogical claims of Christianity and for a religion founded on empiricism and reason.

fundamentalism: Militantly antimodernist conservative Protestant evangelical thought, arising in the early twentieth century with the publication of *The Fundamentals* from 1910 to 1915, emphasizing a strict literalist interpretation of the Bible and a rejection of many forms of "modern" thought, especially Darwinism.

Garvey, Marcus (1887–1940): A mass orator in Harlem in the 1920s who advocated black separatism and was the leader of the African Orthodox Church. A Jamaican by birth, Garvey was an early advocate for some of the themes that later would emerge in black theology.

Ghost Dance: A pan–Native American movement that emerged during the late nineteenth century among the Paviotsos of Nevada and California. The moving spirit was the prophet Wodziwub, who had a vision revealing white influences on his people. Wodziwub's vision showed the followers of the Ghost Dance being resurrected after the earth opened up and swallowed all of humanity and the restoration of the departed ancestors of the Native Americans.

Goddess religion: A late-twentieth-century movement that claims to recover beliefs and practices of ancient times, before the advent of patriarchal religions. The publications and rites of this movement, which is often tied to "neo-pagan" practices, emphasize feminine myths and symbols found in pre-Christian Europe and Native American, Hindu, and Mesoamerican traditions.

Great Awakening: A massive revival that occurred along the entire English-speaking Atlantic seaboard in the late 1730s and 1740s. Emphasizing the personal, intense religious experience of emotional conversion as playing a central role in the process of salvation, the revival helped to create the American evangelical tradition. Leading proponents included Jonathan Edwards, George Whitefield, and Gilbert Tennent.

harmonial religions: Those forms of belief and personal practice in which spiritual, physical, and sometimes even economic health are understood to flow from a person's relationship to the cosmos. These traditions frequently have unusual features, such as charismatic founders, complicated institutional structures, secret doctrines, or elaborate rituals. Harmonial religions cut across traditional lines of religious division by emphasizing different patterns of belief and practice that tend to be highly individualistic.

heresy: A belief or doctrine that varies from established religious belief within a tradition. The term is usually employed as the antonym for orthodoxy.

higher criticism: A scholarly, critical analysis of biblical texts in order to learn their origins and the intention of the authors. This pursuit treats scripture as any other historical source—to be read as a document of its time and region. Beginning in the nineteenth century, it led to a division among Christians as they argued whether its academic approach to what had been understood as an inspired document was appropriate. These divisions eventuated in the fundamentalist movement, a reaction to attempts to read the Bible as a human rather than divine text.

Holiness tradition: Body of theological thought and practice originating from Methodism and popularized in America by Phoebe Palmer, a New York Methodist, in the mid-nineteenth century and later by the Holiness and Pentecostal denominations of the twentieth century. Holiness traditions emphasize the purification of the soul, a quest for sanctification that defines the Christian believer's pilgrimage following conversion.

Jehovah's Witnesses: Founded by Charles Taze Russell in 1872, an enduring movement in the millennialist tradition. It was based on the belief that Jesus had inaugurated a "Millennial Dawn" with his return in the "upper air" in 1874 and an expectation of the millennial consummation of the worldly order in 1914. Jehovah's Witnesses proclaimed that Satan's three great allies were false teachings in the "churches," tyrannies of human government, and the oppressions of business. They are well known for their door-to-door evangelism and their publication *The Watchtower*.

Judaism: The ancient faith of the Jewish people, practiced in the United States through three separate "denominations"—Reform, Orthodox, and Conservative. Reform Judaism was led initially by Isaac Mayer Wise. Deeply influenced by the work of Moses Mendelssohn and the upwardly mobile status of Jews in Germany, nineteenth-century Reform Jews in America emphasized contemporary decorum in worship as opposed to conducting services in Hebrew. Reform Judaism used models found in contemporary Protestant practice; families were seated together, and organs and choirs were utilized. It also discontinued the wearing of the yarmulke and prayer shawl. The Reform Jews are defined as a progressive religion and not inextricably bound by the ancient biblical ideas. The Orthodox movement was dedicated to a traditional emphasis on the Torah and Talmud. Orthodox Jews are generally united by the precept that Jewish law remains binding on Jews. Conservative Judaism provides a middle ground between the Orthodox and Reform sections. A major key to the character of Conservative Judaism is that it views Jewish life holistically.

King, Martin Luther, Jr. (1929–68): African American civil rights leader and Baptist minister. Leader of the Montgomery bus boycott of the mid-1950s and subsequently the organizer of the Southern Christian Leadership Conference, King won the Nobel Peace Prize in the 1960s for his efforts in the black civil rights movement.

Ku Klux Klan: The first Ku Klux Klan was a sort of paramilitary wing of white Democrats in the Reconstruction-era South that sought a restoration of political power and white supremacy. The second Klan reached its height in the 1920s, when millions of white Protestants joined a group avowedly in defense of "100% Americanism" and focused on the dangers posed by immigrants, Catholics, and Jews. The Klan was revived a third time during the civil rights movement in the 1960s, again in defense of white supremacy in the South against black struggles for civil rights.

liberal Protestantism: An impulse in Protestantism beginning in the mid-nineteenth century and taking deep root by the turn of the twentieth century that highlighted themes of a benevolent God (as opposed to a God of judgment), a humanity open to growth through religious nurture (rather than innate sinfulness and the need for conversion), and an emphasis on the ethical components of religion (rather than the metaphysical). Embracing the progressivism inherent in much of modernity, liberal Protestants touted the possibilities for human improvement through institutional and social reform, culminating in the "social gospel" that characterized this brand of Protestantism early in the twentieth century.

liberation theology: Body of thought that emphasizes God's "preferential option" for the poor and neglected of the Third World and of America. It is often associated with Latin American and African theologians of the twentieth century who sought to resist colonialism, economic exploitation, and oppression.

Lutheran: A denomination that emerged first in Germany from the work of Martin Luther in the early Protestant Reformation and later spread worldwide. It is a highly structured denomination with worship rituals that are closer to Catholicism than many other Protestant groups. In America, the Lutheran Church is strongest in the Midwest and other areas settled by German immigrants.

Malcolm X (1925–65): Born Malcolm Little, Malcolm X converted to a version of Black Islam while in prison after a youth of petty crime. In the 1960s Malcolm became internationally known as a fiery speaker, critic of the integrationist thrust of the civil rights movement, and proselytizer for the Honorable Elijah Muhammad and Islam as the true religion of the black man. Shortly before his assassination in 1965, Malcolm visited the Middle East and converted to a more orthodox brand of Islam, alienating him from his many of his allies in the Black Muslim movement.

Methodist: A denomination founded by John and Charles Wesley in the 1740s as a reform movement within the Anglican Church. Methodists later went on to become the dominant American denomination of the nineteenth century because of their emphasis on free will and divine grace and their successful system of itinerant preachers combined with a close church organization overseen by bishops and an elaborate structural hierarchy.

millennium: Literally "a thousand years"; metaphorically, the final end time, usually seen by Christians as the time of the final establishment of God's Kingdom and the end of earthly time. See also "Dispensational Premillennialism" and "Postmillennialism."

Moody, Dwight (1837–99): Famous Chicago-based mass evangelist of the later nineteenth century and founder of the Moody Bible Institute in Chicago. Moody created many of the techniques and forms of what we now consider mass Protestant evangelism, along with a body of music composed and led by his musical director, Ira Bliss, that came to be called "gospel music."

muscular Christianity: A response to Victorian models of religiosity that, some men believed, stripped Christianity of its manly elements. Such individuals as revivalist Billy Sunday and such institutions as the YMCA sought to redefine the sex roles of the faithful by emphasizing the masculine aspects of spiritual discipline and fighting sin.

National Council of Churches (NCC): A transdenominational Protestant agency that addresses social concerns. Begun in 1950, the NCC succeeded the Federal Council of Churches (begun in 1908) as the leading Protestant voice in the cultural arena for the middle third of the twentieth century. Its members include the mainline Protestant denominations, the Eastern Orthodox churches, most of the African American Baptist and Methodist denominations, and a number of smaller denominations. Throughout the 1950s and 1960s, it advised the state and federal governments on religious matters.

Nation of Islam: The official organization of Black Muslims, begun in America by Noble Drew Ali and given prominence by Elijah Muhammad and his protégé, Malcolm X, in the 1960s. The Nation of Islam preaches black self-determination and opposition to white Christianity.

natural theology: A term used in the eighteenth and nineteenth centuries to specify the knowledge of God that comes through nature rather than through scripture or revelation. Most Christians during that period believed that God is revealed both through nature and scripture, the latter being a more precise revelation that taught the way of salvation. Natural theology was especially popular among Deists, who claimed that since nature taught the being and attributes of God (including God's benevolence and power), no further revelation was necessary.

neo-paganism: Contemporary expression of what its believers see as ancient traditions and rituals that pay homage to the natural and feminine forces (including the Goddess, hence the term "Goddess religion") governing earth and spiritual life, those forces that were worshiped in the ancient pagan traditions. Neo-paganism is sometimes associated with witchcraft or with "New Age" religions.

New Age: A movement, more than a formal religion, that tends to have no agreed-on holy text, central organization, or membership, focusing more on private practices in seeking spiritual meaning. Usually these practices incorporate a number of nontraditional means, including channeling, astrology, healing crystals, tarot cards and palmistry, meditation, near-death experiences, reincarnation, ecological mysticism, radical feminism, acupuncture, yoga, UFO cults, and so on.

New Lights: Revivalist wing of the Congregational Church during the Great Awakening of the mid-eighteenth century.

Niebuhr, Reinhold (1892–1971): Considered one of America's greatest theologians of the twentieth century, Niebuhr was a Lutheran parish minister from Detroit and later a professor at Union Theological Seminary in New York. He articulated a body of theology emphasizing the reality of human sin and evil and the necessity of state power to restrain that evil, part of what is often called neo-orthodox theology. Niebuhr's thought was a response to and critique of the more positive social gospel theology of the earlier twentieth century.

parachurch organization: An institution outside traditional denominational structures that focuses on a particular mission under the larger umbrella of Christian service, for example, social reform or foreign missions.

Parham, Charles (1873–1929): A key figure in the development of Pentecostalism. Parham's teaching at a Bible school in Topeka, Kansas, in the early twentieth century became one of the roots of the doctrine of speaking in tongues as evidence of the movement of the Holy Spirit in the soul.

parochial schools: Private schools formed by Catholics in response to anti-Catholic prejudice in public schools.

Penn, William (1644–1718): An English Quaker who prevailed on King Charles II to give him a large land grant to settle debts with his family. This colony was called Pennsylvania—"Penn's woods." Penn and his followers did not restrict this land to Quakers but wanted it open to all.

Pentecostalism: Twentieth-century theological and denominational movement emphasizing the "third work" of the Holy Spirit, evidenced by speaking in tongues, as the final culmination of the Christian journey. It is currently a huge worldwide movement incorporating many varieties of charismatic Christians who embrace bodily expressions of the Holy Spirit.

postmillennialism: The belief that the thousand-year kingdom described in the Book of Revelation would unfold gradually and be climaxed at the end of the millennium by the Second Coming of Jesus.

premillennialism: The belief that the thousand-year kingdom described in the Book of Revelation would occur only after the Second Coming of Jesus.

Presbyterian: Historical "mainstream" denomination that took root in America in the eighteenth century and became one of the major evangelical groups in American history. Usually associated with orthodox Calvinist theology, this denomination places a strong emphasis on the Protestant work ethic and educational attainment and has a form of church government run by local presbyters and regional synods.

Protestant: General name given to Christian groups that emerged from Martin Luther's "protest" against the Catholic Church in the early sixteenth century. Most Protestants emphasize the creed of the "priesthood of the believer" and direct access of the believer to God, without the requirement of the intervention of priests or saints.

Protestant ethic: Term coined by the sociologist Max Weber to describe the historical propensity in Protestant countries for hard work and the accumulation of wealth, all done for the greater glory of God; later secularized into the term "work ethic."

Puritans: Originally a movement of devout English men and women who sought to "purify" the Anglican Church, to excise its remaining vestiges of Catholicism; later the dominant group of English believers who settled New England in the seventeenth century and founded many of the key institutions of the colonial era in the North.

Quakers: Radical religious movement originating in seventeenth- and eighteenth-century England that emphasized a rejection of all forms of authority (including ministers and organized churches) in favor of lay-led spirituality. This spirituality taught the value of silence in listening for the "inner light" that would bring one to spiritual truth. In America, the Quakers under William Penn founded the colony of Pennsylvania.

Reformation: Sixteenth-century challenge to the authority of the Roman Catholic Church. Also called the Protestant Reformation, it was led initially by Martin Luther of Germany, who claimed that (1) the Bible is the sole authority for the believer, (2) one is saved by grace and not by good works, and (3) every believer is a priest before God and need not go through the church for forgiveness. The movement swept through northern Europe and effectively divided Western Christianity into Protestant and Catholic Christians.

Reformed: A term used to refer to the theological system and the membership of a variety of denominational traditions from the Calvinist branch of Protestantism.

republicanism: An influential political ideology that reached its height in America in the late eighteenth century, emphasizing the importance of virtuous leaders and a sense of community in building a stable society. Its rhetoric was continued through much of the nineteenth century, but the assumptions that lay behind the debates between republicanism and classical liberalism were altered by the development of a more democratic society and market economy in the years that followed.

revivalism: Largely a North American Protestant phenomenon characterized by mass evangelistic activities intended to produce religious conversion in the audience.

Sabbatarian: One who observes Saturday as the Sabbath Day. Among the Sabbatarians are Jews and a number of small Protestant groups such as the Seventh-Day Adventists.

sanctification: Nineteenth-century doctrinal development originating in Methodism and emphasizing the dwelling of the Holy Spirit within an individual believer's soul, resulting in the complete cleansing of all sin and a higher state of spiritual life.

scientific naturalism: The belief that everything that exists can be explained in principle by science.

Scopes trial: A 1925 media event in which perennial presidential contender and Protestant spokesperson William Jennings Bryan defended a Tennessee law prohibiting the teaching of evolution and nationally known lawyer Clarence Darrow defended the schoolteacher (John T. Scopes) who had deliberately violated the law as a test case. Although Bryan's side won the case, Darrow's cross-examination compelled Bryan to admit inconsistencies and problems in the biblical account of creation, and it made fundamentalism an object of national ridicule.

Scottish commonsense philosophy: A school of thought that emerged from the Scottish Enlightenment of the mid-eighteenth century and took as its starting point the argument that all humans possess an innate sense ("common sense") that complements the physical senses and can help to acquire knowledge and make judgments. It ran contrary to the skeptical arguments of other philosophies by democratically advocating for a "common" sense shared by all people that uses inductive rather than deductive reasoning and that helps to establish morality common to all people.

Shakers: One of the longest-lived utopian communal societies in American history. Officially called the United Society of Believers in Christ's Second Appearance, they came into being through the life and work of "Mother" Ann Lee, who they believed was the Second Coming of Christ. Among other beliefs, they taught in their "realized eschatology" that since they now lived in the millennium, there was no need for marriage and sex. Shakers became known for craftsmanship and the quality of their work. They combined the Protestant work ethic and "the plain style" of the Puritans with the celibate life of medieval monasticism.

shaman: A Native American religious specialist who functions as, among other things, a healer of the sick. Shamans, who are considered to hold the knowledge of the tradition, also have the ability to engage in trance voyages in the supernatural realm.

Smith, Joseph (1805–44): New York farmer and religious seeker who claimed to have discovered some tablets in the late 1820s that, when translated, became the Book of Mormon. He was the leader of the new sect the Church of Jesus Christ of Latter-day Saints until his execution by anti-Mormon vigilantes in 1844.

social gospel: Theological and social movement dating from the late nineteenth and early twentieth centuries emphasizing the role of individual believers and churches in reforming and perfecting this world in preparation for the final coming of God's Kingdom. The social gospel was a key part of the progressive movement from the 1890s to the 1920s and a political avenue of expression for many liberal religious thinkers and activists.

Southern Baptist Convention: Formed in 1845 as a southern branch of Baptists in America, the Southern Baptist Convention became, in the twentieth century, the largest Protestant denomination in the United States, numbering more than 18 million members at its height. It is generally seen as the major conservative evangelical denomination of the South, but with a strong nationwide presence.

speaking in tongues: Speaking in an unknown language while in a state of spiritual rapture or ecstasy. Speaking in tongues has a long history in Christianity, dating from the Book of Acts, when Jesus' desciples awaited his return and received the gift of the Holy Spirit, then preached to all nations in their own tongues. In American religious history, speaking in tongues is most often associated with Pentecostalism (see earlier entry), which took the practice as one of its defining doctrines.

Spiritualism: A movement that arose in the nineteenth century that claimed it is possible to have contact with the dead through a variety of means, including séances and "spirit boxes." Its chief publicist was Andrew Jackson Davis, whose books helped popularize the movement in Victorian America.

Sunday, Billy (1863–1935): American evangelist who reached his greatest audience around the time of World War I. A former professional baseball player, Sunday became a full-time itinerant preacher, known as "the baseball evangelist," and was a powerful advocate for Prohibition.

televangelism: A term that arose in the late twentieth century to describe the ubiquitous presence of television ministries. Most of the ministers are evangelical in leanings and help to popularize that style of ministry through their programs.

Theosophy: Part of the "New Thought" traditions of the late nineteenth century, generally considered to be among the most important influences of the contemporary New Age movement. Originating from the writings of Russian immigrant Helena Blavatsky and her close ally and associate Henry Steel Olcott, Theosophy emphasizes the higher wisdom of the ancients, who exist in an ethereal realm, and the means humans may use to access that ancient wisdom.

transcendentalism: A literary, philosophical, and religious movement that emerged in the 1830s, centered in Massachusetts but with far-reaching influences, with emphasis on the continuity between the divine, the human, and the natural. Its major proponents were Ralph Waldo Emerson, Henry David Thoreau, and Walt Whitman.

Trinity: Also called the Holy Trinity, the traditional Christian concept that God exists as three persons, as established by the creedal statements of the early church and the first seven ecumenical councils.

Turner, Henry McNeal (1834–1915): Free-born African American minister originally from South Carolina. A Methodist minister, he was later a bishop in the African Methodist Episcopal Church. After a political career that included serving in the Georgia legislature during Reconstruction, Turner later became known as a progenitor of black theology and an advocate for emigration to Africa as the only respite from a hopelessly racist America.

Unitarianism: A Christian movement that denies the Trinitarian nature of God, arguing instead that God exists only as one person. This idea emerged first in Transylvania and then in England in the seventeenth century and traces its religious roots to Reformation-era "free spirits" such as Servetus and Socinus. The movement gained ground in New England Congregational churches in the late eighteenth and early nineteenth centuries.

Williams, Roger (1604–83/84): Early Puritan dissenter exiled from Massachusetts for rejecting the authority of the Congregational Church. Williams was the founder of Rhode Island, a theorist of religious liberty (often claimed as the founder of the Baptist Church in America), and a translator of Native American languages.

utopian communities: Idealistic communities in the early 1800s that lacked sectarian aspirations or were antireligious. One of the most famous was New Harmony, founded by Robert Owen.

Vatican II: The most important modern church council, which met from 1963 to 1965. Called by Pope John XXIII, it addressed more issues than had been addressed since the Council of Trent in the effort of the Roman Catholic Church to come to terms with the non-Catholic world, the non-Christian world, and the modern world. The council redefined the church's character through a much greater emphasis on the role of the laity and an updating of the church's rituals. Some saw this loosening of the Catholic Church's traditions as a result of the growing influence of its American membership.

Virginia Statute for Religious Freedom: Written by Thomas Jefferson in 1779 after the disestablishment of the Church of England in Virginia, the statute was not fully adopted by the state until 1786. The document argues for the freedom of conscience in religious matters and helped to influence the drafting of the religion clauses of the First Amendment.

wall of separation: A phrase in a letter by Thomas Jefferson to the Baptists of Danbury, Connecticut, describing his understanding of the role the First Amendment plays in the new federal government in regard to religion. This argument for separate spheres, secular government and religion without government influence, as well as Jefferson's phrase, was picked up by the U.S. Supreme Court in the mid-twentieth century.

Wesley, Charles (1707–88): English Methodist preacher and hymn writer. His songs defined first Methodism and later mainline Protestantism throughout the nineteenth and much of the twentieth centuries.

Wesley, John (1703–91): English evangelical preacher in the Church of England and founder of Methodism. Wesley's organization greatly influenced religion in America through its theology and evangelical style.

Whitefield, George (1714–70): The "Grand Itinerant" of the First Great Awakening, Whitefield was a young Anglican preacher who turned the revivals into a transatlantic event. Known for his oratory, he became the spokesperson for the evangelical movement first in his well-attended meetings and later in his published journals and sermons.

Winthrop, John (1588–1649): Leader of an early English Puritan migration to New England in the early 1630s, best known for his speech describing the Puritan experiment in the New World as establishing a "city set upon a hill," a shining light for all the world to see.

Woman's Christian Temperance Union (WCTU): Founded in 1874, a reform organization dedicated to the abolition of alcohol. Headed by Frances Willard in the late nineteenth century, the WCTU became the single largest women's organization in American history up to that time and one of the most powerful reform organizations of the progressive era.

World's Parliament of Religions: Worldwide meeting of religious leaders held at the Chicago's World Fair in 1893, often considered one of the first major forums for representatives of Eastern religions, especially Hinduism and Buddhism, to make their case before a broad American public.

Young, Brigham (1801–77): An early follower of Joseph Smith in the Latter-day Saints movement. After Smith's death he was appointed the successor and presided over the movement of the Mormons to Utah and their subsequent growth.

Young Men's Christian Association (YMCA) and Young Women's Christian Association (YWCA): Founded in mid-nineteenth-century England, the YMCA and YWCA soon spread worldwide and were part of social gospel and reform movements designed to address the needs of urbanizing and industrializing countries and the perceived disorder and irreligion that might afflict a generation of young people moving from farms to cities. In the early twentieth century, leaders of the YMCA and YWCA became some of the most important advocates for the social gospel movement.

Zen Buddhism: School of Buddhism popularized by Shunryu Suzuki and the West Coast "Beat" poets of the 1950s, most often associated with the use of paradoxical "koans" (such as "what is the sound of one hand clapping") to communicate ineffable spiritual truths.

Zionism: Late-nineteenth-century movement in Jewish thought led by Theodor Herzl that emphasized a revitalization of the Jewish faith. Eventually it became attached to support for the state of Israel, established in 1948, as the spiritual and temporal home for Jews worldwide.

Notes on the Contributors

Yvonne Chireau is associate professor of religious studies at Swarthmore College.

Amy DeRogatis is associate professor of religious studies at Michigan State University.

William Durbin is associate professor of ecclesiastical history at Washington Theological Union.

Tracy Fessenden is associate professor of religious studies at Arizona State University.

James German is associate professor and chair of the Department of History at the State University of New York, Potsdam.

Philip Goff is director of the Center for the Study of Religion and American Culture and associate professor of religious studies and American studies at Indiana University–Purdue University Indianapolis.

Paul Harvey is professor of history at the University of Colorado, Colorado Springs.

Sue Marasco is lecturer in history at Vanderbilt University.

Winnifred Fallers Sullivan is dean of students and associate professor of religion at the University of Chicago Divinity School.

Roberto Treviño is associate professor of history at the University of Texas, Austin.

David Weaver-Zercher is associate professor of American religious history at Messiah College.

Index

Abolitionism, 51–52, 142, 144, 146, 278, 346

Abortion, 220, 255

Adams, Henry, 279–80

Adams, John, 208, 279, 327

Addams, Jane, 283–84

Adler, Mortimer J., 319

Adrian IV (pope), 167–68

African Americans, 165, 199, 208, 270–71, 288, 297; cosmology and, 113–14, 117, 118–19, 127; proselytization and, 40, 53–54, 63–65; race and, 129–35, 138–42, 144, 146, 148–49, 151–55, 159–60, 189; regionalism and, 336–37, 345–46, 349–50, 357; supernaturalism and, 75, 80–81, 84–85, 91, 96; theology and, 15, 17, 29–30, 33, 34, 148–49, 158, 159, 161–62, 345. *See also* Slavery

African Methodist Episcopal (AME) Church, 54, 118, 141, 152, 350, 356

African Methodist Episcopal-Zion Church, 350, 356

African Orthodox Church, 30, 152

African religions, 42, 65, 132, 133, 139, 147, 151, 159, 271, 298, 330, 336; cosmology and, 104–5, 108–9, 111, 114; supernaturalism and, 75, 80–81, 84,

91, 96; theology and, 8–9, 14–15, 17, 134;

Agnosticism, 232, 293, 310–11, 313

Ahlstrom, Sydney, 72

Albanese, Catherine, 330

Alchemy, 76–77, 79

Algonquians, 205

Ali, Muhammad, 65, 153

Ali, Noble Drew, 152–53

Alpert, Richard, 91, 92

American Academy of Arts and Sciences, 304, 323

American Bible Society, 341

American Board of Commissioners for Foreign Missions, 59, 143–44

American Colonization Society, 144

American Home Missions Society, 341

American Indian Movement, 151, 157

American Philosophical Society, 302–3

American Protective Association, 185, 246

American Revolution, 14, 16, 47, 140, 175, 338–39

American Scientific Affiliation, 320–21, 322

American Sunday School Union, 341

American Tract Society, 51, 341

Amish, 174, 176

Anabaptists, 15, 272

Ancestor religions, 8, 105, 114, 134
Anglicans (Episcopalians), 11, 12, 16, 41–
    42, 46, 52, 66, 75, 136, 141, 142, 144,
    152, 172, 207, 297, 314; economy and,
    270, 272, 276; ethnicity and, 167, 172,
    175; regionalism and, 327, 333, 335,
    337, 338–39, 355, 356; state and, 233,
    235–36, 238–40; theology and, 11
Apess, William, 142
Aquarian Age, 94, 95
Aquinas, Thomas, 29
Arcane School, 89
Arminianism, 18–19
Arnold, Kenneth, 93
Ascended Master Teachings, 89, 93–94
Assemblies of God, 59, 350, 353, 355, 356
Astrology, 76, 94, 97
Atheism, 22–23, 232, 253, 287, 293
Austin, Stephen F., 179–80

Backus, Isaac, 241
Bacon, Francis, 294, 300–301, 306, 318
Ball, Charles, 114
Ballard, Guy, 89
Baltimore, Lord (Cecil Calvert), 236, 270,
    336
Baptism, 9, 27, 107, 108, 138–39
Baptists, 33, 81, 176, 190, 209, 276, 288;
    proselytization and, 49, 52, 53, 60–62,
    64; race and, 53, 139–40, 141, 144,
    148–49, 155, 350; regionalism and,
    327, 333, 337, 339–42, 346, 350–52,
    355–57; state and, 236, 240–41
Barton, Bruce, 39, 285
Bear Tribe Medicine Society, 35
Beat movement, 219
Beecher, Charles, 147
Beecher, Henry Ward, 54
Beecher, Lyman, 144, 177
Bellamy, Edward, 283
Berdaches, 203. See also Two-Spirits
Berkovits, Eliezer, 32
Black, Hugo, 253
Black Legend, 172–73, 180
Black Muslims. See Nation of Islam
Black theology, 54, 288
Blackwell, Antoinette Brown, 216

Blanch, Harriet Stanton, 55
Blavatsky, Helena Petrovna, 86–87, 216
Bly, Robert, 222
Booth, Maud, 216
Boudinot, Elias, 144
Boyle, Robert, 300–301
Branch Davidians, 256
Brinsley, John, 206
Brownson, Orestes, 19
Bryan, William Jennings, 250–51, 282,
    316, 324
Buddhism, 26, 35, 41, 66–68, 86, 88, 92,
    156, 159, 199, 219, 257, 281, 289; eth-
    nicity and, 166, 181, 188–89, 191–92,
    194; regionalism and, 329, 351, 353,
    354, 357–58
Burhoe, Ralph, 323–24
Burkett, Larry, 126
Bush, George W., 257

Calvert, Cecil. See Baltimore, Lord
Calvin, John, 11, 233, 262–63, 333
Calvinism, 45, 49, 169, 205, 238, 333, 337;
    economy and, 269–72, 275–76, 281,
    287; science and, 302–3, 306–7, 310,
    317; theology and, 11, 12, 14, 18–19,
    21, 35, 45. See also Presbyterianism;
    Puritans
Campbell, Alexander, 49
Camp meetings, 48–49, 209–10
Carnegie, Andrew, 279, 280, 281
Carroll, John, 236
Carson, Rachel, 124, 125
Cartwright, Peter, 49, 210
Castenada, Carlos, 95–96
Castro, Fidel, 191, 354
Cather, Willa, 120–21
Catholicism. See Roman Catholicism
Catholic Worker movement, 29, 286–87,
    291
Catlin, George, 104
Celibacy, 198, 202, 209, 213, 223–24, 245
Century sermons, 304–5
Chambers, Whitaker, 286–87
Channeling, 94–95
Chapman, Johnny (Johnny Appleseed),
    78

Charismatics. *See* Pentecostalism

Chauncy, Charles, 13–14, 46

Chávez, César, 189–90

Cheney, F. S., 152

Cherokees, 113, 133, 134, 144

Chicano movement, 189–90

Chopra, Deepak, 66

Christian and Missionary Alliance, 348, 350

Christian Identity movement, 131

Christian realism, 285–86

Christian Right, 289–90

Christian Science, 25–26, 86, 87, 123, 216, 308

Church of Christ. *See* Disciples of Christ

Church of Christ, Scientist. *See* Christian Science

Church of England. *See* Anglicans

Church of God in Christ, 91, 350, 353–54, 357

Church of Jesus Christ of Latter-day Saints. *See* Mormonism

Church of the Nazarene, 348

Civil rights movement, 33, 63–65, 155–56, 255, 288

Civil theology, 6, 54

Civil War, 21, 147, 243–44, 245, 279, 345

Cold War, 93, 124, 352, 353

Columbus, Christopher, 10, 26, 136, 138, 203, 208, 263, 294–95

Commonsense realism, 16–17, 306

Communalism, 110, 116, 213–14, 269, 270

"Community of Christ," 343

Condomblé, 159

Cone, James, 33, 158, 288

Confucianism, 165, 181, 192, 351

Congregationalism, 49, 118, 173, 216, 263, 277, 306–7; race and, 138, 142, 144, 148; regionalism and, 333, 338–39, 344

Conjuring, 71, 72, 84–85, 90–91, 127, 267

Conscientious objection, 254–55

Conservative Judaism, 24, 57, 63, 182–83, 349

Conwell, Russell, 54

Copernicus, Nicolaus, 106, 300

Cotton, John, 137, 206, 233, 235

Coughlin, Charles, 61, 286

Council on Biblical Manhood and Womanhood, 223

Counterculture, 67, 91–93, 95, 289

Counter-Reformation, 42, 237

Covenant theology, 11–12, 45

Cox, Harvey, 32–33

Creationism, 308, 313, 320–22, 324

Creation myths, 7–8, 102, 203, 204

Creation Research Society, 321

Creation science, 321–22, 324

Cridge, Annie Denton, 115

Crowdy, William S., 151

Cuban Catholics, 191, 354–55

Dalai Lama, 67

Daly, Mary, 33–34, 220–21

Darrow, Clarence, 250, 316, 317

Darwin, Charles, 3, 23, 25, 310

Darwinism, 250–51, 280, 312–13, 314, 316, 321, 322, 324

Davis, Andrew Jackson, 83

Dawes Act (1887), 120, 150, 248

Day, Dorothy, 29, 286

Death of God movement, 33

Deism, 16, 47, 238–39, 241, 302; cosmology and, 112, 117, 123, 127

Deloria, Vine, Jr., 158

Denominationalism, 49, 328, 338, 340–42, 346, 358

Descartes, René, 106, 128, 300

Dewey, John, 315, 318–19, 324

Disciples of Christ, 49, 209–10, 342, 351, 355, 356

Disestablishment, 40, 227, 229, 232–36, 239–42, 247, 249, 253

Dispensational premillennialism, 28

Divination, 72, 82

Divine, Father, 153

Douglass, Frederick, 51, 84, 146, 278

Drugs, 91–92, 96, 154–55, 227

Du Bois, W. E. B., 145–46, 148, 151, 153, 154, 156

Dunkers (German Baptists), 176

Dutch Reformed Church, 144, 171, 236, 271–72, 337

Dwight, Timothy, 307, 324

Eastern Orthodoxy, 167, 184, 189, 281, 351

Eastern religions, 40, 66–67, 86, 88, 92, 219, 353

Eddy, Mary Baker, 25–26, 86, 87, 88, 123, 216, 308

Edwards, Jonathan, 13–14, 46, 274, 307, 338

Eighteenth Amendment, 251, 285

Eisenhower, Dwight, 287, 352

Eliot, John, 44–45

Ely, Richard, 58–59, 248, 314, 315

Emerson, Ralph Waldo, 19, 112–13, 277, 308

Endecott, John, 234

Enlightenment, 79, 238, 241, 279, 301–9, 319; cosmology and, 101, 106–7, 112; theology and, 16–17, 19

Environmentalism, 121–22, 124–26, 158

Episcopalians. *See* Anglicans

Eugenics, 315

Evangelicalism, 17–18, 81, 95, 124, 126–27, 147–48; economy and, 271, 273–78, 281–83, 285, 289; ethnicity and, 191; gender and, 197, 207, 209–10, 223; interdenominationalism and, 338, 339, 340, 341; proselytization and, 40–41, 46–61, 63–66, 68; race and, 139, 141–44, 243; regionalism and, 338, 340–41, 343, 348, 354, 356–57; science and, 296, 302, 304–5, 307, 316, 320–21, 324; state and, 242, 243, 246, 257. *See also* Great Awakening

Evans, Hiram Wesley, 60–61

Evolution. *See* Darwinism

Extraterrestrials, 93

Falwell, Jerry, 289

Fard, Wallace D., 30, 153

Farrakhan, Louis, 157

Federal Council of Churches, 219, 249

Feminism, 51, 55, 199

Feminist theology, 22, 33–34, 216, 220–22

Finkelstein, Louis, 319

Finley, Robert, 144

Finney, Charles Grandison, 50–51, 115, 307

First Amendment, 142, 227–28, 232, 239, 246, 248, 251–52, 255, 257, 322

First Cause, 16–17, 300, 309

Fitzhugh, George, 278

"Flood geology," 320–21

Flores, Patricio, 190–91

Ford, Henry, 154, 354

Foreign missions, 59–60, 143–44

Fosdick, Harry Emerson, 28

Fourteenth Amendment, 244–45

Fox, George, 139

Franciscans, 42–44

Franklin, Benjamin, 16, 47, 172, 175, 303, 305, 324

Frazer, James George, 72

Freemasonry, 77, 80, 82, 308

Fundamentalist Christians, 28–29, 31, 62, 285, 287, 289; Darwinism and, 250–51, 316–17, 321; gender and, 218

Gabriel's Rebellion, 17

Gaia hypothesis, 125, 127

Gandhi, Mohandas, 33, 156, 190

Garrison, William Lloyd, 51, 146

Garvey, Marcus, 152, 156

George III (king of Great Britain), 174

German Reformed Church, 174–76

Ghost Dance, 150–51, 155, 248

Ginsberg, Allen, 67, 219

Gnosticism, 80

Goddess religion, 34, 222–23

Gospel of wealth, 54, 280

Graham, Billy, 55, 63, 124

Grant, Ulysses S., 149, 248

Great Awakening, 13–14, 46–47, 50–51, 110–11, 127, 139–40, 302; denominationalism and, 338, 339, 340; economy and, 269–71, 273–74, 276. *See also* Second Great Awakening

Greek Orthodox Church, 167, 184, 189, 281

Grimké, Angelina and Sarah, 146, 212

Hampton Institute, 148, 149–50

Handsome Lake, 48

Handy, Robert, 189

Hare Krishnas, 291

Harmonial religions, 72, 83–84, 89–90, 94, 308, 314

Harrington, Michael, 287–88

Healing. *See* Medicine

Hecker, Isaac, 19–20

Hedrickites, 343

Henry, Patrick, 239–40

Henry II (king of England), 167–68

Henry VIII (king of England), 10–11

Herberg, Will, 189, 219, 254, 287, 352

Heresy, 14, 42

Hermeticism, 77

Herzl, Theodor, 57

Higher criticism, 25

Hinduism, 26, 86, 87, 88, 156, 159, 181, 189, 191–92, 198, 257, 289, 357

Hitchcock, Ethan Allen, 79–80

Hitler, Adolf, 31, 32, 64, 188

Hodge, Charles, 142

Holiness tradition, 19, 348, 350

Holocaust, 31–32, 215

Homosexuality, 198, 202, 221, 223–24

Hopi, 331–32

Howe, Mark deWolfe, 251–52

Huguenots, 170, 236

Humanism, 101, 189, 232, 257, 317–18

Hutcheson, Francis, 16–17

Hutchinson, Anne, 12, 205–7

Huxley, Thomas, 310

I AM Religious Activity, 87, 89

Immigration, 67, 119, 142, 329; economy and, 263, 272, 281, 284; ethnicity and, 56, 59, 163–94, 212–13, 215, 344; proselytization and, 56, 59; race and, 131–32, 146–47, 148, 154, 156, 159–60, 315; regionalism and, 336–37, 347, 353, 354–55; science and, 315; state and, 242–43, 245; theology and, 23–24

Ingersoll, Robert, 310–11

Inquisition, 42, 207, 334

Institute for Religion in an Age of Science, 322–24

Intelligent Design, 322

Ireland, John, 25

Iroquois Nation, 41, 48, 145

Islam, 65, 88, 256–57, 288; ethnicity and, 168–69, 173, 181, 184, 194; gender and, 199, 221, 223; proselytization and, 42; race and, 152–53, 157, 159; regionalism and, 336, 354, 355, 358; theology and, 30. *See also* Nation of Islam

Jackson, Andrew, 145

Jackson, Phil, 67

James, William, 26–27, 92, 280, 314–15

Jefferson, Thomas, 14, 47, 48, 112; disestablishment and, 240–41, 249, 253; science and, 303–5, 307

Jehovah's Witnesses, 252, 254

Jesuits, 42–43, 204, 296, 334

Jews. *See* Judaism

John of Salisbury, 127

Jonas, Hans, 32

Jones, Charles Colcock, 53

Jones, John William, 54

Judaism, 84, 92, 119–20, 315, 319; economy and, 281, 287, 291; ethnicity and, 164, 167, 169, 171, 181–83, 185, 189, 192, 194; gender and, 199–201, 208, 215–16, 220, 221, 223; proselytization and, 56–57, 62–63, 66; race and, 31, 148, 151–52, 153, 154, 156, 159; regionalism and, 62, 337, 343, 348–49, 352, 354, 356; state and, 235–36, 242, 245, 247, 250, 254, 257; theology and, 9, 16, 23–24, 32, 181–83

Kelpius, Johann, 77

Kelso, Isaac, 177–78

Kemp, John Henry, 85

Kennedy, John F., 129, 254, 288

Kenyon, Dean, 322

Kerouac, Jack, 219

King, Martin Luther, Jr., 33, 64–65, 155–56, 190, 255, 288

King Philip's War, 45, 137–38

Kino, Eusebio, 295–96

Knight, J. Z., 94

Kronish, Leon, 62

Ku Klux Klan, 58, 60–61, 131, 154, 182, 250

Larson, Edward, 316

Las Casas, Bartolomé de, 173, 237

Latinos, 117, 121, 126, 156, 160, 172, 179–81, 186–87, 189–91, 353

Latter-day Saints. *See* Mormonism

Laveau, Marie, 81, 147

Leary, Timothy, 91–92

Lee, "Mother" Ann, 209

Lefebvre, Henri, 127

Lehrman, Irving, 63

Leopold, Aldo, 126

Leo XIII (pope), 25, 246

Lewis, Sinclair, 316–17

Liberation theology, 33, 288

Lincoln, Abraham, 21–22, 243–44

Long, Charles, 130, 160

Lost Cause theology, 22, 54, 150

Lovelock, James, 124–25

LSD, 91–92

Luther, Martin, 9–10, 11, 106, 169, 186, 233, 262

Lutheranism, 79; ethnicity and, 171, 174, 176, 184–85; regionalism and, 329, 333, 337, 344, 347–48, 352, 355, 356

MacLaine, Shirley, 66, 95

Madison, James, 240, 249

Malcolm X, 31, 64–65, 156–57, 255, 288

Manifest Destiny, 148, 151

Marriage, 202, 208, 214, 219, 223, 224. *See also* Polygamy

Marty, Martin, 249–50, 252

Marxism, 262, 286–87, 288–89, 290, 315

Mason, Charles Harrison, 91, 350

Mather, Cotton, 12, 45, 110, 138–39, 142, 173, 301, 324

Maurin, Peter, 29

Mayhew, Jonathan, 13–14

McCartney, Bill, 197

McGuire, George Alexander, 30, 152

McIntire, Carl, 287

McKinley, William, 249

McPherson, Aimee Semple, 58, 61, 218–19

Mechanicism, 100, 101, 105, 109, 116, 120, 122–28; Deism and, 112

Medicine, 297–98, 302, 308; alternative, 84–90, 133–34

Medicine bundles, 103, 119

Megachurches, 66

Menéndez de Avilés, Pedro, 170

Mennonites, 15, 16, 171, 174, 176, 254, 337

Men's movement, 222–23

Mernissi, Fatima, 221

Mesmer, Franz Anton, 82

Methodism, 81, 209, 216, 249, 276; proselytization and, 46, 48–50, 53, 56, 58, 210; race and, 53–54, 139, 142, 144, 148, 151, 350; regionalism and, 327, 333, 339, 340–42, 346, 350, 352, 354–58; theology and, 18–19, 22

Mexican Americans, 179–80, 181, 186–87, 189–91, 193

Migrant Ministry, 190

Millennium, 28, 107, 111, 209

Miller, Samuel, 305

Millerites, 49–50, 86

Miracles, 73, 75, 90

Missouri Synod Lutherans, 185, 356

Modernism, 28–29, 31

Monk, Maria, 178, 213

Moody, Dwight L., 54–55, 61, 118, 281

Moorish Science Temple, 152–53

Moravians, 174, 176

Mormonism, 81–82, 100, 189, 276, 308; cosmology and, 116; gender and, 214–15; proselytization and, 50, 59, 62; regionalism and, 329, 343, 351–52, 354, 356; state and, 242, 248–49; theology and, 20–21, 50, 116

Muhammad, Elijah, 30, 65, 153, 157

Muir, John, 121–22, 125

Munger, Theodore, 25, 26

Muscular Christianity, 59, 217–18

Muslims. *See* Islam

National Association for the Advancement of Colored People, 153

National Baptist Convention, 149, 153, 350, 357

National Council of Churches, 155

Nation of Islam, 30–31, 40, 65, 153, 156–57, 159, 254–55, 288

Native American Church, 91, 154–55

Native Americans, 20, 267, 289, 295–97, 307, 337, 341; cosmology and, 99, 102–4, 105, 107–8, 109, 111, 113, 117, 119–20, 125–26, 330, 331–32; economy and, 116–17, 263–68; ethnicity and, 165, 173, 179; gender and, 203–5, 208; proselytization and, 41, 42–45, 47–48, 107–8, 111, 137, 140, 143, 334, 341; race and, 130–38, 140, 141–42, 143–45, 149–51, 154–59; regionalism and, 116–17, 145, 328, 330–32, 336–37, 341; state and, 154–55, 157, 227, 228, 230–31, 235, 237, 242, 248, 255; supernaturalism and, 74–75, 91, 96; theology and, 7–8, 35, 48, 91, 133, 141–42, 150, 203–4, 227

Nativism, 60–61, 147, 175, 177–81, 185, 212–13

Natural philosophy, 299–301, 309–10

Neo-paganism, 96, 100, 125

Neo-Thomism, 29

New Age, 34–35, 66, 72, 95–96, 101, 157–58, 159, 289, 291, 357

New Christian Right, 289–90

New Haven Theology, 18

New Lights, 46, 269–70, 274–75

New Theology, 25

New Thought, 87–88, 95, 153, 189

Newton, Isaac, 106, 300–301

Niebuhr, Reinhold, 31, 33, 64, 285–86, 287, 291

Niles, Nathaniel, 140

Nisei Christians, 188

Norris, Kathleen, 126

Noyes, John Humphrey, 213–14

Numbers, Ronald, 324

Numerology, 123

Oglala Sioux, 330–31, 332

Olcott, Henry Steel, 66, 86–87, 216

Old Lights, 46

Olson, James, 168

Oneida Perfectionists, 213–14

Organicism, 100–105, 107, 109, 111, 115–17, 120–27

Original sin, 9, 201

Orsi, Robert, 187

Orthodox Church. *See* Eastern Orthodoxy

Orthodox Judaism, 24, 119–20, 182, 349

Orwell, George, 124

Osborne, Sarah, 110–11, 128

Our Lady of Guadalupe, 108, 190

Pacifism, 15, 16, 174–75

Paganism, 96, 135, 167, 183, 187

Palmer, Phoebe, 19

Parham, Charles, 27

Parks, Rosa, 155

Parochial schools, 56, 247, 251, 252–53, 344

Patrick, Saint, 73, 167

Paul, Saint, 64, 201, 345

Peace Mission movement, 153

Peale, Norman Vincent, 66, 88

Penn, William, 139, 236–37, 337

Pentecostalism, 57–59, 67, 90, 91, 153, 159, 189, 191, 218, 290, 350, 354; regionalism and, 350, 354, 357; theology and, 27

Personalism, 29

Peyote, 154–55, 157, 227

Philanthropy, 280, 283–84

Pietism, 46, 176

Pius X (pope), 29

Plaskow, Judith, 221

Pluralism, 129–30, 249–50, 257, 328

Polish National Catholic Church, 183

Polygamy, 214–15, 242, 248–49, 253

Pope's Day, 174

Popular theology, 6, 12–13, 73, 77

Postmillennialism, 28

Pragmatism, 280, 314

Predestination, 45, 302, 303

Premillennialism, 28, 348

Presbyterianism, 49, 53, 141–42, 209; economy and, 263, 272, 276, 287; ethnicity and, 172, 175, 190; race and, 132, 141–42, 144; regionalism and, 245,

327, 333, 337–40, 346, 355, 356, 358;
science and, 302, 305–6, 313, 316; state
and, 235–36, 241, 243
Presentism, 130
Primitivists, 49
Prince, John, 304
Progressivism, 59, 118–19, 122, 282, 283,
284–85, 314
Prohibition, 56, 251, 285
Promise Keepers, 197–98, 223
Prophet, Elizabeth Claire, 89
Prosser, Gabriel and Martin, 17
Protestant ethic, 262–63, 281, 287
Protestantism: theology and, 1, 10–17,
22, 25, 28–29; proselytization and,
39–41, 43, 47–50, 53–57, 59, 61–63,
65–66, 111, 118; supernaturalism and,
71, 73, 75, 79–80, 81, 90; cosmology
and, 100–101, 106–7, 109–11, 113,
118, 121, 127; race and, 129–30, 132,
135–37, 142–44, 146–48, 151, 155,
159–60; ethnicity and, 163–64, 168–
70, 172–74, 176–80, 184–85, 188–91,
193–94; gender and, 202, 205–13,
216–20, 223; state and, 228, 232–33,
237–39, 241–43, 245–47, 249–51,
254–55, 257; economy and, 262–63,
270–75, 277–78, 280–82, 284–85,
287, 289–91; science and, 302–3, 310,
315; regionalism and, 328–29, 332–
33, 335–58
Psychedelics, 91–93
Psychic phenomena, 71, 82, 89, 94–95,
97, 315
Pueblo Indians, 43–44, 103
Puerto Rican Catholics, 191
Puritans, 109–10, 129–30, 136–38, 154,
171; economy and, 263–65, 268–69,
271–72, 281, 285–86, 288, 290–91;
gender and, 205–7; proselytization
and, 42, 44–45, 137–39; regionalism
and, 327, 333, 335, 337–38, 340, 358;
science and, 297–99, 301, 316–17, 324;
state and, 231, 233–35, 238, 242; supernaturalism and, 12–13, 71, 75–76;
theology and, 11–13, 16, 35, 42, 45.
See also Congregationalism

Quakers, 15, 49, 167, 171, 208–9, 212,
301, 303; economy and, 263, 272, 291;
race and, 139, 142, 144; regionalism
and, 333, 336–37; state and, 236–37,
241, 254
Quimby, Phineas Parkhurst, 86, 87

Racism, 148, 149, 154, 155–56, 165–66,
315
Randolph, Pashal Beverly, 79–80
Rastafarianism, 159
Rationalism, 47, 243, 277, 308
Rauschenbusch, Walter, 59, 282
Reagan, Nancy, 97
Reformation, 10, 42, 73, 100, 106–7,
127, 135, 169, 174, 177, 202, 232, 245,
262
Reform Judaism, 23–24, 56–57, 62–63,
119, 181–82, 220, 349
Reid, Thomas, 16–17
Religious freedom, 12, 40, 51, 157, 227–
29, 233, 235–36, 237, 238, 240–42,
248, 252–53, 322, 338
Religious Freedom Restoration Act, 255–
56
Restorationism, 342–43
Revivalism. *See* Evangelicalism
Revolutionary War. *See* American
Revolution
Rittenhouse, David, 302
Roberts, Oral, 61, 290
Rockefeller, John D., 279, 280, 281
Roman Catholicism: cosmology and, 73,
101, 105–8, 111, 116–17, 119, 120–21,
122; economy and, 270, 276, 281, 284–
87, 289; ethnicity and, 163–64, 167–
74, 176–81, 183, 186–87, 189–92, 344;
gender and, 202, 208, 212–13, 216–17,
219, 220–21; proselytization and, 42–
44, 47, 56, 59, 65–66, 107–8, 295–97,
334, 341; race and, 129, 135–38, 142,
146–48, 154, 155, 159; regionalism
and, 327, 329, 332, 334, 336, 341, 344,
346–48, 352, 354–56; science and,
295–97, 313, 315, 322; state and, 233,
236–38, 242–43, 245–47, 250, 251,
254–55, 257; supernatural and, 73, 75,

81; theology and, 8–12, 16, 19–20, 24–25, 29, 33–34
Roosevelt, Franklin D., 61
Rosenkreuz, Christian, 79, 80
Rosicrucianiam, 77, 79–80
Rubenstein, Richard, 32
Rush, Benjamin, 302
Russian Orthodox Church, 184, 351
Ryan, John, 251, 284, 286

Sabbatarians, 242
Sacraments, 9, 20, 29, 202
Sacrifice ritual, 8, 96, 103, 105, 107, 112, 123
Sagan, Carl, 293, 324
Saints, 73, 105
Salem witch trials, 13, 206, 338
Salvation, 11, 12, 14, 19, 20, 45, 59, 302
Salvation Army, 216, 281
Same-sex marriage, 223, 224
Santeria, 96, 159, 191
Schechter, Solomon, 24, 183
Schwenkfelders, 176
Scientific humanism, 318–19
Scientific naturalism, 310–14, 315
Scientism, 320
Scopes trial, 250, 316, 317, 321
Scottish commonsense realism, 16–17, 306
Second Great Awakening, 50–51, 81, 115–17, 139, 307
Secularism, 32–33, 232, 312
"Seed Faith" theology, 290
September 11 attacks, 65, 194, 256–57
Serpent gazing, 78
Serra, Junípero, 44, 341
Seventh-Day Adventism, 86, 254, 308
Sexual behavior, 198, 202, 207, 211, 214, 219–20
Seymour, William L., 57, 350
Shakers, 49, 81, 209, 344
Shamans, 8, 74, 94, 95–96, 99, 103, 105, 133–34, 140, 267, 296
Shapley, Harlow, 323
Sheldon, Charles, 283, 285
Sikhism, 57, 166, 181, 192
Simmons, William, 60

Slavery, 130–33, 138–49, 151–52, 156, 165, 237, 297, 336, 345; cosmology and, 108–9, 113–14, 127; economy and, 262, 270–72, 277–79; gender and, 199, 207–8, 212; proselytization and, 15, 42, 49, 53, 65, 132, 138, 139, 271, 336; supernaturalism and, 71, 75, 84, 85, 91; theology and, 14–15, 17, 21–22, 138–39, 140, 146, 151, 243–44, 278, 345–46. *See also* Abolitionism
Smith, Al, 154, 251
Smith, Joseph, 20, 50, 82, 100, 116, 214, 242, 308, 343, 351
Snyder, Gary, 67, 92, 219
Social Darwinism, 280, 281, 313, 315
Social gospel, 28, 58–59, 63–64, 251, 282–89, 314
Society of Sisters, 251
Southern Baptist Convention, 59, 60, 61–62, 355, 356, 357
Southern Christian Leadership Conference, 63, 156, 288
Southern Presbyterians, 245
Space exploration, 124, 125
Speaking in tongues, 27, 90, 350, 357
Speer, Robert, 59
Spiritism, 191
Spiritualism, 51, 82–83, 94, 96, 115–16, 212
Stanton, Elizabeth Cady, 55, 216
Stearns, Jonathan, 211
Stewart, Maria, 141
Stone, Barton, 49
Stowe, Harriet Beecher, 52
Strong, Josiah, 118, 148, 149, 281, 347–48
Stuyvesant, Peter, 171
Sumner, William Graham, 280, 313
Sun Dance, 331
Sunday, Billy, 217, 285
Sunday closings, 241, 242
Suzuki, Shunryu, 67
Swedenborg, Emanuel, 78, 83
Swedenborgianism, 77, 78, 314
Syncretism, 44, 81, 96, 108–9, 121, 137, 147, 329, 357

Taoism, 67, 165, 181
Taylor, Nathan, 18
Televangelism, 61, 63, 66, 127, 289, 290
Temperance movement, 55–56, 149
Tennent, Gilbert, 46, 274, 338
Theism, 22, 23, 310
Theosophy, 77, 86–87, 89, 94, 216
Theravada Buddhism, 67, 192
Third World, 288–89
Thoreau, Henry David, 112–13, 114
Tibetan Buddhism, 67
Tocqueville, Alexis de, 17–18, 228, 261
Transcendentalism, 19, 49, 112–13, 277–78, 307–8, 314, 322
Transcendental Meditation, 353
Transmutation hypothesis, 312
Treasure hunting, 79, 82
Tridentine Catholicism, 180–81
Trinity, 9, 19, 39
Truth, Sojourner, 51, 146
Turner, Frederick Jackson, 122
Turner, Henry McNeal, 54
Turner, Nat, 146
"Two Books" belief, 307
Two-Spirits, 203-5

UFOs (unidentified flying objects), 93, 97
Unification Church, 289
Uniformitarianism, 309
Unitarianism, 14, 19, 216, 277, 322–23, 339, 344
United Foreign Missionary Society, 143
United Methodists, 355, 356, 358
Unity school, 88
Universal Friends, 209
Universal Negro Improvement Association, 152
Utopian communities, 213–14

Vesey, Denmark, 142–43
Vietnam War, 153, 156, 255, 288, 354
Virginia Statute for Religious Freedom, 240–41, 249
Vision quest, 103
Voodoo (Vodou), 71, 75, 80–81, 90, 96, 147, 159

Wanamaker, John, 55
Washington, Booker T., 148
Washington, George, 238
Waters, Frank, 120, 125
Watts, Alan, 66, 67, 92
Webb, William, 84
Weber, Max, 262–63, 265, 274–75, 277, 278, 285–87, 291
Weld, Theodore Dwight, 146, 212
Wells, Ida B., 149
Weninger, Francis Xavier, 56
Wesley, Charles, 139
Wesley, John, 18, 46, 139
White, Andrew Dickson, 311–12, 316, 324
White, Ellen Gould, 86, 308
Whitefield, George, 46–47, 139, 207, 274, 338
Whitehead, Alfred North, 317–18, 319, 323
Wicca, 96, 125, 222
Wilkenson, Bruce, 290
Wilkinson, Jemima, 209
Willard, Frances, 22, 55, 149
Willard, Joseph, 304
Williams, Delores, 34
Williams, Eunice, 41
Williams, Roger, 139–40, 231–32, 234–35, 257
Williams, Walter, 203
Winthrop, John, 44–45, 206, 268–69
Winthrop, John, Jr., 299–300
Wise, Isaac Mayer, 56, 182
Witchcraft, 13, 74, 76, 78, 94, 96, 99, 125, 206–7, 301, 338
Witherspoon, John, 16, 17, 275
Womanist theology, 34
Woman's Christian Temperance Union, 22, 55, 149, 251
Women's Aglow, 223
Women's suffrage, 55–56, 218
Woodmason, Charles, 172
Work ethic, 262–63, 281, 287
World Community of Al-Islam in the West, 157
World's Parliament of Religions, 26, 66, 88

World War II, 31–32, 153, 188–89, 254–
    55, 286
Wounded Knee, 150–51, 157, 248
Wovoka, 150
Wright, George Frederick, 309

YMCA/YWCA, 188, 217
Yoga, 88, 92

Young, Brigham, 242, 248, 343, 351
Young People's Christian Conference, 188

Zen Buddhism, 66, 67, 92, 219
Zionism, 57, 216, 250